D1074667

THE TOOL CATALOG

AN EXPERT SELECTION OF THE WORLD'S FINEST TOOLS

BY THE EDITORS OF CONSUMER GUIDE®

Harper & Row
NEW YORK, HAGERSTOWN, SAN FRANCISCO, LONDON

Contents

Copyright© 1978 by Publications International, Ltd.
All rights reserved
Printed in the United States of America

Published by
Harper & Row, Publishers
10 East 53rd Street
New York, New York 10022

Published simultaneously in Canada by Fitzhenry &
Whiteside Limited, Toronto, Canada
Library of Congress Catalog Card Number 78-4729

ISBN: 0-06-010859-2

This book may not be reproduced or quoted in whole
or in part by mimeograph or any other printed means
or for presentation on radio or television without
written permission from:

Louis Weber, President
Publications International, Ltd.
3841 West Oakton Street
Skokie, Illinois 60076

Permission is never granted for commercial purposes.

Acknowledgements: The Editors of CONSUMER GUIDE® would like to thank Ernie Conover, R.J. DeCristoforo, Matt Zurawski and the many others who contributed their expertise to the tool selections and for their input into the editorial content of this book.

The Editors of CONSUMER GUIDE® have made every effort to ensure the accuracy of the approximate retail prices given in this publication. Please note that prices may vary from coast to coast within the United States and Canada. Additionally, many of the items covered are imported tools and their prices could change with fluctuations in the value of the American dollar.

From the Olduvai Gorge in Africa to the
world of the 20th Century, tools have
ever been man's route to ascendancy.
Therein lies their fascination — which we
now invite you to explore with us.

Welcome To The World Of Tools

Welcome to a world older than recorded history itself. Long before humans left any written testimony about their lives, they bequeathed to future generations their primitive renditions of what today constitute a multimillion-dollar industry. Welcome, in other words, to the fascinating world of tools.

THE TOOL CATALOG is your vehicle for exploring this world, both past and present. Ever wondered how today's saws, planes, drills, etc., evolved from their ancient forebears? If so, then you've come to the right place, for THE TOOL CATALOG covers the genealogy of these items and many more.

As fascinating as the history of tools might be,

however, THE TOOL CATALOG is devoted primarily to examining the realm of hand and power tools as it exists today. It is a realm filled to overflowing, so crowded with products from so many sources that only the experts can stay up-to-date and know what is worthwhile from what is worthless.

Recognizing the need for reliable information on hand and power tools, the Editors of CONSUMER GUIDE® assembled a team of craftsmen and tool experts to create this totally unique catalog. Unlike catalogs intended to sell goods, THE TOOL CATALOG is designed to make sense out of the competing claims of the tool marketplace and to

provide everyone — from novice do-it-yourselfers to lifelong craftsmen — with the knowledge needed to make intelligent purchases.

This knowledge is really two-fold in nature. First, tool buyers must learn what tools are appropriate for particular tasks. Throughout the long history of hand and power tools, inventive minds have created a host of offshoots from the basic sawing, drilling, shaping, smoothing, and other tools that preceded them. Some of these offshoots fell quickly into deserved oblivion, their usefulness being too limited to earn widespread acceptance. But a good many of the variations represented bona fide improvements, and as such have become integral parts of the contemporary tool scene.

The problem, of course, is that all the tools that justifiably fall within a general category (hammers, screwdrivers, pliers, and so forth) are so different from one another and so specific in terms of application that consumer confusion is an inevitable result. THE TOOL CATALOG has been structured specifically to eliminate this confusion.

First, tools are grouped into functional categories according to their primary purpose: e.g., measuring, sawing, shaving, drilling, shaping, smoothing, fastening/tightening, and gripping. Second, a general introduction to each section delineates the types of tools within the category. Finally, a separate and more specific introduction to each type within the category makes clear the precise applications for which the tool is best suited.

Discovering what tool is appropriate to a particular task eliminates a good deal of confusion but not all of it. The question then becomes: What brand should I buy once I know exactly the type of tool I need? It is in this unexplored territory within the realm of tools that THE TOOL CATALOG becomes an especially valuable resource.

Nowhere else can the tool buyer—from inexperienced to sophisticated—find such unbiased, comprehensive evaluations of today's name-brand tools. Of course,

some preselection was necessary; our team of tool experts could not possibly review every tool from every manufacturer. Yet the selection was made in such a way as to present a wide range of each type of tool.

Where appropriate, tools ranging from inexpensive models suitable to the casual user up to costly versions for the demanding craftsman are carefully scrutinized. Strengths and weaknesses are explained in jargon-free terminology, and each tool is placed in the perspective of who should buy it, why, and—as accurately as possible—at what price.

Not everyone needs the best crosscut saw available, for example. There are plenty of good ones at more moderate prices from which to choose, and THE TOOL CATALOG provides a broad selection. Yet some tool lovers will prize the special features which make that crosscut saw the best of its type, and to such individuals the steep price they must pay represents money well spent. And, of course, even those who are not ready—in terms of finances and/or skills—to buy the best can still derive some important information (to say nothing of vicarious pleasure) by reading about the top-of-the-line model.

FOR BROWSERS AS WELL AS BUYERS

THE TOOL CATALOG is not simply a buyer's guide, however. It is an intriguing,

amusing, provocative compendium that's fun to browse through as well as study in detail. Filled with anecdotes, tips, charts, and other visual aids, it reduces the often overwhelming world of tools to one that can be understood and enjoyed by people with absolutely no technical background or training.

It also introduces a host of tool makers who—despite the fact that they produce fine implements at reasonable prices—have not yet received the public attention they deserve. In part, this lack of attention is due to the limited degree of retail distribution these companies enjoy—some of them being mail-order outlets only. If they produce quality tools, though, there's a good chance that they appear in THE TOOL CATALOG, along with complete information on how buyers can order from them. In fact, a very useful "Directory of Manufacturers and Suppliers" —a guide to names and addresses of tool makers large and small—can be found at the rear of the catalog.

One word of caution: the world of tools is a fascinating realm, in some ways almost an enchanting one. Its lure is so potent, in fact, that it can captivate the unsuspecting and never let them go. Therefore, turn these pages at your own risk; we who have prepared THE TOOL CATALOG already know the danger, and we welcome all who would join us in succumbing to its charm.

An old saying goes: "The carpenter cut off the board twice, but it was still too short!" His was a measurement error common in many shops, but one that can be avoided by the use of accurate measuring instruments.

Measuring And Marking Tools

The first problem in any woodcraft project is to measure correctly. Errors in measuring a piece of stock tend to be much less forgiving than mistakes of any other type. If this initial step isn't done correctly, it'll show up somewhere down the line — often with disastrous results.

Measuring instruments range from a simple piece of string and a pencil to a micrometer with a light-emitting diode and digital readouts. Accuracy somewhere between these two extremes is needed by most craftsmen. In furniture and cabinet work, it's the mark of the careful artisan that the piece as a whole is "square." This means that all adjoining surfaces meet at a 90-degree angle, even if the edges of the work have been broken or sanded to a rounded surface. In construction, the work must be "plumb," or level with the ground surface at the site.

For a carpenter to say that his work is plumb and square is to say that he knows what he is doing.

So, measuring and marking is one of the first stages of any crafting, and is called "layout work" in the shop. This can range from simply cutting out a pattern (technically called a "template") to a whole series of measurements — with each successive measurement relying upon the accuracy of the last. Whether you're a craftsman or nail pounder, measuring is a critical initial operation. Shortcuts that creep into the work at this point will ruin the project.

Although the rest of the world, including England, uses the metric system, we in North America persist in using the clumsy English system of measurement. This quaint system is based on the anatomical length of certain parts of a long-forgotten British king. The base measurement is the yard,

which is broken down into feet and inches. Despite its familiarity, this system is an utter nightmare. In precise work, it's unwieldy, and relies heavily on fractions that are difficult to deal with. A good part of the first year of most apprenticeship programs is wasted teaching trainees the intricacies of the English measurement system. But the weight of tradition has kept it around despite its faults.

The metric system is much simpler. It uses 10 measurement units, starting with a "meter." This is further subdivided into tenths (decimeters), hundredths (centimeters), and thousandths (millimeters). There are no fractions — just decimal points. Even though this system is simple, it's only used in scientific and other precision work. Since we still prefer to use the system based on the yard, all the tools discussed in this section will use this system.

A QUICK LOOK AT MEASURING AND MARKING TOOLS

NAME	REMARKS	TYPICAL USES
Flex Tape	available in lengths up to 50 feet — automatic power-return tapes most popular	standard measuring tool for long stock — measures height, width of almost any size work or room
Folding Rule	available in 4, 6, & 8 foot lengths, with 6 foot most common — folds up to small 8" length overall	carpenter and shop tool for measurements on stock — accurate measures within $\frac{1}{16}$-inch on almost all wood stock
Machinist's Rule	available in 6 and 12 inch lengths — flexible — made in extremely thin gauge metal with close markings	most accurate of common rules — use for close tolerance work where precision is required — thin gauge most useful
Squares: **Carpenter's Square**	pressed or cut steel construction — standard sizes are 18 or 24 inches (body) by 12 or 18 inches (tongue) — large number of scales	large number of scales used to figure out board feet requirements and brace (rafter) height — obligatory carpenter's tool for house framing
Try Square	small and handheld with wood or metal body — tongue has maximum length of 12 inches — may have miter corner at joint	tests (trys) edges for squareness in planing and sawing work — miter cut in handle will check right angle layouts
Combination Square	body slides along blade and can be fixed at any point — may incorporate scratch awl and level in handle — blade section reversible with different scales	better than try square for checking for plumb, square surface — adjustable, sliding body permits working in close quarters with small stock
Bevel	sliding blade section can be locked at selected angle	transfers angles in layout work — can be used to reproduce angles already known
Depth/Mortise Gauge	sliding body or fence rides along stem — may have one or two (mortise) spurs — hardwood is normal construction	set lines parallel to an edge — two spur models handy to mark sides of mortise — use limited by length of stem (usually 6 inches)
Level	vials with movable bubble mounted in fixed, rigid frame — lengths available up to 6 feet — ground edges more accurate	check plumb or level surface when compared to rest of structure — necessary tool for any construction task
Chalk Line	small canister or case filled with powdered chalk — string encased — case may be pointed for use as plumb bob	mark long lines on walls or floors — snapped line creates accurate verticals — can be used to make a base line for remodeling work

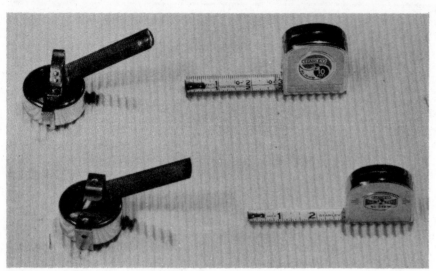

Antique (left) and modern (right) flex tapes.

Flex Tapes

Aside from the yardstick, the most common and popular ruler sold today is the flex tape. Shorter, smaller versions are used in the home, while longer, larger ones are preferred by carpenters and tradesmen. A flex tape is nothing more than a thin strip of steel on which a ruler is marked. This flexible strip is coiled inside a metal housing that protects it and stores it for easy use. Most flex tapes sold today are spring-loaded. You can pull out the amount you need for measuring and lock it. When you release the lock, a spring draws the tape back into the case.

The biggest advantage of flex tapes is that you can bend them to measure oddly-shaped contours. You can also take inside and outside measurements. An outside measurement would be measuring a board or the height of a cabinet. Measuring something like the inside of a drawer would be an inside measurement. Most flex tapes have a small, loosely movable hook at the end of the tape. This is not a sign of poor manufacturing. The movement is designed into the tape to facilitate inside measurement. When the tape is pushed against an inside edge, the hook slides exactly its own width to maintain the accuracy of the measurement. The length of the tape's case must also be added to the inside measurement. No guessing is required—the case length is clearly stated on the housing.

A wide array of flex tapes is on the market. The old stalwart, the 72-inch, 6-foot type is fine for household use, and the 15- to 25-foot models are most suitable for woodworkers. A replaceable blade is a good feature to look for in longer tapes. The blade often takes a beating in construction work; slammed in doors or even cut off inadvertently by a power saw. If you have a replaceable model, the useful life of the instrument does not end when such a mishap occurs, since you can just buy and insert another tape. A bargain tape is no bargain at all if the tape is not replaceable.

Stanley's Powerlock II (PL 425) is a good, 25-foot flex tape that's 1 inch wide. It can take reasonable inside and outside measurements usually required in woodworking. The tape's slightly semi-circular cross section allows it to remain rigid for a length of 7 feet outside the case. This is useful for taking measurements in hard-to-reach places.

The tape is clearly marked in $\frac{1}{16}$-inch gradations. Markings are black on a yellow background, and a plastic coating provides protection from wear. This plastic coating also acts as a lubricant to help the tape slide smoothly. Every 16 inches, the distance between standard wall studs, there's a convenient marking, too. A lock holds the tape in

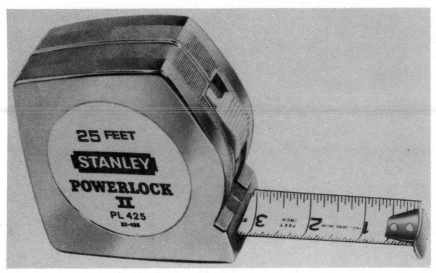
Stanley's Powerlock II Flex Tape

You can see at a glance that 39 inches equals 3 feet, 3 inches. Clear markings appear every 16 inches for stud layout. Like most flex tapes, this one is slightly bowed to allow fairly long sections to remain rigid when extended from the case. A toggle switch locks the blade open to any desired length.

An extra feature not found on most power tapes is a rubber bumper that protects the hooked end against violent closure. Many flex tapes are thrown away because the hooked end has torn out. This bumper prevents such tear-out. Lufkin also offers 8-, 10-, 12-, and 16-foot models. Approx. Price: (Y25) $11.50

position at any length. The Stanley Powerlock II, 25-foot tape is available at most hardware stores. You can also choose from 10-, 12-, 16- and 20-foot Powerlock models. Approx. Price: (PL425) $13.00

contained in a chromed case. In addition to the ⅟₁₆-inch gradations, there is also a dual readout in both feet and inches as well as just inches.

Lufkin's Y25 Mesurlok is a 25-foot power tape, made by a manufacturer of quality measuring equipment. The ¾-inch-wide flex tape is

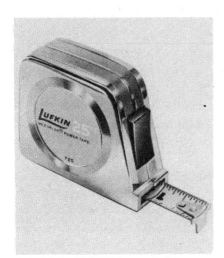
Lufkin's Y25 Mesurlok

If you use flex tapes frequently you will encounter one nagging problem. The little metal hook on the end will often break off, the result of constant snapping against the case when the power feed pulls the tape inside. This means a ruined tape, since the entire length will roll up inside, rendering it useless.

Recognizing this problem, some tape manufacturers have incorporated a little rubber bumper or stop to cushion the impact of the hook. On less expensive tapes, however, this protection is not provided. One simple trick that has been used by carpenters can be easily adapted to regular shop use. During normal use of a power tape the hand encircles the case, with the thumb used to operate the lock that prevents the retraction of the tape. The trick is to extend the forefinger far enough forward so that the bottom surface of the tape rides against the inside of that finger. As it retracts, the tape will be slowed. When it finally reaches the end of the tape the hook will catch against the outside edge of the forefinger, effectively stopping it. Removing the forefinger will allow it to be drawn fully into the case, without snapping against the metal lip.

With a little practice this trick soon becomes a habit, and is quite effective in preventing this common cause of tape damage.

Brookstone's "Gentleman's Tape" is a unique flex tape made in France. This tape is ⅝ inch wide, 10 feet long, and is marked in black on a yellow tape body. Calibrations are marked in ⅟₁₆ -inch gradations, with the first 6 inches also marked off in ⅟₃₂-inch increments. The entire tape is also marked in centimeters and millimeters,

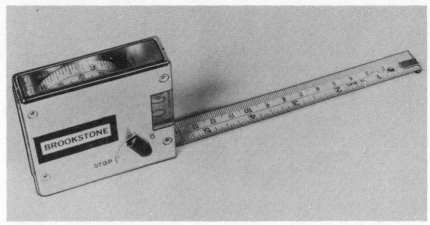

Brookstone's "Gentleman's Tape"

to let you measure in both common systems. Another unique feature is a plastic window with a hairline indicator marked on it. This window lets you make direct readings for inside measurements without adding the length of the tape housing. The tape also locks open and includes a small bubble level in the end of the housing. All these features make it a very handy household tool. Brookstone carries it under the stock number 2805. Approx. Price: $13.00

METRIC/ENGLISH CONVERSIONS

The Most Common Prefixes
milli — .001 (one thousandth)
centi — .01 (one hundredth)
kilo — 1000 (one thousand)

Relationships
10 millimeters (mm)=1 centimeter (cm)
10 centimeters (cm) = 1 decimeter (dm)
10 decimeters (dm) = 1 meter (m)
10 meters (m) = 1 decameter (Dm)
10 decameters (Dm) = 1 hectometer (Hm)
10 hectometers (Hm) = 1 kilo-meter (Km)

Equivalents
1 mm = .03937 inches
1 cm = .3937 inches
1 dm = 3.937 inches
1 m = 39.37 inches or 3.281 feet or 1.094 yards
1 Km = .62137 miles

English Equivalents
1 inch = 2.54 cm
1 foot = 30.48 cm or .3048 m
1 yard = 91.44 cm or .9144 m
1 mile = 1.6093 Km

Conversions
mm X .03937 = inches
mm divided by 25.4 = inches
cm X .3937 = inches
cm divided by 2.54 = inches
m X 39.37 = inches
m X 3.2809 = feet
m X 1.094 = yards
Km X .621377 = miles

Wood Folding Rules

The wood folding rule is the most traditional craftsman's and carpenter's measuring tool. It's sometimes called a zig-zag rule, because of the way it folds, and is popular because it can make more accurate measurements than a power tape.

A folding rule is simply constructed of a series of 8-inch-long wood strips. These strips are bound together by brass pivoting joints. Each strip is bound on a 6-inch center, with a 2-inch overlap at each joint. Commonly, folding rules are 6 feet long, and are made by joining 12 wood sections together. Some 4- and 8-foot models are made, but not usually found in hardware stores.

An "extension end" is practically a necessary feature on any folding rule. This extension end is a brass piece built into the first 8 inches of the rule. It's usually marked on the surface and can be slid out for 6 inches.

Of all its uses, the most important is for inside measurements. You open the rule to within 6 inches of the inside measurement to be taken, and then slide out the extension until the rule fits snugly in the opening. The two readings are then added together to get the accurate inside measurement. Extension ends are also used to draw a line parallel to an edge. It's extended the desired amount, and the end of the ruler is butted to the outside edge. A pencil is held to the end of the extension, and the ruler is drawn along the edge with the pencil following along. This results in a parallel line the desired distance from the outside edge.

Another useful feature found on folding rules is a hook end. This rests against the side of the ruler when not in use, so measurements can be taken in the usual manner. But by pulling the hook open, you can hook it over the piece to be measured. The zero marking at the end of the ruler then falls on the inside of the hook. All you do is keep a slight tension on the hook while marking with a pencil. This is very handy for making outside measurements in hard-to-reach locations or for cutting a board to length.

Six-foot folding rules are the most practical, because 8-footers are too bulky for the pocket. Measurements over 6 feet should be made with a flex tape. When you buy a folding rule, make sure it has an extension on one

Tool users and tool makers are generally very conservative about adopting new designs, a trend which is evident in the design of the traditional folding rule. Two-foot folding rules made of boxwood, for example, are documented prior to the 1650s. Their construction and design were almost identical with rules produced today— many using the same kinds of joints to pin the sections together and with much the same markings.

An offshoot of the standard boxwood rule was made of ivory, with black markings on the white surface. The edges on these rules were often bound with German silver strips, with all joints and hinges made of the same metal. Although subject to shrinkage (due to humidity changes) many of these old rules are still as accurate as when they were made a hundred or more years ago. At present they are avidly collected and bring a high price at tool auctions or antique shops. If you should find one of these rules at a reasonable price, it is well worth purchasing—both as a memento of a long-ago age of tool making and as a symbol of the almost unchanging continuity of tool design.

end and a hook on the other.

The first folding rules were made out of boxwood, which is unfortunately scarce today. Nowadays, most folding rules are advertised as having a "boxwood finish." Such rules are usually made of maple or birch, and stained to look like traditional material.

However, there are still a few companies that make the traditional boxwood rule.

Lufkin's Red End 8-foot folding rule has a joint system that makes it long lasting.

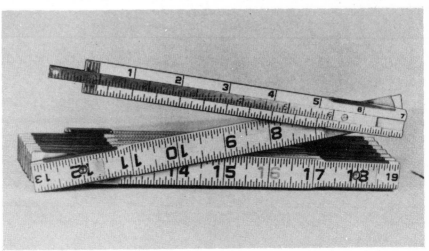

Lufkin's Red End 8-foot Folding Rule

One of the most important factors in the construction of a folding rule is the care and quality put into making the joints. You do have to oil the joints of this rule periodically, but that's true for any folding rule.

The rule gets its name "Red End" from the fact that the end of each wooden section is painted red. Gradations are on both sides in $\frac{1}{16}$-inch increments. They are black, embossed slightly into the wood, and covered with a clear, tough plastic coating. This is guaranteed not to chip, peel, or discolor. The 16-inch stud centers are highlighted in red. The 8-foot Red End Rule also has an extension slide that can be pulled out 6 inches, and a brass-plated steel hook on the other end. Available at many hardware stores and lumberyards, it's also found in the Brookstone catalog (4320). Approx. Price: $9.50

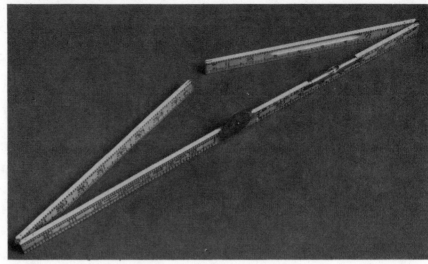

Rabone and Chesterman's Boxwood Rule

Stanley's X226 6-foot folding rule with extension is a quality tool with a boxwood finish—common on domestically made rules. It has black $\frac{1}{16}$-inch gradations and red, 16-inch stud center markings. Joints and hinges are brass, and non-critical parts, like the extension, are brass-plated steel. You can find it at most hardware stores. Approx. Price: $8.00

Rabone and Chesterman of England makes a wood folding rule that's a reminder of the good old days—a fine, boxwood rule made in the traditional pattern. The joints between the wooden pieces are in a scissors pattern, and each arm folds in on itself over a box-type hinge. Most companies have ceased to manufacture rules like this because of the high cost of boxwood and the expense of the hand construction.

The ruler is a 36-inch model, and folds down to 9¾ inches long. It has two exceptionally nice features. One is a protractor built into the scissors joint—although it's only graduated to 5 degrees, and not accurate enough for critical work, it comes in handy. The other feature is a bubble level built into one arm. This isn't made for house framing, but it's fine for leveling picture frames and other household work. The rule is available from Brookstone (4593), Woodworker's Supply (516-002), and Garrett Wade (39N01.02). Approx. Price: (4593) $12.50

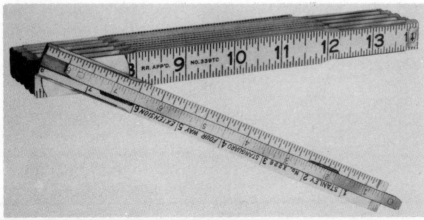

Stanley's X226 6-foot Folding Rule

Steel Rules

Craftsmen involved in metal or wood working to close tolerances may find a wooden rule lacking in accuracy. A wooden rule graduated in 16ths of an inch can be "eyeballed" to half gradations, or 32nds. But for really close work, this is only guessing, and a ruler graduated in 1/64-inch increments may be necessary. A handy rule for work requiring this kind of accuracy is a 6-inch or 1-foot steel machinist's ruler. The 1-foot size is ideal, and it should be made of the thinnest possible stock. Best-quality rules like this can be as little as 1/32-inch thick. The thinner the better, because it's easier for the eye to transfer a marking to the work—especially when working with fine markings in 64ths of an inch.

A good steel rule usually has four scales. One side is laid out with ⅛-inch gradations on one edge and 1/16-inch markings on the other. Flip the rule over and you have 1/32-inch and 1/64-inch gradations. Better machinist's rules also have engraved, or etched, markings; cheap rules have markings stamped on. You can find steel rules in some well-stocked hardware stores and always in machine tool supply houses.

Squares

A "square" is a necessary woodworking tool used to check the accuracy of 90-degree angles and for layout work on a workpiece. Its name comes from its shape—two cuts that are made at a perfect 90-degree angle to each other are said to be square. This tool has two members that meet at a perfect 90-degree angle. The family of squares includes the carpenter's, try, combination, and bevel types. Having at least one, and sometimes all, is required for accurate work.

Carpenter's Squares

The construction of the carpenter's square is simple—nothing more than a piece of steel stamped in the shape of an "L." The steel it's made from is usually 3/16-inch thick. The longer, upright part of the "L" is called the body, while the shorter, bottom part is called the tongue. Standard models have a 24-inch-long, 2-inch-wide body, and a tongue that's 16 inches long

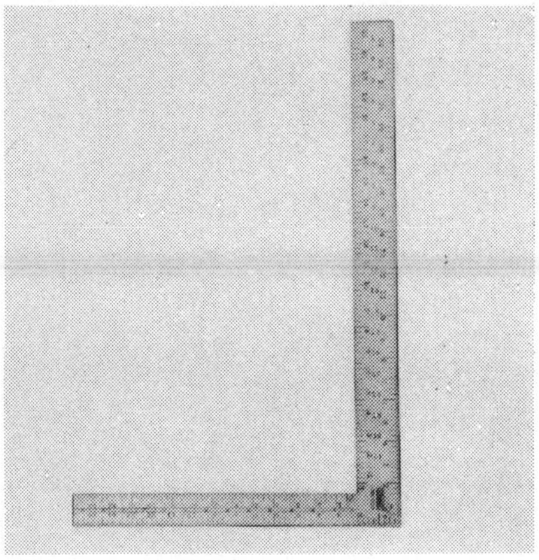

Stanley's #100

and 1½ inches wide.

This type of square appears simpler than it actually is, however. The scales cut into the metal make it considerably more complicated. You can use these scales to figure out "board measure," which is the amount of lumber needed

NOMINAL AND ACTUAL SIZES OF LUMBER

Nominal Size, Inches	Actual Size, Inches
1x2	¾x1½
1x3	¾x2½
1x4	¾x3½
1x5	¾x4½
1x6	¾x5½
1x8	¾x7¼
1x10	¾x9¼
1x12	¾x11¼
2x2	1½x1½
2x3	1½x2½
2x4	1½x3½
2x6	1½x5½
2x8	1½x7¼
2x10	1½x9¼
2x12	1½x11¼
3x4	2½x3½
4x4	3½x3½
4x6	3½x5½
6x6	5½x5½
8x8	7½x7½

for a given job. Also, you can figure out "brace measure" — the hypotenuse of a triangle of which two sides are known. The latter measurement is necessary for rafter and framing work.

Carpenter's squares are relatively inexpensive and virtually indestructible. They're available in almost every hardware store, lumberyard, and major merchandising house. Stanley's #100 is one of the best. Approx. Price: $14.00

Try Squares

The try square is the tool of the cabinet maker and finish carpenter — most commonly used to check a cut edge for squareness. This procedure is called "trying" the edge and is the source of the tool's name. Originally, try squares had a wood handle bound with brass, in which a steel blade was mounted. The handle made the tool easy to grasp. It's still possible to buy a square with a brass-bound, rosewood handle from some mail order houses, but most of these tools have handles made of zinc or other metals.

The sizes of try squares vary, ranging from those with a 4-inch handle and a 6-inch blade to an 8-inch handle with a 12-inch blade. The smaller ones are easier to use and are favored because they fit into an apron pocket. One refinement to look for is a handle with a 45-degree cut along the point where the blade is mounted. This helps when laying out miter corners and checking

them when assembled. The try square is absolutely necessary for exacting furniture and woodwork, and is the type of square you find in most shops.

Stanley Tools' 12TS try square is the company's top-of-the line model. It's

rated "best" in the company's "good," "better," and "best" grading system. This square is available with either English or metric marking systems on the blade, and you can choose from four different sizes. The tool has a black-finished zinc handle and the English version is marked in ⅛-inch gradations. Numbers are engraved into the metal and filled with a fluorescent yellow paint for easy readability. Also, it has a 45-degree bevel at the handle joint for laying out miters. Approx. Price: (8 inch) $7.00

Fisher Tools of Great Britain makes a high-quality try square. All the edges of this square are surface-ground to insure accuracy. The blade is set into the handle with great precision and held by three brass rivets. This method of

Stanley's 12TS Try Square

Fisher's Try Square

attachment is beneficial because you can readjust the tool and tighten the rivets if you happen to drop the tool.

There's also a small spirit level located in the handle. Although spirit levels in small squares are usually not accurate, this one is. The four-way level can be used to check side as well as face surfaces. This square will be carried by local hardware stores and the large catalog houses in the near future. Approx. Price: $8.00

stores and comes in English, metric and English/metric versions. The latter version gives readings in both systems. Approx. Price: $10.00

Combination Squares

A combination square is very similar to a try square, but it has a handle that can slide along the blade. You can lock it at any point, or remove it altogether. A combination square's blade is like a very thick steel rule, with the edges marked off in ⅛-, 1⁄16-, and 1⁄32-inch gradations. Because the head is removable from the blade, an edge with any desired gradation can be placed inside the square for easy reference.

Most combination squares also have a small scratch awl stored in a hole in the base of the handle. This handle also has a built-in spirit level, which is used to check horizontal and vertical members for plumb. The back edge of this type of square is ground to 45 degrees, making it easy to lay out corners and miters. Although combination squares are more expensive than try squares, their workscope is greater. This makes them worth the extra

investment for the serious woodworker.

Stanley's 122 combination square is the company's best model. It features a removable blade marked off in ⅛-, 1⁄16-, and 1⁄32-inch gradations, and the handle has a scratch awl and spirit level. This square can be bought in almost all hardware

Sear's 39543 combination square is not a high-quality tool, but it's serviceable for most woodworking tasks. The blade has the usual ⅛-, 1⁄16-, and 1⁄32-inch gradations. And there's a spirit level and scratch awl in the cast-zinc handle. Approx. Price: $8.00

Bevels

A bevel is a layout tool used to transfer angles. It's not really a square, but if you set it against a surface of known

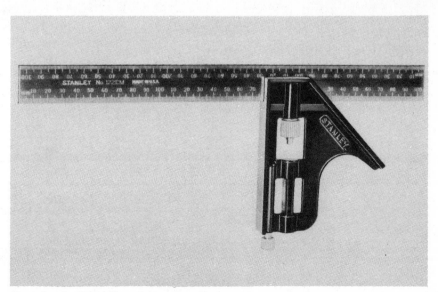

Stanley's 122 Combination Square

15

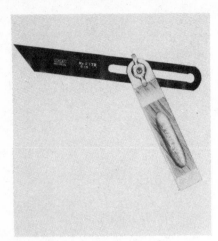

Stanley's 25TB Bevel

squareness and lock it in that position, it can be used as one. The blades of a bevel are adjustable and can be locked at any angle. Quality models have a blade that you can slide back and forth in the handle to some degree. Advanced cabinet work and miter setting make the bevel a necessary tool.

The Stanley 25TB is a quality bevel that has an 8-inch blade and a 5½-inch hardwood handle, bound with brass. The blade is held in place by a thumb screw. It's a pleasant and nice-looking tool. Approx. Price: $6.50

Levels

Once a carpenter has built something that's "square," he has won half the battle.

But in construction work it's also necessary that the building or installation be "plumb." To a scientist, a level, plumb surface is a line drawn tangent to the Earth's surface, or a plane constructed perpendicular to a radial line extending from the center of the Earth. In practical terms, this means that no corner or portion of a surface is higher or lower than any other. In most building, this is done with a tool called a carpenter's or builder's level.

A level is basically a long, rectangular wood or metal body with one or more built-in vials. The vials are filled with colored alcohol and have an air bubble in them. Because the vials contain alcohol, this kind of level is called a "spirit level." When a level is set on a surface that's actually level, the bubble in the vial of alcohol centers itself between two lines scratched on the vial's surface. Most levels have two or more vials set at right angles to one another. This lets you hold the level in various positions to insure that the surfaces or upright members are actually plumb.

The precision of a level is proportionate to its cost, because a lot of work goes into making a good one. In general, inexpensive, household levels are made of aluminum extrusions and have plastic vials. Better-quality models are made with cast-aluminum bodies, and have the edges ground for precision. Vials in this kind of level are made of glass and have glass covers for protection. A quality level also has vials that can be repositioned, should the vials be displaced during rough use.

Levels come in a wide variety of lengths, from 1 foot on up. For shop use, a 2-foot model is about right, but a 3- or 4-foot model may be required for long surfaces. The longer models let you span a greater distance, avoiding any localized dips, but they're hard to store and take a lot of punishment in the field.

The "Sta-True" line of levels, from the Exact Level Company, is intended for the homeowner and do-it-yourselfer. Frames are

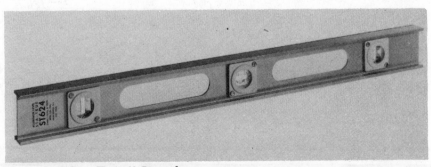

Exact's "Sta-True" Level

made of aluminum extrusions and the vials are plastic. The plastic vials do have an advantage in that they're relatively unbreakable. This line includes models with two, three, and four vials and lengths ranging from 18 inches to 6 feet. Approx. Price: (24 inch) $10.50

Exact's "Professional Series" levels are the kind of precision instruments that are required for expert house building. All of them have a die-cast aluminum body, and can be purchased with ⅛-inch scaled markings on one side. Lengths available are 18, 24, 28, and 30 inches. The six vials on all models make them omni-directional, so no matter how you pick them up, they can be used quickly. They are fine, high-quality levels that give years of trouble-free service. Approx. Price: (18 inch) $17.50

Sands Level Company's line of levels have extruded

aluminum bodies, plastic vials and lengths ranging from 18 to 48 inches. The top surface of most of the levels in this series have scaled gradations of ⅛ inch. Sands also makes a level in the traditional way—of brass-bound, Honduras mahogany. This level is 48 inches long and has six vials. It's marketed as a "mason's" level and is a good choice for the traditional craftsman who prefers tools made of wood. Approx. Price: (24-inch extruded aluminum) $19.50

Special problems usually call for unique solutions and the Mayes 4-way post level is no exception to this. In this case the problem is to sink a post upright in the ground and keep it straight. Using a normal level to do this is tedious because it must be switched from one side to the other to get a reading. The 4-way post level does away with that task, and makes setting a post as easy as jamming a stick into the ground.

The extruded aluminum body of this level has a

Mayes' 4-Way Post Level

unique form, actually two wings joined in a right-angle corner. Four bubble vials are mounted on the outside surface of the wings. When setting a post or timber the level is fitted on the outside surface, with the body of the post inside, between the two wings. Reading the bubble vials on either side gives an instant reading of the post's angle. This is the only level that can give a reading on two sides at the same time, and best of all, it can be used with one hand. It is available in lengths of 6, 12, 18, and 24 inches. Although it will be of interest to anyone in the construction field, its versatility will allow it to be used in any shop. Approx. Price: (24 inch) $20.00

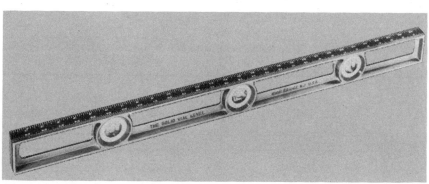

Exact's "Professional Series" Level

Marking Gauges

Marking gauges are used for drawing a line parallel and at a set distance to an edge or face of a piece of wood. Common marking gauges consist of a wood stem with a pointed, steel spur inset in one end. This stem is fitted into a wooden fence or sliding member which can be locked at any point. The inside face of this sliding piece may be solid wood, although on quality marking gauges it's brass-bound.

You use a marking gauge by first moving the sliding member along the stem until it's the correct distance from the fence. Then you lock the fence into place with a thumb screw and run the tool along the edge of the work. The spur cuts an incision along the work as the gauge is moved.

These gauges are used for laying out rabbets, grooves, and dadoes. You can also use them to mark a piece for planing to size. Although an extension rule can also be used for this kind of marking, the marking gauge is more convenient, because it can be used with one hand.

The mortise gauge is a variation of the marking gauge. It's practically identical to the marking gauge, except it has two spurs, rather than one. You can adjust these spurs individually, depending upon the width of the lines required. This kind of gauge is better for laying out two sides of a mortise, and for marking grooves and dadoes. It's much quicker than a regular marking gauge, because you can scribe two sides at once.

Marking gauges are available at most hardware stores, but mortise gauges are harder to find. You can, however, purchase mortise gauges through most large, mail-order tool companies.

The Stanley Tools 65G marking gauge is constructed in a very old, traditional pattern. It's made of hardwood with a brass-bound face on the fence. A modern touch that looks out of place, however, is a locking screw made of plastic, rather than wood or metal. The 1/16-inch gradations on the 6-inch stem are a useful feature. Approx. Price: $9.50

Stanley's 91G mortise gauge has a double-bar design, with two stems sliding through the fence. Each produces one side of the scribed line. Stems are 6 3/16 inches long, and have 5-inch scales graduated in 1/16-inch increments. Approx. Price: $11.50

Marples of England produces a quality, rosewood mortise gauge with a brass-bound fence. This gauge has a single stem, with the second spur being adjustable along a small brass rail. This company is known for its fine touches, which are exhibited by this gauge. It can be ordered from Woodcraft (#12CO2M), Garrett Wade (#10N28.01),

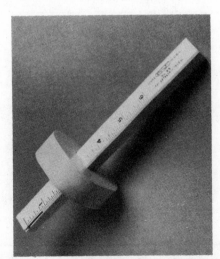

Stanley's 65G Marking Gauge

Marples Mortise Gauge

and Woodworker's Supply (#501-084) Approx. Price: (12CO2M) $12.50

Chalk Lines

A chalk line is a measuring tool used to mark long, straight horizontal and vertical lines. The principle of operation is simple. A long piece of string on a reel is inserted into a canister, and the entire reel of string is surrounded by powdered chalk. The string's free end has a hook attached to it. To mark a line on a surface, the line is drawn from the canister and held taut between two points. Then the string is lifted and "snapped," leaving a clear line left by the chalk. This done, the string is drawn back into the canister with a crank.

Chalk lines are used extensively in remodeling and other work on vertical surfaces where an absolute, straight line is required. When the canister is allowed to swing free, then held taut and snapped, it leaves a perfect line against which measurements can be made.

Although a chalk line is a useful marking device, its use is limited if you don't do a lot of remodeling or construction work. At the nominal price, however, it may be worth having around the shop for occasional tasks.

Stanley's 1050 Chalk-O-Matic chalk line reel is the best offered by the company. It has a die-cast aluminum case and felt gaskets that hug the line to provide a uniform coating of chalk. This chalk line has a hook on the end that you can attach to any projection or convenient slot. Also, the canister is pointed on one end, and can be used as a plumb bob. Line length is 50 feet. Approx. Price: $5.00

The Millers Falls' 8050 chalk line has an interesting extra—a slide-action lock with a spring-loaded line. You pull out the desired

Chalk lines are normally considered tradesman's tools that may not find much use in the average shop. But there is one job they can do better than any other tool—laying out a vertical baseline. This facility comes into particular use if you are applying wallpaper. Even a slight unevenness in the first sheet applied to a wall will be noticeable, and each successive sheet will multiply the original error.

The way to avoid this is to first use a chalk line. Measure out 6 inches from the upper left-hand corner of the first wall to be covered. Attach the hook from the chalk line to a nail hammered in at this point. Unreel the string from the chalkline's case, stopping when you reach the floor. Allow it to swing free until it stops, establishing a true vertical along that wall. Then apply tension to the line and snap it, leaving a mark along the wall. This results in a true baseline vertical from which all other measurements can be taken.

The edge of the first strip of wallpaper is pasted on so that it abuts this vertical line. Each successive strip is matched to the next, going to the right until the starting point. If you work carefully, the wallpaper will be completely even and straight around the entire room—no matter how out of square the corners are in reality.

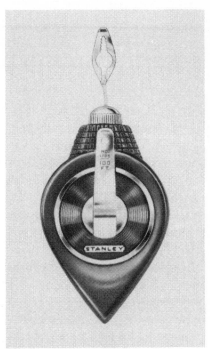

Stanley's 1050 Chalk-O-Matic

amount of line and set the lock before snapping the line. Afterwards, releasing the lock automatically retracts the line into the canister. This eliminates the tedious cranking common with most chalk lines. The die-cast aluminum canister is also pointed at one end for use as a plumb bob. Approx. Price: $5.00

Scratch Awls

These marking tools are smaller versions of the old-time ice picks. They're used to "scratch out" layout marks on wood.
Most woodworkers prefer to use a pencil, however, because a scratch awl leaves a line that usually takes some time and effort to remove. Its only advantage is that it leaves a very fine line, which can be a benefit when working to close tolerances. It takes an especially light hand to use these tools. In most cases, a very sharp, dark pencil will do as good a job and leave a marked line that can be easily erased. Scratch awls are available in most hardware stores and machinist's supply houses, priced at under $5.00

Compasses And Dividers

Compasses consist of a pair of pivoted steel legs with a sharp point on one leg and a pencil on the other. Dividers are the same, except both legs have a sharp point.

For woodworking, the reliable, children's compass is quite adequate. These dimestore-variety compasses are excellent, and cheap. You do, however, have to disregard the scale scribed on the arcing arm. It's much safer to set the correct measurement with a steel ruler, but you have to remember that the radius is only half the diameter of the resulting circle.

Dividers can be purchased cheaply at any hardware store. They're handy for laying out distances, centering holes, and other measuring tasks. You can also use them like a scratch awl, since the points are often hardened. These tools are the quickest way to center a hole on a narrow edge or other tight location, where slight inaccuracies in centering can be very noticeable.

Accuracy with both dividers and compasses depends more upon your attention than on the quality of the tool. As long as you are reasonably sure that the joint where the legs meet will not move while you use the tool, you have made a safe purchase.

Stud Finders

Trying to find a stud behind a wall can be a vexing problem. In house construction, a wall is first framed out with 2x4 lumber (actually 1½x3½). These studs are nailed vertically to form a horizontal lattice at top and bottom, between a series of 2x4s called plates. Out of convention, these vertical framing members are nailed 16 inches apart, or sometimes 18 inches apart if codes allow. This gives structural rigidity, while keeping the amount of material used to a minimum. On outside walls, the exteriors of these studs are covered with siding or other exterior covering, and insulation is put between the studs. The insides of these walls, as well as all interior walls, are covered with some type of plaster material.

Years ago, laths and hand-applied plaster were used, but now it's more often done with large sheets of plasterboard or Sheetrock.

The problem with these modern types of wall coverings is that they're not structurally strong in themselves. If you nail or screw even a moderately heavy object into the wall, it'll soon pull out—usually leaving a gaping hole. For this reason, it's necessary to find a stud first. By nailing through the outer wall covering and into the stud, the fastener is well secured.

Finding a stud is usually a guessing proposition. Once you find one stud, you can find adjacent ones by measuring off 16-inch centers. But doors and windows alter the normal distribution of the studs, making stud finding incredibly difficult—even if you were present when the house was built!

Several useful devices have been developed for finding studs behind plaster. The simplest of these is one or more magnets mounted inside a clear plastic box. This creates a simple compass, and is based on the fact that studs are nailed with iron nails. When the compass-type stud finder is brought near an iron nail in a stud, the magnet moves. Presumably, this tells you that you've located a stud. Actually, this kind of stud finder doesn't work well, and requires a great deal of patience to use. You have to hold the device directly over

a nail to find a stud, which results in a considerable amount of frustrating work.

A new type of stud finder has appeared on the market recently, and this one works quite a bit better. It's really a miniature metal detector, operating off a small battery. You simply sweep this tool over a wall and wait for a small light to go on, indicating a nail in a stud.

The Stanley 47-400 is a better-than-average magnetic-type stud finder. It has a black base with a clear plastic window at the top, through which you can see the magnet. A V-groove cut into the base makes it easy to mark the wall when the stud has been found. Most hardware stores carry it, and it has a reasonable price. Approx. Price: $1.50

The Conover Woodcraft 5000 Metalspy is a unique new stud finder. This compact electronic stud locater has a plastic case measuring 5½x3 inches. The 1-inch-wide case holds the necessary circuitry and a 9-volt battery.

The Metalspy is easily calibrated, and sweeping it across the wall quickly locates any metal behind it. Not only can you locate studs, but also electric wires, conduit, and water pipes. The sensing area of the tool is a full 5x1 inches in area. Plus, there's some overlap at either side to provide quite a large swept area.

It's also useful for discovering "tramp" metal embedded in hardwood. Striking embedded metal with a planer blade can result in a $30.00 repair bill for a new set of blades. So, the Metalspy may pay for itself through this use alone. You can purchase this stud finder directly from Conover Woodcraft, and it's also privately labeled for Brookstone (#5971). Approx. Price: $16.00

Conover's 5000 Metalspy

Wood, unfortunately, was not designed in the correct dimensions — it is always too long, wide, or thick to be used. Handsaws will often remedy this design defect, and do it fast and accurately. Their traditional forms and solid usefulness have earned them not only a place, but the right to be in every craftsman's tool kit.

Sawing Tools

Handsaws appeal to the utilitarian romantic — the person who cherishes the indescribable feel of fine wood. The power saw generally gets the job done quicker — and it frequently does it more accurately — but there is nothing that a power saw can do that a handsaw can't. If not abused, moreover, a good handsaw can last a lifetime.

What North Americans call a handsaw is technically a skewback or sweep-back handsaw. The blade in such a saw can be almost any dimension in length or width; the only essential requirement is teeth. Basically a saw's teeth are indentations cut into the metal blade that can serve to chisel, file or cut the material. Teeth on a good saw blade must be precision ground, and in some cases are hand polished. The coarseness in the cut (the roughness of the finished edge of the material) is governed by the number of teeth-per-inch — often called points-per-inch or PPI. The more points-per-inch, the finer the cut, and vice-versa. The number of actual teeth-per-inch is always one less than the PPI. Most skew-backed saws have a number stamped close to the heel of the blade which indicates the PPI of that blade.

Another characteristic of a saw's teeth is the set. Set is the slight bend of each tooth, in an alternate pattern, to the

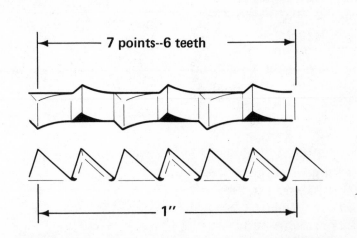

7 points--6 teeth

1"

*The size of a saw's teeth is called out as PPI (points-per-inch) or PTI (points to the inch). There is always one less **full** tooth than there is number of points. The term tells how smooth and how fast the tool will cut. You cut more slowly when the saw has many small teeth but the cut edge will be smoother and more even.*

For cabinet work — 10 to 12 PPI crosscut saw
Rough carpentry ⟨ 7 to 9 PPI crosscut saw
5½ to 7 PPI ripsaw

A QUICK LOOK AT BASIC HANDSAWS

NAME	REMARKS	TYPICAL USES
Crosscut Saw **Ripsaw**	crosscut saws and ripsaws look alike — major difference is in shape of teeth and number of teeth.	sawing boards to length — cutting plywood panels — making angle cuts (miters) in lumber sawing boards to width — cutting *with* the grain of the wood
Backsaw **Dovetail Saw**	reinforced back to stiffen blade — many small teeth for smooth cuts.	cuts for wood joints — use with miter box for picture-frame joints, cutting moldings originally designed for cutting dovetail joints but fine for any precision work
Coping Saw **Deep Throat Coping Saw (Scroll Saw)**	used with thin, replaceable blades — blade is tensioned by tightening handle — blade ends are either looped or pinned — blades adjust for direction of cut	fine fretwork — internal cutouts — accessory cuts on some joint designs — scalloped edges as above but with greater reach
Compass Saw **Keyhole Saw**	both have long tapering blades — typical compass saw is 12-14 inches long — keyhole saw is 10-12 inches long and has a narrower blade — much overlap in function	making openings in walls for electrical boxes — make straight or curved internal cuts by first drilling a starting hole — general curve-cutting — the thinner blade of the keyhole saw makes tighter turns than the compass saw and gets into smaller areas

left or right of the center line of the blade. The reason the teeth are so positioned is to create a kerf (width of cut in the material) wider than the actual width of the blade. The wider kerf prevents the saw from binding while in use. Taper-grinding, usually found in many quality blades, also helps prevent binding. Taper-ground blades are slightly thinner at the toe and back edges than at the edge or heel. Together, the set and taper-grinding help insure a smoother cutting stroke.

Quality saws are also slightly crowned, showing a gentle arc along the teeth from the toe of the blade to the heel. Although it may be as little as ⅛-inch in a 26-inch saw, the crown serves to minimize friction by bringing fewer teeth into contact with the work; it thus frees the stroke. All saws should also have a certain amount of tension, the ability to spring back and stay in a straight line while in use. Tension helps keep the saw correctly positioned and prevents bowing.

The handle of a handsaw can be made of anything, although the feel and grip of a fine hardwood handle tends to be the most comfortable, results in better saw balance, and has remained a traditional favorite. The handle should be securely attached to the blade, and the angle of the handle should contribute to a natural stroke. Manufacturers position saw handles at different angles, so you should try the feel and heft of any saw before

purchasing it. Of utmost importance is that the saw feel right to you. It must help, not hinder, the work at hand.

The surface finish on a handsaw blade does more than contribute to its beauty. A high polish helps the saw glide through the work, making the stroke easier and preventing the blade from binding in the cut. In addition to the conventional finish, some manufacturers now

offer saws with a Teflon-S coating. The coating contributes to easier stroking due to the inherent slipperiness of the Teflon. Since the Teflon also resists rust, it helps keep the blade in good condition over the years. The deep-green color of the Teflon coating fails to match the beautiful finish of polished steel, but the functional advantages Teflon provides cannot be denied.

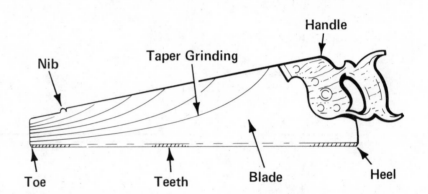

Some Basic Handsaws

Rip and crosscut are the two basic types of handsaws. Ripsaws cut with the grain of the wood. Crosscut saws, as their name implies, cut best across the grain. The basic shape of the teeth, the size of the gullet (the slot between the teeth), the amount of set, and the points-per-inch put a saw in one classification or the other. Fine furniture or hobby work will usually require both. But for general work around the home, a

crosscut is usually adequate for most tasks.

Crosscut saws have teeth that are sharply pointed, are patterned with a mild set, and have a very small gullet. Their teeth actually incise the wood fibers, slicing through each with a clean cut. Since sawdust created by a crosscut saw will be fine and dustlike, the gullets — which facilitate waste removal — need not be deep.

Standard PPI on a crosscut

HOW TO BE AN EXPERT SAW BUYER

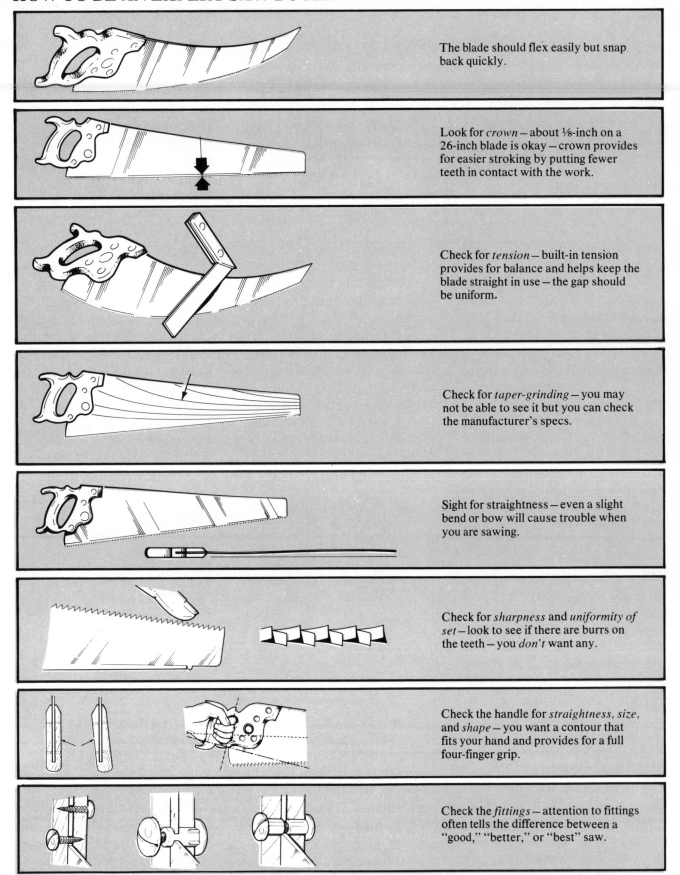

The blade should flex easily but snap back quickly.

Look for *crown* — about ⅛-inch on a 26-inch blade is okay — crown provides for easier stroking by putting fewer teeth in contact with the work.

Check for *tension* — built-in tension provides for balance and helps keep the blade straight in use — the gap should be uniform.

Check for *taper-grinding* — you may not be able to see it but you can check the manufacturer's specs.

Sight for straightness — even a slight bend or bow will cause trouble when you are sawing.

Check for *sharpness* and *uniformity of set* — look to see if there are burrs on the teeth — you *don't* want any.

Check the handle for *straightness, size, and shape* — you want a contour that fits your hand and provides for a full four-finger grip.

Check the *fittings* — attention to fittings often tells the difference between a "good," "better," or "best" saw.

*"This **Setting** of the Teeth of the Saw (as Workman call it) is to make the Kerf wide enough for the Back to follow the Edge: And is set **Ranker** for soft, coarse, cheap Stuff, than for hard, fine and costly Stuff: For the **Ranker** the Tooth is set, the more Stuff is wasted in the Kerf...."*

*Joseph Moxon, **Mechanick Exercises: or the Doctrine of Handy-Works. Applied to the Arts of Smithing Joinery Carpentry Turning Bricklayery.** (London, 1677)*

saw blade is from 5 to 10 points, with the middle ground about 7 or 8. The teeth cut on the forward stroke and give a fairly smooth cut on most materials. For efficient cutting action, the angle of stroke should approximate 45 degrees. Saws of the crosscut type are available in lengths from 16 to 28 inches, with the longer blades easier to use in general cutting because they permit a longer stroke.

Crosscut saws can cut with the grain of the wood, but not as efficiently as a ripsaw. Ripsaw blades have teeth that are sharpened to a chisel point, a wider set, and a larger gullet. Ripsaw teeth don't cut away the wood fibers; instead, they chisel away pieces of the material. Sawdust from a ripsaw contains larger chips of wood, and the function of the deeper gullets is to pull out these bigger pieces.

Common ripsaws usually have a PPI of 5½ to 6 points, and a standard length of 26 inches. Although ripsaws cut only on the downward stroke, they do so very rapidly when held at the correct angle of approximately 60 degrees, providing the best chiseling action.

Some ripsaws of finer quality have a small section near the toe which has more teeth than the rest of the blade. This section is used to start the cut before the relatively coarser teeth in the blade move into the wood.

The brand name on any handsaw is no guarantee that it is the best which that particular company produces. A casual glance through any catalog or store selection will soon show that most manufacturers label their saws with different classifications. 'Good,' 'better,' or 'best' is one such classification system; another is 'standard,' 'premium,' or 'professional.' Even the lowest of these grades will be vastly more durable and usable than a saw picked up at a bargain counter, but it will certainly lack those refinements which distinguish the top-of-the-line tool. Remember that the initial extra cost of a fine handsaw will work out to pennies a year over the life of the tool. Besides being a means to an end—sawing wood—a fine saw can often represent an end in itself.

Rip And Crosscut Saws

Disston's D-95 crosscut saw represents the top line in craftsmanship, plus being an exquisitely balanced saw that shows first-rate cutting performance. The 26-inch blade is made of chrome-nickel steel set off with unique accent stripes; the handle is of carved wood that has a nice walnut finish. The teeth are precision-set and bevel-filed. Eight points-per-inch puts it at about the midrange of crosscut saws and the teeth will retain their sharpness for a long time, especially if you treat this tool with respect. Approx. Price: $18.00

The Disston D-23 is the company's most popular professional handsaw. The D-23 comes with four fittings to hold the walnut handle to the taper-ground blade. In all versions the teeth are precision set and sharpened and come in a wide choice of lengths and PPI. Crosscuts are available in blade lengths from 16 to 26 inches and a wide choice of points-per-inch; the ripsaw has a similarly wide range. Approx. Price: $16.00

Disston's D-23 Handsaw

The Nicholson 300 handsaw should be appreciated on both the amateur and professional level as a fine quality hand tool. A fully taper-ground silver steel blade – with teeth expertly set and hand filed – is fitted with a carved hardwood handle that is really a pleasure to hold because of the tool's above average comfort and balance. Crosscut varieties of the 300 are available in blade lengths of 20 inches with 10 PPI, and 26 inches with 8, 10, 11, or

Nicholson's 300 Handsaw

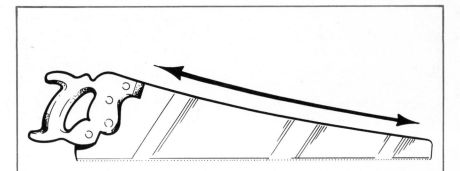

Skew-backed handsaws, standard tools in North America, have had many developments over the years. Some designs were made to deliberately improve the basic sawing qualities of the tool, others were simple embellishments for purely decorative reasons. The best of the designs incorporated both. Henry Disston, the British immigrant who was to found one of the largest handsaw firms of the 19th Century, designed many varieties of the open-frame handsaw. The "skewback" was introduced in 1874 and became one of the most popular variants of this handsaw shape. In this case the back of the saw has been slightly hollowed out. This serves to lighten the saw while improving its balance, imparting at the same time a very graceful appearance. Handsaws with this design are still being manufactured, a tribute to the sense of style and functional utility possessed by Henry Disston over a century ago.

Nicholson's 300 Handsaw

12 PPI. The single ripsaw is 26 inches long with 5½ PPI. Approx. Price: $15.50

"PAX" is the brand name of a Sheffield firm with a 200-year-old tradition of producing exquisite hand tools. PAX blades are electrically melted alloy steel taper-ground to a fine finish. The beech handles are positioned for firm control and balance. Two PAX ripsaws (Models 6P211 and 6P212) are both 26 inches long, with 7½ and 5½ PPI, respectively. Crosscut saws come in seven models (6P208, 6P210, 6P248,

6P260, 6P262, 6P266, and 6P268), ranging in length from 20 to 26 inches with 6 to 12 PPI. They are distributed by the Frog Tool Company. Approx. Price: $20.00

The Bushman Admiral is a professional crosscut saw with a 26-inch blade of cold-rolled steel, taper-ground with 10 PPI. The unusual handle, made of laminated 17-ply veneer and almost impossible to break, is secured to the classical straightback blade by four nickel-plated brass fittings. A quality handsaw made to

handle anything from soft pine to particleboard, the Bushman Admiral is listed as Model 2520 in the catalog of The Princeton Tool Company.
 Approx. Price: $19.50

Buck Saws And Bow Saws

Technically, handsaws like crosscut or ripsaws are known as "open saws," a term now found only in old tool books to describe a saw blade with a permanently attached handle. Bow and buck saws originate from another design, the technical name of which is the "frame saw." Both share the common trait of having a rather narrow metal blade mounted on an open wood (metal in modern versions) frame. Historically, frame saws were popular among early North American craftsmen because wood was simply more available than metal for a saw frame. They bought the blade and mounted it as they wished. Frame saws are also taken apart very easily, and only

PAX Handsaw

> *"The Office of the Cheeks made to the **Frame Saw** is, by the twisted Cord and Tongue in the middle, to draw the upper ends of the Cheeks closer together, that the lower end of the Cheeks may be drawn the wider asunder, and strain the Blade of the **Saw** the straighter. The **Tennant-Saw,** being thin, hath a Back to keep it from bending."*
>
> Joseph Moxon, **Mechanick Exercises: or the Doctrine of Handy-Works. Applied to the Arts of Smithing Joinery Carpentry Turning Bricklayery** *(London, 1677)*

the blade needs to be carried from place to place — a convenient solution to the problems of a metal-poor, but wood-rich world.

Traditionally, the buck saw is made in the shape of a broad "H," with the cross-piece and uprights (called cheeks) of wood. At the lower end of the "H" the blade is held between the two uprights, while at the top is a tensioning device. Original design incorporated a heavy cord or rope stretched between the two ends, and tension was applied by twisting a toggle or stick to create a windlass effect. Buck saws made in this pattern today often have a wire at the top, tensioned by a stud and a wing nut. Further evolution of the buck saw has turned it into a tubular-metal frame made in the shape of a "U," the blade stretched across the open throat and tension applied by either a wing nut or cam lever.

The buck saw was a pioneering tool devised for cutting rough logs and lumber quickly, and was very efficient. Common blade configuration was (and is) alternate chipper and raker teeth separated by deep gullets or slots for efficient chip removal. Most buck saws cut in either direction of stroke for fast cutting. Much to the satisfaction of those whose memory of the buck saw is based on hours of

work on the family woodpile, the advent of the chain saw has all but killed buck saws as a common everyday tool. Tool fanciers mourn their passing because, elegant in their simple design, they were functional tools that did a good job.

Modern buck saws have rigid, tubular frames shaped much like a flattened "U," the relatively heavy, non-adjustable blade gripped tightly across the open end. Tooth shape makes this kind of saw more practical for log cutting and tree pruning, precisely what most of these saws are advertised to do.

Bow saws are also frame saws, but have greater flexibility than buck saws. Two handles protrude from each end of the bow saw blade, allowing the blade itself to be rotated in any direction in reference to the

Construction in the 1750s (Note: Ripsawing on sawhorses)

29

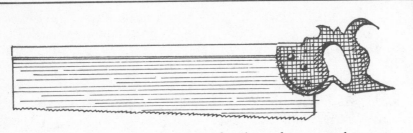

Like most things done with tools, the only way to become proficient at handsawing is by practice. You do not have to do a lot of it to attain proficiency, as learning the proper way to use a handsaw is not difficult. A properly designed handsaw will definitely help you to stroke more smoothly, but even the best will bend or bind if you feel that cutting speed is more important than accuracy. You simply cannot force a saw to take more wood than it was designed to remove. Pressure is required, but technique is more important than muscle. Smooth and correct stroking is more effective, will cut faster, and you will have a superior cut once you have finished.

First, make sure the work is supported correctly and this includes the scrap portion to be removed. Before starting the cut, carefully scribe a line across the face of the material as a guide. Speed and quality of the cut itself are controlled by the angle of the saw's teeth to the surface of the work. When crosscutting this angle should be approximately 45 degrees; ripping cuts should be done at about 60 degrees. Plywood, because of its construction, should always be cut with a crosscut saw; but the angle should be somewhere between regular crosscutting and ripping, perhaps about 50 to 55 degrees. Keep the veneer side of the plywood 'up' and you will minimize the feathering or splintering that will occur in this material.

When beginning a cut, position the blade so that it will cut on the scrap end of the scribed line. Use the thumb of your free hand against the side of the blade to guide the first strokes. On the first few strokes go slowly in order to cut a starting notch; this process is made easier with a quality ripsaw because there are finer teeth set into the toe of the blade to create this notch. Let the weight of the saw do the work as you take care to maintain the proper angle to the stock you are cutting. You can get through knots or hard places more easily if you rock the saw a bit as you stroke it. This puts fewer teeth in contact with the work and you will not have to use as much pressure. Slow your strokes as you come to the near edge and support the waste piece so that it won't splinter away as you finish the cut.

Once the technique is mastered, you will soon be able to cut stock to dimension with a handsaw as easily as with a power tool; saving yourself the setup time that would be wasted on smaller dimensioning tasks.

frame or the work. Tension on the blade can be accomplished by cord and toggle or the modern wire, stud and wing nut arrangement. Bow saws are also much smaller than buck saws, and the turning handles are convenient for holding and driving the saw while in use.

Although the bow saw has largely been replaced in England and North America by the common handsaw, it is still the preferred tool of craftsmen on the Continent — exactly why is a mystery. Bow saws for regular sawing operations have a blade length of 18 to 26 inches, with 6 to 8 PPI. A smaller variety is often called the scroll bow saw. It has a very narrow, thin blade with 8 to 16 PPI. Although bow saws look clumsy and are hard to learn to use, in experienced hands a bow saw will cut at rates comparable to an electric saber saw and with as much accuracy.

Millers Falls buck saws come in three models, all of them alike except for size and weight. The longer blades are heavier, but give longer strokes and faster cutting; shorter units make acceptable tree trimmers or can be taken on camping trips. All three have steel tubular frames with built-in clamping levers to keep the blades taut. Blades are held in place over a pin system, and the action of the lever

Woodcraft's 12B01-M Bow Saw

All village carpenters numbered among their many skills the ability to correctly sharpen their handsaws. Each man had an individual and special way of sharpening and slanting the teeth in his saws, a necessity before precision "saw-sets" and jigs for the correct filing angle. A properly sharpened saw was a source of pride to its owner. Badly sharpened, the saw betrayed to the artisan's fellows that the man who held it was not a skilled craftsman.

Pioneers brought their own tool kits with them to the New World and early ship's manifests show a heavy importation of tools and the material with which to make them. Later, as forges and iron works were established in the colonies, men created their own tools or had it done for them by the village smith. 19th Century tradesmen ordered their tools from the Sheffield catalog or traveling salesmen who carried their wares around on pack animals. By the middle 1800's, companies like Stanley Rule and Level were established in North America; industries whose output would swiftly outrun that of England. The domestic market came first, then the final success at capturing the world market after the First World War.

correctly tensions them. All models also have teeth designed on the "raker and four" system. Four teeth are set in a "bank," and these do the bulk of the cutting. Another tooth called a raker serves to smooth out the cut and remove the waste chips. As with most saws designed for cutting green wood, the gullets are deep. The entire tooth design is meant to provide free stroking and that intent is served in these saws.

Model 9236 uses a 36-inch blade; Model 9030 has a 30-inch blade; and Model 9021 comes with a smaller, 21-inch blade. They all make acceptable replacements for the energy guzzling chain saws, and they warm you twice: once when you use

them and then when you burn the wood.
Approx. Price: (9236) $10.00

Millers Falls' 9236 Buck Saw

Millers Falls' 9030 Buck Saw

Millers Falls' 9021 Buck Saw

Woodcraft's Model 12B01-M is a British bow saw whose graceful shape makes it eye appealing and lends strength to this very traditional saw type. The sidepieces, or "cheeks," are made of curved beechwood, as are the file-type handles for blade adjustment. Tension is provided by a non-stretch cord, and the traditional "toggle stick." This is not a large tool—the blade size is only 12 inches—but it is quite suitable for cabinet work where a coping saw is a little too small. Depth of cut is 5½ inches with 9 PPI. Although technically a crosscut saw, the fineness of the blade and its slim shape make the bow saw ideal for detail work on curves and internal cutouts. You'll like this bow saw—if only because the brass ferrules and formed, wooden construction are reminiscent of traditional woodcrafting.
Approx. Price: $15.50

Frog Tool Company's Model 179E1 at 24 inches, Model 179E2 at 28 inches, and Model 179E3 at 32 inches in length are three versions of the large bow

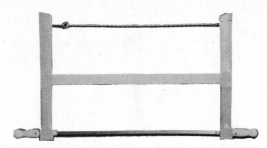

Frog Tool's 179E1 Bow Saw

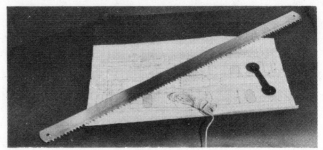

Frog Tool's Bow Saw Kit

saw. These are often called "continental bow saws" and are very popular in Europe (indeed, these particular saws were made in Germany). Blade tension is provided by a strand of twisted wire that is tightened by a wing nut and a threaded eye bolt. Blades for any of these frame saws come in two available widths—either ⅜ of an inch or 1½ inches. PPI's from 5 to 9½ are offered. The wide blades are for ripping and crosscutting heavy stock; the thin ones are for scroll work and curves. All wooden parts are stained and lacquered beechwood, and depth clearance varies with the size of the saw. Nicely made, and the prices are reasonable. Approx.Price:(179E1)$13.00

Frog Tool Company's bow saw kits have blade lengths running from 23½ to 31½ inches and tooth designs in rip, crosscut, or fine. Kits include steel blade tangs (which grip the blades), the blade itself, a non-stretching tension cord and plans for making the wooden frame and toggle stick. It's rare that one has input into any process in our industrial age;

a sad commentary that does much to explain why there is so little craftsmanship in products. Any of these kits lets you shape the frame as you wish and make it out of any exotic species of wood

that you desire, giving yourself a tool for use and an heirloom to pass on. The kits sport product numbers from 971B1 to 971B6 in the Frog Tool Company catalog. Approx. Price:(971B1)$9.50

Rip and crosscut sawing in a 1750s woodshop

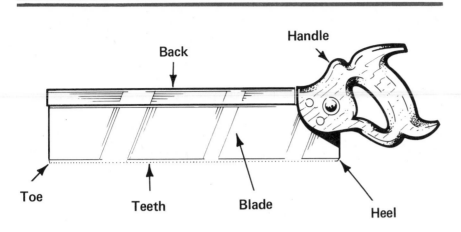

Back
Handle
Toe
Teeth
Blade
Heel

Backsaws

Average handsaws are fine for approximately sizing wood to the correct dimension. But for fine and detail work, more specialized tools are required. Backsaws are invaluable for making intricate outline cuts for dados, halflaps, and rabbets. A backsaw is a crosscut saw with fine teeth and a rigid spine on the back edge. The spine's purpose is to reinforce the saw blade during use to keep it straight. Although most American-made backsaws have a steel spine, the traditional material for this part is brass. A brass spine is not more functional but it excels in beauty. When choosing a backsaw look for teeth with an even set to prevent the saw from wandering during use. Another consideration is "depth of cut," the distance from the teeth to the lower edge of the spine. This is critical when cutting heavy stock, as it dictates the thickness of the material which can be handled. Typical backsaws can be in any lengths from 10 to 30 inches with 10 to 15 points-per-inch.

Brookstone's Model A-3595 is cataloged as a tenon saw, the traditional and historical name still used in Europe for a backsaw. But it's still a backsaw; having, in fact, one of the heaviest brass backs made. This is a precise cutting tool of exceptional beauty and utility. The spine is almost an inch high and ⅛-inch thick on either side of the high-carbon, manganese steel blade. The blade is a mere .032 of an inch thick,

The country carpenter of old made everything from the footstool to the wainscot, from doorpost to shelves and, when the villager he had served came to his alotted span, it was the carpenter who was called upon to make the coffin. Coffin material might be elm, oak, or mahogany depending upon the affluence of its final user. Every family had a distinctive style. Linings were made of swansdown or gingham, only the very poor were laid to rest in an unlined coffin. Occasionally an eccentric would require a coffin years before he expected to need it, taking delivery of the casket for use as a blanket chest or perhaps temporarily installing a glass door so that it could be stood upright and used as a china closet.

Converting a tree into coffin boards would often take two sawyers a full week. Boards were stacked outside to dry, then moved to a loft to season. Planing and finishing would always be done carefully, though it was doubtful that anyone would really appreciate the result for any length of time. Orders from distant villages were accompanied by a length of string to ensure the proper "fit" for the deceased. The advent of the hearse and the development of embalming eventually separated the carpenter's trade from that of the undertaker.

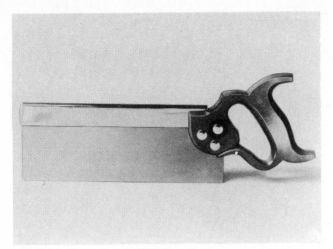

Brookstone's A-3595 Backsaw

Woodworker's Supply 512-005 and 512-006

hardened and tempered for just the right amount of stiffness required in a backsaw. The good polish on the blade reduces cutting friction. Three brass fittings secure the polished beechwood handle to the blade, and it is so positioned as to make firm, positive strokes a pleasure. The saw is 12 inches long and has 14 PPI; the depth of cut is 3¼ inches. Approx. Price: $25.00

Woodworker's Supply offers backsaws in two sizes, Model 512-005 is a stubby 8 inches long with 20 PPI, and Model 512-006 is a more normal 12 inches long with 15 PPI. Both blades are expertly hardened and tempered, chrome nickel steel, with a spine of hand-polished brass. The polished beech handle is fitted to keep the cutting edge close to the work. Both are excellent-quality saws, and the smaller one is perfectly suited for fine cuts. Approx. Price: (512-006) $19.50

The Princeton Company's Model 2521A backsaw is a good choice for the non-professional, and is far less expensive than its top-of-the-line competitors. The blade is tough Swedish Oderholm steel and can be used to cut through non-wood materials like plastic pipe—something you would never do with a quality backsaw. The spine does its task adequately, although the marine plywood handle, attached with only two brass rivets, is acceptable rather than outstanding. At 14 inches long and 11 PPI, this backsaw has above-average quality at a reasonable price. Approx. Price: $8.50

Disston's Model 4B is the company's best backsaw. The high quality steel blade is expertly hardened and tempered, extending well back into the handle. This feature, when combined with the justly famous and comfortable grip, helps any user achieve positive control during precision work. Approx. Price: $11.00

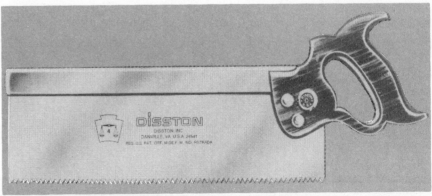

Disston's 4B Backsaw

Miter Boxes
And
Miter Saws

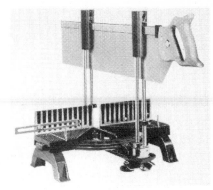

Stanley's "Best" Miter Box

It's tedious and time consuming to lay out a large number of miter or angle cuts, especially if they are identical. As you would expect, manufacturers have developed ways to speed up the process. Miter (or mitre) boxes are essentially adjustable jigs for cutting angles quickly and accurately without requiring continuous measuring operations. Although you can find miter boxes that offer a number of useless gadgets, the basic miter box should accomplish two basic functions. It should support the work securely while it is being cut, and offer a locked guide for the backsaw. Miter boxes make excellent sense if you do a lot of angle work on small dimensional stock. Otherwise you can nail together a small wooden box to perform the same operation and save yourself some money.

Most commercial miter boxes are sold complete with a backsaw, sometimes called a miter saw. The most popular size miter saw is about 26 inches, although the size of these backsaws is dictated by the dimensions of the stock to be cut and the brackets on the box to hold it straight. Quality differences are the same as for regular backsaws, except for the fact that they are usually intended for use by professional woodworking tradesmen, and so are heavier and will resist more wear and tear.

The Stanley Corporation "Best" miter box gives you a choice of accessory miter saws. Available backsaws (Models 2246B, 2358B, and 360B) come in lengths of 26 inches x 4 inches, 28 inches x 5 inches, and 30 inches x 6 inches, and all of them are solid, rugged tools built for a lifetime of use. The box itself offers just about any feature you'll ever need or can imagine a need for: angular capacity of 30 to 90 degrees, infinitely adjustable indexing plate with 11 automatic lock positions, adjustable saw guides to hold the blade, built-in positioning spurs and more. In fact, there are so many gadgets that you could forget about the work at hand and amuse yourself with the machine itself. Capacity is a 90 degree cut on 10-inch boards and a 45 degree cut on 7-inch boards. You will enjoy using this miter box because it does the job—well. Approx. Price: (360B) $150.00

The Frog Tool Company Model 430E Perfecta miter box is not equipped with the conventional backsaw. Instead it has fine-toothed, tensionable blades as the cutting surfaces. This unique design feature lets you cut

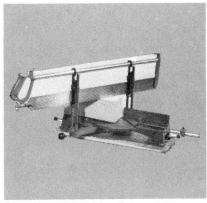

Frog's 430E Perfecta Miter Box

various materials by simply changing the blade. The box itself locks on four automatic settings — 22½, 45, 60, and 90 degrees. An indexing bar and pin lock in the setting. The Perfecta is the largest tool of this design, with a capacity of a 10-inch board at 90 degrees down to a 6½-inch board at 45 degrees. This is more than a woodworking tool, capable of cutting angles quickly and accurately in any material from wood to soft metals. Approx. Price: $238.00

The Jointmaster
(distributed by Brookstone Company mail order firm) is not actually a miter box. But used in conjunction with any backsaw, it can accommodate stock up to 2 x 2 inches in the full 45 degree miter position. Basically a metal jig that holds the wood and guides the saw, the Jointmaster is for the casual woodworker whose highest ambition is to make an

occasional picture frame. You can make lap joints or bridles, but prolonged use is soon liable to send it to a scrap yard for a premature burial. Still, it is a clever tool that won its inventor a gold medal at a Brussels fair, and the 20-page instruction manual tells you all you ever wanted to know about how to cut a joint.
Approx. Price: $25.00

Stanley's Miter Machine Model 100MM is no exception to the fact that miter boxes are prone to being coupled with a variety of gadgets. This box is designed so that any miter joint can be cut, nailed and glued while in the machine. The work is secured by clamps that can hold anything less than 4 inches wide. A 24-inch backsaw is included. Of good quality, the saw is mounted in and guided by roller bearing supports. Rotatable in a full circle, you can even tilt it a full 90 degrees. Both are useful

The Lion Trimmer

features. It won't replace a miter box, but if you need to frame a few hundred pictures, this will do the job.
Approx. Price: $282.00

The Lion Trimmer
(Pootatuck Corporation) is an unusual supplement to the traditional miter box. This tool can create a finish on a cut that is so smooth that often sanding is not required. Two hollow-ground blades are activated by a large steel handle and will cut just about everything put on the bed. The material to be trimmed is first sized in a miter box, and then given the finish cut. The Lion Trimmer can be used for either left- or right-hand cuts at any angle from 45 to 90 degrees on stock up to 5 inches wide (miter trim cuts) or 3⅞ inches wide in trim-bevel or cross miter cuts. The Lion Trimmer can be ordered directly from the Pootatuck Corporation.
Approx. Price: $168.00

Brookstone's Jointmaster

Stanley's 100MM

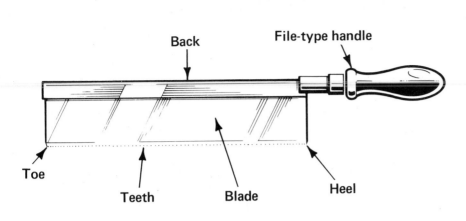

Back   File-type handle

Toe

Teeth   Blade   Heel

Dovetail Saws

In the early days of carpentry everything was done with hand tools, every carpenter's shop had a variety of saws, and in each category there was a size for the particular task at hand. Dovetail saws actually are nothing but very small backsaws designed to cut intricate joints like dovetails, tenons, and dados used in cabinet work. Often called cabinet saws for this reason, dovetail saws are a necessity for inlay or veneer work and for the small model builder. Most dovetails do not exceed 10 inches in length and the depth of cut is only about 1½ inches. The PPI ranges from 15 to 21; this, combined with the exceptionally thin blades, produces an extremely fine cut. Dovetail saw handles are usually round and may be offset to get the hand out of

the way of obstructions. Being specialty tools, dovetails perform a very limited range of cuts, but they do so with an accuracy unmatched by any hand or power saw.

The Sanderson Newbould "PAX" dovetail saw listed in the Frog Tool Company's

catalog is a departure from the traditional dovetail. Its blade is deeper, spine heavier, and the handle is not the conventional file type — in fact, it looks like (and is) a slightly smaller version of the standard backsaw. But the teeth (21 PPI) are set on a special anvil, the blade material is a special electric furnace Sheffield steel, the spine is mirror polished brass, and the handle is carefully angled for precise stroking action. Expensive yes, but they are made only in small quantities and each saw gets a lot of personal attention. A cabinetmaker's precision tool that is as nice to look at as it is to use. Approx. Price: $19.50

Disston's "professional" Model 68 is a conventional dovetail saw — a good, no-nonsense, basic tool priced so it won't shock anyone, not even the occasional user. The blade is good steel with a quality finish, and the spine, also steel, is heavy enough to keep the saw straight. Its

PAX Dovetail Saw

hardwood handle is the traditional file type, and is set to lead into the correct cutting action. Length is 10 inches, with 15 PPI. No beauty this, but a solid tool at an affordable price. Approx. Price: $7.50

Disston's 68 Dovetail Saw

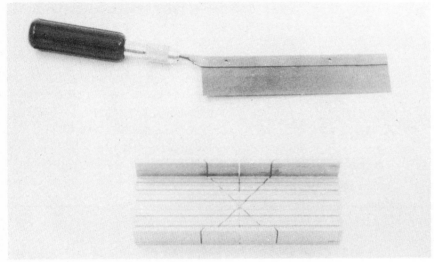

Woodworker's Supply Razor Saw

Woodworker's Supply, Inc. offers a very small backsaw with extremely fine teeth and a thin-gauge blade. Technically, it is a razor saw, which is a variation of the dovetail saw, and it has an unusual accessory—a miter box designed expressly for the saw. This razor saw is a mere 1¼ inches wide and has 30 PPI, and cuts a kerf so thin (.010 of an inch) that it appears finer than a pencil line! The box itself is aluminum, with precut 45 and 90 degree saw-guide slots. Although the box is an extra accessory, together they make such a fine and delicate pair that it would not be right to own one without the other. The blades are also replaceable, a handy feature. Approx. Price: $7.50

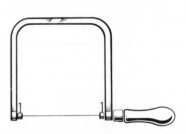

Coping And Fret Saws

Most handsaws are designed to make straight-line cuts. This intention is very clear in the construction of the

> *"Admiration for the artefacts of bygone civilizations should not lead us to overlook the merits of many common tools and utensils of trade in present-day use. Tool-making seldom produces an ugly object, for the design is a culmination of centuries of trial and error; and, as if by instinct, experienced tool-smiths tend to produce tools of graceful appearance. This tendency is apparent not only in conventional tools, such as the hedge-slasher and chisels and axes, but in some of the tools made for newly developed trades—for instance, in the garage mechanic's bi-hexagon ring-spanner (a direct descendant of the coach-builder's wheel-cap wrench) which, with its elegant curves, is an example of good industrial design."*
>
> R.A. Salaman, "Tradesmen's Tools c. 1500-1850" in **A History of Technology**, ed. by Charles Singer, Vol. III (Oxford: Clarendon Press, 1957)

various kinds of backsaws and, despite the disbelief of many woodworkers, is the real purpose of any handsaw. Straight backsaws, however, will not cut or follow a radius smaller than the width of their blades; backsaws will cut no further than the bottom of the spine. Coping saws and the smaller fret saws were developed to solve this problem. They may come under a wide variety of names—jig, scroll, fret, or deep-throat saws—but they are alike in construction and purpose. All are basically U-shaped frames that grip a thin, narrow blade across the open jaws of the "U." Using one of these saws makes it possible to follow curves and angles impossible to cut with other saws. These are the types of handsaw used to do intricate scrolling and fretwork on the sounding boards of many instruments.

The average coping saw is about 12 inches long, with a frame made of spring steel and an attached, file-type handle. The distance between the mounted blade and the bottom of the saw's back is called the "throat." This may be anywhere from 4½ to 7 inches deep on standard coping saws; fret saws are smaller, and some deep scroll saws have throats up to 11 inches deep. Deeper throats allow cutting to the center in larger pieces of work. Blade length is usually about 6½ inches, width under ⅛th inch, and the PPI may be anything from 10 on up. The blade can be fitted into the frame to face the teeth in

either direction with respect to the handle, allowing cuts with either direction of stroke. It is this feature which makes coping saws so useful. For inside work, a hole may be drilled in a waste area, the blade detached from the saw and passed through, and then reattached. This technique is called "piercing" and is a way to make internal cutouts without a lead-in hole from the edge of the stock. Most coping or fret saws also allow you to change the angle of the teeth with respect to the plane of the saw, thus permitting cuts with the saw held in any position. Never sharpened, coping saw blades are cheap and disposable—a virtue, since even in experienced hands they sometimes break during use.

Fret saws are for more delicate work than the standard coping saw. They are not made to handle work heavier than about ¼ inch. For larger stock the regular coping saw should be used. They do best on materials

that require a fine degree of accuracy with a minimum of waste.

Generally you cannot make too many mistakes when buying a coping or fret saw. They are simple tools that are hard to make incorrectly. The frame must have the necessary spring to keep the blade taut and the handle must be comfortable to grip during use. One additional feature that is nice to see is a provision for a positive grip on both ends of the blade, but that is not necessary. In any case, you cannot put too much pressure on these saws without snapping the blades. Coping and fret saws are made for delicate work, not felling trees.

Trojan Tools (Parker Manufacturing Co.) offers two coping saws: Model 50 with a 5-inch throat depth and Model 75 with a 6¾-inch throat. Both have a strong,

Veneer sawing with frame saw, circa 1800.

39

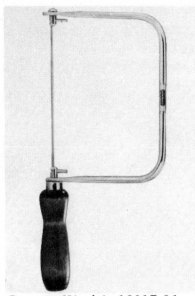

*Garrett Wade's 10117.01
Coping Saw*

one-piece frame, with smooth birch handles. The unique feature of these coping saws is a blade-locking mechanism that helps to prevent blade twisting while using the saw (the most common reason for blade breakage). Good, serviceable saws for the professional or the hobbyist, they do what they are designed to do and do it well. Approx. Price: (50) $4.00

Garrett Wade lists the Model 10117.01; they call it "a fine, English-made, professional-quality coping saw," but it is actually rather run-of-the mill. Its price, however, is quite competitive with standard coping saws offered at most hardware stores. Throat depth is 4¾ inches; the supplied blade is 6¾ inches long and has 12 PPI. A straight beechwood handle is unadorned, but

functional and comfortable. It may not do the job any better, but it does have the *cachet* of an English tool. Approx. Price: $5.50

The Woodcraft fret saw comes in two models— Model 16J40-AV has a 3½-inch-deep throat, and Model 15001-AV has an 11½-inch one. Both use blades that are 5 inches long and which are interchangeable with either frame. Available blade thicknesses range from .011 inch (32 PPI) to .022 inch (16PPI). These blades

must be used with care, since they are quite brittle. The frames are strong and rigid, with wing nut clamps to grip the blade and keep it taut. Capacity of the larger fret saw is quite impressive, and will permit cutting to the center on workpieces that are of very respectable size. Approx. Price: (16J40-AV) $5.50

There really isn't any way to overburden a simple coping saw and so most manufacturers make a basic saw and leave it at that. The following saws share the

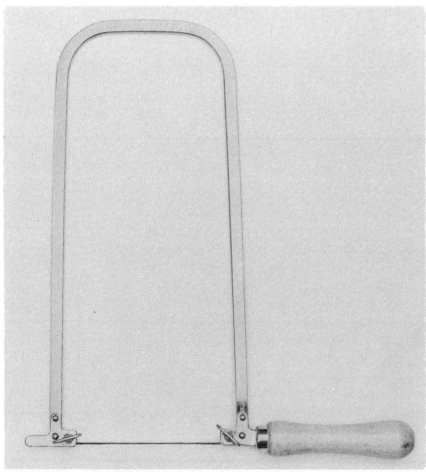

Woodcraft's 15001-AV Fret Saw

characteristics of being functional and adequate tools — they do the job at hand and that is what they were made for.

Disston's Model 10 and Model 15 have 4¾-inch and 6¾-inch throat depths respectively. Both tools take 15 PPI blades that are 6⅜ inches long.
Approx. Price: (10) $3.50

Stanley's Model 39-104 comes with a 4¾-inch frame depth and Model 39-106 has a 6⅜-inch throat. Blade length is 6⅜ inches and 25 PPI.
Approx. Price: (39-104) $3.00

Millers Falls Model 52 has a 5-inch throat; Model 49 comes with a 6¾-inch throat.
Approx. Price: (52) $3.00

Jeweler's Saws

People often confuse a jeweler's saw with a coping or fret saw, perhaps because there is a certain overlap in function. The shape of a jeweler's saw is also very similar to that of the coping saw. The frame of a jeweler's saw is also U-shaped; it has a file-type handle and some method of attaching fine, disposable blades at either end. Jeweler's saws are used for extremely fine cutting — either to cut materials with a minimum of waste (as in working with precious metals) or to make intricate cuts. These fine-bladed saws find extensive use in making cuts in bone, ivory, plastic, and horn where the heavier blade of the coping/fret saws would soon fracture or split such brittle material.

The one basic difference between a jeweler's saw and the larger coping/fret saws lies in the fact that the frame is adjustable and blades in lengths from 2 to 7 inches can be mounted in it. This feature is important because the very fine blades used in these saws break easily. Instead of discarding the broken blade, the frame is adjusted to fit the shortened blade. Jeweler's saws are very sharp and care must be used in working with them because they are not made to withstand heavy pressure. If, however, you are working on materials which require little waste in the cut, close tolerance, or accuracy, the jeweler's saw is the one to choose.

Garret Wade's 10I14.01 is described in the catalog as an "adjustable fret saw", but the shape and form make it a jeweler's saw. The frame on this tool allows adjustments up to 6 inches long, but any blade shorter than that can also be mounted and used. The blade is held in place by two clamps and there is a tensioning screw to keep it taut. Depth from the blade to the back of the throat is 2¾ inches. Almost any blade can be fitted into this saw, and it comes with one 32-PPI blade as part of the package. Blade economy and the ability to work in constricted spaces make this saw valuable; the price makes it a reasonable tool to have in the shop.
Approx. Price: $7.00

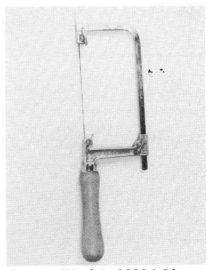

Garrett Wade's 10I14.01

The X-Acto Model 7043 is technically a jeweler's saw but can be fitted with coarser blades than most, which adds to its versatility. The adjustable steel frame accommodates blades from 2 to 7½ inches. A wing nut and clamp hold the small blades firmly and allows a fine stroke without the excessive bowing of the blade that can be a problem with jeweler's saws. Throat depth is 2½ inches. The handle on this saw is of the file type, nicely finished, and it allows a comfortable grip. Blades available to fit this excellent frame range from an extremely fine blade (.006-inch thickness with 96 PPI) to a coarse blade (.024-inch thickness with 16 PPI), allowing a wide range of work.
Approx. Price: $8.00

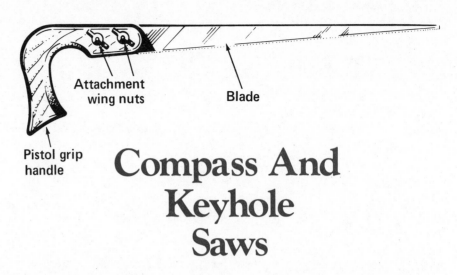

Attachment wing nuts

Blade

Pistol grip handle

Compass And Keyhole Saws

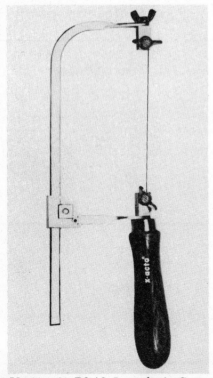

X-Acto's 7043 Jeweler's Saw

Except for their size, compass and keyhole saws look like twins. Both saws have wedge-shaped blades that taper to a sharp point at the toe end, with the blade of the compass saw being longer by about 2 inches. PPI on a compass saw is either 8 or 10; the range on a keyhole is from 10 to 14 PPI. Both saws have pistol-grip handles made of a variety of materials. A quality saw of either type must have a blade that's tempered to provide tension and fairly springy feel, a characteristic

*"The **Compass-Saw** should not have its Teeth **Set** as other **Saws** have; but the edge of it should be made so broad, and the back so thin, that it may easily follow the broad edge, without having its Teeth **Set**; for if the Teeth be **Set**, the Blade must be thin, or else the Teeth will not bow over the Blade, and if it be thin, (considering the Blade is so narrow) it will not be strong enough to abide tough Work, but at never so little an irregular thrust, will bow, and at last break; yet for cheapness, they are many times made so thin that the Teeth require a setting. Its Office is to cut a round, or any other Compass kerf; and therefore the edge must be made broad, and the back thin, that the Back may have a wide kerf to turn in."*

Joseph Moxon, **Mechanick Exercises: or the Doctrine of Handy-Works. Applied to the Arts of Smithing Joinery Carpentry Turning Bricklayery** (London, 1677)

important to the saw's function.

These saws cut with or across the grain and due to their shape, can easily follow an arc or circle. The small points of the blades allow cuts to be started from a hole drilled in the center of the workpiece, which is why this kind of saw is the workhorse of the electrical and plumbing trades. A compass saw fitted with a heavy, flexible steel blade can cut through drywall, wood, or even light metal sheeting. The blades on both saws are easily replaceable and, equally important, they can be inverted so the cutting edge is on the top side of the handle. Many compass or keyhole saws are marketed under the name "drywall" or "panelling" saws, and this indicates their most common use — cutting access holes for electrical connections in those materials. Both saws are very handy around the shop, since they can do certain tasks which are impossible or awkward with other types of handsaws. Utilitarian in looks, a quality compass saw will do several specialized tasks and do them well. You won't feel the urge to display it with your finer cabinet tools, but it will be the one you reach for when faced with home repair work.

Nicholson's Model 10
compass saw is made for the professional; its heavy-duty blade designed for prolonged and possibly severe use. It's available in blade lengths of 12 or 14 inches with 9 PPI, and the blade material is excellent-quality steel. The "comfort-designed" hardwood handle is sculptured to mate nicely with the user's hand and minimize strain and fatigue. The blade locks very securely into the handle with a heavy stud and wing nut, but it's also easy to change or invert the saw blade. A top-of-the-line tool.
Approx. Price: $5.00

Nicholson's Model 30
illustrates the difference between an average tool and a quality one like its catalog mate above. Blade length and PPI are the same as the Model 10 (12 or 14 inches, 9 PPI); but the handle is one-piece polystyrene plastic shaped into a pistol grip. A hole through the handle allows the forefinger to curl snugly around trigger

fashion, and the design leads to secure and comfortable sawing. Obviously made for the craftsman, it can do an acceptable job on any usual home task that requires occasional use of a compass saw.
Approx. Price: $3.00

Disston's Model 15 is a keyhole saw for the professional, at a price which makes it affordable to all. This saw is available in two blade lengths, 10 and 12 inches, both with 10 PPI. These blades taper to a much sharper point than usual in keyhole saws and the hardwood handle has a comfortable grip design that is a pleasure to hold. This handle is designed with two easy to remove screws so that the blades can be interchanged or an additional blade added. This is a saw for rugged use in intricate or close work on inside corners.
Approx. Price: $5.00

Nicholson's 30 Compass Saw

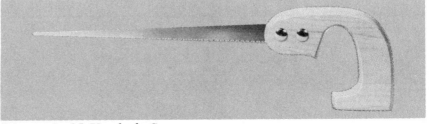
Disston's 15 Keyhole Saw

Pad Saws

Pad saw is really the English name for a keyhole saw, perhaps because "pad" is the English name for a wood handle. They are also called mini-hacksaws; but all the names describe the same basic thing: a hollow, hardwood handle about 7 inches long that is fitted with a strong brass chuck. You can fit a variety of blades into this chuck and the blade will be held in place by two set screws. The protrusion of the blade from the handle can be adjusted to accommodate the work at hand. Any cutting or sawing tool that is not more than ½-inch wide or ⅛-inch thick can be mounted in these handles; the standard blade is usually about 10 inches long and has 8 PPI. The advantage of the pad saw is that it will fit in places where other saws cannot and the chuck's ability to handle different types of blades makes this an all-around tool for general use.

Three companies market saws that are essentially the same product:

Garret Wade #36I01.01 – called a pad saw. Approx. Price: $4.50
Consumer Bargain Corporation #T-84 – called a mini-hacksaw. Approx. Price: $5.00
Brookstone's #A-2346 – called a keyhole saw. Approx. Price: $5.50

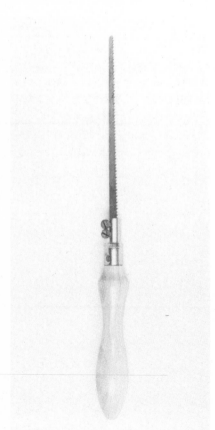

*Garrett Wade's 36I01.01
Pad Saw*

*Consumer Bargain's T-84
Mini-hacksaw*

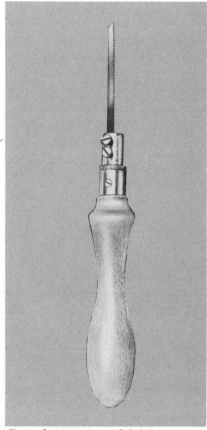

*Brookstone's A-2346
Keyhole Saw*

assortment in relationship to the contemplated scope of the work is more important than blade quality.

Detail from 1750s print — ripsawing with a frame saw.

The Disston Model No. 102, a "nest of saws," is quite typical in terms of blade assortment. Blades include a 12-inch compass, 10-inch keyhole, and a 12-inch, specially tempered blade that can even cut through a nail (not recommended with your average wood saw). The latter type of blade is often called a "plumber's blade" because when cutting access holes in old buildings a lot of nails are encountered that would destroy a regular blade. The sturdy plastic handle has fully enclosed grips, and the blades are mounted on a stud and held

Sets of Saws

The most important part of any saw is the blade. The handle, provided it is comfortable and well situated, is relatively unimportant. Sets of saws reflect this fact, being a set of interchangeable blades designed to fit into one handle. Quite clever, when you think of it, and a truly economical way to do a variety of sawing tasks without having to purchase an individual saw for each. Most sets of saws come with three blades. Typically the assortment has a keyhole and a compass blade, while the third one is some version of a hacksaw for light metal cutting. If your need for any of these saws is not extensive, a set of saws is a useful alternative to individual saws. When choosing a set of saws, remember that the blade

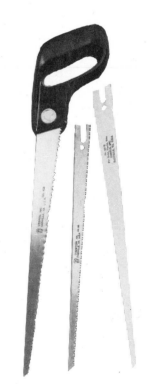
Disston's 102 Nest of Saws

with a wing nut. An excellent, versatile tool of professional quality. Approx. Price: $6.00

Stanley's P100 "saw nest" is a general utility set of saws designed for the casual woodworker/gardener. It comes with three blades, but the design is such that you can perform four sawing functions. There is a conventional 14-inch compass blade, a 10-inch panel blade, and a 16-inch dual-purpose blade. The panel blade is a stubby tool with 10 PPI that works well for sawing cutouts in plywood or paneling. The dual-purpose blade has teeth on both edges; one side for pruning chores in the garden, and the other for crosscutting in rough lumber. The hardwood handle is nicely lacquered, but the wing nut and bolt for securing the blades are merely adequate. A light tool for chores, but able to do a wide variety of them. Approx. Price: $6.50

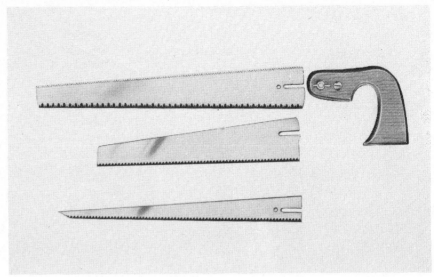

Stanley's P100 Saw Nest

steels. The third blade is very different — short, slim, and tapering to a point. Just right for cutting openings in sheetrock (drywall), a material that will quickly dull most blades. The pistol-grip handle has a unique feature called a "turret head." This quick-change locking device is made so that the blade can be secured in any one of eight positions for convenient sawing in tight quarters. Approx. Price: $8.50

Millers Falls Multi-Purpose Model 9095 goes beyond the usual; indeed, it is a cornucopia of cutting functions. Four blades provide a better assortment, and the handle is in a full grip design that you'd expect to find on a conventional crosscut or ripsaw. Blade styles are a 10-inch keyhole, 15-inch pruning, a 16-inch general purpose panel saw, and a 12-inch backsaw. This combination should allow

Stanley's 175C is a set of saws for the remodeler. All three blades are specially tempered to hold up under considerable abuse. The keyhole blade can be used on wood and materials like asbestos; the second, "metal blade" will cut metal lathing, BK cable, and even mild

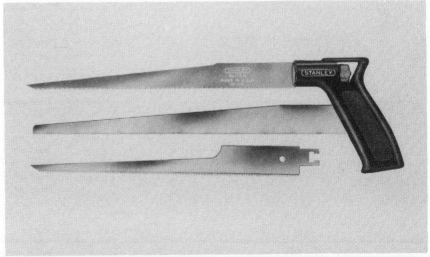

Stanley's 175C Set of Saws

you to do just about any sawing you could encounter around the home. Approx. Price: $11.00

The Millers Falls Saw-Knife Set Model 789 C includes an assortment of useful cutting tools in addition to saw blades. The tool is small—none of the blades is longer than 7½ inches—but this is an asset where room for a conventional-size tool is lacking. The single handle is shaped much like that of a normal utility knife and will grip, in addition to the knife-type blades, metal cutting blades (18 and 24 PPI) or a wood cutting blade with 9 PPI. The metal cutting blades are a good substitute for a hacksaw; the wood cutting blade resembles a very small keyhole. The knife blades enable you to score sheetrock, open packages, or even trim a horse's hooves! Approx. Price: $7.00

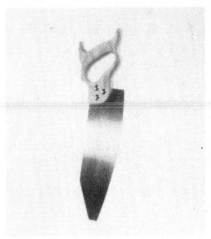

Woodworker's Supply 512-004 Flooring Saw

Flooring Saws

Flooring saws are funny looking tools—stubby and with a wide blade only about 12½ inches long. They have teeth on two edges, with the main cutting edge having a pronounced curve, and the shorter, slanted top having teeth on the forward section of the blade. The design lets you cut through the center of a board or panel without a starting hole (such as is necessary for a compass or keyhole, their closest equivalents).

They are husky tools made for heavier applications than are the compass or keyhole, and are of particular interest to those involved in home construction and remodeling work. The teeth on the forward end of the blade are often used with the saw inverted, especially where it is necessary to make a full length cut in a panel that abuts another, and where only short strokes can be made. Hardwood handles are the conventional, full-grip type seen on regular crosscut or rip saws; and the typical blade is very rigid, hardened, and tempered to take a lot of

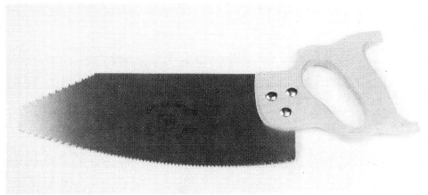

Garrett Wade's 87104.01 Flooring Saw

abuse. Although not usually available in most retail tool outlets, many craftsman's catalogs carry it as a regular item. Garrett Wade's Model 87I04.01, Woodcraft's Model 15B30-AC, and Woodworker's Supply Model 512-004 are all essentially equal in quality and are fine examples of this specialized construction tool. Approx. Price: (87I04.01) $11.00 (15B30-AC) $10.50

Leichtung's Model 314 laminate/veneer saw looks like a flooring saw but is basically a finish saw for cabinet work. It has much smaller teeth than the flooring saw and can make much more delicate cuts in veneers, plywoods, and

Leichtung's 314 Laminate/Veneer Saw

even plastic laminates. The saw's length is 12½ inches; it has 14 PPI, and the handle is set at an angle to permit freer stroking when using the forward edge to start a cut. The main cutting edge is straight, while the second set of teeth are on the forward, gently curving edge of the

blade. The latter are used to begin the starting hole without a lead-in from an edge or drilled hole, which can be very handy for finer cabinet work. An easy saw to work with in these applications, it is a fine specialty saw for anyone doing this kind of work. Approx Price: $5.00

Pruning Saws

Pruning saws, like most well-designed tools, have a form which is dictated by function: to cut green wood containing gummy sap. The main problem with cutting green wood is "binding." The wood presses against the saw blade and prevents free stroking. Pruning saws have comparatively large teeth and wide gullets (spaces) between them to facilitate chip removal. A tree pruner is more concerned about speed and free cutting than the finesse of the cut. Shape of the blade can be either straight or slightly curved, with various PPI for limb cutting or simple trimming. Some blades will have teeth on both edges for those hard-to-reach spots.

Blade lengths vary, and a choice is made in anticipation of the cutting at hand.

Nicholson's Model 20 is a curved pruner made for small limbs, and is a favorite of professional

Nicholson's 20 Curved Pruner

pruners in citrus groves and vineyards. The 14-inch blade has a very gentle arc, and cuts on the pull stroke, a cutting action that is common to many pruning saws. In combination with the curved blade, pull-stroke cutting helps to maintain contact with the wood. The blade is finely polished and firmly attached to a knife-type handle. On the whole, it's a slim, convenient tool that is easy to position and hold in place.
Approx. Price: $6.50

Nicholson's 316 Pruner

The Nicholson Model 316 is a double-edge pruner. Blade length is 16 inches. The small, fine teeth on one side are for light trimming, while the coarser, deeply gulleted teeth on the other are for heavier limbs. The blade is straight and tapers from a full-grip handle down to a narrow toe to permit easy use in narrow spaces. Finish on the blade is very good and does much to eliminate the friction problem presented by green wood.
Approx. Price: $6.00

as a pocket knife and is held open by pressure on the saw's teeth while in use. It

cannot be locked open, however, and could cause injury should the saw close over the hand.
Approx. Price: $7.00

Disston's Model 260 SS is called a safety camp saw. The blade practically disappears into the handle when it is closed. And when in use or stored, a built-in lock keeps the blade securely in position. Another fine feature is the Teflon-S coating on the blade. This finish is superior to regular polishing, providing a lubrication that helps the saw move freely in green or wet wood. It also prevents rust.
Approx. Price: $11.00

Disston's 260 SS Safety Camp Saw

Nicholson's Model 24 is a small folding pruner, with a blade only 10 inches long. But this is perfectly adequate for light garden pruning and camping chores. The blade pulls out in the same manner

Nicholson's 24 Folding Pruner

Stanley's P341 Pruning Saw

The Disston Model 270 SS is a lightweight pruning saw made for close work in orchards and groves. This is a professional-quality tool that works very efficiently. A slim, 14-inch blade is securely attached to a knife-type handle to permit close work among tightly crowned foliage. The Teflon-S coating frees the stroke and protects the blade from weather damage and sap, a decided plus in an outdoor saw. Approx. Price: $10.00

Stanley's Model P341 is a professional, heavy-duty pruning saw that is excellent for anyone with large trees to trim. The 26-inch blade is made of specially tempered spring steel, and the teeth are designed for fast, clean cutting. These teeth are arranged in banks (sets) of four with a deep gullet for sawdust removal and to prevent the saw from binding. The full-size, firm-grip handle is securely attached. It cuts on the pull stroke, and this helps to keep the saw on the work instead of bouncing around. Aside from regular pruning work on heavier limbs, this saw can also be used for cutting wood for the fireplace. Approx. Price: $14.50

Pole Tree Pruners

The difficult part about trimming or pruning larger trees is getting up into them to do the job, an athletic task that is usually left to the professional.

Pole tree pruners were developed to take the danger out of the job (though replacing it with the possibility of a cracked skull from a dropping branch). These tools are basically curved pruning saws attached to a hollow socket that can be mounted on a long pole. Some pole pruners also incorporate a lever-activated shear that can be worked from the ground with a cord, enabling you to saw heavier branches or cut as you would with a conventional pruning shear.

Disston's Model 114 is a professional-quality pole tree pruning saw. The blade is specially hardened and tempered—15 inches of curved blade that eats tree limbs. This is also replaceable, a feature that will be appreciated if this saw is used extensively. Designed to cut branches of under ¾-inch, the 114 comes without the necessary pole, though any 1¼-inch diameter pole will work. Approx. Price: $12.50

Stanley's Model P167 is a pole pruning saw/shear that has a built-in hook to grab branches that might otherwise fall on the operator. The saw portion is 15 inches long and has extremely sharp,

Stanley's P167 Pole Pruning Saw/Shear

needle-pointed teeth. This design ensures fast cutting, an important factor when you consider that you are stroking with a saw mounted on a 10-foot pole. The design is such that you can easily work among closely spaced branches. A pole is not included (a closet pole can be had from any lumber supply), but it does come with 10 feet of braided polyethylene rope for pulling the shear. Another model of the same tool, Model P 330, comes with a two-section, 1¼-inch diameter, weatherproofed hardwood pole that extends to 10 feet. With or without a factory pole, pole tree pruners can be heavy and awkward to use. Unless you have a lot of trees over 15 feet high you may not find much use for one of these specialized saws.
Approx. Price: $15.50

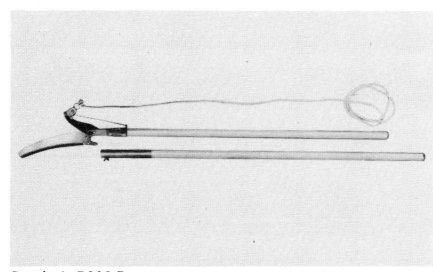

Stanley's P330 Pruner

*Ornamental tree pruning —
Detail from 1760's print*

51

Kitchen Saws

Kitchen or butcher saws are not a common, everyday item that many people want around the house, let alone would have occasion to use. If, however, you are seeking a saw that will cut through fresh or frozen meat or bones in quantity, then this is the tool for you. One reported story has a woodshop owner using his band saw for these same tasks, though he is careful to spread wax paper on the table before doing so. This is not recommended. If you have a need for it, it's better to buy the special tool, keep it clean, and use it only for such kitchen work.

Butcher saws are made by many saw manufacturers, but are usually designed for professional application. Their normal blade lengths run from 18 to 24 inches, which makes them a trifle oversize for the average kitchen. Quality kitchen and butcher saws are designed to do a minimum of shredding when cutting frozen meat. And they have easily replaceable blades because the blades dull with use. Even if you don't use one, just the sight of such a saw hanging on the kitchen wall will give pause to anyone wishing to comment about the quality of your cuisine!

Brookstone Company's Model E-4062 frozen food saw is shaped and used like a knife. The tool has a 12-inch stainless steel blade with teeth on both edges. One edge is made to cut through normal frozen meat, fish, and poultry; encounter a bone and you just flip the blade over. The hardwood handle has a nice contoured grip and a thong hole so it can be hung up out of the way. Overall length is 18 inches, and boiling water or a dishwasher will not harm the tool. A neat way to package a special purpose saw, but its smallness may create difficulties if you are sectioning anything substantial.
Approx. Price: $11.00

Disston's Chef Saw Model 16 resembles a hacksaw in frame shape and mounting system for the replaceable blades. Very light, the plated-steel frame is easy to clean and the teeth (11 PPI) cut with a minimum of shredding. With a blade length of 14 inches, the whole saw is fairly compact and will fit nicely into the average kitchen drawer. Although small, it can be used effectively on big cutting jobs.
Approx. Price: $7.00

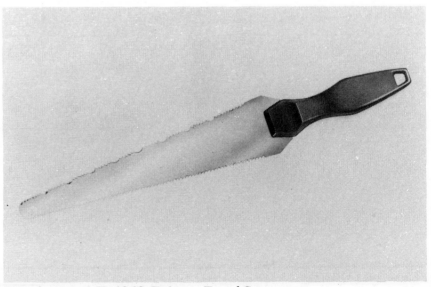

Brookstone's E-4062 Frozen Food Saw

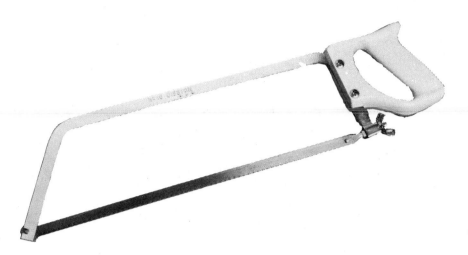

Disston's Chef Saw Model 16

Logging Saws

Short of a summer backpacking trip across the Mohave Desert, absolutely nothing will work up a sweat more quickly than using a logging saw. Although it will make you bone tired at the end of a day of use, it also gives a fine sense of accomplishment. You will have definitely earned your bread by the sweat of your brow. Until the advent of the heavy chain saw, most timber was felled using some variety of the logging saw —typically 5- to 6-feet long, with a large, two-fisted handle at either end, and sharp teeth and deep gullets for chip removal.

Today's interest in wood burning as an alternative source of energy has brought renewed interest in this type of saw. You can find them in larger display racks, usually next to the chain saws to give a good contrast. They're a romantic alternative to the chain saw unless you have to use one extensively, in which case you'll probably hire a couple of kids from across the road and let them work up a sweat.

The "Peerless" is a logging saw manufactured by the Pennsylvania Saw Corporation and distributed by Stanley Tools as Product P 800. This is an impressive example of the two-man saw and is made in lengths of 5, 5½, and 6 feet. Most logging saws are made with a straight back and a curved tooth edge; in the case of the Peerless, this is 5¾ inches at the center and tapers to 3¼ inches at the ends. This shape assures that only those teeth doing the actual cutting are in contact with the work and facilitates the natural rocking motion that occurs

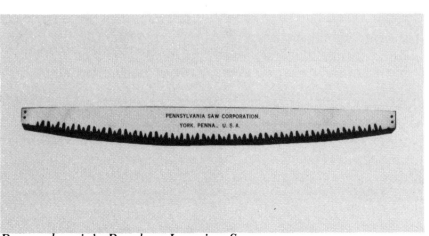

Pennsylvania's Peerless Logging Saw

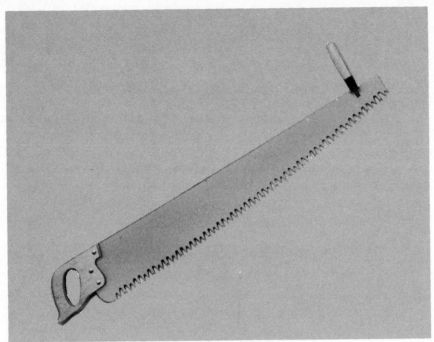
Woodcraft's Model 18 K 21-AL Logging Saw

(Product P 65) for these blades. These are 13 inches long and come equipped with the necessary mounting hardware. If you need a logging saw that can handle any conceivable cutting job on rough timber (and have two, very healthy adults to operate it) the Peerless is a good choice.
Approx. Price:(5') $40.00

The Woodcraft Model 18 K 21-AL is a saw that is similar to the two-man logging saw, but is designed for either one- or two-man operation. The blade is three feet long with the Champion tooth pattern of two cutting teeth and alternate raker with deep gullets. It's equipped with the conventional handle found on regular saws, and an accessory handle that can be attached to the blade in several places. This extra handle permits the tool to be stroked by two people, or it can be used as an auxiliary grip when one man is sawing. The blade has a straight back and slight curve to the toothed edge, tapering from 6¼ inches wide at the handle down to 2⅝ inches at the toe. A nice, small functional saw that can handle all but the largest timber with ease.
Approx. Price: $26.50

Garret Wade's Model 94I02.01 is another version of the one-man logging saw, this time with a double bite. The

when two people work such a saw. The teeth are set in the "Champion" pattern—each bank of two cutting teeth is divided by a raker tooth and deep gullets. This design keeps the kerf free of wood chips and promotes smooth stroking. The blades are sold without handles and come packed in a heavy envelope stitched with wire that can be reused as a protective cover. Stanley also markets handles

Throughout recorded history, logging and the timber trade have started with the same basic beginning: felling trees. This was (and is) done in winter because the sap is down and they are easier to cut. Carpenters, wheelwrights, and woodworkers came to choose and cart away their supply from the logging camps; afterwards this was hauled to the "sawyer's pit." Two men, one above and one below the log (called tiller and box man, respectively), would mark the tree with a chalk line after roughly squaring it; then using a pitsaw they would turn it into planks and boards. These would be stacked and seasoned, a year being considered about average for each inch thickness of the plank. Though modern lumber processing has made the sawyer's pit obsolete in industrial areas, in many parts of the third world this back-breaking labor is commonplace. While the rasping chain saw will never match the clean music of a two-handed pitsaw, it is doubtful that anyone would willingly throw out a power-tool's ease just to listen to it.

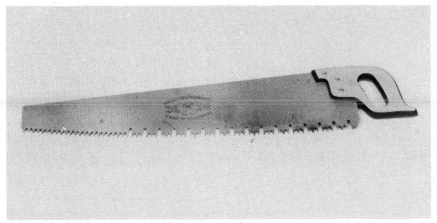
Garrett Wade's 94102.01 Logging Saw

Special Purpose Saw Types

"Every job has its own tool" states an old craftsman's adage. This is as true of saws as any other tool type. The tools in this section are all saws, at least in the sense that they are made to dimension material, but they have some kind of special use that makes them hard to categorize. Yet they are invaluable for the special purposes for which they were devised, often being the only tool that will do the job. Having that one, particular tool around the shop can sometimes make the difference between a quick job or one that is tedious or impossible.

28-inch blade has two types of teeth. Approximately three-quarters of the serrated edge has banks of three teeth separated by very deep gullets; the remainder are diamond-points with V-shaped gullets between. The latter are "starting teeth," and by using short saw strokes the user can quickly establish a kerf for the major cutting teeth to ride in. This avoids one of the major problems with any log saw—the large teeth are often quite hard to start in the beginning of a cut. The red beech handle is of the conventional, one-hand, full-grip type, and the blade is highly polished to reduce friction and binding in the kerf. This design feature facilitates starting a cut, and makes this saw a nice addition to the tools of the woodworker, especially if you have a fireplace.
Approx. Price: $18.50

"The sound of tools properly used is as a pleasing tune. The craftsman has no need to examine a saw to know if it is sharp or if it is handled properly. Nor need he look at a plane to know if it functions at its best. The ill-used tool makes a discordant noise which is agony to the trained ear. The sound of a hammer driving a nail, or releasing or securing the wedge of the plane, in each case has its separate and distinctive note. The blow of the mallet on the chisel tells by its sound alone whether or not the user has confidence of ability. The multitude of sounds of tools at work on wood is a separate language known to the woodworker, and each separate note is recognized with satisfaction or dislike. An unexpected note at once arrests attention; especially the shriek of protest from the saw that has struck an unsuspected nail. This is the horror of horrors to the wood craftsman; it sends a shudder through the whole workshop."

Walter Rose, **The Village Carpenter,** *(Cambridge: The University Press, 1952)*

Pocket Saws

Consumers Bargain Corporation makes what they call a "pocket saw," Model V-149, that's a handy little gadget made for either the

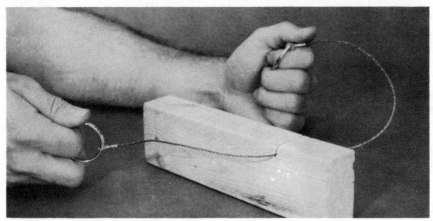

Consumer Bargain's V-149 Pocket Saw

tool box or survival kit. It's nothing but an 18-inch piece of fine, flexible wire with a finger ring at each end, but this wire is coated with tungsten-carbide particles. This "blade" will cut in any direction of pull and through just about any material from wood to ferrous metals. It is very handy for those jobs where a conventional saw will not reach, such as when cutting a large pipe nested in a wall. You can also use it for cutting up firewood on a camping trip. Coiled up, it fits in a small place inside a pack. A length of green stick, notched at both ends and fitted into the rings converts it into an instant bow saw. Flexibility, though, is limited and wrapping it around too

narrow a diameter will break it, but it's sufficiently flexible to adapt to a wide variety of functions. It's inexpensive, too! Approx. Price: $3.00

Veneer Saws

These saws are often called veneer knives, since they are used for making

extremely fine cuts with maximum smoothness in thin wood veneers. In use they are guided by a straightedge, and cut so clean that glue joints between adjoining pieces are practically invisible. These little saws are usually about 3 inches long and come with a firmly attached, file-type hardwood handle. The blade has two edges. One edge forms a saw-type kerf because of its straight teeth, and the other edge is tapered for very fine cuts. Although not a common item in most hardware stores, many craftsman's catalogs list it. Among them are: Craftsman Wood Service Co. (Model 1137), Woodworker's Supply (Model 508-013), Garrett Wade (Model 19I06.01), and Woodcraft (Model 15S05-EG). All of these are highly recommended, and are necessary for the craftsman doing close tolerance work with thin woods or veneer. Approx. Price: (1137) $5.00

The term craftsman, incidentally, is a modern term which refers to a carpenter or other worker who gives loving attention to his work; but in earlier times these same men referred to themselves as "tradesmen" or "mechanicks." To have a craft was to know the various practices of one's trade. It was taken for granted that if you were a master carpenter, you would practice your craft lovingly and well.

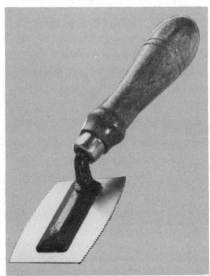

Craftsman's 1137 Veneer Saw

Say "power saw" and nine times out of ten you mean a portable model. Lightweight and versatile, they are the workhorses of the tradesman and craftsman.

Portable Power Saws

Power was the greatest boon to tool users since the first hammer whacked the first nail. Initially, though, man's ability to harness the power of wind, water, steam and electricity had a negative effect on craftsmanship. The craftsman couldn't compete with the low-cost, factory produced products. But in recent years the introduction of power hand tools has brought about a renewed interest in hand-crafted wood products. Today, the craftsman can handle a wider variety of work with more speed than ever before. Although some may mourn the passing of an era when wood shavings and sawdust meant sweat and elbow grease, there's probably not one serious craftsman who doesn't own at least one power tool. Even if only used for rough work, the power tool reduces tedious labor and lets the craftsman concentrate on fine fitting and finishing with traditional hand tools.

If you were to choose just one power tool for a general shop, it would likely be a power saw. Whether you're building a cabinet or a house, portable circular saws, reciprocating saws and saber saws have distinct advantages over hand tools. And no one can argue the advantages of the chain saw over the bucksaw for cutting timber. Power handsaws do the hard work of cutting, while you just guide them. Also, cutting jobs that once took hours now take only minutes, with power hand-saws. Traditional handsaws may have the edge in accuracy in some cases. But if the job doesn't call for accuracy to $\frac{1}{32}$ nd of an inch, the power handsaw— especially with a fence—is the logical choice for sizing lumber.

Power saws come in three grades. Designations vary from one manufacturer to another, but the most common are "commercial," "craftsman," and "homeowner." These terms reflect the durability and design features incorporated into the saw in relation to its intended purpose. In general, the higher the grade, the

more frills—like extra power switches and handles. Higher price tags accompany the higher grade saws, too. In some cases, the difference in price between commercial and homeowner versions of the same saw can be double or more. These facts should be considered carefully when choosing a power saw. While it's handy to have a saw that will cut through 4-inch dimensional stock in one pass, you must judge whether or not your work scope justifies the extra cost. Additional frills also make the saw more complicated to operate and increase weight. Buying more saw than you can use conveniently is a mistake. The idea is to save time and labor, not add to the basic burden.

Regardless of the grade of the saw, always make sure that it is "double insulated." This goes for all other power hand tools as well. Double insulation means that no electrified portion of the tool can come in contact with the user to cause a shock. This feature is especially important in outside

A QUICK LOOK AT PORTABLE POWER SAWS

NAME	REMARKS	TYPICAL USES
Circular/Contractor's Saw	motor drives circular blades at high *rpms* — mounts a wide variety of blades depending upon work application — blade guard is automatic	both trade and crafts tool — most common power saw in any shop — widely used for cutting lumber — both cross, rip, and dimension cuts can be made with right blade
Saber/Jigsaw/Scroll Saw	motor drives a relatively short (4 inches or less) blade in up/down reciprocating motion — disposable blades — no guard	fine line or contour cutting — cuts both with or across grain — intricate cuts and will follow a small radius — plunge-cutting from center of panel
Reciprocating/Bayonet Saw	motor drives straight blades up to 12 inches in length — in/out, straight line reciprocating motion — disposable blades — no guard	contractor's tool for use in heavy duty remodeling or repair work — long blades can be used for pruning or cutting firewood — often finds applications in sectioning heavy lumber
Chain Saw	either gas engine or electric motor powers endless cutter chain around a fixed guide bar — minimal guards — electric models cheaper to buy and use than gas ones — can be dangerous	pruning or limbing trees — felling trees or brushing out timber — cutting firewood — dimensioning cuts in heavy structural timber or thick lumber

applications, where dampness and the chance of shorting out the tool are particularly prevalent. Many early power tools were equipped with three-prong grounded plugs, as are many commercial models today. If properly grounded, the need for double insulation is eliminated. Unfortunately, over half of all American homes do not have the grounded three-prong outlet required. Double-insulated power tools are safer to use regardless of the outlet.

saw, builder's saw and Skilsaw. The first three names reflect the great popularity of this saw in the construction trade, where its introduction drastically reduced the labor in house building. The last term is actually a trade name that has almost become generic. Skil Corporation was the first to mass market these handy power tools, which will do a wide range of straight cutting tasks in diverse situations.

Even a wood shop with a full complement of stationary power saws will usually have a portable circular saw. When sawing materials like standard 4 x 8 foot sheets of ¾-inch plywood, the portability of this saw is a great convenience. Such large panels are difficult for one person to handle on even the largest table saw. Supporting the sheet on two sawhorses and cutting it with a portable circular saw is easier, faster, and safer. For trimming and rough work, the utility saw is very useful and it's this versatility that makes it so popular in the construction field.

All circular saws are basically a housed motor turning a circular blade. The upper half of the blade is shielded by a fixed guard. The lower half (the section of the blade that encounters the work) is covered by a retractable guard. This guard swings up when the tool is in use and automatically swings down to cover the blade when sawing is completed. The blade projects through an adjustable part of the saw's frame called a

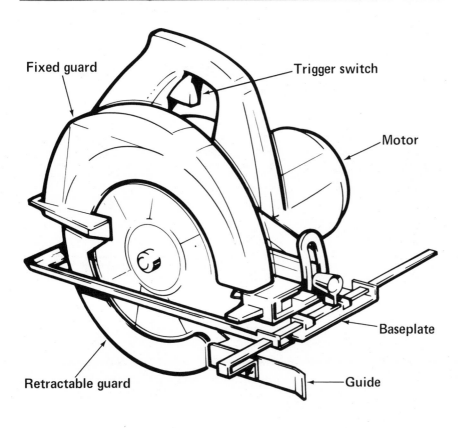

Fixed guard

Trigger switch

Motor

Baseplate

Retractable guard

Guide

Portable Circular Saws

The portable circular saw is the powered equivalent of the handsaw. Both are designed to make straight cuts on panels and dimensional stock. These circular saws are known by a variety of names: cutoff saw, utility

"baseplate." You can adjust the baseplate to set the depth of cut. The spinning blade will always be exposed beneath the work, but safety dictates that the blade should project a minimum distance—perhaps as little as ¼ inch. Greatest efficiency, however, is attained when the teeth project far enough so that the bottom of the gullets (spaces between the teeth) clear the work. Professionals usually set the blade in this manner because it helps the blade run faster and cooler. This practice is not recommended for the average user. Always remember that you're dealing with a tool that can take off an arm faster than it can cut through a 2x4.

When considering a portable circular saw, remember that blade diameter and motor horsepower are two separate factors. A large blade will bind or burn the wood if the motor cannot spin the blade at the correct cutting speed. For the average user, the most important factor is capacity, which is the thickness of material the blade can cut at 90 and 45 degrees. A common norm is a capacity of at least 2-inch nominal stock at either setting. There are not many saws made today which can't handle this amount.

Quality saws have a wide range of additional features. Some of these features are designed to prevent "kickback," a constant hazard when using a circular saw. Kickback is the quick

Circular saw blades are the ones used in portable electric circular saws, as well as on table and radial arm saws. These blades are all similar in shape, the only difference being the diameter of the blade. Several different designs are available—each made to cut with maximum efficiency in a certain material. Although some blades are more all-purpose than others, it is not advisable to use one blade for every sawing task. The right blade, used for the cutting task it was designed to do, will produce a superior cut and will retain a sharp edge far longer than a single blade used to do everything.

One basic difference in circular blades is how they are designed to provide a clearance for themselves when they are cutting. This is necessary to minimize friction and insure a clean, neat cut without splintering. The object is to cut a kerf or groove formed by the blade that is wider than the gauge or thickness of the blade's body. Two methods are in common use to achieve this aim.

Like handsaws, some blades are designed with a set, with each alternate tooth bent slightly away from the blade's body. Only the cutting teeth contact the work, with the body of the blade running free. Set blades cut fast, but do not leave the smoothest edges. The greater the amount of set and the fewer the number of teeth, the rougher the cut. Edge smoothness improves as the number of teeth increases and the set decreases. Plywood blades, for example, usually

and sudden backward movement of the saw toward the operator. This happens when the saw binds in the kerf (cutting groove), as is common during long rip cuts, or encounters a nail or knot in the wood. While many circular saws have some sort of design feature that helps keep the kerf open, better quality saws go a step farther. Some have a safety clutch that helps keep the blade from kicking back by slipping the blade. Others have a safety brake that stops the blade almost instantly when you release the switch. Either, or both, is worth

having, but the braking feature is rare on saws with less than a professional classification and a premium price.

As with any cutting tool, a properly sharpened blade of the correct type will allow you to get the most from a circular saw. In addition to wood-cutting blades, circular saw blades are available for cutting masonry and thin metals. If you plan to use the saw for extensive cutting, investigate the available guides and attachments. For example, "rip fences," sometimes called "edge guides," allow you to make

have a large number of small teeth and minimum set to avoid splintering this material.

The other way to provide clearance is to hollow-grind the blade. There is no set, but the gauge of the blade body is thinner from the teeth to some middle portion of the blade. This produces a concave area that provides the required clearance, resulting in a superior cut. For this reason hollow-ground blades are often termed planer blades. Since there is more production work involved in producing this kind of blade there will also be an increase in price.

Aside from the different means of sharpening the blade teeth, some circular saw blades are available with carbide tips. The cutting teeth on this kind of blade are faced with tungsten carbide. These blades can be used for crosscutting, ripping, or pocket cuts in just about any wood material. They will also stay sharp despite the abrasive effect of cutting plywood or particle board—notorious destroyers of regular blades. Tungsten carbide is tough, will hold a keen edge for a long time, and blades faced with it will cut almost any material. But it is brittle and must not be abused. Banging it against a hard surface can chip the teeth. These blades should not be used to cut ferrous or hard metals, or in applications where they are likely to encounter buried nails. They are also very expensive, although they will stay sharper and last considerably longer than conventional blades.

parallel cuts in long stock. Precise miter cuts in most stock can be accomplished with a "radial cutting attachment," which also helps hold the work. Both of these accessories greatly increase the utility of the circular saw, and make it invaluable in the field or shop.

The Black & Decker 7300 is relatively new on the portable circular saw scene. It's the mighty mite of the field, weighing only 5½

pounds. Although compact and lightweight, it's not a toy. The saw's ½-hp motor spins the small 5½-inch blade at

Black & Decker's 7300 Circular Saw

4000 rpm—letting you handle nominal 2-inch-thick stock (actually 1½ inches thick) when cutting at 90 degrees. Cutting at a 45-degree angle reduces depth of cut to a rather small 1⅛ inches. Its capacity may be limited, but then the saw was not designed for cutting house framing. Its forte is slicing through paneling, plywood and trim with minimum effort on the part of the operator. A nice design feature of this saw is its wraparound shoe pattern base—not unique, but valuable. The base, which is the part of the saw that rests on the work, gives extra support for the tool. The saw blade projects through a slot in the baseplate. A combination blade is supplied to let you do either ripping or crosscutting with equal ease. Double insulation protects you from shocks when working outside or when standing on damp basement floors. The Black & Decker 7300 is not the tool to buy for rough framing or heavy-duty work. But its light weight makes it easy to handle when involved in finishing or paneling work. Approx. Price: $35.00

The Black & Decker 7356 is designed for the craftsman, but its quality often makes it the choice of construction trade professionals. This saw's 2-hp motor turns the 7¼-inch blade at a speedy 5300 rpm—definitely in the heavy-duty class. And it has

*Black & Decker's
7356 Circular Saw*

cutting capacity to match its muscle power. At 90 degrees you can cut as deep as 2 $\frac{7}{16}$ inches. At 45 degrees your limit is 1⅞ inches. For this impressive power and capacity, however, you pay the price in weight. The saw weighs a hefty 10½ pounds, and after a day's continuous use you'll be aware of every ounce. Heavy saws have their assets and drawbacks. A heavy saw provides stability, although the weight can be tiring. On the other hand, a light saw gives you less exercise, but can tend to chatter, bounce and kick back. This requires more care when operating the tool.

A second handle in front of the saw's baseplate allows two-handed operation for better control. Other features include double insulation, a wraparound shoe and a detachable 10-foot cord. To prevent dangerous accidental starts, a special safety button cuts off power completely. The saw comes complete with a good-quality combination rip and crosscut blade, plus a rip fence. All in all, this is an uncompromising saw that can handle a wide variety of sawing operations. Approx. Price: $85.00

Combination crosscut and rip blades are the usual ones provided with the tool. This is the standard blade used in construction work, with a lot of set so that it cuts freely. For quality work the edges of the cut material have to be smoothed later. A compromise design, these blades will crosscut or rip, but they will not do so as efficiently as blades designed for these specific purposes. Combination blades are good ones to leave on the saw for all basic sawing procedures.

Crosscut blades have a minimum set and many small, fine teeth. These are the blades to mount in a saw for cutting across the grain of the wood when a smooth edge is an important factor. This blade will do a much better job of cutting plywood than most others because the small amount of set reduces the splintering common with this material. It is not suitable for ripping.

Rip blades are designed for fast cutting with the grain of the wood—and that's about it. They have much larger teeth than a combination blade and deep gullets or spaces between the teeth for fast waste removal. Although rip blades are handy if there is a large amount of ripping to be done, a combination blade also does an acceptable job in this regard. Ripping is made much easier with one of these blades, but the average user can get along without it.

Hollow-ground or planer blades usually have a combination type design and thus are usable for all types of wood cutting. This kind of blade makes the smoothest cuts and should be regarded as the best blade where precision is necessary. Initial sizing cuts should be done with one of the above blades because of the characteristics of the blade manufacture. The slightly concave shape of the hollow-ground blade means that it requires more projection above or below the work surface than other blades. Neglecting to watch this can result in excessive friction,

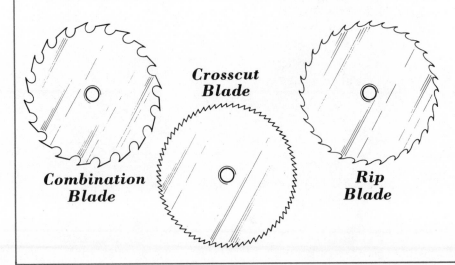

Crosscut Blade

Combination Blade

Rip Blade

slow cutting, and possible burning of either blade or wood. It is better to use the hollow-ground blade for final assembly work where attention to such details is more important than the amount of wood that is being cut.

Abrasive *blades lack teeth, being essentially a metal or fiber disc impregnated with abrasive particles. Masonry, metals, and other difficult-to-cut materials are the forte of this kind of circular blade. The hardness of the abrasive bonded to the blade depends upon the material that has to be cut. Which kind to purchase depends upon the job to be done.*

In addition to the above blades, there are other designs made for specific cutting tasks. As a general rule they should only be purchased if the job requires it, as they are essentially limited use tools.

Thin-rim *blades are so-called because the perimeter of the blade is much thinner than the body. The heavy gauge body provides stability while the thin rim cuts an exceptionally fine kerf. The fine and smooth cut produced by these blades is necessary when cutting fancy and expensive veneers because the design minimizes waste. The depth-of-cut with this circular blade is limited to the width of the thin area. One and a quarter inch or smaller is common, but that is all that is necessary for the work the blade is made to do. This blade would be a virtual requirement for fine furniture work, though it has a limited application for other types of cutting.*

Plywood *blades are really crosscut blades with a minimum set and a large number of smaller teeth. These are used on plywood because they leave a respectable edge and cut with a minimum of disruption of surface fibers. These blades can be used for general crosscutting, but are liable to dull rapidly if pressed too hard in everyday work that they are not meant to do.*

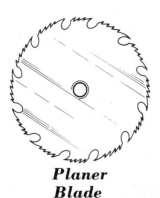

Planer Blade

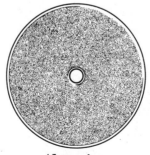

Abrasive Blade

Skilsaw is the trade name of Skil Corporation's circular saw product line. The company pioneered the production of portable circular saws, and the trade name has become synonymous with this type of saw. These saws are justly famous because of their quality. They are built to industrial standards and, with reasonable care, will last for a long time. If you seek top functional quality in a portable power saw, these are the ones to select.

Skil's drive system is different from those of other manufacturers. The blades are not mounted on a motor shaft. Instead, they are driven by a gear train that transmits the power from the motor. As a result, they can take shock loads, like running over a series of knots, that would damage other saws in short order. The motors are also specially designed to reduce the incidence of "burn out" during severe usage. Also, the gear train is constantly lubricated because it runs in an oil bath. Another feature clears chips and sawdust from the cutting line. This is done via a stream of air which is sucked in through rear vents, flows over the gear case and motor and is discharged out the front of the saw.

As would be expected in a quality line of power saws, Skilsaws have a safety feature called a "Vari-Torque" clutch. It permits the blade to slip if it jams in the kerf, protecting against motor and gear damage and reducing the

Skilsaw 77 Circular Saw

Skilsaw 825 Circular Saw

kickback hazard. The Vari-Torque clutch is, however, a user-adjusted device, and its performance depends upon how you adjust it. Since it is not automatic, you must follow the instructions carefully.

Skilsaw bases are of the wraparound type, but an extension in the front allows seating the saw firmly before the blade contacts the work. Double handles are standard, as is common on such heavy-duty and heavyweight saws. The saws also come with a combination rip/crosscut blade, and rip fences are extra cost accessories. There are three sizes of professional-quality Skilsaws to choose from:

Skilsaw 77 has a 7¼-inch blade that turns at 4400 rpm. Depth of cut at 90 degrees is 2⅜ inches; at 45 degrees it is reduced to 1 ⁵⁄₁₆ inches. Weight is 15 pounds. Approx. Price: $180.00

—

Skilsaw 367 turns a 6½-inch blade at 4600 rpm. Straight line cutting at 90 degrees is 2 inches and 1¾ inches at 45 degrees. This saw weighs 14½ pounds. Approx. Price: $170.00

—

Skilsaw 825 is truly heavy-duty, having an

8¼-inch blade that turns at 4300 rpm. Capacity is 2⅞ inches on 90 degree cuts; when set to 45 degrees it can still handle 2¼-inch stock. With this size and power comes weight. This model is heavy at 18½ pounds. Approx. Price: $195.00

—

Skilsaw 559 is not a professional quality tool, but bears mention because it gives you many of the features of the heavier-duty Skilsaws at an attractive price. This craftsman-quality saw has a 2-hp motor that turns a 7¼-inch blade at 5500 rpm. Depth of cut is 2 ⁷⁄₁₆ inches at 90 degrees and 1⅞

Skilsaw 367 Circular Saw

Skilsaw 559 Circular Saw

inches at 45 degrees. This saw has more than adequate power and capacity and has a surprisingly light weight of only 9⅛ pounds. Standard features include double insulation, ball-bearing construction, sawdust blower, wraparound shoe and baseplate and Skil Corporation's Vari-Torque clutch and emergency power shutoff button. A decent, combination rip/crosscut blade is also standard. The Skilsaw 559 is one of the best of the craftsman-quality saws and deserves consideration. Approx. Price: $80.00.

The Rockwell 4525 is a top-quality, 7¼-inch portable circular saw built for comfortable and efficient performance. It falls into the "craftsman" category, but is one of the best in its field. There's power here for many heavy-duty applications, yet the saw's light weight makes it a pleasure to use by the

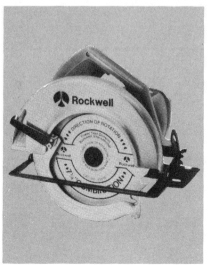

Rockwell's 4525 Circular Saw

Sharpening a handsaw is a relatively easy task that can be handled by any competent shop owner, but this is not true for circular saw blades. The teeth must be filed to the correct bevel and angle and properly set — have each alternate tooth slightly bent to provide clearance for the blade itself. This is necessary with all saws. But most users do not recognize that several other actions must be done with circular blades. On every third or fourth sharpening the gullets or U-shaped depressions between the teeth should be filed. These must be made deeper, but still retain the same shape. Another problem with hand filing of these blades is that great care must be taken in filing the teeth so that the distance from the center of the blade to the top of each tooth remains the same. Both of these tasks are better accomplished on automatic machinery or at least jigs and fixtures. Unless you do a lot of sawing with circular blades, the cost of the jigs to "do-it-yourself" is not justifiable. For the price of the jig and fixture the circular blade could be professionally resharpened many times. This would carry the average user through a lifetime of use. You may lose something in self-satisfaction, but the job will be done correctly and you will save a lot of time.

average man or woman. And it's priced so that you needn't be Midas to purchase it. The motor develops 1½ hp and turns the 7¼-inch blade at 5800 rpm. Maximum projection of the blade allows cutting 2⅜-inch-thick stock at 90 degrees and 1⅞-inch stock at 45 degrees. Other features include double insulation, ball-bearing motor construction, a large wraparound base, a chute in the upper guard to dispose of sawdust, and a sturdy case for durability. This is a functional, well-designed tool capable of breezing through the toughest tasks expected of a saw in the "craftsman" category. Approx. Price: $50.00

The Makita 5402 is a Japanese-built circular saw that would satisfy Paul Bunyan. Its 16⁵⁄₁₆-inch diameter blade is backed up with the power to cut through 6-inch-thick stock! This is undoubtedly the largest saw of its type, and the heaviest. A working tool for the heavy construction field, its weight of 31 pounds is not excessive when the saw's size and capacity are considered. The huge blade rotates at 2200 rpm, and can cut through stock of 6³⁄₁₆ inches when set at 90 degrees or 4³⁄₁₆ inches at 45 degrees. The wraparound base is large, and two exceptionally large and sturdy handles are conveniently set for the two-handed operation mandatory with a saw of this caliber. A combination blade and a rip fence are part of the package, and an extra-cost accessory saw stand lets you use the tool as a table saw. While this isn't the saw you'd buy to repanel the kitchen, if you want to own and use the biggest in the field, this is it. Approx. Price: $298.00

Some Circular Saw Accessories

The Sears, Roebuck and Co. Craftsman 25963C is a table that lets you use a Craftsman portable circular saw as a stationary table saw. This table measures 15½ inches wide by 26¾ inches long. Its 12¼-inch height makes it ideal for use on a bench, or for normal use by a Lilliputian. The legs fold for easy storage and good portability. To use, you just invert the saw and attach it to the table so that the blade projects through a slot in the tabletop. One nice feature of this accessory is a safety switch that's easier to turn off than on. Anyone wanting to do some table saw work without investing in a separate machine will find this accessory useful. Portable circular saws made by other manufacturers can be used with the table, but it might be a good idea to check for fit before purchasing. Approx. Price: $40.00

The Panel Crafter, from Minnesota Versatil, Inc. is a sophisticated guide that lets you cut large panels with greater accuracy and convenience than can be done freehand. You can use this guide with any saw whose baseplate is shorter than 13 inches. For all practical purposes, this means just about any saw now on the market. An edge guide spans the open end of the tool's U-shaped, tubular frame. An adjustable platform, to which the saw is secured, slides along the two frame members. You set the width of the cut by placing the edge guide on the edge of the panel, and moving the platform to a chosen position on the frame. One leg of the frame extends beyond the edge guide, and is fitted with a rubber grip. In use, the operator places one hand on this extension and grips the saw with his other hand. The tool's size permits cutting to the center of a 4-foot-wide panel, the standard width in the construction industry. This is one of those easy-to-use accessories that provides safety and accuracy during long cuts. It can be especially useful when many identically sized pieces are required. Approx. Price: $60.00

Minnesota Versatil Panel Crafter

KerfKeeper

Adjustable Clamp Company's KerfKeeper is a clever accessory that licks the most common problem of circular saw users. On long cuts, the kerf tends to close behind the blade, resulting in binding. Many workers insert small pieces of wood or a screwdriver in the kerf to keep the cut open. But there's no need for such makeshift arrangements when the KerfKeeper is at hand to keep the kerf open. In addition, the tool bears against both surfaces of the stock, and helps to keep the wood from sagging—a common cause of kickback. KerfKeepers are made of heavy-gauge steel and plated to resist rust. At the price, it would be useful to have several on hand, since you can use them with handsaws and table power saws as well. Approx. Price: $3.00

Strate-Cut, from R.A.K. Products, is a portable guidance system for circular power saws. It's actually a telescoping straightedge that clamps to the work surface to eliminate errors that can occur when sawing freehand. The extruded aluminum sections telescope from 51 to 102 inches, which is longer than a standard 8-foot panel. It can also be clamped to the work in any position—a definite advantage. Parallel, taper, and miter cuts can all be guided by the tool. This accessory is very versatile, since it also makes a good guide for routers and saber saws. But it can't be used with handsaws because the teeth will damage the guide's edges. It's one of those handy accessories you'll wonder why you never had before. Approx. Price: $20.00

Craftsman's 17151N Miter Arm, from Sears, Roebuck and Co., is one of the more sophisticated portable power saw accessories. It's usable with Craftsman and other brands of saws whose baseplates are not larger than 6 inches. This unit has a specially shaped platform on which is mounted a track where the circular saw rides. Stock is clamped in the platform and the saw is moved along the track to make the cut. Even accurate angular cuts can be made, because the track pivots. Work size is limited to 12 inches wide and 2 inches thick, which does not qualify it as a replacement for a radial arm saw. But it's quite adequate for the work it's intended to do. The accessory can also be used with the saw blade in a tilted position for cutting bevels and compound angles. It's a very handy accessory for finish work, or for the remodeler who lacks a full-size radial arm saw. Approx. Price: $37.00

R.A.K.'s Strate-Cut

Trik-Trak, from Brett-Hauer Co., Inc., is a guidance system for portable circular saws and other power tools. With it you can make long straight cuts, angular cuts, and those of the fancier variety—like simple or compound miters, rabbets and dadoes, bevels and chamfers. You can use Trik-Trak on a bench, sawhorse, or on a special folding stand which you construct yourself. The aluminum track bars adjust to fit the baseplate width of any saw, and an integral safety bar prevents the saw from kicking itself out of the stock. Once installed, this guide allows cuts in wide panels and stock up to 2 inches thick, and it can be turned left and right for angular cuts. This tool's great versatility makes it a great asset where shop space is limited. In fact, it's possible for a person with a Trik-Trak and a circular or other power saw to get by without many of the conventional stationary saws. It's a useful gadget in a shop where floor space and funds are limited. Approx. Price: $70.00

The Saw Mate SM 2460 is the professional model in Saw Mate Corporation's line of track systems for portable power saws and routers. The difference in the several different models is size, and the SM 2460 is the largest and most useful—accommodating a 4 x 8 foot panel. All models are available as complete units with table, or in kit form. The kits save you money, but you must supply your own plywood table or platform. As with most accessories of this nature, work is placed in a fixed position, and you move the power saw along the track to make an accurate cut. Using this accessory it is possible to perform rip, crosscut, miter, bevel, groove, and angle cuts in many standard materials. It will make work easier and your cuts more accurate. Approx. Price: $80.00

Circular Saw Angle Guide, Adjustable Cut-Off Guide, Saw Guide and Protractor—these names all identify a small, economical accessory which is a necessity for extensive portable circular saw work. They are valuable for the circular saw's most common functions, such as squaring boards, cutting them to length, and crosscutting boards at an angle. These tools are alike in that they have a fixed arm and an adjustable one. To make an accurate cut, one arm is held against the edge of the work, while the other serves as a guide for the saw's baseplate. The guide arm is adjustable in relation to the cut needed, either straight or to any angle within the tool's range of adjustment.

Montgomery Ward's 9305 and Sears, Roebuck's 1719 are essentially the same product. Both have a fixed arm with an attached semi-circular protractor and a lockable pivot arm which can be set

Saw Mate SM 2460

according to the gradations stamped on the protractor. You can set either tool from 0 degrees for straight cuts to 72 degrees left or right for cutting angles. Approx. Price: (9305) $6.00; (1719) $6.00

Black & Decker's 1918 is identical in function to the Ward and Sears models, but it doesn't have a protractor setup. Instead, both arms pivot around a common anchor point. After being set, both arms are secured in position by a locking crossarm. This design's advantage is that it can be used as a layout tool to measure or transfer shapes of inside corner angles. Approx. Price: $6.50

Switch

Baseplate

Blade

Guide

Saber Saws

Saber saws, also known as electric handsaws or portable jigsaws, are perhaps the most versatile of any of the portable power saws. They are the motorized equivalents of the traditional compass or keyhole saws, but saber saws are capable of much more than these parent handsaws. Many sawing tasks for which there is a specifically designed tool—ripsaw, crosscut saw, compass or keyhole saw, stationary jigsaw and bandsaw—can be done faster and easier with a saber saw. With one you can perform a wide variety of sawing operations. Straight cuts, curves, internal cutouts without a pilot hole (through a technique called "plunge cutting"), and with the right blade, even metals and other materials can be cut. This power tool will not do everything well, but it is extremely useful for many jobs which would otherwise require many separate saws.

Almost all saber saws operate with the same mechanical action: a short reciprocal stroke provided by an eccentric or cam system. A short blade is fastened into a "chuck" or gripping collar at the end of the stroke arm. Standard blade size is about 3½ to 4 inches long, though oversize blades are available. The blade teeth point upward, and cutting is only done on the upstroke. This prevents the blade from jumping or chattering by keeping the work snug against the saw's baseplate. Better-quality saber saws usually have an adjustable baseplate to permit a certain amount of bevel cutting, though this tool is not designed to do this particular job with ease.

One of the saber saw's biggest sales points is plunge cutting. By using this technique, you can start a cut in the center of a panel or board without drilling a pilot hole first. While saber saws have this capability, it's still better to drill a pilot hole and then use the power tool as you would a keyhole or compass saw. Typical saber saws are 5- to 10-pound lightweights and jump around considerably when the entire tool rests on the front part of the baseplate, as in plunge cutting. This can result in a snapped blade, or even worse, a marred work surface. There's no advantage to cutting a hole quickly if you have to spend an hour cleaning up a marred surface afterwards.

All saber saws can also do scroll work, but a variety are called "scrollers" or scroll-type saber saws. These saws have an adjustable knob on top of the blade, which lets you turn the blade as you cut. Turning tight corners, for example, while working with the baseplate close to a vertical frame member, is considerably simplified. This feature is not expensive, and makes the saw much more versatile.

Saber saws are rated according to several factors, the most important of which is strokes-per-minute or SPM. This is the total number of upstrokes and downstrokes. Of course, cutting strokes are half this number, because the saber saw only cuts on upstrokes. Saber saws are offered in single-speed, two-speed, and variable-speed models. Blade speed is important because different materials require a faster or slower cutting action. Single-speed models (3000 to 3400 SPM) are adequate for most woodworking operations. Two-speed models have the same high speed (3400 SPM), and a low speed from 1800 to 2500 SPM. The lower speed gives you greater accuracy when cutting thinner materials and when cutting curves. Variable-speed saber saws offer an infinite range up to the highest cutting speed. These are the best saber saws for metal and plastic cutting, which are best done at 1200 to 1700 SPM. Obviously, variable-speed models offer the widest range of application, and are the ones to choose if you have many varied tasks to perform.

The type of blade mounted in the saber saw is as important as the speed at which it works. Blades should be chosen according to the type and thickness of the material being cut, the intricacy of the cut, and how smooth the final edge should be. Wide blades with few teeth-per-inch (5 to 7 TPI) operate much like crosscut saws, and are best for cutting heavy stock where the quality of the cut's edge is not critical. Narrow blades with 10 TPI or more leave smooth edges and can turn smaller radii. Although they cut more slowly, the quality of the cut is superior. Metal cutting blades are usually "wave-set" and look much

*Although normal sawing operations are the same with any saw, **plunge cutting** is a term associated with saber saws. What this means is to start a cut in the center area of a board or panel without first having to drill a hole to insert the blade. This capability is a big sales point with saber saws, but it is usually easier to drill a hole first and start the cut through the hole. However, there are occasions when this cannot be done, and where using plunge cutting can be very handy in tight situations.*

To make a plunge cut, the front end of the saw should be rested on the baseplate at an angle that keeps the saw blade above the surface of the work. Start the motor. Slowly, very slowly, tilt the tool until the blade contacts the material and starts to saw through it. As the blade cuts out its own slot the saw is slowly pushed down until it is in normal sawing position. A considerable amount of vibration can occur if this is rushed. Forcing the cut can cause the blade to break or jump around and mar the surface. To avoid these negative results the saber saw should be worked slowly into the cut with the highest motor speed available. The shortest and stiffest blade that will do the job should be used. If possible, avoid doing this cut at all and take the time to drill a hole in the waste area of the wood. It will result in a much finer cut with a minimum possibility of damaging the result.

like small hacksaw blades. At slow speeds, they can cut most metals and plastics. Saber saw blades are never resharpened because they're cheap enough to throw away when dull.

Selecting a saber saw isn't difficult, once you know what type of material you'll use it on. Motor size is not a critical feature, since the motor's operating speed dictates its cutting capabilities. For all-around use, a variable-speed model is probably the best, and it is the type usually selected by the professional. But for remodeling and some types of general work around the shop, a single- or two-speed model is perfectly adequate. Unlike the relatively dangerous portable circular saw, saber saws are safe to use. It's difficult to damage the work or your body with one of them. Handy tools, they should be a general piece of equipment in almost every shop or tool kit.

Rockwell's 4301 single-speed saber saw is listed by the company as a "jigsaw." It has one of the best features of any power tool for home use—a reasonable price. The small motor turns out .25 hp and drives the blade at 3300 strokes-per-minute. This is enough capacity for cutting 2-inch wood, composition materials, and some light metals. But your workscope will be limited somewhat by the saw's single speed. The

Rockwell's 4301 Jigsaw

baseplate is adjustable to 45 degrees, and casual users will appreciate the saw's light, 4-pound weight. Double-insulated, this tool has a slide-type, on-off switch located at the top of the handle. One additional feature makes this tool stand above its competitors. It has a device called an "anti-splinter" insert that minimizes the opening around the saw blade and bears down closely to prevent the blade from lifting surface fibers. Although this device is prone to wear, it's an attractive feature that makes this saw stand out among those offered for the small shop owner or casual user. Approx. Price: $18.00

The Craftsman 1717, from Sears, Roebuck and Co., has a price comparable to that of a good handsaw. This single-speed saber saw is not suited for heavy-duty jobs, but is fine for making a bookcase or cutting openings in wall paneling. The 1/6-hp motor provides a 3200 SPM

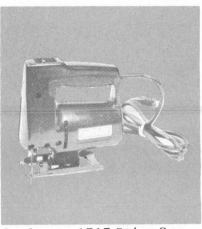

Craftsman 1717 Saber Saw

blade speed, and the tool is double-insulated, with the sliding on-off switch inserted into the full-length handle. The base tilts to the right and left for bevel cutting, and there is a built-in blower to keep sawdust from the cutting line. You won't be able to trim out a house with it, but it will cut adequately through light work. Approx. Price: $9.00

The Wen 531 has a variable-speed control that makes it one of the best of the breed. A push-button control allows a choice from between 0 to 2800 strokes-per-minute,

Wen's 531 Jigsaw

and the husky, ⅔-hp motor gives ample capacity for almost any cutting job. Standard features include double insulation, the "scroller" control, plus an infinitely adjustable base for bevel and flush cuts. A combination rip-guide/circle-cutter fence comes with the saw, too. Variable speeds make this tool extremely useful for cutting everything from heavy stock to thin-gauge materials like laminates and veneers. Approx. Price: $50.00

The Black & Decker 7530 is a basic two-speed saber saw. It lets you choose from 3200 SPM for sawing wood or composition materials, and 2500 SPM for cutting plastics and metals. Speed is set with a slide switch located on the side of the tool's handle. The setting must be made before the saw is turned on. Power comes from a ⅓-hp motor that's double insulated and connected to a 6-foot

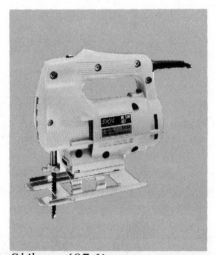

Black & Decker's 7530

detachable cord. This detachable feature makes the saw easy to store. A calibrated, adjustable protractor on this machine lets you make angular settings quickly and easily. This is a good, two-function saber saw with a reasonable price tag. Approx. Price: $18.00

The Skilsaw 487 is another two-speed saber saw, but has a baseplate that can be locked in three positions — a nice feature. Aside from the normal position, the baseplate can be locked in a second position to allow "flush-cutting" next to vertical members. The third position situates the blade in a small slot to minimize surface splintering without the need for a special add-on adapter. This tool's motor is fairly small at ¼-hp but it provides a blade speed of 3500 SPM on "high" and 2800 SPM on "low." Like most Skil products, this saw has most of the popular

Skilsaw 487 Jigsaw

modern features, like double insulation, a tilting baseplate for bevel cuts, and a built-in blower to keep the kerf line clear. It is also offered in a package (No. 487-2) that includes the saw itself, a blade assortment, a rip fence and circle-cutting guide, and a sturdy case to hold all the components. Sturdily constructed, the Skilsaw 487 can fill the requirements of most saber saw users. Approx. Price: $33.00

The Craftsman 1728, from Sears, Roebuck and Co., is an example of a heavy-duty saber saw designed for all-purpose performance and use. The "scroller" mechanism allows the blade to be turned a full 360 degrees, while the variable speed dial at the rear end of the housing can be turned to select any of 12 speeds from 1300 to 2700 strokes-per-minute. Speed is locked in with a push-button control adjacent to the tool's trigger switch. Although this tool does weigh more than 8 pounds, the extra weight contributes to stability when sawing. Features include a double-insulated, ½-hp motor, tilting baseplate, sawdust blower, removable chip guard, and a specially designed chuck that will even hold a broken saw blade. This is a tool for the advanced woodworker who plans to tackle major projects or who just wants to have this saw's impressive capacity on

Craftsman 1728

hand for occasional tough jobs. An optional Side Cutter Attachment (No. 27715) is available. This allows the saw blade to be gripped on one side of the baseplate, allowing cuts flush to a wall or other vertical obstruction. Although not particularly useful in the shop, the attachment can be very handy in remodeling work. This additional accessory makes the Craftsman 1728 saber saw useful for any conceivable cutting task in the home or on a construction site. Approx. Price: (1728) $74.50 (27715) $6.00

The Craftsman 17251 (a product of Sears, Roebuck and Co.) is an attractive saber saw for those who want good features but not the weight of the Craftsman 1728. True, the approximately 2½-pound difference — 6 versus about 8½ pounds — may not seem especially significant. But it can be meaningful in overhead work or heavy use

by a remodeler. Horsepower does decrease, from ½-hp down to ⅓-hp, but the price also decreases by $15. One different and sometimes advantageous feature is that the variable speed is controlled by the amount of pressure on the trigger. The more you depress the trigger, the faster the blade strokes. Blade speed can vary from 0 to 3200 strokes-per-minute. The extra scroller handle locks for straight cuts and doubles as an auxiliary handle for two-handed operation. Other features include double insulation, a tilting baseplate for bevel

Craftsman 17251

cuts, and a sawdust blower. All in all, it's a very useful tool with most of the available features at a reasonable price. Approx. Price: $59.50

Saber Saw Accessories

A combination edge/circle-cutting guide is virtually required equipment for a saber saw. Models are available for all types of saber saws, and may be offered as standard equipment or as an extra-cost option. This gadget is nothing more than a slim metal bar with a short fence attached to the free end. A practical item, it allows you to make accurate cuts in situations where a freehand attempt would result in a botch. It's good insurance for $3 to $4.

Used as an edge guide, the bar is locked into the

baseplate so that the distance from the edge of the blade to the fence equals the width of the cut to be made. The fence rides on the edge of the stock to guide the saw in the parallel cut. This is very handy for making either rip or crosscuts. But be sure to check the straightness of the edge the fence follows. If this edge isn't fairly straight, your cut may be angled or out of line.

For cutting circles or arcs, a hole in the fence end of the accessory permits you to use a nail as a pivot point. The usual procedure is to start with a plunge cut, then tap in a nail to secure the fence to the wood or other material. With the saw's baseplate secured to the bar, you make the cut by pivoting around this central point. The distance from the nail to the saw blade determines the radius of the circle or arc cut. This is an easy way to make very neat internal openings.

Saber Rasps, from Arco Products Corporation, have a conventional saber-saw blade shape, but their cutting teeth are similar to those of a cabinetmaker's rasp. Designed especially for the woodworker, they can be used to file smooth the edges of materials like wood, wallboard, and plastics. They are very good for removing that extra smidgen of material to make an opening just right. The rasps come in three shapes: flat, for any straight edge; round, for curved edges and holes; and wedge, for cleaning out sharp corners. They can be

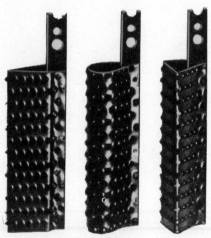

Arco's Sabre-Rasps

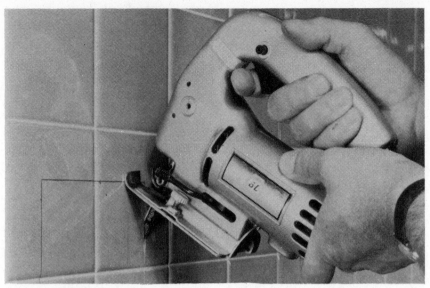

Remington Grit-Edge Blade

purchased individually, or in sets containing all three shapes. Approx. Price: $1.50 each

---

"Grit-Edge" blades, manufactured by Remington, have no teeth. Instead, hundreds of tungsten carbide particles are fused to the edge of the blade. Although you can saw materials like slate, glass, marble, and ceramic tile with regular blades, tungsten carbide blades take such work in stride and last longer. Cutting with these blades, however, is slow going because they cut by abrading. So, it's better to stick with regular saw blades for woodworking. Extremely fine cuts on very hard materials is this type of blade's forte, especially when edge quality and accuracy are more important than speed. Fine, medium and coarse grits are available. Approx. Price: $3.00 each

The main reason for buying a saber saw is its portability. But sometimes the saw can be used more accurately if it's fixed to an accessory table. Secured to one of these tables, the saw can duplicate some of the work of a table saw, band saw and jig saw. But it's not a replacement for these stationary saws, because the saber saw's motor lacks sufficient power and the table lacks stability for heavy-duty chores. With all accessory tables, you simply mount the saber saw underneath so that the blade projects through a slot on the table surface. The work is placed on the table and moved into the blade to make a cut. To make an internal cutout, you first drill a hole in a waste area of the material, place the work over the blade and cut away.

The Craftsman 25444, a Sears, Roebuck and Co.

product, is a rather sophisticated saber saw accessory table. It's rigidly constructed and has an aluminum table supported by steel legs that can be bolted permanently to a bench top. An adjustable fence and miter gauge help out when performing rip and crosscuts, but they're removable for unobstructed freehand scroll work. The table is made for Craftsman products, but any brand saber saw will fit. In fact, if you have a portable router, you can mount it on this table to form a small

Craftsman 25444 Table

shaper. Functional, this table is adaptable to a wide variety of light-duty shop tasks. Approx. Price: $40.00

front of the motor, the tool is sometimes called a bayonet saw.

This is a heavy-duty contractor's tool that's undaunted by heavy construction timbers, steel pipe, conduit, composition materials, plastics and plaster board. It'll even cut through a house wall without trouble. Around the house, it's handy for pruning and sectioning small logs. Typical blade sizes range from 3 to 12 inches, and a second handle is provided for a two-handed grip.

When judging the quality of a reciprocating saw, scrutinize the motor size, speed control and the foot brace that rests on the work. Generally, reciprocating saw motors are built to take a lot of abuse, but for heavy-duty work, a ½-hp motor is a minimum requirement. Blade speed is controlled by either a two-step high/low switch or a variable-speed control that gives you infinitely adjustable speeds within a given range. Foot brace design is a matter of personal preference. If possible, try out the saw before buying to find out how the particular foot brace works for you. Large foot braces make it easier to control the tool, which has a tendency to chatter. Smaller foot braces help you fit the tool into odd corners. Placement of the second handle is important, too, since it aids in safely controlling the saw.

Unless you do a lot of remodeling work, the saber saw is more useful than the reciprocating saw. But if your

Motor

Auxiliary handle

Blade

Handle

Shoe

Reciprocating Saws

On the power tool family tree, the reciprocating saw is closely related to the traditional compass saw. It's a portable, handheld saw that has a reciprocating blade like that of a saber saw, but the blade movement is horizontal to the motor housing, rather than vertical. Because the reciprocating saw's blade projects from the

game plan calls for extensive remodeling, the reciprocating saw is a good investment. It does many tasks well, and the cost of a quality product is not prohibitive.

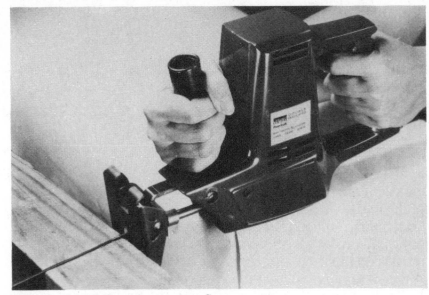

Ward's 8932 Reciprocating Saw

Montgomery Ward's 8932 is not an industrial machine, but it can handle everything short of the heaviest-duty chores. This reciprocating saw has an attractive price, too — costing less than a top-rated saber saw. It's powered by a ⅔-hp, double-insulated motor with a two-speed switch that provides either 2200 or 3000 strokes-per-minute. This is entirely adequate for most work found in an average shop. The switch is located in the main handle and has a push-button lock that holds the selected speed. The saw also has a feature that licks one of the most common problems connected with reciprocating saws. Most reciprocating saws have a short blade stroke — in this case it's 1 inch. Repeated cutting of the same size stock soon wears out those teeth in contact with the work, while the rest remain in good condition. A special feature of the Montgomery Ward 8932 lets you shift the blade back and forth in the chuck to bring the other teeth into play. This greatly extends blade life. The saw's three-position auxiliary handle can be set vertically for normal use, or to the left or right of the housing.

Pivot-mounted, the foot brace automatically adjusts the saw against the work. Except for the two-speed control — which limits the saw's flexibility — this saw is a performer with a good price. Approx. Price: $45.00

The Black & Decker 7574 is a top-of-the-line tool with a matching price tag. Its ½-hp

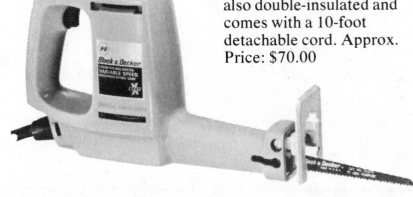

Black & Decker's 7574 Reciprocating Saw

motor is teamed with a trigger-switch that gives variable speeds from 0 to 2600 one-inch strokes-per-minute. A built-in counterbalancing mechanism helps reduce vibration for better control while sawing. Unfortunately, there's no auxiliary handle, but you can grip the small, cylindrical front end of the tool. This provides additional stability, but it's not the safest way to hold a reciprocating saw. Due to its light, 5-pound weight, the Black & Decker 7574 is relatively maneuverable. It's also double-insulated and comes with a 10-foot detachable cord. Approx. Price: $70.00

The Craftsman 1706, from Sears, Roebuck and Co., is an impressive reciprocating saw with professional quality. This saw is powered by a ½-hp motor, and the trigger-controlled variable speeds range from 0 to 2000 strokes-per-minute. Blade stroke length is outstanding. The full 1¼-inch stroke brings more teeth into play and is a distinct advantage in all kinds of woodworking tasks. Direction of the cut can be regulated by either turning the saw or rotating the blade clamp—a plus when working in narrow or confined places. An auxiliary handle mounts on either side of the housing, though not in the vertical position. There is a projection in the front, which is molded so that your free hand can curl around it comfortably. Double-insulated, this saw weighs under 9 pounds and comes equipped with three different blades. It's a good tool with all the desired quality features, at a price that will not seriously "cut" into the pocketbook. Approx. Price: $64.50

The Sawzall 6531, from Milwaukee Electric Tool Corporation, is often considered the best professional-quality reciprocating saw. A selector switch on the inside of the saw's handle provides two speeds—2400 and 1700 SPM. Blade stroke length is on the short side at only ¾-inch, but it doesn't hamper

Milwaukee Electric Sawzall 6531

this saw's cutting efficiency. In fact, by selecting the proper blade from the eleven available, you can cut through just about anything. This saw is also made to last, incorporating heavy-duty ball bearings and a nylon handle. Standard equipment includes a selection of eleven blades, adjustment wrench and an extra blade clamp and retaining screw. A 240-volt motor in place of the standard 120-volt model is available, and a steel carrying case is also an option. Approx. Price: $121.00

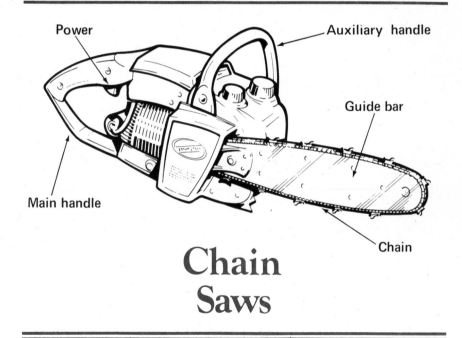

Power

Auxiliary handle

Guide bar

Main handle

Chain

Chain Saws

A wood-burning fireplace fills a room with romantic light and cozy warmth. But sawing logs by hand is backbreaking work that can put a damper on your hearth-side enjoyment. In recent years, many portable chain saws for the casual user have appeared on the market, partly due to the energy crunch. The crunch did more than increase the cost of gasoline. Faced with the prospect of short heating fuel supplies, many people rediscovered the wood stove and fireplace as practical heating alternatives. As the price of a cord of wood doubled, fireplace owners quickly discovered the convenience of the new, smaller chain saws and sales figures for these reasonably priced tools skyrocketed.

Of course, if you live in the middle of a large city, you won't find much use for this type of power saw. But suburban and country homeowners have come to appreciate the chain saw for many chores like pruning, brushing out scrub, and cutting firewood. If you're faced with chores like these, the chain saw can take much of the labor out of land maintenance.

There are two types of chain saws — gasoline and electric. Both types are alike in that the motor moves a continuous toothed chain along a guide bar. This chain, moving in a circular motion around the edge of the guide bar, is what cuts the wood. Although some pressure is required to keep the saw cutting, it is relatively minimal. When the chain is sharp, as it always should be, the saw can cut wood about four times faster than can be done with a handsaw.

When buying a chain saw, the power put out by the engine assembly, called a powerhead, should be at the top of the list of your considerations. Gasoline chain saws have two-stroke, air-cooled engines that run on a mixture of gasoline and oil. Like an airplane engine, the gasoline chain saw motor is designed to run in any

*Unless you are experienced, it is better never to use a chain saw to cut anything larger than the length of the guide bar. Burying the nose in wood is almost asking for kickback, and controlling the saw is critical. For large tree felling it may be better to let a trained tree man do the work. There are occasions when such a person is not available, however, and with practice it is fairly easy to cut a tree whose diameter is not more than twice the length of the guide bar. The procedure is relatively simple, **but** you have to be careful. Tree felling is dangerous!*

A notch is first cut into the side of the tree. This is cut on the side where you want it to fall. Check carefully to make sure that there are no lines or other obstructions to block the tree from falling properly.

The first cut will use a pivoting motion. Rest the base of the guide bar about two inches back from the bottom of the notch and slowly pivot the guide bar into the tree. Because you are actually boring into the tree this must be done carefully. Withdraw the saw when the guide bar is horizontal into the wood. Do not cut through the hinge.

The second cut is done on the same line as the first, only

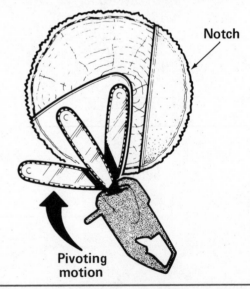

From left to right: first, second and third cuts

Notch

Pivoting motion

position. Motor size is measured in either cubic inches or cubic centimeters. And you'll find that the majority of chain saws have motors ranging from 1.5 cubic inches or 25 cubic centimeters on up. The more displacement, the more power and the heavier the

saw. Electric chain saws are rated by either horsepower or amperage draw, and have circuits designed for either 110 volts (the most common) or 220 volts. Usually, the higher the amperage draw, the more powerful the saw.

The size of the guide bar, which is the bar on which the

this time draw it around the opposite side of the tree. The tree will now have about two-thirds of it completely cut through.

The third cut is the actual felling cut. Place the guide bar so that it will cut in the same direction as the second cut. Behind the saw insert a felling wedge to prevent the tree from falling toward the back of the cut and pinching the blade. Draw the saw across the remaining wood, but leave the hinge intact. At this point, driving the wedge into the back of the cut will allow you to remove the chain saw from the tree. Continue to pound the wedge into the back of the cut to force the tree over.

*You can also yell "**Timber!**" at the top of your lungs — it's traditional and also warns everyone around. Be careful to stand clear of the tree as it is falling. The butt end is liable to jump around considerably and there will be branches and other debris around the area. It would also be wise to practice this technique on several small trees before starting on forest giants. There is a certain amount of danger in any operation with a chain saw and practice will considerably lessen the chance for accidents.*

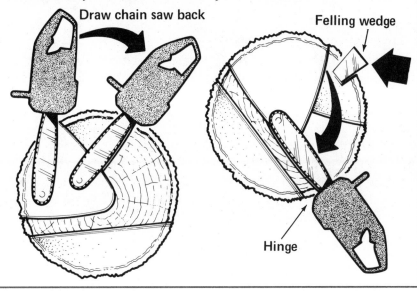

Draw chain saw back

Felling wedge

Hinge

chain revolves, is important, too. In saws designed for the home user, guide bars range from 8 inches to 4 feet in length, but the most popular sizes range from 12 to 20 inches. Select a guide bar length on the basis of the largest diameter log that you'll cut regularly. The bar should be 2 inches longer than the diameter of the log. It's possible to cut a log that's wider than the length of the guide bar, but this takes practice. Some chain saws accept interchangeable guide bars of different sizes. Not only is this convenient because it makes the saw more versatile, but it gives you extra value. This is because the powerhead is designed to power the largest guide bar available for the saw.

Weight of a chain saw varies, depending upon the motor size and the length of the guide bar, but most fall into the 8 to 15 pound range. Don't count on finding the actual weight of a saw in manufacturers' listings, because the weight of the guide bar isn't always included. The added weight of gas and oil is never included. Lighter-weight saws are easy to handle and are great for small pruning jobs. Their disadvantage is that the user may attempt to force the cut by applying too much pressure. For tree felling, larger pruning jobs and cutting firewood, choose a saw weighing between 10 and 20 pounds. Be sure to match the saw to the job. It makes the job easier and safer.

All chain saws have either automatic or manual chain oiling devices, or a combination of the two. The oiler speeds cutting and keeps the chain running smoothly. Automatic oilers save you the trouble of pressing a button periodically during a cut to keep the chain lubed. If you forget to press the button, you may be faced with a lethal flying chain.

Additional features found on some chain saws mainly ease cutting chores or increase safety. A "sprocket nose" is an additional toothed wheel set into the nose of the guide bar. It keeps the chain tracking correctly. Automatic chain sharpening is a handy feature, since chain saw cutters dull quickly, even if not abused. But even with this feature, you'll have to touch up the cutters with a file once in a while to keep them sharp. Electric chain saws start with the push of a button, but gasoline-powered models also offer a variety of ignition systems to make starting easier. Electronic ignition, which does away with contact points, is one. Another is a compression-release system that lets the engine crank easier when starting. If you plan to use your chain saw in the woods, a spark arrestor may save you from finding yourself in the middle of a forest fire in dry areas. You should remember that these accessories increase the price of the saw and may be completely unnecessary for backyard work.

Chain saws are dangerous devils that can put you in the hospital if you use them carelessly. In fact, they are among the most dangerous of portable power tools, due to their rotating chain. Kickback is the most common hazard. Let the guide bar's nose contact a log or stone while cutting, and your body is in jeopardy. The blade kicks up and back in an arc toward your face, often resulting in loss of control and serious injury. While you can avoid most kickback situations by carefully clearing the work area beforehand and using standard safety precautions, extensive use of a chain saw makes kickback inevitable at some time.

If all this sounds scary to you, as it should, opt for the kickback prevention devices offered by some manufacturers. One of these is a guard that covers the end of the guide bar to prevent contact with an object that could cause kickback. Unfortunately, this device limits the effective cutting area of the guide bar. While the limitation may not be important when sectioning logs for firewood, it is when felling trees. For this reason, industrial chain saws never have this guard. Another safety feature is an integral chain brake. It consists of a safety paddle mounted on the second handle on top of the saw. The theory is that when the saw kicks upward and back, the operator's hand comes in contact with the paddle and the chain stops in a split second. This device is fairly effective when adjusted correctly, and should be on every quality electric or gasoline chain saw.

The choice between a gasoline and electric chain saw depends upon your work location and the type of sawing you intend to do. In bar lengths under 14 inches, both cut the same. If you need a longer guide bar, choose a gasoline model because they have more power. The noise of gasoline models may infuriate your neighbors; they need to be refueled and may present starting problems. Electric saws are quieter and start at the press of a switch. But they require an electrical outlet, and you are limited by the length of their power cord or extension. For heavy cutting and work in the woods or brush, a gas chain saw is the one to choose. If you only anticipate backyard work like pruning and cutting small firewood, give your neighbors' ears a break and opt for an electric model. Electrics also cost less than comparable gas models. Whatever your choice, a well-manufactured chain saw should give you years of trouble-free service and lighten many of your heavier chores.

Stihl's E 10 electric chain saw is expensive, but worth the price. This fine German import compares favorably with gas-powered models of the same size, and sports many additional standard features. It can operate on either 110 or 220 volt current, though the fuse must be changed when switching voltages. Rated capacity is 10 and 5.3 amperes, respectively. The Stihl E 10 is one of the few electric chain saws that accepts guide bars of different lengths. A 10-inch bar is standard, but a 12-incher is available, either with or without a sprocket nose for added stability. The small guide bar is great for limbing trees or sectioning small logs. The larger one lets

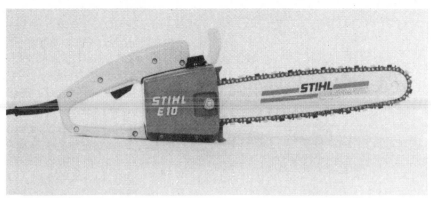

Stihl's E10 Chain Saw

tubular auxiliary handle slants toward the main handle. This makes it easy to grip, but awkward to hang onto for extended periods of time. The Village Blacksmith G9104-11 is outclassed in power by gas-powered models of the same size. But it'll do an efficient job, even if a bit slowly. Approx. Price: $70.00

you fell trees up to 2 feet in diameter. Chain oiling is automatic and governed by motor speed — the higher the speed, the more oil it delivers. For its size, the Stihl E 10 is a lightweight. It weighs just a bit over 8½ pounds with the 10-inch guide bar. It is, however, also a lightweight in the safety feature department. A handguard for the front handle is the only real safety device. But this is not a critical drawback when you use the saw carefully for around-the-house chores. Approx. Price: $175.00

Village Blacksmith's G9104-11, from McGraw-Edison, is an electric chain saw for the person who doesn't need a heavy-duty model, but can't get by with a bottom-of-the-barrel machine. This double-insulated tool weighs close to 11 pounds, has a 1.6-hp motor and a 14-inch guide bar. It also has a "sprocket nose" on the guide bar. This is a sprocket insert

in the nose of the bar. The chain rides on this sprocket, eliminating a lot of friction and helping to keep the chain on the bar. You do have to grease the sprocket occasionally, but it's labor well spent. Other important standard features include an automatic oiling system and "bucking spikes." These spikes are V-shaped teeth on the front of the motor housing that help anchor the saw into a horizontal log. "Bucking" is the old-style term for cutting firewood, and shows up in the word "bucksaw." Although the saw is loaded with good features, there is a hitch in its design. The wraparound,

Skil Corporation's 1602 is one of the best electrics at a reasonable price. It's a heavy-duty chain saw that draws a lot of juice. In fact, its 13-ampere rating crowds the limit of most home circuits. Yet it only weighs slightly more than 9 pounds. This power, combined with the 14-inch guide bar makes it hover right on the line between amateur and professional. This was undoubtedly one of the reasons the saw was designed to run on both AC and DC current. In the field, it can be powered by a portable generator. This tool has just about anything you'd want in a chain saw: double insulation; a safety switch to prevent accidental starts; sprocket-nose guide bar; and bucking spikes to anchor the saw for horizontal cutting.

Village Blacksmith's G9104 11 Chain Saw

Skil's 1602 Chain Saw

Chain oiling is manual, but it isn't a hassle once you condition yourself to press the button at regular intervals during a cut. One design feature puts this saw in the deluxe class. The wraparound handle is set so that in normal use, the operator stands out of line of the saw's chain. A possible kickback is deflected away from the body line. Unless you plan heavy-duty, constant usage, the Skil 1602 will satisfy your chain saw needs.
Approx. Price: $130.00

okay. Chain oiling is manual, with a small window functioning as an oil sight gauge. The secondary handle is situated forward of the motor housing. The position is a necessity with such a featherweight tool because you will definitely have to apply pressure if you are going to cut anything heavier than a popsicle stick. This chain saw has sufficient capacity for average pruning chores or cutting light firewood. Anything heavier will require the use of a larger tool, and it may pay to purchase one at the outset.
Approx. Price: $29.00

Homelite's XL-2 is small, spunky and easy to use. It's well-suited for lesser chores like limbing small trees, yet lets you cut cords of firewood without ruining the motor in the process. The powerhead displaces 1.6 cubic inches and the guide bar is available in a 12-inch length. The 12-inch bar extends this saw's versatility close to the range of heavier models. Chain oiling is automatic and the saw weighs a little over 7 pounds without fuel or oil. Homelite's patented "Safe-T-Tip" shields the front end of the guide bar's nose. If you want to fell a tree that's wider than the length of the guide bar, you have to remove the guard. But it effectively prevents the most common cause of kickback — striking the guidebar nose against a solid object when cutting small logs. The secondary handle is the standard wraparound type, but the main handle has an unusual feature — two trigger switches. When you need optimum leverage, you use the rear switch. The front

Montgomery Ward's Powercraft 30031 is a small, lightweight electric chain saw which has only one thing going for it — price. It's very inexpensive. This model has an 8-inch guide bar, and 1¼-hp motor. It weighs under 5 pounds, which is less than many saber saws. Obviously this is not a fast-cutting, tree-felling giant powerhouse. But if you need to clear out a small brush patch in the backyard, it's

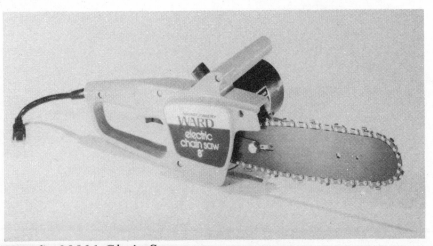

Ward's 30031 Chain Saw

Homelite's XL-2 Chain Saw

McCulloch Mac 320 Chain Saw

comes into play when a shift in balance is required for light cutting jobs. Of course, all these features add dollars to the price. But they do increase the usefulness of this tool, which is one of the best small gas chain saws designed for the amateur. Approx. Price: $145.00

McCulloch's Power Mac 320 is a tool for many reasons in all seasons—perfect for the homeowner and professional landscaper. This chain saw does it all: small tree felling, limb pruning, general trimming work, and firewood cutting. The combination of a 2.1 cubic-inch engine and a 16-inch guide bar provides the capacity for tough cutting chores. Weight is close to 12 pounds, including bar and chain. Both manual and automatic oiling systems are present. The latter operates whenever the trigger switch is depressed. The former is for tough cutting jobs where extra oiling can mean the difference between easy cutting and a stalled engine or kickback. A semi-automatic

chain sharpener is standard, too. You simply press a button on the right side of the handle and a grinding stone hones the moving chain. This doesn't completely eliminate hand sharpening, however, since periodic handwork is necessary at the sides of the cutters, where the sharpener doesn't touch. An automatic chain brake is the principal safety feature. It stops the chain in seconds or less when the safety bar is tripped—effective, but not a guarantee against kickback. Ignition is the solid-state, electronic type for ease of starting. All in all, the Mac 320 is one of the best chain

saws in its class. It does everything short of felling mighty oaks. Approx. Price: $170.00

The Skil 1646 is a heavy-duty model. You could build a log cabin with this chain saw. Its rugged construction makes it attractive to ranchers, farmers, and professional tree trimmers. Engine displacement is a hefty 4 cubic inches, and available guide bars with built-in sprocket nose range from 16 to 20 inches long. This saw has everything: chain brake for automatic stopping in

Skil's 1646 Chain Saw

Many people make a curious distinction between standing trees and cut lumber—one grows in the forest, while the other is material you buy in the lumberyard. Although the raw material is known to come from a tree, it is always assumed that without the services of a mill one always has to take what is available at the lumberyard. Experienced craftsmen are accustomed to going to a specialty house to obtain exotic woods like mahogany or teak, which can be gotten no other way. But the common North American hardwoods are now becoming difficult to obtain at the corner lumberyard, especially if some odd size or special graining is desired. Yet, short of finding a tree and hauling it to a mill for cutting, there was not much one could do about it. One took what was available and paid the price.

Portable chain-saw mills have forced a change in this situation. Chain-saw mills are actually metal jigs on which are mounted one of two chain-saw engines. Cutting is done with a chain ground for ripping cuts. These chain-saw mills enable one to cut a tree into planks or dimension lumber right where the tree has fallen, instead of hauling it to a mill. The principle is simple: rather than the log moving through the mill—the customary practice in a sawmill—the operator pulls one of these sawmills through the log!

Using one of these mills, it is possible to do three things: obtain the size and dimension of lumber you want, get quarter-sawn or crotches (something the lumberyard will usually cut out), and get it at a cheaper price than you would pay at a yard. Although the last would not be a factor unless you use a lot of lumber, in a heavily wooded region it could even pay for the initial cost of the saw and your labor.

Chain-saw mills are safer than conventional chain saws, practically feed themselves into the cut, and do not require backbreaking labor to operate. They are not cheap, however. Typical units range from $800 on up, which includes the cost of the engine(s) to operate it. But they are interesting and, in these days of mass processing, offer an alternative that is practical and has greater variety than simply going to a yard and taking what is available.

Portable chain-saw mills are available from:
Sperber Tool Works, Inc.
Box 1224
West Caldwell, NJ 07006

Granberg Industries, Inc.   *Haddon Tools*
200 S. Garrard Blvd.   *4719 W. Route 120*
Richmond, CA 94804   *McHenry, IL 60050*

case of kickback, automatic oiling, a throttle that can be preset for easier starting, bucking spikes to lock in solid contact during horizontal cutting, and solid-state ignition. A special handle attachment lessens operator fatigue by reducing vibration, and is welcome in a saw this large. Along with these features comes the inevitable—weight. Fourteen pounds may make it too much saw for the average homeowner. However, if you need to thin out five acres of pine, it's the right choice. The Skil 1646 works efficiently, and has the weight to make speedy cuts. Approx. Price: $380.00

The Husky 32 is the smallest chain saw in the company's line of professional woodcutter's tools. But Husquvarna's extensive experience in chain saw making has given even this small model all the features of a lumberjack's dream tool. Powerhead displacement is just under 2 cubic inches, and weight without chain and bar is 9 pounds. An optional 14-inch guide bar is available in addition to the standard 12-incher. Chain oiling is automatic, and standard equipment includes a kickback guard. A chain brake is an optional feature, and is highly recommended for safe work with any chain saw. A Swedish import, the Husky 32 is one of the best small, professional chain saws. Approx. Price: $180.00

In doing almost any kind of shop work, the first machine to be used is usually one of the stationary power saws. The operation may be as simple as cutting a board in half or as intricate as precision joinery; but these are the tools to do it.

Stationary Power Saws

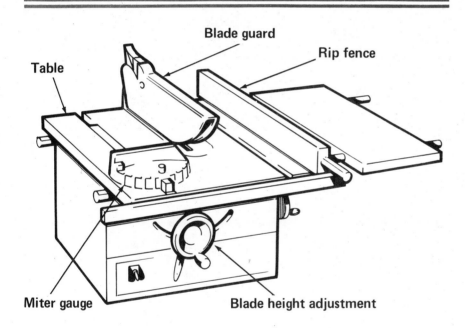

Blade guard

Rip fence

Table

Miter gauge

Blade height adjustment

Table/Bench Saws

It's easy to set up a woodshop in your home, but you do have to decide which power tools to buy. For many years, the table, or bench, saw has been the home craftsman's first choice. Recently, the radial arm saw has challenged the table saw's first-place position, but the old favorite is still the mainstay of furniture and cabinetmakers. Long ripping cuts on wide stock, dimensioning lumber to the correct size, groove and dado cutting—all can be done on the table saw. Sawing tasks that take laborious minutes with a handsaw are done in effortless seconds with a table saw. And the quality of the cut increases with the cutting speed. So, the table saw is one of the few great equalizers; novices and professionals get similar results. If you want a versatile woodworking tool, the table saw is the tool for you.

All table saws work the same way. A motor, either connected directly or via belts and pulleys, turns a circular saw blade. The blade projects through a slot in the table and is adjustable for height, which determines the thickness of wood that can be cut. A second adjustment either tilts the blade or the table to allow bevel cuts. The tilting blade is the most common type of angular

A QUICK LOOK AT STATIONARY POWER SAWS

NAME	REMARKS	TYPICAL USES
Table/Bench/Contractor's Saw	uses circular saw blades — size of saw based on blade diameter — work is passed over turning blade — tilting table or tilting arbor — mounts dado and shaping assemblies in place of saw blade	cross or rip cuts to dimension stock — accurate dadoes and grooves with correct assemblies — best stationary saw for cutting panels or plywood to dimension
Radial Arm Saw	uses circular saw blades — size of saw based on blade diameter — saw is pulled *across* work to be cut — auxiliary spindle can be mounted with router bits and drum sanders — will mount dado assemblies	accurate crosscutting in very long stock — poor ripping capacity — cuts accurate dadoes and grooves — limited shaping possible with router/shaper cutters mounted on auxiliary spindle — can mount drum sanders or boring tools
Band Saw	operates with continuous blade in endless loop — greatest depth-of-cut in any stationary power saw — can be used for long rip cuts — crosscutting limited by throat depth of saw	curves and other shapes — pad sawing of thick stock (6 inches or more) — resawing for textural effects — scalloped edges — rough shaping for subsequent lathe treatment
Jigsaw/Scroll Saw	uses short (6 inches or less), straight blades in reciprocating up/down motion — cuts very thin kerf — removable upper arm permits mounting of saber saw blades — very safe saw to use	extremely fine cuts in thin material — "piercing" or internal cutouts in the center of stock — intricate pattern or inlay work — machine used to create the thin separations in "jigsaw" puzzles

adjustment. Machines that use this method are called "tilting arbor" saws, since the spindle, or arbor, on which the blade is fastened, tilts as a unit while the table remains stationary. If the table tilts while the blade remains stationary, the saw is called a "tilting table" bench saw. Neither method alters the scope of the work you can do on the saw, but each has certain advantages if certain kinds of cuts are performed extensively. You can hold a workpiece to the table of a tilting arbor saw more easily, because the table remains horizontal. Bevel cuts, on the other hand, are easier to do on a tilted table, because the rip fence makes a secure cradle for the work. Which type of saw you choose depends upon the kinds of cuts you anticipate. But remember that some multipurpose saws, like those made by Shopsmith and Inca, must have a tilting table. These saws have arbor-driven accessories, such as mortising attachments and sanding drums. The table must tilt out of the way to use some of these accessories, or it has to be in a certain position to support the work. The versatility of these saws far outweighs any drawbacks due to the tilting table.

Besides motor and table, bench saws have two standard guides—the "rip fence" and the "miter gauge." The miter gauge fits into one of a series of flat grooves cut into the top surface of the table, and slides along the table in the same direction as the blade spins. It's adjustable from 0 to 45 degrees or more, and holds the work in the correct sawing position. A straight setting of 0 is for making crosscuts, while the angle settings are for making miters. In use, both the work and the gauge are moved as a unit toward the spinning blade. This operation is called "making a pass." On a quality saw, this miter gauge comes equipped with automatic stops, so it can be set quickly for the most common angular cuts.

The rip fence fits across the face of the table and can be locked at any point. It functions as a guide when stock is being cut to a certain width. The width of the cut is determined by the distance between the saw's blade and the rip fence. Usually, ripping operations are done on wide boards or panels, but there is some danger in this operation. It's possible for you to cut your hand badly on the blade when guiding the stock into the saw. The other problem is "kickback," which happens most often when the width of the cut is narrow. The rotating saw blade can move stock caught between the blade and the rip fence back toward the operator, with considerable force. To avoid both dangers, it is advisable to use a pushstick to move narrow work into the blade. This is a slim piece of wood, notched at one end to fit over the end of the work. It is good practice to use a pushstick whenever the distance between the blade and the fence is less than 6 inches. On wider cuts you can use your hand, but be careful to keep it close to the rip fence as the work goes into the saw. Table saws are not to be played with, and you can be severely injured if you are careless.

The size of a table saw is determined by the diameter of its blade. Although this gives some indication of the saw's depth-of-cut, blade diameter is not an adequate measure of the tool's size or power. You can't assume that a 10-inch table saw has more power or a larger table than a 9-inch one. In many cases, table size, which determines the maximum rip cut possible, is much more important than whether the saw has a 9- or 10-inch blade.

One acceptable cutting capacity norm is the ability to cut through at least nominal 2-inch stock (actually 1½ inches thick) when the blade is set at either 45 or 90 degrees. Almost all modern saws can do this. You should also check the distance from the blade to the front edge of the table. When the blade is raised high enough to cut through nominal 1-inch stock, this distance should allow crosscutting 12-inch boards with the miter gauge head resting solidly on the table at the beginning of the cut. A distance of 14 inches or more is best.

Almost all stationary saws are equipped with a blade guard. In most cases this is a pivot-mounted

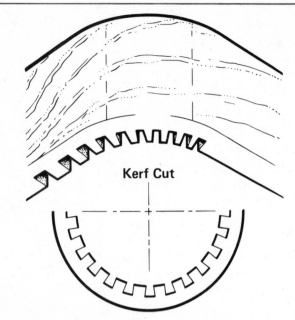

Kerf Cut

One of the interesting techniques that can be used on a table saw involves wood bending—normally a time consuming process involving jigs and steam. This is usually not practical for the home shop, but for wood bending jobs where the full strength of the stock is not required there is an alternative. This is called "kerf-curving."

The object in this kind of operation is to make a number of deep, adjacent cuts in the face of the stock. These cuts will form the inside of the bend, while giving the opposite face flexibility. The material between each pair of saw cuts becomes a reinforcing rib to strengthen the resulting bend. The closer the kerfs are spaced on the underside of the bend the more sharply the wood can be bent. Depth of the kerf in the wood is a factor, but it is best to leave at least ⅛ inch of solid wood to avoid needless breaking. It is also good practice to cut at right angles to the grain. Although this makes bending the stock more difficult, it helps to prevent the stock from fracturing.

To figure out how to space the kerfs for any given radius, cut a kerf in a piece of scrap wood with the same thickness as the one you want to bend. Fasten this piece to the bench and on the free side of the kerf measure out the distance of the desired radius of the curve. Lift the scrap piece until the kerf closes. Height from the underside of the board to the bench top at the radius mark is the correct kerf spacing for that particular radius.

When bending the wood do it slowly; on stubborn or tough woods it may help to wet down the unkerfed side. With a little practice, a wide variety of curved and irregular shapes can be formed. When used as project components they add a nice, professional touch to almost any cabinet or furniture work.

system attached to the rear of the table in line with the saw blade. The guard lifts up and rests on the surface of the work, covering the part of the blade that projects above the wood. Some guards include a "splitter" and "anti-kickback" fingers. The splitter keeps the saw cut (kerf) open, so the wood will not bind on the blade. The anti-kickback fingers are strips of metal with a serrated edge. They are pivot-mounted to ride freely on the surface of the wood when the cut is made in the proper direction. Should kickback develop, they dig into the wood and help prevent it from moving back toward you.

Unfortunately, some sawing operations can't be done with the guard in place because it interferes with the free movement of the wood, especially large pieces. Some manufacturers design the guard so it can be lifted out of the way. Many woodworkers damn the guards as a general nuisance, and toss them on a shelf, never to be seen again. Although removing the guard is not a safe practice, it's true that it can give you a false sense of security. If wood being fed into the saw can lift the guard, so can your finger—and get snipped off in the process. Respect for the machine and knowledge of its operation is more effective than any guard made. Read your owner's manual carefully.

Before you shop for your table saw, measure the room

where it'll be placed. The size of the wood you plan to cut is important, too. With a table saw you move the wood into the blade, so there must be clearance around the saw. Even a very large saw won't require more than 3 or 4 square feet of floor space. But if you plan to slice through the entire length of a 4x8-foot plywood sheet, you'll need 8 feet of clearance in front and behind the machine, plus standing room for yourself. You also have to position the saw correctly in the shop. You can mount the unit on casters and roll it around the room as necessary, but it's better to position the saw correctly to begin with. Casters decrease the unit's stability and defeat the purpose of this heavy saw, which is designed to sit solidly on the floor to make accurate cuts.

Rockwell's Unisaw 34-466 is an industrial-quality bench saw of good repute. Built to take it, this saw is often found in school shops and commercial cabinet and furniture-making establishments. With its 10-inch blade it has a capacity of 3⅛ inches at 90 degrees and 2⅛ inches at 45 degrees. You can add extensions to the 20x27-inch table to stretch the width from 20 to 36 inches. Since the extensions double the standard 25-inch rip cut possible on the standard

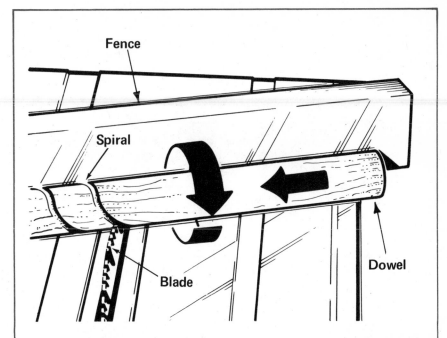

The most difficult shape to get on round stock is a spiral. This can be either a square-cut groove or a shallow, beveled edge. The traditional method used to get this effect was to mark out the stock with pencil lines and then cut with a handsaw along the lines. Often the result was uneven or irregular due to the inherent inaccuracy of the eye or difficulty in holding the stock to assure an even spiral effect.

A table saw makes it easy to add this decorative effect to almost any size round stock. If a slanted guide is attached to the miter gauge on the saw and the round stock rotated slowly against it, a spiral "pitch" will be established by the angle of the guide. Depth of cut is controlled by the projection of the saw blade above the table top. Using this method requires some experimentation on scrap, but once mastered it produces a very unusual effect that is hard to duplicate in any other way. Table saws are like any other power tool in that you will never find out just how much can be done on this machine until you experiment. Often a user can obtain unusual effects that even he did not anticipate, adding to his own repertoire while learning a new shop technique.

table, you should consider the extensions if you plan a lot of wide ripping. Distance from the fully projected saw blade to the front edge of the table—critical for certain crosscutting operations that

require use of the miter gauge—is 12¼ inches. This is quite enough to handle a nominal 12-inch wide board.

The fully enclosed base of the Unisaw conceals the motor and drive belts and

Rockwell's Unisaw

acts as a sawdust depository. A large door in the front of the cabinet allows you to shovel out the accumulation quickly. The interesting drive mechanism incorporates three matched V-belts that cut down vibration and practically eliminate power loss from belt slippage. A front lever locks the rip fence at both ends, and handwheel controls take care of the blade tilt and projection. You have the option of power from 1½- to 3-hp. Unless you own a professional shop where a lot of ripping is done, opt for the 2-hp motor, operated on a 220-volt circuit. The Rockwell Unisaw is a leader in the basic bench saw field, and is designed for years of hard use. Approx. Price: $883.00

Inca cabinetmaker's saws are a special breed. These Swiss-made bench saws are made specifically to perform precise, accurate cabinet work and accept a wide array of accessories. Because the accessories are driven off an extension of the arbor, the saw has a tilting table instead of a tilting arbor—not a handicap with these tools. You can add accessories like a belt sander, an attachment for making mortises and tenons, an abrasive disc, and a drill chuck to increase the saw's versatility.

There is a drawback to Inca tools, however. You can't just stroll down to your local hardware store to buy blades. Inca tools have a standard Swiss metric arbor. North American blades won't fit, so you must purchase blades from the Inca dealer. Also, the tables are made of die-cast aluminum, rather than the common cast iron, and won't tolerate a lot of scraping and banging. You have to treat these expensive tools with care and respect.

The Inca 10-inch Cabinetmaker 250 has a working area of 20⅝x33¾ inches and a rip capacity of about 23¼ inches wide. You can add extension rails to increase the table size to 47½ inches, but this is still too short to allow ripping through the center of a 4x8-foot panel. Highest blade projection is just a trifle more than 3 inches. This is small, but quite adequate for any form of precise cabinet work. Motor size is optional, but a 1½-hp unit is recommended. Approx. Price: $570.00

The Inca Modelmaker 150 is a smaller, 7-inch bench saw for the person who specializes in precise, small-scale work. Its 16½x22½-inch table allows a rip width of 11¾ inches. The blade projects a little more than 2 inches, and a 1-hp motor is recommended. It

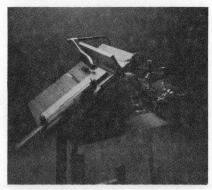

Inca Modelmaker 150

90

doesn't offer as many accessories as the Cabinetmaker, but that's to be expected in such a small saw. Approx. Price: $320.00

These saws require a big outlay of cash, especially when you add the accessories. They are a lifetime investment, but only if you plan to specialize in making quality furniture and cabinets. Just as you wouldn't use a pair of dog clippers to trim a hedge, you shouldn't consider these machines for remodeling a house. They will do it, but you'll ruin a fine machine in the process.

Toolkraft's 4106 is a 9-inch, tilting arbor saw that's a prime candidate for the home workshop. This is a "motorized" tool, which means that the motor transmits power directly to the saw's arbor instead of through conventional pulleys. The advantage is that the saw comes completely assembled, and power loss from belt slippage is eliminated. Also, since there are no exposed pulleys, you can't catch a shirt tail or finger in the mechanism.

The standard table gives you a work area of 17x20 inches, but you can extend this to 20x50 inches with extensions. Toolkraft's saw table is made of "ferrolon" instead of the common cast iron or aluminum. It looks like a good deal, since the strong, lightweight material won't rust, wears almost as well as cast iron, and costs less. Blade projection at 90 degrees is 2¾ inches; tilting the blade to 45 degrees reduces this to 2 inches. The table does have one bad mark against it. The area in front of the blade is only 9¾ inches, which is not enough to mount a nominal 12-inch board.

Blade projection and tilt are controlled by handwheels, and you can slap a padlock on the on-off switch to prevent the children from playing carpenter. At first glance, the ⅞-hp motor might seem small, but it's quite adequate for a saw with no power-robbing pulleys or belts. This package comes ready to use, complete with saw, table extensions, motor and stand. The neat package saves you the time and trouble of selecting and mounting a proper motor. Approx. Price: $270.00

Rockwell's 34-388 table saw is a contractor's tool, but also a good choice for extensive remodeling or deck construction. This is a 12-inch, tilting arbor machine that can be fitted with motors up to 2-hp. Since depth-of-cut is 4⅛ inches, you can buzz through 4-inch

Toolkraft's 4106 Table Saw

Rockwell's 34-388 Table Saw

nominal material (actually 3½ inches thick) quite easily. With the supplied extensions, table size is 27x42 inches — more than enough to halve a standard 4-foot-wide plywood panel. If you plan a lot of heavy construction work, then the Rockwell 34-388 is a good choice. For average shop use, however, it's overkill. Approx. Price: $500.00

Craftsman's 29818N5, from Sears, Roebuck and Co., is a 10-inch, tilting arbor saw with above-average depth-of-cut capacities. With this saw's power and capacity, you can handle all normal-size projects and occasional larger pieces of work. Depth-of-cut is 3⅜ inches at 90 degrees and 2¼ inches at 45 degrees. You can extend the 20x27-inch

cast-iron table to 27x40 inches with side extensions. This saw is a champ for cutting wide boards, because there's an extra-wide 15¼ inches between the front edge of the table and the blade. Rip capacity is 24 inches. The saw comes equipped with a 1-hp induction motor, which is quieter than the standard universal type. But don't expect the noise to be reduced to a whisper, because blade type and the thickness of the material being cut are more important factors in noise production.

A couple of standard features enhance the value of this saw. Controlled crosscutting is more accurate because of a feature called "Exact-I-Cut," a small, adjustable circular insert in the table in front of the saw blade. By marking the stock to be cut, and lining up with a guideline on the insert, you

know exactly where the blade is going to cut. This eliminates some of the human error that can result in wasted stock. Another feature is an on-off switch with a special, removable key. A locking switch is a definite asset if children are around the house. This is a shop tool for the craftsman, and you get everything you need to set up the saw and keep it running. Approx. Price: $388.00

American Machine & Tool Company's 21645 B table saw is for people who are watching their pennies. This tool is not the high watermark of craftsmanship, but if you want a no-frills saw and don't mind filing off a burr or two, it's certainly adequate. No fancy knobs or chrome here, just what is

Craftsman 29818N5 Table Saw

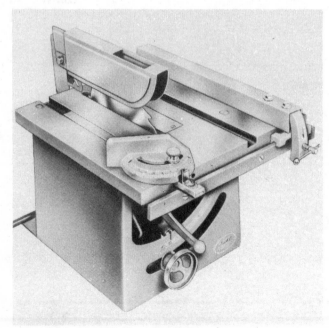

AM&T's 21645 B Table Saw

required to saw wood. The basic table size is only 10x13 inches, and distance from the 8-inch blade to the front of the table is 5 inches. This table size imposes some limitations unless you are going to do modeling work. But construction plans are provided for a cabinet-type base that increases the usable table area to about 24 square inches. Maximum blade projection at 90 degrees is 2¼ inches. At 45 degrees it drops down to 1¹¹⁄₁₆ inches—just enough to cut through nominal 2-inch material. This is a good second saw for light work, miniatures, and mitering. How good you want this saw

to be depends on how much additional work you want to put into building a larger cabinet. Approx. Price: $49.00

Dadoes

Dadoes and grooves are trough-shaped depressions cut into wood so that two pieces can be fitted and joined together. They're really both the same, except that a dado goes across the grain, and a groove goes with

the grain. As far as these cuts are concerned, the bench saw owner has it made compared to the old-time craftsman. In the past, dadoes and grooves were made by first cutting with a backsaw to the desired depth, and then chiseling out the waste between the two kerfs. With a bench saw, these cuts are easy to make right on the table. You use a normal saw blade for the most common method. Adjust the blade to the desired cutting depth and make successive passes until the groove or dado is of the correct width. Even for a moderately wide shape, you have to make several passes, since each pass only removes as much wood as a normal kerf. This method takes time, and you need a certain amount of skill to do it accurately. If you think this is too difficult, take a look at the following specialized tools. Even the neophyte can do a good job with them.

A dado set, sometimes called a dado assembly, consists of "chippers" sandwiched between two thicker-than-normal circular saw blades. The chippers are special cutters, commonly available in ⅛-, ¹⁄₁₆-, and ¹⁄₃₂-inch cut widths. By selecting different size chippers, you can vary the width of the cut. For example, two outside blades with two ⅛-inch chippers between will produce a cut ½-inch wide.

Dado sets mount on a saw's arbor just like regular saw blades, but you need a special table insert to

---

List price on large, stationary power tools is always negotiable. Much like the sticker prices on new automobiles, the list price should be a figure above which you should not pay. It is almost a sure bet that any brand name product will have a large number of dealers in any given area. They will always be in competition. Shopping around will usually turn up a reasonable spread in prices. Specials on power machinery have come to be one of the leading marketing tools for full-range hardware stores. It is quite possible to pick up a saw that will be a hundred or more dollars cheaper than the everyday price.

In the case of specially ordered machinery that is not kept in stock—often the case with those power saws or tools that are designed for the contractor's market—almost any dealer will be willing to dicker a bit on the price. This will usually include the cost of the shipping from the warehouse, a minimum saving of $25.00 on up. Manufacturer's closeouts are another way to pick up good quality machinery at reasonable prices. Setting up even a small shop is not a cheap proposition, even if one takes into account the fact that power machinery has a long life. Every fifty dollar saving is something which can aid in equipping the woodworker's dream shop.

accommodate the wider assembly. All table saw and radial arm saw manufacturers sell the sets and they are usually interchangeable between brands. Diameters of 6, 7, and 8 inches are available, and most offer a maximum cut width of slightly more than ¾ inch. For average use, you can stick with a 6-inch diameter set.

Dado sets have either "flat-ground" or "hollow-ground" blades. Flat-ground blades are the same gauge (thickness) from the center to the tips of the teeth. This puts more blade in contact with the wood and produces more friction. The result can be burning of the blade or wood, and the temper can be drawn from the metal. Hollow-ground blades are slightly concave from the tips of the teeth to the main body of the blade. Since only the tips of the teeth contact the work, the result is less friction, a smoother cut, and cooler running. If you plan extensive dado and groove cutting, spend the money for the more expensive sets with hollow-ground blades. They're better equipment and contribute to finer work.

Flat-ground dado sets:
Rockwell 34-334 (6-inch)
  Approx. Price: $43.00
Nicholson 80916 (6-inch)
  Approx. Price: $24.50
Toolkraft 1127 (6-inch)
  Approx. Price: $30.00
Disston 3 (6-inch) Approx.
  Price: $33.50; (8-inch)
  $53.50

Hollow-ground dado sets:
Rockwell 34-333 (6-inch)
  Approx. Price: $69.00

Sears Roebuck 3257 (7-inch)
  Approx. Price: $35.00
Montgomery Ward 8371
  (8-inch) Approx. Price:
  $35.00

Adjustable dado tools, often called wobbler-type dado tools, do the same job with one blade. As the blade rotates, the teeth wobble from side to side to cut a wider-than-normal kerf. The width of the kerf depends upon how much the blade is offset. An advantage of this tool is that it is infinitely adjustable between a minimum and maximum setting, typically between $\frac{3}{16}$ and $\frac{13}{16}$ inch. Another advantage is that you can adjust the width of the dado without removing the tool from the saw's arbor. This makes it easier to work with

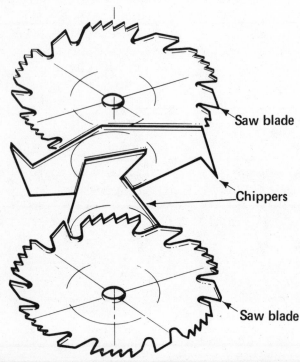

Dado Set

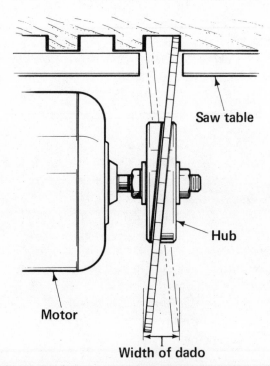

Adjustable Dado Tool

than the blade/chipper dado assembly.

Most adjustable dado tools consist of a heavy blade mounted between two eccentric hubs, which can be turned to adjust the degree of offset. By turning the two hubs 80 degrees in relation to one another, the blade will run true and can be used as a regular saw blade. Adjustable dado tools are not as interchangeable among brand name saws. Sometimes they're not even interchangeable between different models of the same brand of saw because of clearance problems and inserts. Check carefully to make sure that the tool you buy fits your particular saw.

Adjustable dado tools with steel blades:
Rockwell 34-955 (6-inch, 24 teeth) Approx. Price: $30.00

Montgomery Ward 2295 (6-inch, 12 teeth) Approx. Price: $22.00

Shopsmith 505548 (6-inch, 82 teeth) Approx. Price: $30.00

Adjustable dado tools with carbide-tipped blades:
Montgomery Ward 8309 (6-inch, 12 teeth) Approx. Price: $35.00

Rockwell 34-980 (6-inch, 12 teeth) Approx. Price: $25.00

Sears, Roebuck 3262 (7-inch, 32 teeth) Approx. Price: $47.00

Molding Heads

You can mount molding heads on your bench saw's arbor and duplicate some of the work normally requiring a specialty tool called a "shaper." Molding heads accept a variety of formed knives that cut special shapes in wood—frame moldings, and fancy edges on furniture and cabinet doors. But this isn't the only use for this tool. The assortment of cutting knives available makes it practical for making many standard forms used for joining wood.
Tongue-and-groove joints, dadoes and grooves, and rabbets (L-shaped cuts) can all be done with this accessory when it's fitted with blank knives.

The molding head itself, often called a cutterhead, is available in several forms. All grip various patterns of knives which do the shaping. Depending upon the design, these cutterheads may have one to three blades, each holding a knife. There are both single-purpose and combination knives. Combination knives make a variety of cuts possible, depending upon which part of the knife's profile is used. A common combination knife, for example, is called a "cove and quarter round," and can be used to form either a concave or convex arc. There's an endless variety of cutterheads and knives available. And there's probably a tool to put any shape you dream up into wood. Like dado cutters,

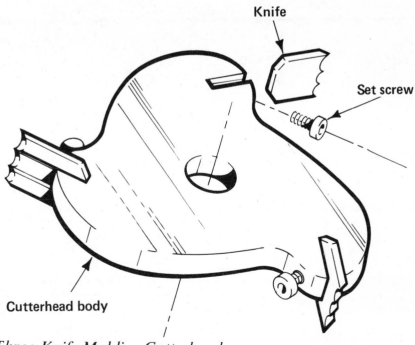

Knife

Set screw

Cutterhead body

Three-Knife Molding Cutterhead

molding heads are not completely interchangeable between brands of table saws (or radial saws, which they also fit), and you have to check before buying. In addition, a different insert must be purchased to fit over the cutterhead, since the slot in a regular table is not wide enough to pass the knives.

Molding Heads (cutterheads):

Rockwell 34-562 (3-knife design) Approx. Price: $32.00

Sears, Roebuck 3217 (3-knife design; includes 8 sets of knives) Approx. Price: $40.00

Sears, Roebuck 3215 (single-knife design; includes 18 different knives) Approx. Price: $35.00

Shopsmith 505553 (3-knife design) Approx. Price: $30.00

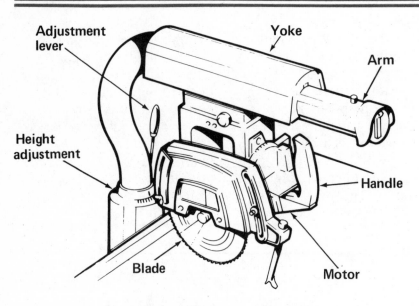

Adjustment lever

Yoke

Arm

Height adjustment

Handle

Blade

Motor

Radial Arm Saws

The radial arm saw is the most versatile of all stationary power saws. Until quite recently, it was typecast as a contractor's tool because it was mainly used for cutting house framing. With a suitable setup, you can use a radial arm saw to dimension stock over 20 feet long. When the portable circular saw came on the scene, however, the radial arm saw lost favor with contractors. Since then, the radial arm saw has become a favorite of the home workshop owner, as a replacement for, or adjunct to, the table saw. With the addition of a large selection of accessories, the radial arm saw can be used as a molder, shaper, sander; can cut dadoes and grooves; and even do limited drilling and planing. It can't perform these tasks as well as a tool specifically designed for the job, but the saw can widen the workscope of the person with limited shop space and plenty of time. And using a radial arm saw for these tasks is cheaper than buying many separate machines.

The function of a radial arm saw and a table saw is very similar. One primary difference between the two is that when crosscutting on a table saw the work is moved into the blade, while the operator of a radial arm saw moves the blade into the wood. The fact that the workpiece remains stationary during the cut contributes to stability and accuracy. This feature is accentuated by available table extensions that let you crosscut lumber that's as wide as the table. Crosscutting wide workpieces is tough to do on a table saw because you have to move the work into the blade.

When ripping, however, the work must be moved into the blade of a radial arm saw, just as is done on a table saw. And the radial arm saw is not as efficient for ripping operations because the stock can be only as wide as the throat depth of the saw's arm. In most cases, you are limited to cutting stock less than 4-feet wide. This means that the saw cannot cut standard 4x8-foot-wide panels conveniently. For most general work, either the table saw or radial arm saw will work out well; but the owner of a radial arm saw gains the edge in versatility.

Basically, a radial arm saw consists of a heavy, vertical column supporting an arm that projects toward the operator and is parallel with a table. The arm has a yoke that's movable along its length. A motor is attached to the bottom end of the yoke. A shaft, extending from the motor, serves as an arbor for a circular saw blade. In many cases, the shaft extends from both sides of the housing. As viewed from the operator's side of the machine, the left extension is for the blade and various types of molding/dado tools; the right extension is for other accessories like a flexible shaft.

The adjustments on a radial arm saw give it great flexibility. You can raise or lower the arm for depth adjustment, and swing it left or right for angle cuts. The motor on the yoke also swivels to tilt the blade. By keeping the blade vertical and swinging the arm left or right, you can set the saw up for simple miter cuts. Swing the arm and tilt the blade, and it makes compound miter cuts, which are often required for some kinds of shadow box frames.

Automatic stops for common angular settings are found on many radial saws. These stops provide for swinging the arm 45 degrees for standard miter cuts; for tilting the blade 45 or 90 degrees, the latter placing it parallel to the table for some specialized cuts; and for swinging the motor 90 degrees so that its blade is parallel to the rip fence located against the column. This last position is for ripping operations where the work is fed into the saw. The saw may offer automatic stops for other operations, too. But remember that vibration and wear tend to change the settings in a short time, no matter how accurate they were in the beginning. You should always check the settings carefully with a gauge before use. Then test the setting on a piece of scrap stock before cutting good stock.

At first glance, a brand new radial arm saw may look odd because it seems that you can't make a cut without cutting into the table. Although this may seem self-defeating, it is true. You do cut the table along with the stock. But the tables are usually made of particle board or heavy plywood, and are designed to be tossed and replaced as necessary. The same goes for the "rip" fence. It's just a strip of discardable material that runs parallel to the table's back edge. It can usually be placed and locked in two positions. In its forward position, the rip fence is used for crosscutting, securing the work in place. A pass with the saw goes right through both the work and the fence. When the fence looks like it was attacked by a horde of crazed beavers, you just replace it. The second position of the rip fence is used for rip cuts. In this procedure, the saw blade is turned 90 degrees from its normal position and locked. The rip fence is set back into its rear position and locked in place to serve as a guide. Width of the cut is determined by the distance between the blade and the rip fence. You move the work into the radial saw as you would with a table saw, only the work slides along the rip fence for the length of the cut.

Although a radial arm saw's size is listed by its blade diameter, this isn't the most important buying information. Crosscut and rip capacity are more interesting. Pay attention to the length of a saw's arm, because this tells you how long a crosscut you can make. Usual crosscut capacity is 1½ to 2 feet. The length of the arm also dictates the rip-cutting capacity of the saw. Most radial arm saws have a sufficient capacity at 2 feet to rip-cut a 4x8-foot plywood panel in half lengthwise. Although it's possible to halve a panel of this size on a radial saw, it's extremely cumbersome to hold the work.

Used incorrectly, you can hurt yourself on any power tool, and this is especially true of saws with rotating blades. Theoretically, the design of radial arm saws should make them safer than table saws. This is mainly because the blade is in sight at all times. Of course, if your body is in the workshop and your mind is elsewhere, this won't keep your hand from straying into the blade.

Complicating the matter is the position of the controls for altering the blade and motor position. These are usually located either on the column behind the blade, or very close to the motor. For this reason, *never* make adjustments when the motor is running. And, since the location of the blade or other cutters is variable, be aware of their location at all times.

All radial arm saws have a guard that covers the top of the blade, and many manufacturers offer an additional "leaf" guard. The leaf guard is usually a semicircular piece of plastic or metal, attached to the stationary top guard. It automatically rises as the blade goes into the work, and lowers when the cut is finished.

Adjustable anti-kickback features are sometimes incorporated into this design, but you have to adjust them carefully before sawing to make them effective. Because you feed the work into the blade while ripping, against the direction of the blade's rotation, chance of kickback is equal or greater than when using a table saw. So, always use a pushstick to feed narrow stock into this or any other stationary power saw. Guards can help prevent kickback and can help shield your hand from the blade, but they can't keep a finger out of the cut line.

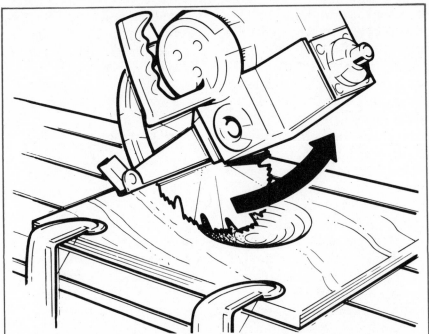

A unique operation that can be done on a radial arm saw is called a "saucer cut." This cut takes advantage of the radial arm saw's tilting ability, and rather than an actual cut into the wood it is more in the nature of a scraping action. The result is a depression or saucer-shape cut into the wood surface. If the machine you are working with has the full range of auto-stops, stopped or sloped saucer cuts are also possible.

To make a saucer cut, first raise the blade—while it is in the crosscut position—high enough so that it can be swung through the full tilt range without hitting the work surface of the table. Clamp the work stock to the table. Lower the arm about ⅟₁₆ of an inch and swing the blade through the tilt while the blade is turning. Full depth-of-cut in the stock is achieved by repeat passes until the desired depth of the saucer is reached. It is important that the work remain firmly clamped during this repeat process, because the saw blade is not so much cutting as it is scraping the wood out of the depression. Some very unique effects can be had using this method, especially with layered woods of contrasting color. The layers will form a sloping, concentric pattern that is pleasing to the eye.

At one time, the blades of many radial arm saws would continue to rotate for as long as a minute after you shut off the saw. This is a safety hazard you shouldn't stand for today. Many current models have built-in manual or automatic brakes that stop the blade in seconds. Make sure there's a brake on the saw you buy.

One of the reasons that home workshop owners like

the radial arm saw so much is because you can place it up against a wall. A table saw usually needs lots of room all around it, but the only critical work space required with a radial is on the sides. You need about 4 or 5 feet on either side of the machine, with either homemade or manufactured side extensions or cabinets to support the work. With space and extensions like this, you can firmly support work up to 10 feet long. Of course, you also need some floor space in front of the machine for yourself.

The radial arm saw's compactness makes it a favorite of people with limited shop space. This versatile tool has only one drawback—lack of rip capacity on wide stock. But for all other applications it's as good as, if not better, than the table saw.

The Craftsman 1977N, sold by Sears, Roebuck and Co., can keep the average craftsman happy for years. It has enough power and capacity to handle all normal radial saw cutting. The 10-inch blade gives a cutting depth of 3 inches at 90 degrees and 2¼ inches at 45 degrees. Depth-of-cut isn't enough to slice through 4-inch nominal stock in a single pass, but that's no problem. Just make one cut, flip the stock over and cut the other side.

Ripping capacity is 26

Craftsman 1977N

inches—pretty good for this grade of saw. And it has a respectable crosscut capacity of 15 inches with stock up to 1 inch thick. The table measures 27½x40 inches, and it's a full inch thick. This thickness gives a firmer and more stable work surface and lengthens the intervals between table replacement. The motor puts out 1.5 hp and is wired for a 120-volt circuit. You can change it to 240 volts by merely changing a plug and two terminals—a handy feature when cutting a lot of heavy stock or green wood.

This well-designed saw gives you a nice package of standard safety features: automatic blade brake; anti-kickback fingers with a "splitter," which rides in the kerf to prevent blade binding; front-located controls and a lockable push-pull switch. A second, leaf-shaped guard is available at extra cost.

Like the bulk of radial arm saws designed for the craftsman, this saw has a

double-ended motor shaft. The arbor on the left accepts regular blades, dado tools and molding heads, while its partner is for special accessories like a router and drum sander. Another feature could save you from a big repair bill after years of use. The guide tracks in the saw's arm are replaceable. Even though they would need to be replaced only after extensive use, it's nice to know you don't have to replace the entire arm.

This radial arm saw isn't the largest in either capacity or ripping-cut depth that's commercially offered. But it's fine for average shop work. The same saw (#19776N8) is sold complete with cabinet stand and work light, and is a good choice if you want a ready-to-use radial arm saw. Approx. Price: $380.00

De Walt's 7790/3431, from Black & Decker, is a lot of saw. This rugged, industrially rated, 12-inch saw has a 1½-hp motor wired for a 208- to 240-volt circuit. Depth-of-cut at 90 degrees is a full 4 inches. This drops to 2¾ inches when you tilt the blade to 45 degrees. Maximum rip cut on the 29⅜x38½-inch table is 27 inches, and you can crosscut stock 16 inches wide. This is the kind of capacity you should expect from a saw this size, but it's actually a rarity.

The saw does have one drawback. Controls for the

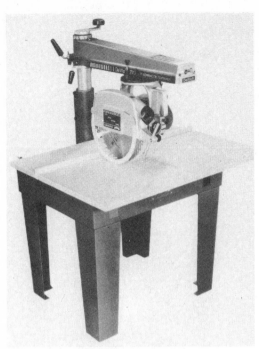

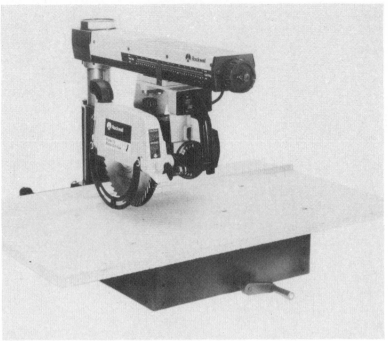

DeWalt 7790/3431 Radial Arm Saw   *Rockwell's 33-215 Radial Arm Saw*

miter stops and the column-adjustment elevator handle are located at the back of the machine. This is not the safest place for them to be. You must make sure the blade is completely stopped before reaching back to adjust these controls. Good safety features include a standard blade brake and secondary, leaf-type guard.

This De Walt tool is a no-frills machine, designed for continuous, heavy-duty use. It's often found in contractor and commercial wood-product shops, and in schools. If most of your work consists of making small cabinets, it may be too much saw for you. Approx. Price: $650.00

The Rockwell 33-215 is a 10-inch radial arm saw

designed for the home user, but professionals often choose it for its rugged construction. Rockwell, which has a well-deserved reputation for producing quality tools, has created an extremely versatile home shop machine. For a home shop saw, it has an unusually large motor, rated at 1½ hp. Although it has plenty of power, the saw's cutting capacity is not exceptionally large. It has a 3-inch depth-of-cut at 90 degrees and a 2¼-inch capacity at 45 degrees. These capacities are adequate for most home shop work, but you can't cut through nominal 4-inch-thick stock in one pass. Crosscut capacity is rather small at 12¾ inches, and the ripping width, at 24 inches, is enough to cut down the middle of a length of 4x8 paneling. Table size is 24¾x42 inches.

Like most nonprofessional

radial saws, all adjustment controls are located up front, and a removable safety switch prevents unauthorized use. A leaf guard supplements the basic, fixed, upper-blade guard, and an adjustable splitter and anti-kickback fingers help prevent accidents.

Additional features that add to this saw's value are an extra spindle in the back, for mounting accessories, and solid, cast-iron construction. This is a compactly designed saw that'll do just about any cutting chore asked of it. Approx. Price: $400.00

De Walt's 7710, from Black & Decker, has minimum capacity and a reasonable price. This machine has only an 8-inch blade. So, if you're

DeWalt 7710 Radial Arm Saw

looking for a full-service radial, you're better off looking elsewhere.

Despite the small diameter blade, this saw still boasts a 2-hp motor. Depth of cut at 90 degrees is 2 inches, and 1⅞ inches with the blade tilted to 45 degrees. Both capacities are enough to handle nominal 2-inch-thick stock. Crosscut capacity is small at 10½ inches. Similarly, you can only rip to 19½ inches. Table size is 22x32 inches.

This saw carries an extremely reasonable price tag, but has many features found in larger, more costly machines. All the controls are in front, and an automatic blade brake, supplemental leaf guard, anti-kickback fingers, and a key-controlled switch are standard.

Weighing in at only 58 pounds, it's just about the only radial saw that can be called portable. Small shop owners and hobbyists may find this an attractive feature. In any case, the De Walt 7710 is a small, but not dainty, saw that's useful for most basic radial saw work. And you'll like the price, too. Approx. Price: $190.00

Radial Arm Saw Accessories

There are many accessories available for radial arm saws. But, like most stationary power tools, the accessories are not interchangeable between brands of saws. Different arbor sizes and spindle chucks can make what seems to be a bargain a useless purchase. So, make sure the accessory fits your machine before buying it.

Dado and groove cutting attachments are made for most radial arm saws. These cut flat-bottomed, trough-shaped cuts, necessary for many joining operations. The various types of accessory cutters are discussed extensively in the table/bench saw section. Both dado assemblies and adjustable dado tools are available for radials, but they should be purchased from the manufacturer of the particular saw.

Molding heads are mounted cutters that shape wood into preset forms for decoration or joining. A large number, with many styles of cutting blades, are available. Molding heads mounted on a radial arm saw are not as efficient as a "shaper," the tool specifically designed for the job. But they'll do the work, even if a bit raggedly. The function of these cutters is also discussed at length in the table/bench saw section, so it won't be repeated here. But you should note that molding heads should be purchased from the manufacturer of the saw to assure a good fit. If they aren't mounted firmly, they won't do a good job and you could become the victim of a flying blade. These accessories can be more dangerous than a regular circular saw blade.

Drum sanders usually mount on the saw's auxiliary spindle, and are used to sand straight and curved edges.

Also, because the saw's motor head can be raised and lowered, sanding drums are handy for smoothing internal cutouts. Sanding drums come in 2- and 3-inch diameter sizes, and the abrasive sanding sleeves are available in most common grits.

Disc sanders are merely flat, round discs of rubber with a circular piece of abrasive paper on them. You can use them for smoothing board ends, convex curves, miter cuts, and other jobs. The sanding paper is either self-sticking or attaches to the rubber disc with an application of adhesive. All standard grits are available.

Router chucks and bits are high-speed cutting tools, often used with a special machine called a router. You can mount them on the auxiliary spindle of a radial arm saw, but the cuts will be ragged and require a lot of sanding to smooth out. This is especially true when cutting across the grain of hardwoods. The reason for their inefficiency when mounted on a radial arm saw is that the auxiliary spindle of most saws cannot operate in the 20,000 rpm range of most routers. So, if your saw can't match this speed, router chucks and bits are a useless accessory. Cutting fancy edges, carving bas-relief patterns and cutting mortises for a mortise-tenon joint are easy with a router, but can't be done on a radial arm saw. Slow motor speeds and lack of maneuverability are the reasons.

Shaper adapters with cutters also depend upon high speed for efficient operation, and most auxiliary radial arm spindles fall short in the speed department. If your saw does have a high-speed spindle, however, these accessories can be valuable. They consist of three identical cutting blades mounted on a central hub. This hub holds them in position and allows you to mount the unit on the saw's auxiliary spindle.

Rotating at speeds in the 20,000 rpm range, they cut a contour in wood in the reverse shape of their blades. Shapers have many decorative uses and are also one of the easiest ways to form a tongue-and-groove joint. Although a molding head can sometimes duplicate the shapes of shaper/cutters, sometimes only the latter can make a particular cut. Yes, shaper/cutters are wonderful tools, but if your auxiliary spindle is too slow, using them is an exercise in frustration.

Compound angle or miter cuts are some of the most difficult cuts to make in woodworking because of the perfect accuracy they require. Unless you build a special jig they are hard to do with a handsaw, but are one of the easier cuts to make with a radial arm. If the arm is swung in any direction of angle other than 90 degrees, the result is one component of the miter; tilting the saw blade achieves a compound angle cut. Fast and accurate cuts are the result. It is important, however, when making these cuts that the operator does so with precision. Constructing a jig is one way to achieve this, but the most important factor is attention to the work at hand. Mastering the compound angle cut is one of the techniques which distinguishes the novice woodworker from the craftsman.

SETTINGS FOR COMMON COMPOUND-ANGLE CUTS

Work Slope, Deg.	Four-Side Figure		Six-Side Figure	
	Blade Tilt, Deg.	Arm Angle, Deg.	Blade Tilt, Deg.	Arm Angle, Deg.
15	43¼	14½	29	8¼
25	40	23	27¼	13½
30	37¾	26½	26	16
40	32½	32¾	22¾	20¼
45	30	35¼	21	22¼
50	27	37½	19	23¾
60	21	41	14½	26½

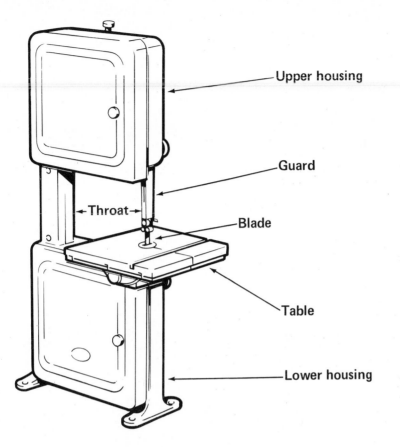

Upper housing

Guard

Throat

Blade

Table

Lower housing

Band Saws

The band saw cuts faster and deeper than any other power saw. Giant-size band saws are used in the lumber trade to convert logs into boards. Of course, band saws made for the small shop are miniscule compared to these gargantuans, but most can cut through wood that's 6 inches thick or more. This alone makes the band saw useful in the small shop, but it has other specialized applications, too. The design of these saws lets you do jobs that would be difficult and awkward with other tools.

Plus, the band saw can accomplish a few tasks that no other tool can do.

Viewed from the side, a band saw has a shape somewhat like that of a C-clamp. An endless band of metal with teeth runs through the C-shaped housing, spans the gap, and goes through a table. Within this housing are two, or sometimes three, rubber-rimmed, blade supporting wheels. The one at the bottom is powered, and the rest at the top are idlers. The blade runs on these wheels, through the housing

and through an adjustable table.

To assure correct blade-band travel, the upper wheel tilts and adjusts vertically. The tilt adjustment is necessary to make the blade "track" correctly — to remain centered on the wheel and not jump off. Vertical adjustments of the wheel provide proper blade tension for efficient and smooth cutting. Both adjustments are necessary, because the width of the bands varies from 1/8 to 3/4 inch. These adjustments are made by removing one side of the saw's housing. Quality band saws have scales and pointers built into the upper housing to facilitate adjustments.

The size of a band saw is based on the diameter of the blade supporting wheels. Wheel diameter dictates the distance from the blade to the saw's vertical supporting member. And this "throat" measurement tells you how wide a board you can cut. Small home shop band saws have throat measurements of at least 12 to 14 inches and a depth-of-cut capacity of about 6 inches. Saws for the small commercial shop usually have an 18-inch throat and 12-inch depth-of-cut. In some cases, you can add a larger, accessory support in the back of the saw to increase depth-of-cut substantially. However, this does not increase the throat measurement.

All band saws have an operator-adjusted, sliding guard that projects down from the upper wheel

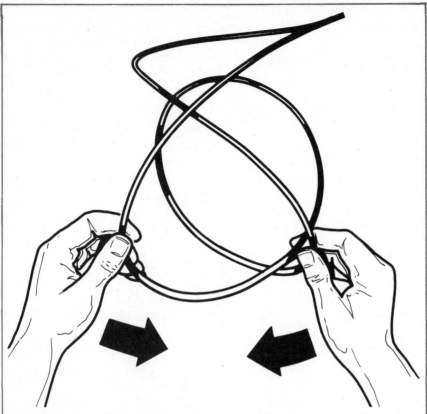

Like most stationary power saws, band saws can have a large variety of different blades mounted on them. However, one problem arises when you go to store the blades that are not mounted on the machine. These endless, toothed bands are subject to kinking if they are twisted or folded incorrectly; hanging them loose on a peg requires a lot of storage space. An easy way to get around this problem is to fold the blade so that it falls naturally into three evenly-sized loops. It takes practice to master this trick, but once learned it can save storage space and blades.

The first step is to hold the blade in a wide loop with the teeth away from the body. The edge of the blade should be cradled inside the thumbs on both hands.

The thumbs are then used to fold the upper half of the blade down toward the floor. At the same time the fingers of both hands should twist a bit to turn the teeth outward.

As the blade is twisted it will begin to fall into three loops. Allow the upper loop to fall into the lower one, while bringing the hands together. Trade the loop that is held in one hand for the other.

As this is done, bring the now coiling blade back against the body. It will fall into three natural coiling loops. The blade can now be tied with tape or soft wire and stored until needed. It will take some practice to master this, but you should be careful not to kink the blade as it is done. Eventually it becomes a habit that your hands will follow automatically.

housing. It covers the portion of the blade that's not contacting the wood. Setting it about ¼ inch above the work is about right. Band saws, like any other power tool, are dangerous. So, you must be careful to adjust the guard properly. A band saw usually has a small table that makes it awkward to hold large pieces of work. It's tempting to leave the guard up, so you can watch the cut. But, if the blade snaps, the exposed section of blade will create a situation you want to avoid. The guard is there for a reason. Place it correctly at all times.

Even installing a blade can be dangerous. Never install a blade with the power on. Check tracking and make tension adjustments by handspinning the wheels a few times with the blade installed and checking visually. Then, replace the housing cover and try the machine under power. This way, if the blade jumps the track or snaps, you minimize the chance of injury.

Two pairs of blade guides are found on every band saw. One pair is attached to the bottom of the sliding guard; the other pair is fixed in place beneath the table. Each guide assembly consists of two metal blocks and a bearing wheel. The blade rides between the blocks, and the back of the blade rests on the bearing wheel when a cut is being made. These blocks keep the blade from twisting and the back-up bearing wheel prevents the blade from being pushed off the drive wheels.

After adjusting the blade for correct tracking, you must adjust the blocks and back-up wheel. The blocks are easily adjusted by placing a sheet of paper between the blade and the blocks before they're tightened. You have to set the back-up wheel so that the clearance between it and the back of the blade is $\frac{1}{32}$-inch. The wheel shouldn't turn when the blade is running free, only when material is being cut on the saw.

Most band saws come equipped with cutting guides. Usually, a miter gauge fits in a slot on the table, and often a rip fence is present. But these guides don't make the band saw a replacement for the table or radial arm saw. The band saw is no match for the straight cutting ability of these other saws, and its throat depth greatly limits the size of the work that can be cut.

However, no saw can cut curved lines in thick stock like a band saw can. When fitted with narrow, $\frac{1}{8}$-inch-wide blades, it can even rival the jigsaw and saber saw for some kinds of scroll-type work. It doesn't quite equal the intricate cutting ability of these saws though, because the blades would have to be so thin that they would snap. Nor can the band saw do "piercing" cuts, because the band is continuous. But in medium-curve cutting, the band saw's depth-of-cut puts it in a class by itself. You can, for example, form a scalloped edge on a 4x6-inch piece of lumber as easily as you could

Band saws, like any other power saw, have certain peculiar traits that are characteristic of the saw and its method of operation. One of these is known as "washboarding," meaning that the blade leaves a characteristic mark in the surface of any wood it cuts. This may be slight or heavily pronounced, but a wavy pattern will be there no matter what is done. Some control over the amount of washboarding can be obtained through a choice of blades. The smoothest cuts are made possible by choosing a blade with minimum set, which will cut down on the washboard effect.

Band saws cut better across the grain than with it. In ripping cuts the actual speed of the saw is reduced and there is a definite tendency for the blade to follow the grain rather than some marked or scribed line. This must be watched carefully when making rip cuts with a band saw, or else the cut will be wavy whether you want that effect or not.

on ¾-inch stock with the other saws. Other applications for this impressive depth-of-cut are:

Pad sawing: If you needed six identically-shaped brackets to support a shelf, it would be difficult to assure all would be the same when using a saber or jig saw. With a band saw, you can tack these six pieces of wood together and cut the entire "pad" as if it were a solid block. Each piece, once separated, would be identical. Even if each piece of lumber were nominal 1-inch stock (actually ¾-inch), the total pad thickness would only be 4½ inches—an easy cut on most band saws.

Resawing: This means slicing thin boards from a single thick piece. A 1½-inch thick piece of stock can be

halved to produce two ¾-inch-thick pieces. Although the width of the board would be limited by the tool's depth-of-cut, on some of the larger machines this can be as much as 12 inches. Resawed boards are often used as exterior home siding and as fine-wood, interior paneling with decorative textures.

Multiple pieces: In this procedure an initial contour is cut into a thick piece of stock. Then the stock is resawn to as many individual pieces as required. This can be very handy for certain kinds of repetitive cutting used for decoration.

Compound cuts: This operation involves cutting two adjacent sides of a square piece of stock, to form stock with a rounded shape that can be worked on a lathe. After marking the adjacent sides of the stock, the first side is cut. Then the waste is reattached to provide a firm support on the table. Next, the adjacent side is cut. When all waste is removed, the wood has a rounded shape. The most practical application of this technique is in the production of cabriole legs often found on classical furniture.

Like most stationary power tools, the band saw does not take up much floor space, but does require work space. In this case, work space is necessary on all sides except the throat side of the machine. This means that the band saw can be placed with its throat side close to a wall without interfering with its usefulness. Space needed parallel with the wall depends upon your workscope. Cutting a 6-foot board, for instance, requires at least 6 feet on either side of the machine. Or, you may want to mount the machine on casters, so you can roll it to the center of the shop when you need more room for long boards.

Rockwell's 14 (catalog #28-285) band saw is an above-average machine, whose basic design has stood the test of time and use in many commercial workshops. The throat measurement is 13¾ inches, giving you an excellent width-of-cut capacity. Depth-of-cut is about average for a small shop

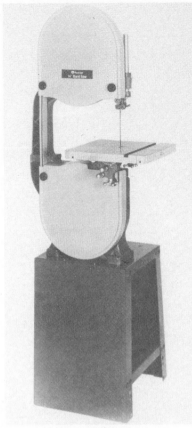

Rockwell's 14 Band Saw

machine—6¼ inches. It has a 14-inch-square table that tilts 45 degrees for bevel cuts. This table has the machined grooves to accept a rip fence and miter gauge, but these cutting guides are extra-cost accessories. The Rockwell 14 accepts a good range of blades, from ⅛- to ¾-inch wide. For tighter curves, the ⅛-inch blade is dandy, while the ¾-incher is perfect for resawing. This saw comes complete with pulleys and belt, one blade, stand, and motor.

When buying the saw, you should consider several optional accessories. One accessory package (#28-984) is called a "height attachment." It allows you to lift the upper wheel housing

about 6 inches. Although this means you have to install a larger blade, it increases the saw's depth-of-cut to 12¼ inches—very useful when resawing boards up to 12 inches wide. Throat capacity stays unaltered.

The sanding attachment (#28-810) is a practical accessory, too. It's an endless abrasive belt that replaces the blade. This setup can't compete with a belt sander with a 3- to 4-inch-wide belt, but is handy for smoothing curved edges. And it sure beats laying out the cash for a separate belt sander. Approx. Price: (28-285) $470.00

The Craftsman Band Saw-Sander (Sears, Roebuck catalog #2435N) comes with everything you need to install an abrasive sanding belt.

Craftsman 2435N

Width-of-cut capacity is 12 inches and depth-of-cut is 6 inches. The table, which measures 14x12½ inches, tilts 45 degrees for bevel cuts. It also has provisions for a miter gauge and rip fence, but the cutting guides are optional at extra cost. The saw uses blades from ³⁄₁₆- to ½-inch wide, which is the middle range in band saw blades. They impose some limitations, but can handle most average work. In spite of the small range of blades available, this is quite a tool at a reasonable price. Several standard features make it very easy to use. A built-in light illuminates the work area, and a dust chute can be connected to a vacuum cleaner to suck away much of the sawdust. Price includes ½-hp motor, saw, pulleys and belts, one blade, and accessories for installing the sanding belt. Approx. Price: $300.00

A speed reducer (#23896) is an extra-cost option. It's installed in conjunction with the regular motor, so that you can adjust the blade's speed at will. It gives about a 21.5 to 1 reduction. This lower blade speed, when used with special metal-cutting blades, lets you cut metals like copper and steel. Approx. Price: $85.00

Shopsmith Incorporated's 505641, 11-inch band saw could be the best saw of its type for the home workshop. It certainly has design

Shopsmith's 505641

features that put it above its class. Actually, it's meant to be an accessory for the Shopsmith multipurpose tool, but you can also mount the saw on its own stand and power it independently. One of the notable features of this saw is automatic blade tracking adjustment. You just provide the correct blade tension with a built-in scale, and the blade moves into the correct tracking position automatically. This saw also has a variable width-of-cut. The normal width-of-cut is 11 inches, but you can adjust the blade guides to "offset" the blade by about 45 degrees. This lets you crosscut long stock at any point, without interference from the machine's throat. It would be nice to see this feature on other machines, since it widens your workscope considerably.

Depth of cut is 6 inches, and is nonvariable.

The table measures 11¾x12 inches. It tilts 45 degrees for bevel cuts and has two miter gauge slots at right angles. The supplied miter gauge can be used in one slot for crosscutting and locked in the other slot for use as a rip fence. Blades accepted range in width from ⅛- to ½-inch — a slightly wider range than most tools. You don't get a motor with the saw. Independent of the Shopsmith, it needs a motor of at least ½-hp. Whether you own a Shopsmith or not, this is an excellent band saw for the home shop. Approx. Price: $250.00

Gilliom Manufacturing, Inc. markets a 771-K band saw that's unlike most models — this one you build yourself. The kit supplies all the necessary metal parts — drive wheels, tracking and tensioning mechanisms, blade guards and guides, table mount and tilt accessories, and so forth. You also get detailed plans for assembly, and for making a wooden frame/stand. Many of these tools have been built and enjoyed by people who followed the plans to the letter. And some people have used fancy materials like hardwood and veneer plywood to make a classier-looking frame/stand.

This tool is not the equal of a steel-framed unit of the same size, which can use higher horsepower motors

Gilliom's 771-K Band Saw

and wider blades. Maximum blade width is ½-inch and the motor should not exceed ¾ hp. But the saw does have a 12¼-inch throat measurement, and the depth-of-cut is an above-average 7 inches. The supplied table is 20x20 inches and tilts 45 degrees. And an extra-cost speed reducer lets you cut metals.

These aren't bad capacities, and the tool can function well for all average home shop projects. Besides, you get a band saw at about half the cost of a production model—not a bad deal in this world of high prices. Approx. Price: $70.00

Toolkraft's 4502 is one of the smallest of the production band saws. Its 9½-inch

throat and 4½-inch depth-of-cut make it only suitable for light sawing chores on small stock. Despite its small size, though, it has a cast-iron frame and table. And it offers all the basic band saw features.

The table measures 10x11 inches, and tilts 45 degrees for bevel cuts. It accepts saw blades with widths from 3/16 to ½ inch. This model comes with everything you need to set up the saw: stand, ¼-hp motor, frame, and a pushbutton on/off switch with a key lock. If you plan extensive resawing of thick stock, constant heavy-duty work or want maximum band saw capability, this is not your machine. But it would be hard to find a better saw for small jobs at such a low price. Approx. Price: $290.00

Toolkraft's 4502 Band Saw

Emco's BS-2 Band Saw

The Emco BS-2 band saw has three blade-supporting wheels instead of the usual two. Its housing is also more angular than other band saws, which provides a large, 14-inch width-of-cut capacity in a machine with a very low profile. Depth-of-cut is a little smaller than 6 inches, but that's enough to handle 6-inch nominal lumber.

The three-speed control is a particularly nice feature of the Emco BS-2. Using the low speed, you can cut metal without an accessory speed reducer. The middle range is perfect for cutting plastics. Power is supplied by a ½-hp motor that's completely built into the unit. Another valuable feature is a spring-loaded mechanism on the wheel support that sets the blade tension automatically. The table measures almost 16 inches square, tilts, and is formed to accept the optional miter gauge and rip fence.

The Emco BS-2 is compact and capable. Its only flaw is that it's built in Austria to metric standards, which may make blades hard to find. Approx. Price: $500.00

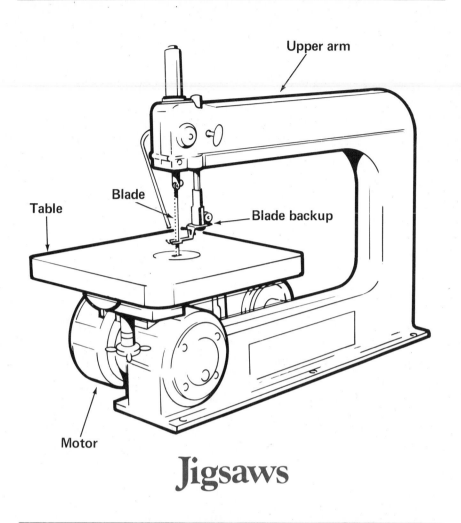

Upper arm

Blade

Table

Blade backup

Motor

Jigsaws

The jigsaw is the powered, refined version of the coping, or scroll, saw. Very specialized, the jigsaw has a limited range of sawing operations. For example, you can't cut anything thicker than nominal 2-inch stock. On the other hand, it has no peer for inlay work. Also, it's great for fine woodworking because it lets you perform internal cuts of extreme intricacy. The thin blades available for this machine make cuts so fine that you can reassemble the cut parts as if they were sliced with a knife. Although this specialized application leads people to dismiss the jigsaw as a hobbyist's tool, it can be used for other sawing work. Some models have lower chucks that grip short metal files and rasps, which makes them suitable for a wide variety of tasks.

The frame of a typical jigsaw looks somewhat like an elongated, horizontal "U." Its bottom arm is connected to a metal case containing the drive mechanism — a motor and crank drive a piston in a

vertical motion. A blade-gripping chuck is attached to the top of this piston. At the end of the upper arm is an assembly that usually consists of a spring-loaded cylinder with another chuck at the bottom end. You can adjust this cylinder vertically to apply the correct amount of tension to the blade. Thin blades usually require more tension than heavy ones. On better jigsaws, this tension is set by a built-in, graduated scale.

Between the two arms, a tiltable table is secured to the top of the bottom case. The saw blade, locked into the top and bottom chucks, passes through a slot in the table. It's this feature that makes internal cutouts so easy. First, you drill a hole in a waste area of the stock. Then you release the blade from the top chuck, pass it through the hole, and reattach the blade to the chuck. Finally, you make the cutout. This procedure can be repeated as many times as necessary to perform intricate scrollwork.

A blade guide assembly is attached to the bottom of a rod that's adjacent to the top cylinder arm. The rod can be adjusted up and down, according to the thickness of the work being cut. This guide assembly consists of a metal disc with various-size slots around its perimeter, a backup wheel, and a stock hold-down. You adjust the metal disc by rotating it until you find a slot that matches the thickness of the blade in the machine. The narrowest slot in which the blade rides

The forerunner of the home jigsaw was actually a small hand-powered saw called a "scroll saw" patented in 1923. This machine sold for a little bit over $6.00. Jewelers' blades in 5 inch lengths were used in this unit, and it was designed to cut very thin kerfs in a variety of wood and other soft materials. Later the machine appeared with an integral motor that had a retail price of less than $20.00. During the Depression era these little motorized scroll saws sold to such an extent that production was often behind sales—in spite of the fact that production of almost all other machine goods had virtually ceased.

One of the curious social happenings that developed during the Depression years was the jigsaw puzzle craze. It is not clear if this craze was caused by the ready availability of the small machine, but in any case many professional and blue collar workers used the small tool to augment their income. Many people dropped everything else and went into business, running small plants and hiring operators to turn out the puzzles. As with all fads, the craze eventually petered out, but not before a whole generation of future craftsmen gained practice and familiarity with a home-owned power tool.

should be adjusted to hold the work firmly, but not so tightly that it interferes with the movement of material fed into the saw.

Jigsaw size is listed according to the throat depth—the distance from the blade to the back of the U-shaped frame. This distance dictates the normal width-of-cut capacity. Sometimes the listing states that a jigsaw can cut to a certain-size circle. If cuts can be made to the center of a 36-inch circle, for example, the tool has an 18-inch throat. Depth-of-cut is never very large. Most jigsaws can cut through nominal 2-inch wood (actually 1½ inches thick), which is quite adequate for work done on most machines.

Some machines have an upper arm that's detachable, or which you can swing out of the way. Since removing this upper arm also removes the upper blade chuck, special saber saw type blades are mounted in the lower chuck. These blades are heavy enough to do most work without the top chuck or guide assembly, but they can't make as fine a cut. However, with the upper arm out of the way, you can cut any size workpiece—even standard 4x8-foot plywood panels.

The jigsaw is probably the safest of all stationary power saws. Since the blade moves up and down in short strokes, with the teeth angled toward the table, anything held against the blade tends to be held against the table.

freely is the right one. This part of the guide assembly is designed to prevent the blade from twisting. The roller-type backup wheel should be barely touching the back of the blade, to prevent the blade from bending

backwards when work is moved into it. The spring hold-down is notched and straddles the blade. This hold-down is necessary to keep the workpiece from jerking up and down, due to the action of the saw blade. It

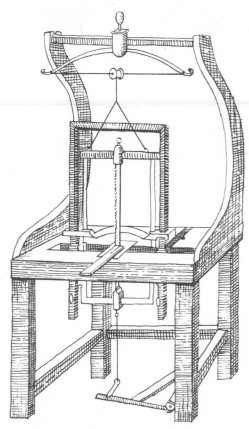

Lengthwise spring saw of the 1700s

The hold-down reinforces this tendency and helps to keep the work flat on the table. Because of these features, there is no guard on the blade. But this doesn't make the saw completely safe. As with all power saws, you have to be careful when using a jigsaw. They're not as harmless as they look.

Even the largest jigsaws require only 4 to 5 feet of floor space, plus a couple of feet in the front of the machine for the operator. Using it as a stationary saber saw means you'll need more work space. If you think you'll be using it in this fashion, mount the tool on casters. This way, you can move it around as needed and store the machine in a corner.

Rockwell's 24-inch scroll saw is a heavy-duty, full-function jigsaw with the finesse to handle projects that require a light touch. For this reason, it's the type of tool often found in commercial and school woodshops. Home craftsmen with a wide workscope appreciate its capabilities; and its 24-inch cut width and 1¾-inch cut depth are only the beginning.

Additional features remove all work size restrictions except wood thickness. You can cut boards as long as 12 feet by rotating the blade chucks 90 degrees and cutting parallel to the saw's throat. The upper arm is removable, too. Cutting saber saw fashion, all length and width restrictions vanish.

Full-function capability includes a three-way tilt, 14-inch square table. It tilts 45 degrees right, 15 degrees left and 45 degrees to the front. The front tilt, in combination with removable arm or rotating chuck feature, lets you perform bevel cuts on stock longer than 24 inches.

Part of the saw's capability to handle both heavy-duty and light jobs comes from its blade-speed variability. The saw is available with either four-step pulleys that let you choose from 610, 910, 1255 and 1725 cutting strokes per minute, or a variable-speed device providing infinite settings between 650 and 1700 CSM. Slower speeds, used with heavier blades, allow you to cut through thick wood without blade bog-down. Faster speeds and thinner blades zip through thin wood and metals.

Rockwell's 24" Scroll Saw

This saw does everything that can be done with a jigsaw and more. In addition to the features described, it also has a chuck that securely grips round-shank accessories like sanding attachments and metal-cutting files. The Rockwell 24-inch scroll saw is so versatile that the serious home craftsman will find no "trading up" necessary until, perhaps, they give one away free! Approx. Price: $767.00

Powermatic's 95 scroll saw isn't for the wood inlay artist or model maker. Using it for these functions would be like using a sledge hammer on a finishing nail. But for light to heavy-duty woodcrafting jobs it gets high marks as a full-function, heavy-duty jigsaw.

Its size and features are quite similar to the Rockwell scroll saw. You get a three-way, 14x15-inch tilting table, 24-inch throat,

1¾-inch cut depth and a removable upper arm. It's available with four speeds—610, 910, 1255 and 1725 CSM. Or you can opt for variable speed capability of 807 to 1653 CSM. Of course, the chucks rotate 90 degrees for handling stock too long for the throat to accommodate.

If you're looking for a capable, full-function jigsaw that'll give you years of good service, the Powermatic 95 is a good bet. Approx. Price: $594.00

The Dremel Moto-Shop can transform your kitchen into a workshop. You can store this light-duty machine in a closet and secure it to a kitchen counter via its rubber suction cups. Its forte is cutting delicate scroll patterns in light wood, but it can also handle 1¾-inch-thick soft woods.

The blade-drive principle is different from that of bigger machines. It features a U-shaped rocker arm, shrouded by the tool's frame. This rocker arm pivots on a shaft and is moved up and down at high speeds by a built-in electric motor. The saw blade holder pivots 90 degrees left or right for unlimited length cutting.

Only "fine" and "coarse" blades are offered, yet these two blades give you a wide scope of workability—from scroll work on thin stock to cuts through nominal 2-inch wood, 18-gauge copper and ¼-inch aluminum and steel.

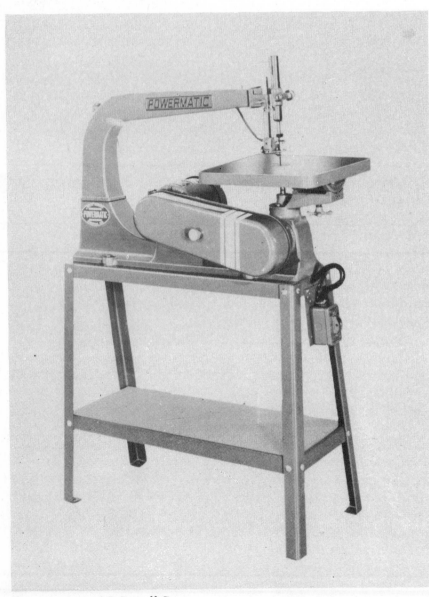

Powermatic 95 Scroll Saw

112

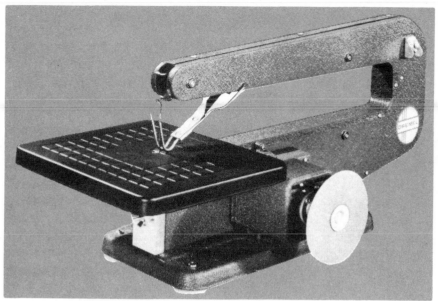
Dremel's Moto-Shop

The Dremel Moto-Shop is actually more than just a jigsaw, as its name implies. Apartment dwellers and others with limited work space appreciate its power take off feature, which gives you many tools in a compact package. The power take off is essentially an extra shaft that projects from the back of the motor. This handy shaft accommodates a 4-inch, rubber-backed sanding disc, polishing wheels, grinding wheels and a flexible shaft. A chuck at the drive end of the shaft grips many cutters used on portable grinders for woodcarving and drilling small holes.

The basic Moto-Shop includes disc sander capability. Dremel's Deluxe Moto-Shop comes with many accessories, including a flexible shaft with cutters and a grinding wheel with a special guard. The tools are also listed in Sears, Roebuck and Montgomery Ward catalogs. Approx. Price: (Basic) $65.00

Because of the setup on the jigsaw it is possible to do one cut that is almost impossible with any other type of stationary power tool. This technique is called "piercing." What it means is releasing the blade from the upper gripping chuck, passing it through a previously drilled hole in the workpiece, and then resecuring the blade. This permits the operator to make an internal design without a lead-in cut from the edge. The usual cutting procedure is followed once the blade is resecured into the chuck. Of course, the blade must be reinserted for each separate cutout in the design. The result is often quite interesting visually, as nice pattern and shadow effects can be achieved by this method.

Although the insertion hole may be drilled in any part of the waste, it makes for less time if it is drilled close to one of the lines that will be part of the pattern. Square corners are produced by following the line down to the corner, then backing out and coming in down the other side. It is possible with a thin blade to simply turn the corner, but the result will not be square. This is usually not critical; though if the work has to be accurate it would be better to practice this technique on some scrap before trying it on good stock.

The Sprunger 20-inch jigsaw from Sprunger Bros., Inc., is a jigsaw, period. And it's built like a tank. No frills here — the frame is cast in one piece, and the very solid, 1-foot-square table tilts only two ways, 30 degrees left and 45 degrees right. And you are stuck with one fixed speed.

But, although a basic tool, it's not primitive. The Sprunger has a 20-plus-inch throat and 90 degree rotating chucks for longer cuts. Mounting blades in the chucks is a quick pleasure. The back edge of any blade butts against a positive stop so the backup roller doesn't have to be adjusted for different width blades. In

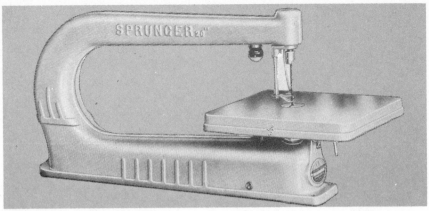

Sprunger's 20" Band Saw

The Shopsmith 18-inch 505644 jigsaw is specifically designed for the multipurpose Shopsmith, but it can also be operated with its own stand and motor. Used as a separate tool, it's equipped with three step pulleys that give three specific speeds. Shopsmith power provides continuously variable speeds.

This jigsaw has a lot of enticing features that put it in the same league with full-function machines. It has a built-in sawdust blower, rotatable chucks, and the lower chuck grips round-shank accessories. The 11x11-inch table tilts one way to 45 degrees; cut depth is more than enough to get through nominal 2-inch wood.

addition, the blade backup guide has a built-in blower to whisk sawdust from the cut line. Other tools with blowers use a separate air tube.

It's not fancy, but if you're looking for a rugged, simple-to-operate, moderately priced jigsaw that handles up to 2-inch stock, it fills the bill. Approx. Price: $345.00

It's frame, however, is its outstanding feature. This unique frame incorporates a sturdy, U-shaped arm made of tubular steel, instead of heavy casting, which connects at one end to the machine's base. It holds all of a jigsaw's topside components—including upper chuck, blade tensioner and blade guides. The tubular arm makes the machine a snap to organize for saber sawing. You merely unlock the arm at the base and swing it down out of the way. It can also be removed entirely, leaving only the base, table, and lower chuck.

If you own or intend to own a Shopsmith multipurpose tool, the Shopsmith 505644 is a wise choice. Approx. Price: $184.00

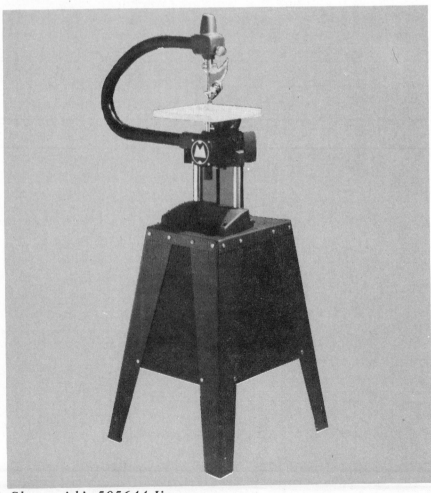

Shopsmith's 505644 Jigsaw

After a piece is cut to approximate dimension, usually the next task is to drill one or more holes. Dowel holes for assembly, access holes during construction, and pilot holes for screws or nails can all be drilled with a hand drill. Although slower than power drills, they cannot be beat for quick, accurate hole drilling in wood, plastics, and many composition materials.

Drilling Tools

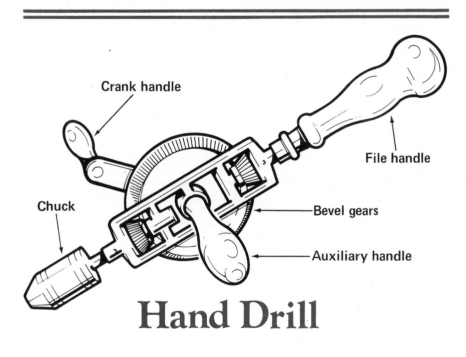

Crank handle

Chuck

File handle

Bevel gears

Auxiliary handle

Hand Drill

Before Edison, consumer electricity, and the portable electric drill, all holes were drilled by hand. This was done by various methods, several of which have stood the test of time and are still used—even by people who have a full complement of power tools. A craftsman or tradesman would as soon be without a hammer as he would be without a manual drill. This is because a power drill requires electricity and a certain amount of setup time. Also, sometimes you find yourself in situations where an electrical drill is inconvenient to use—as in wet locations. Hand drills avoid these problems, and for small tasks they do as good a job as power equipment.

Hand drills also give you a "feel" for the material; as you work, you feel more personally involved in the project, and your interest escalates as the project takes form. Power tools are great time and work savers, but it's hard to get romantic about them. Hand tools, including manual drills, have a certain *cachet* of workmanship and interest inherent in them. They bring out an awareness of tradition and craftsmanship that's sometimes not evident when you use modern power tools.

The hand drills in this section demand attention for

A QUICK LOOK AT HAND DRILLS

NAME	REMARKS	TYPICAL USES
Hand Drill	eggbeater shape—drive handle moves bevel gears to turn chuck —mounts twist and other small, round shank bits—limited capacity for large holes	small diameter holes in wood or soft metals—limited diameter possible —shallow depth
Breast Drill	same drive mechanism as hand drill—longer main handle braced against chest for increased pressure—uses twist and other small round-shank bits	larger, deeper holes in wood and soft metals—weight of body on back of drill permits increased force and deeper holes
Push Drill	push handle drives shallow spiral on shank to turn snap-grip chuck—bits kept in handle—small holes with bits that produce flat bottomed holes	pilot holes for wood screws—easy to use for small holes around the home—handy to set hinges or other hardware because only requires one hand to use
Brace	rotating offset handle turns a chuck with ratcheting mechanism—uses square-shanked "auger bits"—main wood boring tool for large diameter holes	bores very accurate, large diameter holes to 1½ inches—ratcheting mechanism allows work in limited access areas—widely used to bore access holes in plumbing/electrical work
Gimlet	small handle mounted crossways on auger bit—operated by turning handle—self-feeding screw-cuts, rather than punching hole—separate size bit for each hole	small pilot holes for nails or screws—least expensive way to drill small diameter holes up to ⅜ inch—requires more time and effort than other hand drills

these reasons. All of them are relatively inexpensive compared to most power tools, and do an excellent job when used correctly. Useful, inexpensive and easy to operate—what more could you ask from a tool? Look them over. You may find something that suits your fancy, or you may find an explanation for a tool you found in granddaddy's old tool box.

The hand drill is a purely American invention dating back to shortly after the Civil War. It looks something like an old-style eggbeater, a utensil near extinction due to electric mixers and whipped cream in a can. The hand drill may look clumsy, but it can drill a clean hole with a minimum of fuss.

Most hand drills are simple, cast-iron affairs, on which a large handwheel drives a set of bevel gears. In turn, the gears move an arbor with a self-centering, three-jawed chuck. On the end opposite the chuck there's a file-type handle for holding and controlling the tool. On better quality hand drills, the handle has a screw-in cap. Inside there's a compartment for storing extra drill bits. There is also a small knob or handle opposite the turning handwheel. On quality tools, this handle is removable to facilitate drilling in blind corners or close to obstructions.

Hand drills are available in a wide choice of prices and construction. Poor quality ones are less than a joy to use, and prove to be a poor investment in the long run. In particular, avoid drills with plastic gears because they inevitably bend and slip in high-torque situations. It's curious but true that a good hand drill can often cost more than a run-of-the-mill electric drill. But you should recognize that a hand drill is often a lifetime investment. It can be used where there is no electricity, and is sometimes handier than an electric. If you buy one, you'll certainly find a use for it.

In some situations, a hand drill can give you performance superior to that of an electric drill. It's usually much quicker for drilling one or two holes because you don't have to drag out an extension cord. For light, precise holes in wood, plastic, and other soft materials, hand drills are much more controllable than even variable-speed electrics. Also, it's quicker to fasten a bit in a hand drill because the chuck is the keyless type, which locks a bit in by simple hand tightening. These are all assets and reasons why you should consider adding a hand drill to your woodworking equipment.

Millers Falls makes a ⅜-inch hand drill that is an American

Artisans were fairly ingenious—a practical necessity in a world where almost everything had to be made rather than bought in a store. One problem they encountered was drilling large diameter holes in thick hardwood stock. This is not easy to do with a brace, even with very sharp bits available today. The solution of these craftsmen was to make a breast bib, a device whereby the weight of the body could be used to increase pressure on the bit.

Breast bibs are nothing but a piece of hardwood shaped to fit the chest, and held there by some kind of harness. There is a saucer-shaped recess on the front surface in which the head of the brace is fitted. Using this distributes the pressure of the head of the brace over the entire chest, and aids in helping to steer the brace at the correct angle.

Making this particular bib is not difficult. Any piece of scrap wood about a foot long will do, although hardwood is liable to last longer. Shape a concave depression across the back of this piece of wood, fitting it to your chest as you work. In the center of the face chisel out a circular depression for the brace head, or if you own a radial arm saw, scrape out a saucer cut with the machine. Straps to secure it to the body can be made of almost anything, but if prolonged use is anticipated it may be best to have someone sew up a couple of straps of webbing. Staple or nail them to the bib, slip it on, and you're ready to bore a lot of large holes!

Brookstone's E4684 Drill

(#E4684) and can often be found in larger hardware stores. Approx. Price: $28.00

The Craftsman 4231, from Sears, Roebuck and Co., is a quality hand drill with a keyless, ¼-inch capacity chuck. The wood handle is made in two sections to store the eight drill bits that come with the tool. Bit sizes range from ¹⁄₁₆-to ¹¹⁄₆₄ -inch in diameter. Gearing is all metal to stand up to punishment. Its 11½-inch length and reasonable price let it fit the toolbox as well as the pocketbook. It may not last

Craftsman's 4231 Hand Drill

as an heirloom, but it'll give you good service. Approx. Price: $12.00

masterpiece of craftsmanship. This tool has all the classical lines of the original hand drills and is constructed of top-quality materials throughout. The wearing parts of its keyless chuck are plated for rust resistance. This chuck can hold bits up to ⅜ inch in diameter, with either round or hex shanks. Inside its two-section handle are eight supplied drill bits ranging from ¹⁄₁₆-to ¹¹⁄₆₄ -inch in diameter. Gearing allows 4.5 turns of the chuck for every rotation of the handle to give you ample torque for most soft materials. You can drill light sheet metal and soft, nonferrous metals with this hand drill, though it takes longer. At 14 inches in length and weighing 2½ pounds, this drill is expensive, but you're getting your money's worth in quality. It's carried by the Brookstone Company

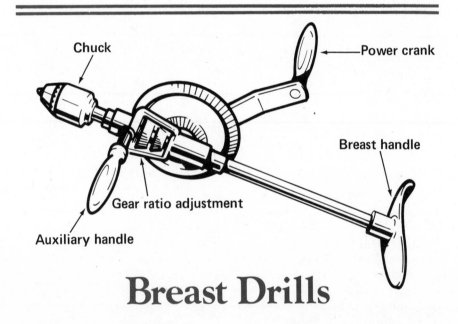

Breast Drills

The breast drill historically antedates the hand drill and is a larger version of that tool. These drills are also the eggbeater type, but have

heavier construction and a larger cranking radius for higher torque. In place of the file handle of the hand drill, there's a metal extension that ends in a curved plate. In use, you hold this plate against your chest and use your body weight to put greater pressure on the drill bit. The auxiliary handle opposite the hand crank is also longer than that of a hand drill to afford better control. Older versions of the breast drill often had an integral spirit level, which helped the operator keep the tool straight. Quality breast drills often have a means to switch speeds—that is, alter the amount the chuck turns for one revolution of the crank handle. The higher speed is for drilling soft materials like wood, while the lower gear ratio is selected for metal or turning large bits in hardwood.

Breast drills are relatively specialized tools. They're not often found in woodworking kits because most of the drilling they're designed to do can be done better by an electric drill or other variety of hand tool. Even the traditional craftsman finds little use for this tool, but the fact that they are still made and sold indicates that some people do use them.

Woodcraft Supply's 04S11-EE is one of the few quality breast drills available. Except for a spirit level, the drill exhibits all the features that should be on this type of tool. The two speeds let you choose from a 1-to-1 or 3-to-1 gear ratio. The three-jawed, keyless chuck has a ½-inch capacity— something to be expected on this heavy tool. This drill is also expensive, and is a good choice for the person who has a constitutional dislike for power tools. Approx. Price: $46.00

hanging pictures and installing hinge hardware. They are admirably suited for drilling small pilot holes for screws, and this is why they are so popular with craftsmen. A push drill is better for such work than an awl, which merely pushes aside wood fibers rather than actually drilling a hole. Use of a push drill results in more holding power and less splitting.

This type of drill is simply constructed and looks somewhat like a screwdriver. The handle is like that of a file, and is hollow for storage of drill bits, which are usually supplied. The working end of the tool is a simple plunger, which ends in a spring-loaded chuck for holding bits. This plunger is also spring-loaded in the handle and has a series of spiral grooves cut into the outside surface. When you place the bit against a solid surface and push on the handle, the plunger collapses into the handle and turns due to its spiral grooves. Releasing pressure on the handle causes the plunger to return for another stroke. You use a push drill by pushing down on the handle and releasing. This in-and-out motion is continued until you have a hole of the appropriate depth. The return stroke causes the drill bit to turn in the opposite direction, but push drill bits are designed to cut in either direction and can swiftly drill a hole through soft material. Unlike most other wood drill bits, push drill bits aren't cut with spiral flutes for chip

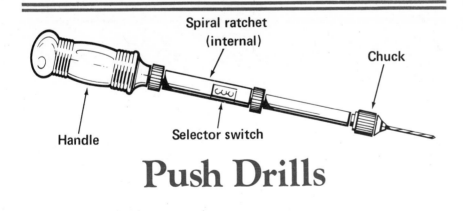

Spiral ratchet (internal)

Chuck

Handle

Selector switch

Push Drills

The push drill is a hand-drilling device that's equally at home in the advanced artisan's toolbox and the housewife's utility drawer.

The typical low price of these drills makes them worthy of consideration for the homeowner whose drilling requirements are limited to

clearing. So, they have to be removed from the hole often to clear them. In soft wood, and with sharp bits, push drills work at speeds comparable to a power drill—without a lot of setup time.

Two fine push drills are manufactured by Stanley Tools under the trade name "Yankee." These drills are available almost everywhere in retail stores and catalog houses. The company also private labels these tools for the larger catalog houses, so there's an excellent chance that any push drill you buy will be made by this firm.

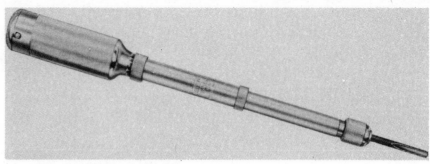
Yankee 41YC Push Drill

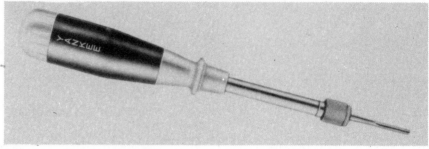
Yankee 45Y Push Drill

The Yankee 41YC is Stanley Tools' best push drill, and features all-metal construction. The drill's magazine holds eight bits, ranging in size from ⅟₁₆- to ¹¹⁄₆₄ - inch. You gain access to this magazine by undoing a knurled ring at the base of the handle and sliding the entire length down the shaft of the tool, thus exposing the bits. It's a good-looking tool, with a bright chrome finish. Functionally, they come no better. Approx. Price: $18.00

Yankee's 45Y push drill may not be as durable as the Yankee 41YC, but it works as well. Rather than all-metal construction, this drill has a plastic handle with a die-cast,

plated cap. Access to the bit magazine is obtained by undoing this metal cap piece. Bits that come with the tool range from ⅟₁₆- to ¹¹⁄₆₄ - inch.

The construction of this push drill is somewhat cheaper than the Yankee 41YC, but then so is the price. Approx. Price: $12.00

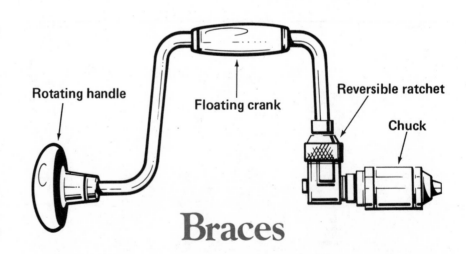

Rotating handle

Floating crank

Reversible ratchet

Chuck

Braces

The brace is a boring tool. This doesn't mean that it's uninteresting, however. In

woodworking jargon "boring" is the term for drilling a hole that's about

¾-inch or more in diameter. The brace has a very ancient lineage and first appeared in Europe in the 1400s, though the form was known in China before the birth of Christ. The fact that this tool is still made and used testifies to the ingenuity of ancient woodworkers.

A brace's design is very simple. The tool is really nothing more than a crank. At the top of this steel crank there's a doorknob-shaped wood or plastic handle that fits the palm of the hand. This handle rotates freely on top of the crank mechanism, and better models include a simple bearing with an oil hole to reduce friction at this point. At the working end of the crank there's a shell-type, self-centering chuck that accepts both square and round shanks. The ability to handle both types of shanks is important because it greatly increases the workscope of this simple tool.

Just above the chuck there's usually a reversible, ratcheting mechanism. You can lock this ratchet to allow either clockwise or counterclockwise turning of the crank. This permits you to use the tool where space is limited for a full turn of the crank, because when the ratchet is locked for operation in one direction, it can swing in the other direction without turning the bit. The ratcheting feature is handy, and should be on any brace chosen for extensive use.

At the center of the offset

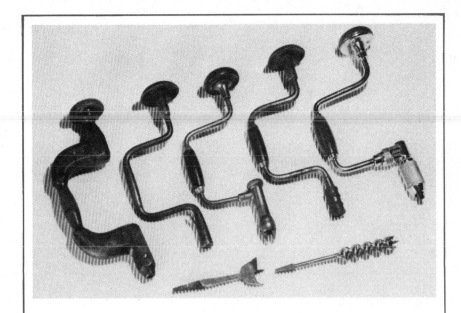

The design of the brace is among the oldest still in current use, testimony to the utilitarian sense of the old-time artisan. In spite of developments since the late 1800s, the shape and basic working principles remain the same. This picture details the progressive development of this common woodworking tool.

On the left is the older pattern bit brace made of wood with a square, metal socket chuck. By the 1860s chucks were developed with a pin-locking device and the iron bow was added. The revolving handle came next, easing the turning problem, and then movable jaws to hold various size bit tangs. Universal jaws were then used to hold round or square, straight or tapered shank bits. The ratchet brace—pictured on the far right—is now the common pattern. The ratchet eliminates the full swing, a necessity on old-style bit braces.

The two bits in this picture also capsulize this development in tools. One is the early, flat spade variety; while the other is the modern, double-twist auger bit.

portion of the crank there's a wood or plastic handle that is free to float as you turn the crank. The amount of offset in the crank is called the "throw." The greater the throw, the more torque you can deliver to the chuck and bit. But as the throw increases, the tool becomes more cumbersome and difficult to use in confined areas. The "sweep" of a brace is the diameter of the circular area needed to revolve the crank a full turn. It is twice the measurement of the throw. Braces are available with sweeps ranging from 6 to 12 inches, with a 10- to 12-inch sweep best for average use.

Braces are generally used with special, square-shank auger bits. An auger bit has a point—a tapered screw thread that feeds itself into the wood. This is a help when boring because it pulls the bit into the wood and lessens the pressure you have to put on the back of the brace. The square shank of the bit locks positively into the chuck of the brace and won't turn under high torque. While most modern brace chucks also grip round shanks, this capability is only an advantage if you wish to use attachments designed for electric drills. One excellent use of this feature is driving screws with the brace. By placing a "Yankee" type screwdriver bit in the chuck, you can apply a high degree of torque to large wood screws with less danger of slipping (which happens with an electric drill). Stanley, maker of "Yankee" tools, also offers square-shank, screwdriver bits for use in braces.

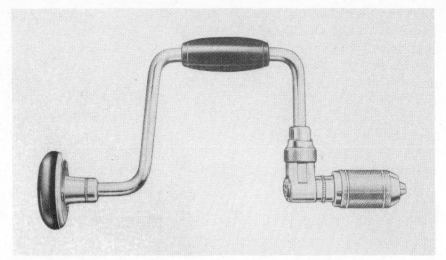

Stanley's 100 Plus Bit Brace

brace is available with either a 10-or 12-inch sweep, and both are adequate for just about any hole-boring job. Approx. Price: (10") $36.00

Woodcraft Supply's 09C07-I is a fine quality bit brace, available in sweeps from 12 inches downward. One interesting model has a sweep of only 8 inches. It's

extremely useful for working inside cabinets and in other confined areas. Capacity is ⅛- to ½-inch square- and round-shank bits. Approx. Price: (8") $34.50

Garrett Wade's 23J03.01 is a handy brace with an ultra-short swing of only 6 inches. This tool is excellent for confined spaces, but its

Stanley's 100 Plus is the company's best quality bit brace and is available in most hardware stores. This fine tool has a ball-bearing head under the handle, which can be lubricated. The universal chuck holds either round- or square-shank bits between ⅛- and ½-inch diameter. All metal has a bright nickle finish and handles are high-impact plastic. This

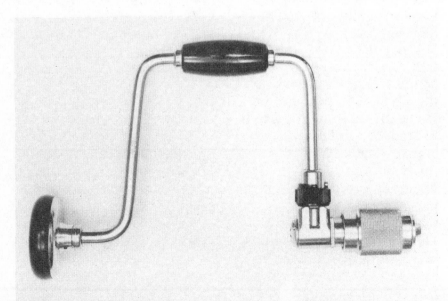

Woodcraft Supply's 09C07-I Bit Brace

general use is limited, because the short sweep limits the amount of torque you can apply to the bit. The tool is beautifully constructed. All metal parts are heavily nickel-plated and highly polished. Smooth and positive, the ratcheting mechanism features a ball-bearing mounted head. The universal chuck holds bits ranging from 1/8- to 1/2-inch diameter. Handles are composition and can take a lot of knocking around. Altogether, it's a fine tool for working in areas where space is limited. Approx. Price: $28.50

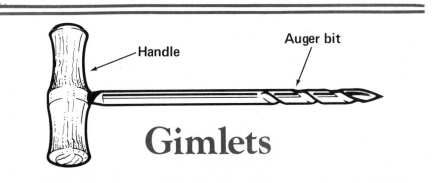

Gimlets

Although a gimlet is a cocktail to most people, it's also the name of a little-known hand tool that's useful for drilling holes from 1/8- to 3/8-inch in diameter. Inexpensive and lightweight, apartment dwellers with very basic and infrequent drilling needs can find them valuable. You can buy a good quality set of these tools for less than $5. It requires patience to use them, and you won't want to bore many holes at a stretch, but they'll do the job.

A gimlet is just a miniature auger bit attached to a handle mounted at right angles to the shank. The gimlet's point has a tapered screw thread, which pulls the tool into the work while the handle is turned. It's like an awl in that it initially pushes the wood fibers aside, but the flank of the tool's sides do actually cut and pull out some of the wood's fibers. This results in a hole that's tapered to a point and conforms to the shape of a standard wood screw. English-type gimlets have a straight wood handle, while in Continental-style tools the shank of the tool is twisted into a D-shaped handle. Both work well, and can drill small holes accurately.

Brookstone's E3623 is an excellent set of Continental-style gimlets. This five-piece set contains gimlets that can drill holes in the following diameters: 1/8, 5/32, 3/16, 1/4, and 5/16 inch. These are about all you need for small hole drilling. The tools range in length from 4 3/4 to 7 1/2 inches, and the entire set weighs a mere 6 ounces. It's a nice little package for the price. Approx. Price: $6.50

Garrett Wade's 37J03.01 is a set of two English-style gimlets. The two sizes, 1/8-and 3/16-inch, are just about standard for small wood screws. If the sizes are too small for the screw you intend to use, you can soap the screw threads to help compensate for the smaller diameter hole. Approx. Price: $3.50

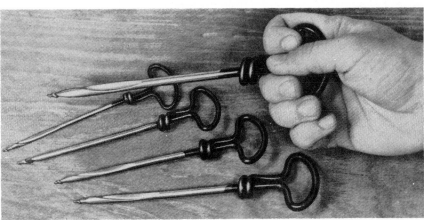

Brookstone's E3623 Continental-Style Gimlets

Drilling Accessories

Auger Bits

These tools are specially designed to bore deep, clean holes in wood. Typically, they're used in a brace (hence, "brace and bit"). So, they have a design different from wood bits used in an electric drill. The chuck end of the auger bit is square for secure attachment to the brace's chuck. The business end has a screw point that self-feeds the bit into the work—giving good control with minimum pressure on the back end of the brace. Diameters of auger bits are usually standardized in $\frac{1}{16}$-inch gradations. They can be purchased separately, but most people buy an entire set that includes most standard sizes under an inch. A complete set of auger bits requires a considerable investment, so shop with care. A good set will last a long time, but quality bits are not available at a cheap price.

Greenlee Manufacturing's new set of "Jennings

Greenlee's Auger Bits

Pattern" auger bits gives you the best bits of this pattern on the market. Russel Jennings was an old Sheffield toolmaker who devised the most common pattern of auger bits used today. Jennings is now to auger bits as Kleenex is to facial tissue. This pattern uses a double twist in the shank flutes, which produces quick cutting

and excellent chip clearing ability. The double twist pattern has always been the standard in the industry, and in demand by serious craftsmen. Greenlee's new set includes 13 auger bits, ranging in size from $\frac{1}{4}$-to 1-inch, with a $\frac{1}{16}$-inch difference between sizes. The whole set is packed in a wooden box that makes the kit a joy to own in itself, if you love fine tools. This set is also marketed by the Princeton Company and Conover Woodcraft. Approx. Price: $95.00

Stanley's 100 Plus auger bit set (#BXD32½) is also based on the Jennings pattern. This set includes 13 bits that range from $\frac{1}{4}$-to 1-inch diameter, in $\frac{1}{16}$-inch gradations. This pattern has good chip clearing ability and can bore a clean hole in a

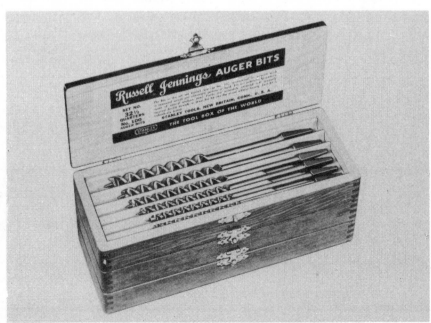

Stanley's 100 Plus Auger Bit Set

minimum amount of time. The whole set is packed in a wooden chest and is available in most hardware stores. Approx. Price: $121.00

Greenlee Multi-Spur bits have a shape somewhat like a round cookie cutter. The circumference of the drill bit, rather than the point, is used to center the bit and guide it while drilling. The great advantage of the Multi-Spur pattern is that it can cut large, flat-bottomed holes. However, it can't bore exceptionally deep holes. Greenlee's Multi-Spur differs from the traditional pattern in that it has a serrated lip for better cutting, with one chipper (chisel-like surface) to cut away the waste in the circular area enclosed by the lip. Bits of this style are available in a wide range of sizes from all major tool catalog houses. They have round shanks, so you can also use them in portable and stationary power drills. Approx.Price:(149-½)$14.00

Expanding Bits

If you're involved in woodworking for any time at all, you'll eventually need to drill a hole that's an oddball — not conforming to standard-size bits. This can be particularly vexing after having spent a small fortune on a complete set of auger bits. You can solve the problem simply and inexpensively with an expanding bit. This type of bit is also useful if you only drill a large-diameter hole once in a while, since it saves you the price of a complete set of standard bits.

An expanding bit is like a standard auger bit, but it has a movable wing cutter. The cutter slides in a dovetail just behind the standard point, and is adjusted with a small setscrew. Some adjust by way of rack-and-pinon, and others by worm gear — the latter is slightly more desirable because it permits more sensitive adjustment. To use the bit, you expand this spur cutter to the desired radius and then bore the hole. You can cut a hole any size within the movable range of the tool. Most expansion bits come with a set of two cutters to allow a more comprehensive range of adjustment. Expansion bits work reasonably well right off the store shelf, but for superior performance, some fine tuning may be necessary.

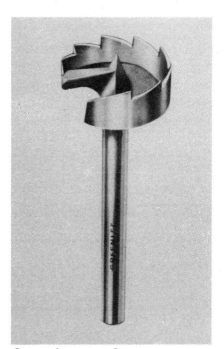

Greenlee's Multi-Spur

The simplest and most widely used drill in the ancient world was the "bow drill." This consists of a long stick, called the bit-stock, which is rotated by the string of a bow that is wound around it. In use, the cord is wrapped around the bit-stock — whose point has some kind of hard drilling implement attached — and the bow rapidly sawed back and forth to impart a rotary motion by means of the cord. While this would seem to be very inefficient, for drilling small holes it works quite well. Often a breast plate or bib was used to brace the end of the bit-stock to impart pressure to the point while it was cutting. Even the advent of small power tools has not superseded the use of this kind of small drill. Much of the intricate jade work done in the Orient is still done by this traditional method — which, while tedious, time-consuming, and inefficient, will not seriously damage the precious material if a mistake is made.

It's usually a good idea to take the bit apart and remove any burrs from the adjusting mechanism for smooth operation. Then use a slip stone to hone the cutters to a razor edge. This will greatly improve the quality of the bored hole.

Stanley Tools' 01-710A and 01-711A are two excellent expanding bits. Each comes with a set of two cutters and both are 9½ inches long and end in a square shank for bit brace chucks. Model 01-710A bores holes between ⅝ and 1¾ inches in diameter; model 01-711A has a ⅞- to 3-inch range. Both models have positive rack-and-pinion adjustment. One full turn of the adjusting screw enlarges or decreases the hole diameter by ⅛ inch.

Together, the pair answers any need you may have for boring large-diameter holes. Approx. Price: (01-710A) $13.50

Bit Extensions

Stanley's 180 bit extension increases the shank length of any standard auger bit by 18 inches. This greatly aids in drilling through walls or in blind spots like the backs of cabinets. Admittedly, you won't use this tool often, but when it is needed, it can save the day. At the price, it's expensive for only occasional use. Approx. Price: $19.00

Dowling Jigs

Modern furniture construction now often involves dowling two pieces of wood together, rather than using the time honored, but time consuming mortise-and-tenon joint. In the dowling joint, blind holes are drilled in the adjoining faces of both pieces. Dowl pins are glued and inserted in these holes and the adjoining surfaces of the stock are butted together. This results in a strong joint and good fit if done properly. One problem, however, is that the dowl holes in the two corresponding surfaces must register exactly and be drilled in one common line. And, to obtain a good fit, the holes must be absolutely square to the work surface. A dowling jig is a device that makes this task easier. In its simplest form, it's a hardened steel fixture that screws onto the workpiece to guide the drill bit. This results in a square bore at a specific point.

The Dowl-It is one of the best dowling jigs on the market. This jig lets you drill holes in the five most popular dowl sizes — ¼, ⁵⁄₁₆, ⅜, ⁷⁄₁₆ and ½

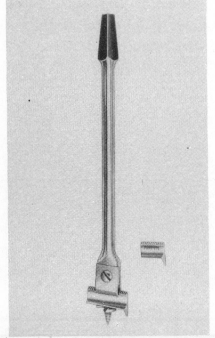

Stanley's 01-710A

Stanley's 180

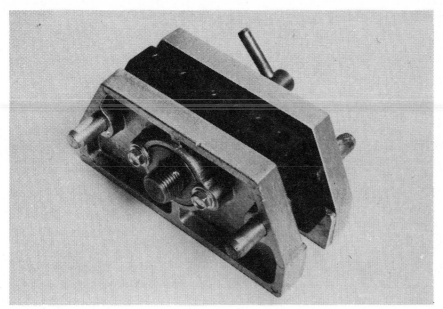
Dowl-It

Stanley's 59 is a dowling jig specifically designed for twist drills. This is unusual, since most jigs are designed for use with auger bits, special dowling bits, and only incidentally with twist drills. Stanley's jig has guides for drilling holes in the following diameters: 3/16, 1/4, 5/16, 3/8, 7/16, and 1/2 inch. This jig is not elaborate, but useful, and can see you through most dowling projects. It's also fairly handy for just drilling a hole square to a surface when the need arises. Approx. Price: $25.50

inch. It has a heavy steel center section which serves as the drill's guide. On either side of this section are mounted two heavy, cast-aluminum wings that close by means of a turnscrew. This turnscrew works like a turnbuckle and closes both wings simultaneously. The design makes this jig self-centering, which is not true of other jigs. Dowl-It's self-centering capability is its main virtue, although it also lets you drill off-center holes if you need to.

The jig has a mark for registering each size hole at a specific point. In use, the two pieces of wood to be dowled are usually butted together for a fit and a line drawn on each piece. Then you place the dowling jig over the piece and line up the mark with the pencil line on the piece. After drilling, the holes are perfectly square and in register. This is also the only jig available that can drill a crosshole on center through a piece of round stock. Dowl-It is available from Brookstone Company

Stanley's 59 Doweling Jig

Portable electric drills are one of the most useful
shop or field tools — not only for drilling holes,
but also because of the wide variety of
accessories which can be fitted into their chucks.
You can stir paint or smooth wood, cut a mortise or
route a decorative design with one convenient tool.

Portable Electric Drills

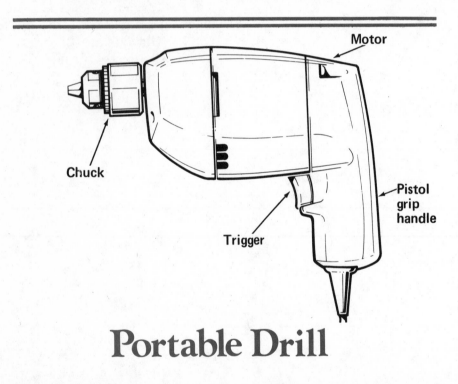

Portable Drill

If there's one power drill that should be considered a necessity for the home and shop, it's the portable electric drill. It's almost as basic as a saw or hammer, and is sometimes more useful than either. This may be hard to understand, since this is basically only a tool for drilling holes. But, if you ever worked with a brace-and-bit or eggbeater-type hand drill, you'll appreciate the portable drill's speed at boring holes in wood, metal and composition materials. These jobs can be done with a minimum of time and effort on your part. Also, there are some types of drilling that can't be done at all on a conventional hand drill or brace — like drilling concrete. Until fairly recently, such tasks were done with a tool called a "star drill" and a heavy hammer. The end of the star drill was given several sharp blows, after which the drill was rotated, and the procedure continued. This takes a lot of time and work, and eventually results in a black and blue fingernail. Today, you can do such work much more easily, with a conventional electric drill or new impacting model, turning a carbide-tipped bit. This can be done quickly, cleanly, and without the typical ragged holes that a star drill usually leaves in these materials.

The portable drill is also a convenient power source that can drive a fantastic array of accessories. These range from sanding, polishing, and grinding tools to gadgets for stirring paint or turning screws. Accessory stands hold the drill to make it a miniature piece of stationary equipment, or turn it into a small drill press. An attachment can convert it into a saber saw, a small pump can be added to move water, rotary rasps can be gripped for shaping wood or metal, and there are even sharpening devices for kitchen knives and lawnmowers. So many accessories are available, that it's easy to get confused. And the cost of all these accessories can easily outstrip the original cost of the drill itself.

When you add it all up, this tool is a necessity for any shop, no matter how elaborate or well-equipped.

This is true even if the portable drill is used in situations where it's more convenient to bring the work to the tool. It's perfect for the woodworker who lacks space but not interest. Any portable drill and the necessary accessories can be stored in a drawer or on a closet shelf. And you can use it wherever there's an electrical outlet.

The size of an electric drill is determined by the largest diameter bit that can be secured in the drill's chuck, or gripping device. Common models include those with ¼-, ⅜- and ½-inch capacities. The size gives you a rough indication of the tool's drilling capacity in steel. A ¼-inch drill, for example, can form holes in

steel up to ¼-inch in diameter. This is doubled in wood, to about ½-inch in hardwood. The same formula applies to the other two standard drill sizes. A ⅜-inch drill can handle ⅜-inch holes in steel and ¾-inch holes in wood. A ½-inch drill can form holes up to ½ inch in steel and about an inch in hardwoods. Of course, this formula is only a rough estimate of capacity and power, since drills of the same size may have motors with considerably different power ratings. A tool that can drill a ½-inch hole in steel has to be more powerful than one that can only drill a ¼-inch hole in the same material.

So, chuck size is a general statement, and not meant to

A QUICK LOOK AT PORTABLE ELECTRIC DRILLS

CHUCK SIZE	CAPACITIES	REMARKS
¼ Inch Chuck	¼ inch in metals, ½ inch in wood— smallest of the electric drills— limited range of drilling operations possible—no hammer mode— reversing feature of limited use— highest revolutions per minute, low torque	cheapest of portable drills—good for homeowner use in limited hole-drilling applications—not recommended for extensive use—will drive wire brushes and other auxiliary equipment
⅜ Inch Chuck	⅜ inch in metals, ¾ inch in wood— best all around shop size— hammer mode permits drilling in concrete—reversing feature handy for removing screws—midrange in revolutions-per-minute and available torque	middle range in price, but has extensive usefulness in both home and shop—some models will take heavy-duty use—mounting spade bits in chuck allows for deep, clean hole boring in wood
½ Inch Chuck	½ inch in metals, 1 inch in wood— largest of portable drills— hammer mode and different chucks— concrete drilling and other large boring jobs in thick material—low revolutions-per-minute and high torque	highest price of all portable electric drills—contractor's tool used for very heavy duty applications .. high torque and auxiliary handles allow accurate and heavy drilling in thick, tough materials

Wherever man travels, he takes along his tools and technology: even to the moon, as this Apollo Lunar Surface Drill by Black & Decker, proves.

incorrectly. Occasionally, an underpowered drill can handle a tough job if the operator applies only enough pressure to keep the cutting tool working. But you must frequently break contact between the drill bit and the work to allow the drill to cool down by running without a load. You must apply enough feed pressure (how hard you bear down on the tool) to keep the cutter working, without overtaxing it. The amount of material the cutter bit removes may be minimal, and the job may take some time. A small drill with moderate rates of speed and feed pressure can sometimes be substituted for a larger capacity drill, but patience is a requirement.

All size electric drills are available in one-speed, two-speed, and variable-speed models. Variable-speed models let you select any speed up to the highest rpm of which the drill is capable. The speeds provided relate to the general rule: "Drill small holes at high speed and large holes at slow speed." Drills with a ¼-inch chuck capacity have the highest speeds. Those of ½-inch capacity have the slowest speeds, and ⅜-inch models span the gap between the two.

"Torque" is the most useful measurement of a drill's power. It's a measurement of the actual turning force used to rotate the drill. Drilling a ½-inch hole in steel requires a lot more torque than drilling a ¼-inch hole in wood. High

indicate that a particular drill can do a particular task. Even a small ¼-inch drill, with the proper accessories, can have more capabilities than its specifications indicate. Used correctly, with a fine-quality, well-sharpened spade bit, this drill can drill holes up to 1½ inches in diameter in wood. A hole saw can increase this capability even more. It is possible, however, to overtax a drill by trying to stretch its capacity. A light-duty, ¼-inch drill turning an oversized bit can be abused to the point of failure if the operator applies too much pressure. This will reduce the tool's turning speed excessively, so that the work will not get done or the motor will stall. Small drills are not built to handle this kind of pressure and will quickly show it by overheating—a warning that you're using it

torque and low speeds are necessary partners in heavy-duty, ½-inch drills. These tools operate in low gear, like a car does when climbing a steep hill. If the drill were not geared down this way, it couldn't do the job.

Single-speed drills are okay for some jobs, but for many they're just a compromise. Such a drill can get most jobs done, but the overall quality usually suffers. The material, hole diameter, and type of cutter can all influence drilling speed. So, the ability to select the right speed for a particular accessory used in the drill is important. A hole saw, when cutting at a particular speed, may do an excellent job in wood, but barely scrape the surface of metal. Look for adjustable speeds in quality drills of any size.

You usually control the speed of a variable-speed drill by depressing a trigger switch. The further you press the trigger, the greater the speed. Some tools have a preset speed control that you can adjust to limit how far back you can depress the trigger switch. This is a convenience when a certain speed is used for a long period of time. Ordinarily, this control is a small button, mounted on the shaft that passes through the trigger. You set it for the correct speed by turning the button to a set point. This prevents the trigger from being depressed further.

Another interesting feature

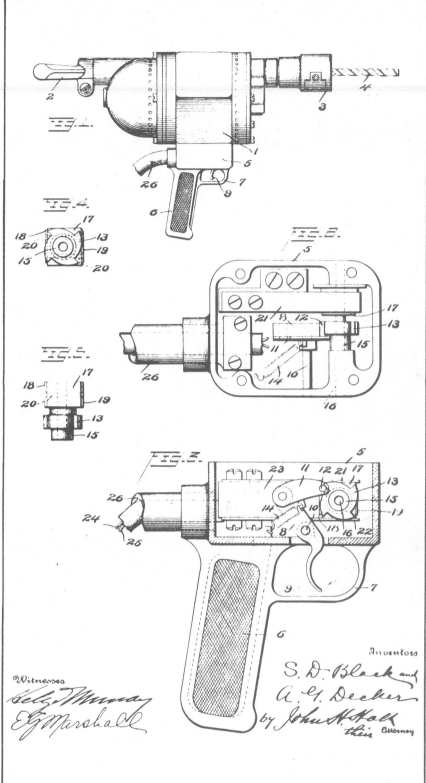

We take for granted the pistol grip power switch on electric drills; however, they are a fairly recent innovation. This patent application is for the original Black & Decker switch mechanism for electrical tools (1917).

becoming common on portable drills is "reversing"—the ability to change the direction of the drill's rotation. You do this by way of a sliding switch. The reversing feature is a noticeable advantage with a variable-speed drill, because it allows you to remove as well as drive screws, using the proper bit. It also lets you loosen drill bits easily if they jam in a hole. However, this reversing feature is often overplayed as a sales point, with claims that wire brushes and other accessories will last longer if their working rotation is reversed occasionally. Running a drill bit in the opposite direction for any length of time will destroy it. And the only value to a reversing switch is for removing screws or removing an occasional jammed bit. This expensive little feature may add as much as $10 to the cost of the drill, and offers convenience only once in a while.

Lock buttons let you lock the trigger switch, so you don't have to depress it continually. This feature reduces operator fatigue, and lets you pay more attention to the work at hand. The lock is released by merely pressing the trigger switch again. Locks are also very useful when the entire drill is mounted in a stand for use as a stationary tool.

Many models of all sizes come with an extra handle or offer one as an option. This is most important when using large, heavy-duty tools, since they afford much better

control. The fact that they can usually be mounted on either side of the drill is appreciated by lefties.

Cordless, battery-powered drills have invaded the market recently, and they free you from the need of a nearby electrical outlet. These drills are available in ¼- and ⅜-inch sizes. They vary in speeds available, power, and the amount of work they can do before recharging. Cordless drills should be considered only light-duty tools—good enough for driving screws or drilling holes, but not sturdy enough for a wide variety of accessories. Some heavy-duty models are made, but these are specialized

tools and should only be chosen when you have jobs that warrant their expense and heavy weight.

To make a choice between the various sizes of drills, you must consider your workscope. A ¼-inch drill isn't a bad choice for the homeowner who wants an inexpensive tool for lightweight chores. It lets you drill small holes, put up a shelf, remove scaled paint from wrought iron, and even mix paint. It's a good tool as long as you can accept its limitations.

A ⅜-inch drill, especially a variable-speed model, is the best choice for home maintenance and the small shop. It has enough power

The use of screws in woodworking is a relatively new innovation dating from the time when automatic machinery was developed to produce accurate screw threads. It is not often recognized that using screws requires careful preparation of the work before they are put in. It is not enough to simply drill a hole. Flat headed wood screws require at least three holes.

These holes correspond to the three sections of the typical wood screw. The first hole is a "pilot" hole. Drilled slightly smaller than the threaded portion of the screw, it serves to provide a pathway and a surface for the threads to grip. A "body" hole is drilled the same size as the diameter of the unthreaded shank of the screw. This is to prevent splintering or forcing as the screw pulls itself into the wood. Last, a countersink is used to create a depression the same size as the screw head's diameter. This is done to allow the screw to fit flush with the surface of the workpiece—a mark of the careful woodworker.

Special combination drill bits are available so that the correct pilot, body, and countersink holes are formed in one drilling operation. These correspond to the commonest sizes of wood screws. If they are not available the same effect can be had with three separate bits. The pilot and shank holes are drilled with regular bits, while the countersink is done with a special rosehead or countersink bit.

for most jobs and is more suitable as a drive source for accessories. This drill can do anything a ¼-inch model can do, and with a minimum of time and trouble.

The ½-inch drill is a borderline tool for the homeowner and small shop owner. Most buyers of this tool do lots of construction and remodeling work. Power varies, but they can be had with ¾-hp and more. Typical applications are drilling large holes in concrete, brick, and steel; forming access holes in framing members for plumbing, and cutting vents in a wall. The average woodworker won't find the ½-inch drill very useful unless he contemplates this kind of work.

A good ⅜-inch drill can easily compete with ½-inch models in the lower horsepower range. So, it's the best choice for average use. Many woodworking enthusiasts equip their shops with both a ¼- and ⅜-inch drill, which prepares them for 99 percent of the work they're likely to encounter. This course is feasible today, because while drill features have increased, prices have gone down considerably.

Drills, regardless of their size, are often used too casually. One bad procedure is to hold the work in your hand while you drill. If the bit jams in the hole, as does happen, the drill's torque can spin the work and injure you. A ½-inch, heavy-duty drill has so much torque that it can literally spin the operator if the bit jams in a hole.

Especially when drilling large holes in concrete and metal, *always* grip the tool with both hands — one hand on the main handle, and one on the auxiliary handle. And make sure you always have a firm stance when drilling. Heavy drills are only portable for convenience. They're not toys and should never be considered as such.

Skils' Xtra-Tool comes in two sizes — ⅜-inch (#599) and ½-inch (#600). Both have the same speeds and features, but the ½-inch model is slightly more powerful. Clever engineers will probably dream up more

features to pack into an electric drill, but it'll take some ingenuity to top the Xtra-Tool. Both these machines have good power, removable auxiliary handle, reversibility, and trigger-controlled variable speeds from 0 to 800 rpm. What makes this tool so neat is a feature called a "hammer mode." When you twist a collar, short, choppy blows are delivered by the rotating chuck at about 36,000 per minute. You'll appreciate this feature if you drill holes in concrete — a tedious task even with a carbide bit and regular drill. The hammer mode increases the impact and momentary torque on the bit to make such cutting and drilling jobs much easier.

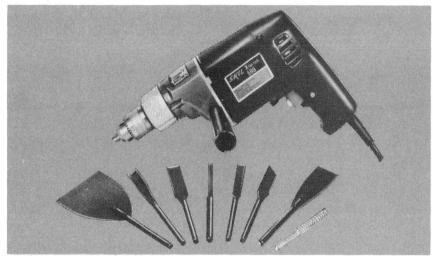
Skil's Xtra-Tool 599

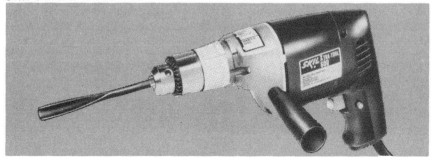
Skil's Xtra-Tool 600

This special mode can be used with or without the standard rotary action. Other specialized bits allow you to use the hammer mode to remove scale and scrape off wallpaper.

In itself, the tool is a good, functional, portable drill, capable of handling any available accessory. The hammer mode does make it something else. This feature is not unique, since it's found on other drills, but it's very useful. The gadget does take some getting used to, so it's worth your while to practice on some scrap material first. Also, the hammer mode is a bit noisy, so ear protection may be advisable if you plan extensive use. Approx. Price: (599) $60.00; (600) $70.00

Black & Decker's 7156 is a ⅜-inch portable drill with all the features a full-function drill this size should have. This is the tool for the homeowner who works with one drill and wants to get the most from it. And it's also for the professional who seeks a nonfailing, lightweight tool for some heavy-duty work.

Speed is variable, and trigger-controlled from 0 to 1200 rpm. A locking switch lets you set it at one particular speed. The drill also has a reversing switch, double insulation, and the trigger switch can be locked in the "on" position when necessary. It has a little over ⅜-hp, and basic capacities of ⅜-inch in steel and ¾-inch in

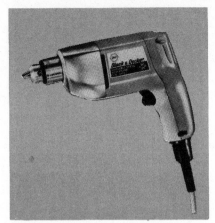

Black & Decker's 7156

hardwood. The 10-foot cord is much longer than that of most portable drills, and the cord detaches for easy storage. This is your basic drill with most of the frills, and should give years of use. Approx. Price: $45.00

Shopmate's T215111 is a top-performing ⅜-inch drill with all the features that identify the full-function tool. This one is often selected by professional tradesmen, which is often a tipoff to a tool's quality and durability. And it should be a good choice for the average woodworker.

Shopmate's T215111

The shape of this drill departs from the standard pistol-grip design. The handle is at mid-point position under the tool's housing—a location some consider to be better, since it provides better balance and lessens fatigue during long periods of use. This is arguable, because proponents of the conventional pistol-grip handle claim that it allows better control and makes it easier to apply feed pressure. So, handle location is basically a matter of personal preference, and you should select the one that feels best to you.

This Shopmate drill has speeds ranging from 0 to 1000 rpm, variable via a trigger switch, and it also has a reversing feature. Motor is ⅓-hp—adequate for almost any work task. An additional feature is an auxiliary handle that can be used on either side of the main housing. This is a feature that lefthanders of the world will appreciate. Approx. Price: $30.00

The Craftsman 1140, ¼-inch drill from Sears, Roebuck and Co., works with a ⅙-hp motor and has a single speed of 2000 rpm. That's about it. It's a basic tool for drilling small holes, and is a good choice for the hobbyist who does modeling work. Construction is merely adequate for its range of job applications, and it can serve nicely if not abused by

Craftsman's 1140

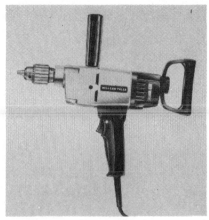

Millers Falls' SP352

motors of smaller drills. It's commonly used by tradesmen to drill concrete and brick and for making access holes through house framing components. Even with all this capability, the drill weighs only about 7 pounds — pretty good for such a heavy-duty drill. Approx. Price: $95.00

heavy-duty work. The one outstanding feature of this tool is its price. For under ten bucks, you get a small drill that uses electric power instead of muscle power. Approx. Price: $8.00

The Craftsman 1142 falls in the same category as the Craftsman 1140, but offers a little more power and capacity. This is a ⅜-inch, minimum drill with a single speed of 1200 rpm. Power is provided by a ⅕-hp motor. The tool is double-insulated and has an extremely cheap price tag. Approx. Price: $11.00

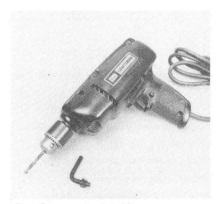

Craftsman's 1142

Millers Falls' SP352 is a really rugged, powerful ½-inch drill designed for professional electricians and plumbers. Although it's an industrial machine, this tool is not out of line for the shop owner who wants a complete set of equipment and who wants a drill that will drive every conceivable accessory. This double-insulated, single-speed drill (450 rpm) has the basic capacity to drill ½-inch and 1½-inch diameter holes in steel and hardwood, respectively.

The tool has a design which permits a positive grip, no matter what the job being done. Its main handle, with a trigger switch and lock button, is under the main housing. A back handle, shaped much like the letter "D," is removable and adjustable to the chuck's angle of drilling. A third handle can be mounted on either side or the top. Really, this arrangement lets you hold the drill in any position, as long as your strength holds out!

This drill is for tough jobs that would damage the

Black & Decker's Mod 4 (#9092) is a cordless, battery-powered electric drill that is the nucleus of a variety of accessories for the homeowner. The ⅜-inch drill is actually a two-part package. The removable handle unit contains the rechargeable energy pack, and can be attached to a wide variety of accessories in the Mod 4 line. The handle becomes the power source for grass shears, a hedge trimmer, a lantern and a small vacuum cleaner. A main advantage is that you can use these tools without the need of an electrical outlet, and the

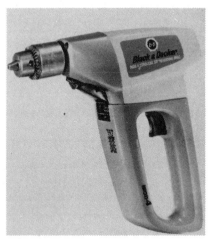

Black & Decker's Mod 4

nuisance of a trailing electric cord.

In its drill mode, it's a nice tool. It is reversible, but like any cordless tool, it's not made for heavy-duty use. The drill's novel design doesn't interfere with efficient use, because weight distribution favors the chuck end of the tool. This drill could be the basis of a homeowner's care kit, since the accessories are useful. Approx. Price: $35.00

Skil's 2002, ⅜-inch cordless drill has amazing power for a battery-operated tool. The two speeds — 100 and 300 rpm — are low, but the double-reduction gearing and available power gives more than enough torque to drive wood screws. It can also remove them, since the drill is reversible. The powerpack enables this drill to bore from 90 to 100 ¼-inch diameter holes through 1½-inch wood before recharging. Basic

drilling capacities are ⅜ inch in wood and ¼ inch in steel, which means it is a heavy-duty model among the cordless drills. A couple of nice features in this drill are a safety lock on the trigger switch that prevents accidental starts, and a little cavity in the housing to hold the chuck key. One of the optional accessories is a charger (#71871) that plugs into a car's cigaret lighter outlet. Field work can continue without a worry about depleting the drill's energy source. If you're looking for a cordless drill with above-average power, this is it. Approx. Price: $40.00

Rockwell's 4101 is a low-cost, ⅜-inch electric drill that performs impressively. It has a single speed of 1400 rpm, and it does not reverse, but it behaves well for general-purpose work

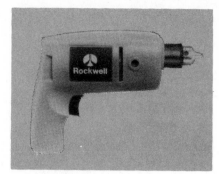

Rockwell's 4101

— including polishing, sanding and wire brushing — when equipped with the right accessories. Construction is admirable when you consider the price. Double-reduction gears contribute to durability, and the drill has ball thrust bearings. Other features include high-impact housing, double-insulation and capacities of ⅜ inch in steel and ¾ inch in wood. The single speed does impose some limitations. For instance, you can't bore holes in masonry. But it's a good choice for the person who wants a good drill at a reasonable price. Approx. Price: $18.00

Portable Drill Accessories

Drill alignment accessories include drill stands that transform a drill into a stationary tool, and products like "Portalign," which act as a guide when the tool is hand held.

Skil's 2002 Cordless Drill

Drill stands convert the drill into a small drill press. They consist of a base, a column, and a device that secures the drill in a vertical position and lets you move the drill up and down the column. They're good for the person who wants drill press capability, but who doesn't have the space or cash for a standard model. But they're not a substitute for a full-function press, and can't be used for operations such as mortising or routing/shaping. You must also remember that they're only as good as the drill you mount on them, since the drill is the main power source and heart of the unit.

Most drill manufacturers offer accessory stands that fit their own products, as well as other drills. But since the stand listing often states, "fits most electric drills," you should make sure your drill fits before you buy the stand.

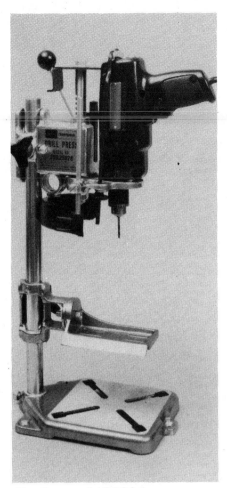

Craftsman's 25926

The Craftsman 25987C, from Sears, Roebuck and Co., is a heavy-duty drill stand designed to work with almost any portable drill of any chuck size. This stand has a small table that tilts for angular work, and swings aside so that the base can support larger workpieces. A stop-rod attachment on the drill mount can control the depth of the hole drilled. This is quite useful if a large number of identical holes need to be drilled. Approx. Price: $50.00

The Craftsman 25926, from Sears, Roebuck and Co., is made to accept all ¼- and ⅜-inch drills with pistol-grip handles. It works like the Craftsman 25987C, but has one additional and useful feature. The drill mount can be turned 90 degrees to put the drill in a fixed, horizontal position. This makes it convenient to use buffing and polishing accessories in the drill's chuck. Approx. Price: $28.00

"Portalign" is not a drill stand. It's a cradle with a base in which the drill is held so that the bit is perpendicular to the work surface. This portable jig also has a stop control so holes can be drilled to a specific depth. The base can be organized to position round stock, either tubes or solids, for radial drilling. It can be adjusted for angular drilling. Also, you can set Portalign so that repeated holes can be drilled exactly in the center of a workpiece without having to measure or draw guide lines.

This accessory can be used with any ¼- or ⅜-inch drill that has a removable chuck (a common design feature, since chucks wear rapidly) as long as the drill housing is not more than 3 inches wide. Most drills in these chuck sizes fit the Portalign. The accessory is available at most retail outlets and catalog houses. Approx. Price: $20.00

Portalign

Pumps use the portable drill as a power source to help you remove water from basements, stopped up tubs, fish tanks, and the like. You should remember, however, that water and electricity create a potentially dangerous combination. So, even if your drill is double insulated, you should be careful. You may not be shocked by electricity, but you may be shocked to find that you've destroyed a perfectly good drill with one mistake.

Arco Products' 1590 electric drill pump has a shaft that locks in the drill's chuck, and has a claimed capacity of up to 250 gallons-per-hour. This is a simple, plastic-encased mechanism that's used with an ordinary ½-inch garden hose. In combination, they allow use in a wide variety of draining situations. Approx. Price: $6.50

Saber saw attachments consist of a small case with a

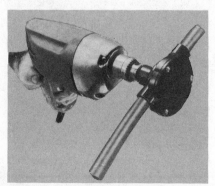

Arco's 1590 Drill Pump

Arco's 560

handle and a shaft that locks in the drill's chuck. The mechanism inside the case converts the rotary motion of the drill into a reciprocal, up-and-down movement that drives the saber saw blade. This saw/drill combination is not as convenient to use as a regular saber saw, but it does a job after a fashion. Although these attachments may be used with single-speed drills, they are more useful if your drill is a variable-speed model.

Arco Products' 511 and 560 are saber saw attachments that change your drill into a saw. The 511 has a design flaw in that the handle of the drill must be gripped securely before it is turned on, to prevent the attachment from spinning. A more elaborate model, the 560 includes a flexible clamp that girds the body of the drill and prevents this from happening. This model also includes a rip gauge to guide the tool. Approx. Price: (560) $11.00

Drill bit sharpeners are useful accessories, too. Twist drills must be sharp to perform efficiently and to produce clean holes in wood or metal. Keeping them in the correct form and angle to the bit's sides requires a considerable amount of skill when done on a grinding wheel. Drill bit sharpeners may be mounted on any ¼- or ⅜-inch drill, and make anyone a quick expert at this task. A sharpener is basically a small case attached to the top of a stand which serves as a cradle to hold the drill in a vertical position. A shaft at the bottom of this case locks into the drill's chuck and turns a grinding wheel that sharpens the bits. What makes this whole procedure simple are the various guides and controls that are used to position the drill bit exactly right.

Black & Decker's 79-800 is a drill bit sharpener attachment

Black & Decker's 79-800

that accepts bit sizes from ¼ to ⅜ inch. It can't be operated at speeds greater than 3000 rpm, and you can't use it to sharpen carbide-tipped twist drills. But within these limitations, it does a good job. Approx. Price: $12.00

Most of the following accessories are commonly available from local retail outlets and catalog houses. They are essentially the same products used with drill presses, except where noted.

Drill fixtures or stands (not to be confused with a stand that converts the drill to a small drill press) are simple devices which mount on a bench top. A clamp holds the drill in a horizontal position, creating a small stationary power source for tasks like sharpening, wire brushing, and polishing.

Drill stops are small gadgets that slip over a drill bit and lock into place. These are necessary when a large number of identical holes must be drilled to a specific depth.

Drum sanders. Usable with drill presses also. See page 149 for a complete description.

Fly cutters should *not* be used in a portable drill!

Hole saws. Usable with drill presses also. See page 148 for a complete description.

Paint mixers consist of a shaft with fan-type blades at one end that turn as the drill chuck rotates. This accessory has to be put into

the paint before it is turned on. Otherwise, you and the walls will be dotted with paint. These accessories work best when the drill is moved up and down and the direction of rotation is reversed occasionally. Reversible drills obviously work best here.

Right angle drives mount in the chuck to make it possible to drill holes at right or acute angles to the normal line of the drill chuck. This is very useful in tight places. Some of these accessories accept polishing bonnets and pads, as well as drill bits. Extremely sophisticated types are geared to run at either double or half the drill's normal speed, depending upon which way they are mounted. This permits a wider range of operations than can be done with the normal speeds available in the drill.

Rotary rasps and files can shape wood and metal, remove burrs from cut metal edges, and enlarge holes. In fact, they can do just about any chore that can be done with a conventional rasp and file. They clog with waste particles quickly if they are not watched, but they sure beat doing the job by hand when there is much material to be removed.

Spade bits. Usable with drill presses also. See page 148 for a complete description.

Sharpeners are usually two matched grinding wheels mounted on a shaft that is gripped, and turned, by the drill chuck. Various types are available for sharpening

kitchen knives, scissors, and even lawn mower blades.

Twist drills. Usable with drill presses also. See page 148 for a complete description.

Wire brushes are used to clean metals, remove scaled paint, create a satin finish on soft metals, or a rustic finish on woods. Two varieties are available. Wheels with brush wire on the rim are for general use, while cup types are especially good for getting into corners and other hard-to-reach places. They come in coarse and fine grades.

Woodscrew bits are special hole drilling tools which make it easy to install a wood screw correctly. Normally, three operations would be required. A "pilot hole" would be necessary for the threaded portion of the screw. Then you'd have to drill a "shank hole" for the unthreaded portion beneath the head. Finally, an indentation called a "countersink" would have to be made so that the screw could be driven flush with the wood surface. Woodscrew bits are shaped drilling tools that accomplish all three operations in one stroke. These save time and increase accuracy. They are available individually, to match a particular size screw, or in sets that span the full range of woodscrews you're likely to use.

Some of these bits also cut a "counterbore" — a hole which permits the screw to be driven beneath the surface of the wood. The hole is then filled with a cut wooden plug to conceal the screw.

Although precise, accurate hole-drilling in all sizes of stock is the *forté* of the drill press, it can also be used to mortise, sand, and cut plugs.

Drill Presses

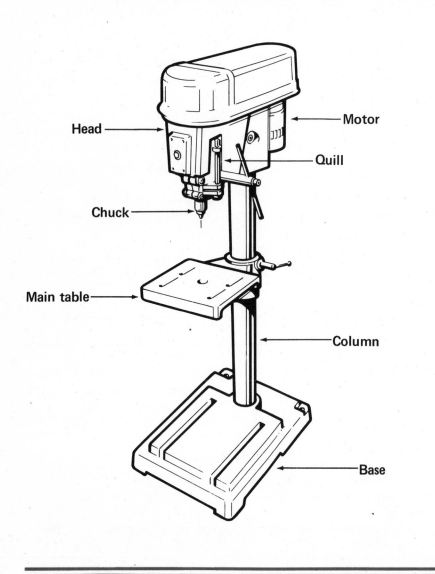

Head

Motor

Quill

Chuck

Main table

Column

Base

available for it. Sanding drums, rotary planers, router bits, rotary rasps, shaping cutters, mortising equipment, plug cutters, and hole saws are just some of these accessories. This is why many shop owners consider the drill press second only to sawing tools in importance.

The drill press makes it fairly simple to complete some of the more sophisticated woodworking projects, like forming the mortise-tenon joint. This joint is one of the most durable connections for wood, and indicates dedicated and prideful craftsmanship. The mortise is a rectangular cavity cut into the wood; it requires skill, time, and a lot of effort when done with hand tools. The tenon is the extension on the other piece of wood, which fits into the mortise. If you have a drill press equipped with mortising bits and chisels, this chore becomes relatively easy. With a little care, almost anyone can do an accurate job.

Drill presses are made up of three separate parts—head, column, and one or more tables. The head is a cast-iron housing, fixed at the top of the column. Encased in front of the head

No tool can bore holes in wood and other materials as quickly and accurately as a drill press. It was originally a metalworking tool, and still sees extensive use in that field. But woodworkers now find it a very versatile machine, due to the vast number of accessories

is a heavy-steel tube called a "quill." It adjusts up and down by way of external levers and is either spring-loaded or counter-balanced to return to a neutral position.

A rotating "spindle" is centered and supported inside the quill, and moves up and down with it. There's a bit-gripping chuck at the lower end of the quill. This is usually a variety of the three-jawed chuck, which adjusts with a special key and holds round shanks of various diameters. Some expensive, multipurpose drill presses have a chuck that can be replaced with a specialized gripping unit. A router chuck, for example, will hold router bits; an adapter can hold shaper cutters.

The capacity of a drill press is expressed by the number of inches the quill and spindle can travel. Manufacturers usually list drill press capacity as "quill travel" or "spindle travel." These are interchangeable terms, since the quill and spindle move as one unit. You may also see this measurement expressed by the term "stroke." In any case, if the quill travel, spindle travel or stroke of a machine is 4 inches, the machine can drill a hole 4 inches deep. Normally, drill presses have a quill travel ranging from 3 to 6 inches. You should note, however, that a drill can bore a hole that is deeper than its quill travel measurement. One of the techniques is to drill from

When drilling through any kind of wood a certain amount of wood splintering will happen at the breakout point. This is true regardless of the type of bit used, since wood has a composition that causes it to fracture, rather than break. To prevent this breakout splintering the proper procedure is to backup the stock with a piece of scrap, with either a clamp if the work is large, or a vise if it is small.

Using auger bits presents a different problem, because the point will always break through before the cutter lips. To avoid splintering when using these kinds of bits, drill the stock from both sides. The exposed point in the first operation will mark the center of the hole on the opposite side. This makes it easy to complete the job accurately. However, there will not be too much wood left for the pilot screw to grip during the second operation. When drilling in this way it is wise to be careful, or the hole will not be bored cleanly.

both sides of the workpiece on a common centerline. This way, you can drill an 8-inch hole with a drill press having a 4-inch quill travel. Or, you can use extension bits, which are much longer than regular bits. First, you bore a hole to the maximum depth of the quill stroke. Then you raise the work table until the bit bottoms out in the first hole, and you drill again. Although it's rare to drill such a long hole, it is sometimes required. For instance, you might want to hollow out a cypress knee for an electric cord to form a lamp.

Power is supplied to the spindle by an electric motor attached to a movable plate located at the back of the machine's head. This plate may be hinged or mounted on twin shafts so it can be adjusted. The adjustment is necessary to change the belt's position and tension. On most drill presses, the

belt runs from a step-pulley on the motor shaft, to a similar pulley on top of the spindle. You change the rpm of the spindle by moving the belt to various positions on the pulleys.

The length of the column depends a lot on whether the machine is a free-standing or bench model. Most models have a column secured on the bottom to a heavy, cast-iron base. This is often called the "lower," or "bottom" table. The main table, where work is placed for most normal operations, moves up and down the column and locks at any point. Often, you can swivel the main table out of the way and use the bottom table to support bulky workpieces. Some better machines also have tilting tables for various types of angular drilling and drilling into the end of a workpiece. The work is usually secured to the table with clamps.

A drill press has a variety of controls. The "quill lock" secures the quill in any extended position, to hold the tool in the chuck stationary. You need to lock the quill when performing operations like routing, shaping, and using a drum sander, where the work is moved into the tool. A "depth control" limits quill travel to allow you to drill holes of a certain depth. This comes in handy when drilling holes to make a dowel joint, which is often used when joining boards edge-to-edge.

The "quill feed" consists of one or more levers that are used to move the quill and chuck downward for drilling. When you release the feed lever, the quill normally returns to a neutral position. Better machines have an adjustment to compensate for the different length and weight of tools in the chuck. The quill return should be smooth and quick, without bounce or force.

Efficiency of a drill press depends upon its speed range and the number of speeds available. Various operations require different speeds. Metals call for slow speeds, while wood drilling may require a variety of speeds, depending upon the density of the wood. Routing and shaping are done most efficiently at very high speeds. For drum sanding, the speed must be a good match for the density of the wood and the sanding sleeve's abrasive quality.

Speed adjustments are made either of two ways. The oldest method uses step or cone pulleys, which let you change the position of the belt to attain a specific speed. Each time a different speed is required, you must move the belt and retension the motor to prevent slippage. A newer method provides infinitely variable speeds, by way of a mechanical speed-changing wheel or electronic circuits. The electronic method is the most expensive of the two and is commonly found on machines designed for the small shop. For utmost flexibility, a variable-speed mechanism is a must, especially if you plan to use many accessories.

Drill presses come in a wide variety of sizes and shapes, and some models have better advantages than others. Bench, floor, radial, and portable models are available. Bench and floor models are the same, except for the size of the column. The longer column of the floor model increases vertical capacity for working with large stock. More important is the fact that floor models take up less space in a small shop because bench models must be mounted on a sturdy stand or take up valuable bench space.

Radial drill presses are fairly new. This type of machine has the head and motor plate mounted at opposite ends of a horizontally mounted, heavy steel tube. The tube can travel back and forth, swivel, and swing up and down. In fact, you can position the head in any location within the arm's range of travel. The advantage is that the maximum distance from the spindle to the column (throat dimension) is greater than that of conventional tools. Also, the sliding head permits a wide number of operations that would be difficult on a regular drill press. Drilling a hole at an angle, for example, is simply a matter of tilting the machine's head to the desired position.

Portable drill presses are also relatively new. These tiny presses fill the gap between large, standard machines, and handheld power drills. These lightweights weigh only about 10 pounds, but they have a head, column, and base, plus a built-in motor and variable-speed mechanism. Small and compact , these tools can store neatly in a cabinet or closet, and can be carried to wherever needed. They are not substitutes for a full-size machine, but they are handy where space is limited and cost is an important factor. These small drill presses give you automatic accuracy for hole drilling and drum sanding, where use of a handheld drill could cause mistakes.

Drill press size and capacity is expressed as twice the distance from the column to the spindle. A 15-inch drill press, for instance, can drill to the center of a 15-inch wide panel.

Chuck capacity is often expressed as the largest and smallest shank that can be gripped. Usually, this capacity on the high end is ½-inch, although this only refers to the shank diameter of the bit, and not to the maximum size of the hole that can be drilled. Most drill bits have shanks that are smaller than their cutting heads. Spade bits, for example, can drill holes up to 1½ inches in diameter, but their shanks fit comfortably in a ½-inch chuck. Hole saws and fly cutters have extremely small shanks in comparison to the size of the hole they can drill. Holes as large as 6 inches can be cut in wood with a fly cutter, and a hole saw can bore holes up to 3 inches in diameter. The low-end rating of a drill press chuck tells you the smallest diameter the chuck can grip securely. Zero to ½ inch means that the chuck can grip anything from a hair to a ½-inch shank. A $\frac{1}{16}$-to ½-inch chuck can't hold anything less than $\frac{1}{16}$-inch in diameter. A low-end capacity of $\frac{1}{16}$-inch isn't a big drawback for woodworking, but higher-quality tools usually have a zero low end.

Chuck-to-table and chuck-to-base capacities are also usually mentioned in drill press specifications. They tell you the maximum size of the work that can be placed under the head. All machines give you enough of this type of capacity to be functional through a wide range of operations. Floor models give the most capacity, because their columns are longer. Some bench models, however, have heads that can swing 180 degrees. If the machine is positioned correctly, you can swing the head so that the spindle clears the edge of the bench or stand supporting the tool. Vertical capacity then becomes the distance from the chuck to the floor — very useful if you want to drill into the top of a chair leg or the edge of a door.

A drill press needs little shop space, and this is especially true of floor

A QUICK LOOK AT SOME COMMON DRILL BITS

NAME	DRILL TYPE	USES
Twist drill	H,P,D	bores small diameter holes in wood and metal
Spade bit	P,D	bores holes up to 1½ inches in wood
Auger bit	H	bores holes up to 1½ inches in wood
Expansion bit	H	bores holes up to 3 inches in wood
Fly cutter	D	bores large diameter holes, up to 6 inches in wood
Hole saw	D	bores large holes up to 3 inches
Mortising chisel	D	cuts mortises
Plug cutter	D,P	forms short dowels or plugs
Countersink	H,P,D	makes depressions for wood screw heads
H-Hand drill/P-Portable electric drill/D-Drill press		

models. You can place any drill press against a wall or in a corner without limiting its usefulness. Radial types, however, need clearance to swing the head 180 degrees, and there must be some room behind the column to allow for the back-and-forth movement of the head.

Room for the operator is only required in front of the machine; space to the right and left can be minimal for routine work. But, of course, if you wish to drill dowel holes for joining wood slabs of a 5-foot-long table, you need 5 feet of space on either side of the machine. The press should be positioned in accordance with the particular tasks you'll do on it. Floor model drill presses are not designed to be mounted on casters. They have heavy bases to fix them solidly to provide a stable platform. Bench models, with their lighter weight, can be made mobile without affecting their normal work range.

A drill press may look mild-mannered, but it can injure the careless operator. Always clamp the work to the table, because if the drill or tool snags in the work, it can spin with enough force to break your fingers. The heavy motors of floor models have a lot of torque, so clamping the work down is especially important when drilling large holes. Be very careful when using fly cutters. These tools consist of a vertical shank connected to a horizontal arm equipped with a cutting bit. They're

adjustable tools for cutting holes in wood and metal. Although fly cutters are used at low speeds, the cutting bit is only a fast blur. It can damage an operator severely. And, if you have long hair, you can actually scalp yourself if it's caught in the spinning tool. Long hair should be bound behind the head when working with this machine.

After a stationary power saw, the next machine you buy should be a drill press. The wide variety of jobs that can be done with a full-function machine are impressive. But even smaller models are valuable for their hole-drilling accuracy. When you begin working with a drill press, you'll wonder how you ever got along without it.

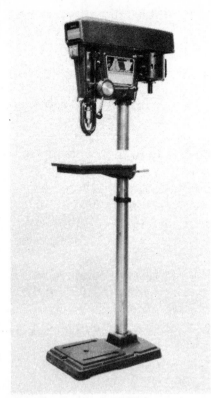

Craftsman's 2137N

Craftsman's 2137N, from Sears, Roebuck and Co., is a 15½-inch drill press that's full of features for the advanced woodworker. This full-function, floor-model tool is designed specifically for the home shop, but it's also acceptable for light industrial use.

Spindle travel capacity is 4 inches, and the standard chuck capacity runs from 0 to ½ inch. Specially designed step pulleys and a belt system provide eight specific speeds from 380 to 8550 rpm. This gives you extra speeds at both the high and low range. These extra speeds contribute to very efficient operation. You can use the

lowest speeds for drilling large holes in metal, and the highest speeds for smoother, faster routing and shaping cuts.

The standard 10x12-inch table doesn't tilt, but an optional tilting table is available at extra cost. Other features include a scale at the side of the head, which details how to position the belt on various pulleys to attain a particular speed. There's a work light over the table, and the push-pull power switch has a removable locking device. Length of the column (and length of the work that can be put under the machine) is just slightly over 4 feet. This is enough for virtually any project. You can also choose from a full line of accessories for metal and woodworking operations: planers, routing chucks, mortising bits, and even a dovetail attachment. Although this drill press is not as heavy or powerful as industrial machines, it's a nice tool for anyone interested in turning out quality work. Approx. Price: $290.00

Toolkraft's 4452 floor-model drill press is chock full of built-in conveniences. It's different from conventional machines in that all mechanisms necessary for motor operation are located in the head when you buy the machine. It has an electronic, solid-state, variable-speed control. You have no belts to change, and speed is adjustable by simply turning a dial. The head rotates for angular drilling. Also, a high-speed spindle protrudes from the top of the head. With the head in its normal position, the spindle has variable speeds ranging from 600 to 2500 rpm. By rotating the head to bring the second spindle into working position, the range becomes 4000 to 18,000 rpm. This high-speed spindle has speeds comparable to machines designed specifically for shaping and routing. So, you can have a wide workscope without buying separate machines.

Spindle travel is a full 6 inches, and chuck capacity is 0-to ½-inch. You can't tilt the 10⅝x14-inch table, but it doesn't matter because the

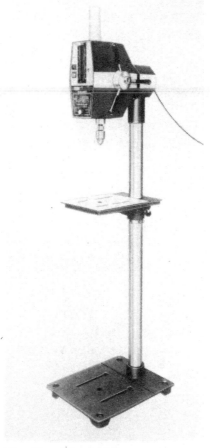

Toolkraft's 4452

head tilts. One excellent safety feature is that the machine won't start unless the handle of the chuck key (which tightens and loosens the grip on the bits) is inserted in a hole in the machine's head. You can't accidentally leave the key in the chuck, allowing it to spin out dangerously when you turn the machine on. And you can hide the key to child-proof the drill press.

If you're looking for all the conveniences, this is a good drill press to buy. And this full-function, compact machine is also available in a bench model (#4453). Approx. Price: (4452) $400.00

Sprunger's DP1218 is a 12-inch, bench-model drill press that was designed with two things in mind—full function capability and low price. Physically, it's small. But it handles most of the accessory equipment available, including a mortising attachment.

The spindle can travel 3¼ inches and chuck capacity is ½ inch. This tool stands slightly less than 30 inches high, but it has both a lower base and adjustable 8x7-inch table. With the table swung aside, the maximum distance from the chuck to the base is a bit under 13 inches. These are small dimensions, yet this press can handle most of the jobs its larger, heavier counterparts can do. Using step pulleys, you can select from nine speeds ranging from 600 to 5200 rpm. This speed range does limit routing and shaping

Sprunger's DP1218

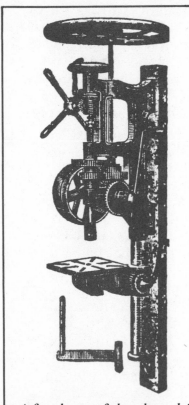

A forebear of the shop drill press was this 1916 "Combination Post Drill". Wards listed this drill at $38.00. It could do everything that a modern drill press can do.

operations, but it's fine for general woodworking.

A larger, 14-inch version of the same machine is offered as DP1418. Bearings on this machine are supposedly "lubricated-for-life," although the "lifetime" usually depends upon how long and hard the machine is used. This model has a larger quill, table, and base. Other than that, it's the same as Sprunger's DP1218. Both are functional and work out well where shop space is limited. Approx. Price: (DP1218) $225.00

Rockwell's 11-072 is an industrial, radial drill press that's as clean and compact as any such tool can be. And it's as rugged as this reputable manufacturer could make it. This machine satisfies both the amateur and professional who are interested in the flexibility of a radial drill press. With it, you can drill to the center of a 32-inch circle, and like all radial drill presses, the head is adjustable in all directions. You can swing it 360 degrees, and tilt it 90 degrees to the left and right. And these adjustments can be made individually or in combination to give you the maximum in workscope.

Spindle travel is 3⅝ inches and the chuck capacity is ½ inch. Step pulleys provide four speeds from 700 to 4700 rpm. Since this is a bench model, the distance between the base table and the chuck is a short 14⅜ inches —

Rockwell's 11-072

somewhat limiting for larger work. The chuck key has a nice safety feature. Spring loaded, it automatically ejects from the chuck. So, you can't accidentally leave it in the chuck while the machine is turned on.

Due to the radial design of this press, you have to move the table out of the way for certain operations. The basic table measures only 8½x9 inches, but the saw also comes with a 15⅞x23⅞-inch chipboard table. It can be attached to the press for larger operations. The Rockwell 11-072 is a well-designed radial drill press that's built to please. Approx. Price: $260.00

Shopmate's T2741-11 is so small that you could almost store it in a drawer. This drill press isn't made to bore through 6 inches of lumber, but it lets you do a lot of drilling with more precision than would be possible with a handheld drill. It's a good tool where there is minimum shop space, but to be happy with it, you have to recognize it's limitations. It can handle a few accessories like drum sanders and wire brushes, but it doesn't accept router or shaper bits or equipment for mortising chisels.

Overall size is only 18 inches tall by 10 inches deep, and the whole outfit weighs but 12 pounds. However, the built-in, double-insulated motor provides the power to drill a ⅜-inch hole through

Shopmate's T2741-11

steel and a ¾-inch hole through wood. It's definitely not a toy, despite the small size.

Quill travel is a little over 2¼ inches and chuck size is ⅜ inch. And you can dial any speed you want between 700 and 1800 rpm. Also, the tool cannot be operated unless you place the chuck key handle in a slot in the motor housing. This is a safety feature that's becoming standard on better drill presses. Distance from the chuck to the base is under 10 inches, and this base serves as the standard table. But you can buy an optional, tilting table (T8026-11) that allows you to drill angular holes. This drill press is no substitute for full-function machines. It does, however, fill a need when portability and compactness are important. Approx. Price: $65.00

The Rockwell 15-069 is an industrially-rated 15-inch drill press that has the heft and power to handle all basic drill operations. It also accepts a wide range of accessories. Four step pulleys give you a selection of 680, 1250, 2400, and 4600 rpm. The chuck has a 0 to ½-inch capacity. Quill stroke is 4$\frac{7}{16}$ inches, which is about standard for other 15-inch machines. And drilling a ⅜-inch hole in steel or ½-inch hole in cast iron are not unreasonable.

All working mechanisms are well-guarded, and the spring-loaded chuck key ejects automatically, so you can't forget it in the chuck when you flick the switch. It also has a tilting table that's slotted and edge-ledged for easy clamping of work. This is a serious tool for people

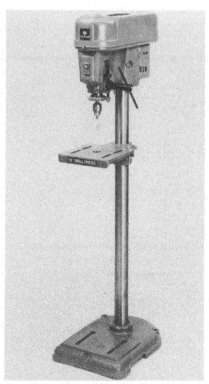

Rockwell's 15-069

who use a drill press to its fullest advantage. Approx. Price: $350.00

The AM&T 2532 is a radial drill press that's basic in both design and in price. At the price, don't expect massive castings or anticipate super power or extensive features of higher-priced tools. It's not recommended for routing, and it doesn't accept mortising attachments. It is, however, a radial drill press with excellent capacity (16 inches from spindle to column), and which performs in fine fashion for vertical and all sorts of angular drilling. Spindle stroke is 2 inches and the Jacobs geared chuck has a capacity of $\frac{5}{64}$ to ½ inch. Distance from spindle to base is 10 inches. This is one of the no-frills tools manufacturered by AM&T. Many have been sold and much has been accomplished with them—even though they're not fancy. Approx. Price: $70.00

AM&T's 2532

Drill Press Accessories

Beside the regular bits used for simple hole drilling, there is a wide variety of accessories that can be used on a drill press. These bits and tools fall into two categories: those which can be gripped in the conventional, three-jawed chuck, and those that require special chucks. The former fit on any drill press, but those requiring special chucks must be purchased from the manufacturer of your particular press. Many of these specialized tools are quite expensive. If you don't check for fit before buying, you could be throwing your money to the wind.

Chuck Accessories

Twist drills are usually designed for metal, but can be used for some wood drilling. The sizes of these drills are expressed in either fractions, decimals or letters, depending upon the manufacturer. Fractional drills are commonly available from 1/64- to 1-inch, with increments of 1/64-inch between sizes. Numbered drills, with the size designated as a decimal, cover the sizes between the fractional drills up to .228 inch. Letter drills complement the fractional drills from .234 to .413 inch. This admittedly confusing system arose out of the wide variety of tasks the drills perform. Fractional drills are the most common and most available. Numbered drills can be used for modeling work in very small material. Letter drills are mostly used in tool-and-die shops, and are not required by the average shop owner.

Spade bits are specially designed for drilling clean, smooth holes in hard and soft wood. Sizes range from 3/8 to 1½ inches in diameter. You can buy them in sets or individually. They are different from other drills in that they break the rule that states: "Slow speed for large holes and fast speeds for small ones." These bits work best, regardless of their size, at a speed between 1500 and 2000 rpm. Superior bits are manufactured by Irwin Hand Tools.

Brad point bits are designed for drill press drilling and offer many advantages. They're more expensive than spade bits, but drill a cleaner, more precise hole. These bits can also be used through a doweling jig (a device for precisely centering holes), where a spade bit cannot. And the special fluting clears away the chips better in deep holes. If brad point bits are operated at moderate speeds under 1500 rpm, you can get excellent results and prolong their useful life.

Hole saws are specially formed holders that can grip any one of a number of circular bands that have saw teeth cut into one edge. One

TWIST DRILLS EQUIVALENCY CHART	
Sizes: Inches-Numbers-Letters	Decimal Equivalents
1/8	.1250
29	.1360
9/64	.1406
25	.1495
5/32	.1562
20	.1610
11/64	.1719
15	.1800
3/16	.1875
10	.1935
13/64	.2031
5	.2055
7/32	.2187
A	.2340
15/64	.2344
C	.2420
1/4	.2500
F	.2570
17/64	.2656
J	.2770
9/32	.2812
M	.2950
19/64	.2968
N	.3020
5/16	.3125
P	.3230
21/64	.3281
R	.3390
11/32	.3437
T	.3580
23/64	.3594
U	.3620
3/8	.3750

product, for example, has seven such bands and can form holes from 1 to 2½ inches in diameter through ¾-inch stock. Other varieties of this saw can cut through up to 1¾-inch wood stock. Arco Products is one of the best manufacturers of such equipment.

Drum sanders are just rubber drums that grip replaceable abrasive sleeves. These drums are used for smoothing straight and curved edges, and on the drill press can be adjusted to sand off the rough spots in internal cutouts. Drum diameter ranges from about ½ inch on up to about 3 inches.

Drum rasps are round Stanley Surform tools that function much like any hand rasp for woodworking. They are excellent for bringing any straight or curved edge to the point where final smoothing can be done with sandpaper and a sander. Also, these tools are often used on flat or curved surfaces to produce a rustic texture. They measure 2 inches in diameter and may not be used at speeds greater than 4000 rpm.

Plug cutters are used to cut short, wooden cylinders that are used to conceal screw heads in fine furniture. Sometimes these plugs are sanded flush and finished; often they are allowed to project from the surface of the work to provide additional decorative detail. Stanley makes a wide variety of diameter sizes. Rockwell makes a set of plug cutters that produces a longer plug, a convenient way to obtain a

set of dowels for gluing and joinery work.

Specialized Attachment Accessories

Shaping/routing cutters are tools which require a special chuck or adaptor that is mounted in the drill press spindle in place of the regular chuck. Besides the special chuck and cutters, you also need to install a special fence on the table for shaping work. When organized like this, the drill press is a reasonable substitute for a shaping machine. It's no match for a full-function shaper, because the drill press lacks speed and flexibility in this area. The drill press does, however, work out quite well for occasionally putting a fancy edge on a table, if you recognize its limitations.

Routing adapters are used with flat, straight cutting bits

that resemble flat-end drilling bits. You can use these on a drill press to form dadoes (U-shaped cuts or troughs) and rabbets (L-shaped cuts) — both used for making joints. Usually, these cuts are made on a stationary power saw, but there are times when such a saw isn't available, or when the operations are more convenient on the drill press. You can also use these bits to incise or decorate wood surfaces, and to perform some of the simpler routing operations.

When using shaping/routing bits in a drill press, many people make the mistake of making a cut that's too deep for the machine to handle. It's asking a lot of a drill press to cut a ½-inch dado in any material in one pass, especially if the wood is dense, like maple and birch. You should perform this operation in two or three passes, extending the quill between passes until the desired depth is achieved. Even when using a tool specifically designed for these jobs, you only obtain accurate work if you're careful.

Mortising equipment is a means to making a

Stanley's Drum Rasp

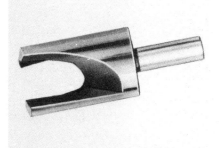

Stanley's Plug Cutter

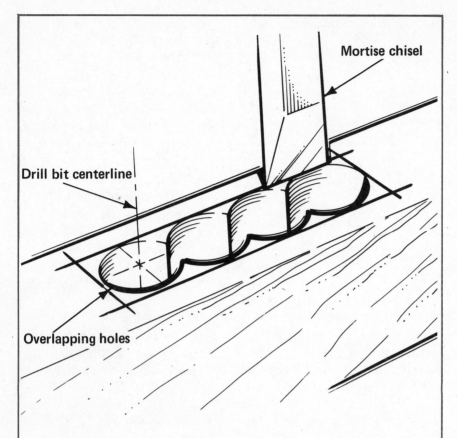

Mortise chisel

Drill bit centerline

Overlapping holes

Mortise-tenon joints are one of the marks of the experienced woodworker. Because of their strength, they are much used in professional cabinet and furniture work. The tenon is a rectangular, projecting piece that is usually cut with a saw and then sized to fit with a plane; while the mortise is the hole in which this projecting piece fits. Over the years several methods have been devised to create this rectangular space. Chiseling out the wood is probably the most basic way to do this; while using a mortising attachment on a drill press is the easiest and most modern.

But if you don't have a drill press, there is another way to create the mortise hole. This is done with a hand or portable drill fitted with spade or auger bits. It is an extremely fast method of producing these holes.

First mark out the size of the mortise you want to cut, being careful to make the lines square. Mark a center line between the two long edges. Cut around the outline with a sharp knife. Using an auger or spade bit, drill overlapping holes along the center line. Size of the bit will depend upon the width of the mortise. If the mortise is blind (does not go through the stock), a stop-gauge must be used to control the depth of the holes. A chisel is used to clean out the waste remaining after the boring is done. The result will be a clean, neatly square mortise.

rectangular hole in wood to form a particularily strong joint. This is a special device that locks at the end of the drill press spindle and, together with the regular chuck, permits both to grip a square, hollow chisel and an off-beat drill bit. As the quill is moved downward, the bit rotates *inside* the chisel and forms a hole while the chisel cleans out the corners. The result is a square cavity that can be made larger by repeating the procedure until a hole as large as necessary is made.

The mortise-tenon joint is one of the classics of all woodworking, producing an exceptionally strong connection between wood components. A mortising accessory for the drill press makes this joint easier for anyone to do. Mortising bits and chisels come in various sizes, ranging from ¼ inch on up, and are readily available. It may be, however, that a certain brand of equipment will only fit one particular type of press. You should check carefully before any purchase.

The tenon—a rectangular projection which fits into a mortise and is the component part of the joint— is usually cut with a saw. One common error is to make this joint too large, making it necessary to force the joint and create stresses that can cause splits and cracks. This tenon must slide into place—not too tightly or too loosely. The best procedure is to make the mortise first and then size the tenon to fit into it.

Shaving Tools

Hand planes are precision woodworking tools—
be the work heavy "hogging" cuts or
slices as thin as a sheet of paper.

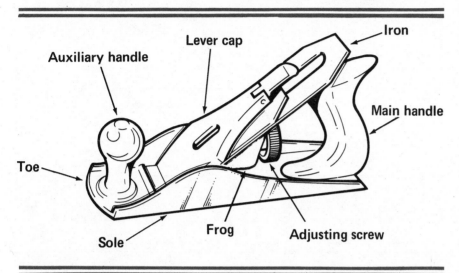

Lever cap

Auxiliary handle

Iron

Main handle

Toe

Frog

Adjusting screw

Sole

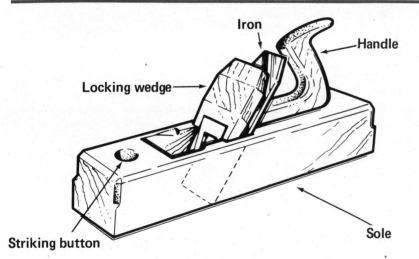

Iron

Locking wedge

Handle

Striking button

Sole

Hand Planes

imaginable. Sure, there are power tools that can duplicate the hand plane's results, but there are few tools that can give you the same kind of satisfaction.

Hand planes are a fairly recent hand tool, dating from Roman times. Yet they shave wood better than any other hand tool. Some tool collectors are so enamored with the plane that they devote all their energy to the acquisition of odd, old planes. As a common everyday tool, the hand plane's popularity has declined slowly since about 1850. And since the end of World War II, the decline has hit bottom—to the point where many carpenters carry only a small block plane in their tool box. This small plane has been relegated to trimming small imperfections during the final fitting of cabinets and casements. At one time, every carpenter had a separate plane for specific shaving and smoothing operations, but now the plane has been reduced to one small trimming tool.

Yet, there has been a revived interest in the plane—due mainly to a renaissance in handcraft woodworking. Far too many

The two basic problems facing a woodworker are cutting wood to an approximate size, and squaring and smoothing it.

The first job is for the saw, while the second is the hand plane's duty. A hand plane can handle any smoothing or shaving operation

technical schools and shops get students involved in power tool operation without first giving them a basic knowledge of corresponding hand tools. There are distinct advantages to knowing how to use a hand plane well. First is personal satisfaction—the on-hands experience that only hand tools can give. Second, any craftsman who knows how to hand plane is better able to do fine machine work simply because he understands the process better. Third, it is often easier to hand plane because no electricity or setup time is required—just a bit of elbow grease. And, you often obtain a better finish with a hand plane than with a machine. For all these reasons you should consider purchasing and learning to use a hand plane. You may find the experience very rewarding.

Planes are based on a simple concept. A metal blade or cutter, called an "iron," is fitted inside a metal or wooden body. This is held or "bedded" at a certain angle so that the sharpened edge of the blade projects through the base of the body to cut or shear away wood. The amount that the iron projects below the base or "sole" of the plane determines the thickness of the shaving that will be removed. On planes with wooden bodies this adjustment is made with a hammer; planes with metal bodies are adjusted by a series of screws and levers. Such adjustments are

A QUICK LOOK AT HAND PLANES

NAME	TYPICAL USES
Scrub/Roughing Plane	initial rough shaping of stock—heavy hogging cuts—blade ground convex—sole 10 inches long
Bench Planes: **Jack Plane**	brings surface of stock to trueness and smoothness—first plane used after scrub—12-14 inches long
Jointer Plane	trues up long and critical edges for gluing—typical sole length in excess of 20 inches
Smooth Plane	brings surface to final finish—cleans up in close, confined areas—6-9 inches long
Rabbet/Fillister Plane	workpiece—may use fences and spurs for crosscutting or specialized work
Plough Plane	cuts grooves and slots in faces for panel construction—uses interchangeable cutters of different width in same body
Block Plane	cuts endgrain—low blade angle allows clean endgrain cutting

necessary to make sure that the iron's edge is square with the sole of the plane and that the tool removes the correct amount of wood. No matter how expensive a plane may be, if you can't make these adjustments correctly, the plane is useless.

Wood-bodied planes are favored in Europe in much the same way that bow saws are favored there—as holdovers from a tradition. Although wood-bodied planes perform the same as their metal-bodied cousins, there is a certain knack required to adjust them. Once you master this, though, they will do the same shaving task as metal planes with many separate adjustments. Some wooden planes now have adjusting mechanisms incorporated into their design. Reform wood planes also have provisions for adjusting the throat opening, via a sliding plate in the sole.

The purpose of this

NAME	TYPICAL USES
Spoke Shave	shapes round and long staves — used for final fitting of hammer handles
Scraper Plane	not true plane — finishing tool used for surface work — blade held vertically or inclined forward — burnished edge
Combination/Multi-Plane	uses vast number of interchangeable cutters — will do: plough, bead, dado, rabbet, and tongue & groove work — replaces single purpose planes
Compass Plane	curved and shaped cuts — flexible sole allows it to fit convex/concave shapes — 10 inches long with metal sole
Palm/Finger Plane	delicate instrument work — fine detail shaving with close tolerance — used where accuracy and not amount of wood is important
Toothing Plane	rough up surfaces prior to application of face veneers
Bullnose Plane	cleans up work surface close to vertical obstructions — iron fixed forward and close to front end of plane

is to aid in curling and breaking up wood chips. Wood-bodied planes are usually finely crafted tools with beautiful finishes. They often get as much attention in their manufacture as a piece of fine furniture.

Metal planes are the favorite in North America. Aside from their greater ease of adjustment, they have other features. Instead of resting on the body of the plane (as is the case with wood planes), the iron rests on a mechanism called a "frog." This frog is adjustable and can control the opening size of the "throat," the slot cut into the bottom of the sole where the blade projects. This helps to prevent the occurrence of "tear out," a situation where the wood is raised instead of smoothly shaved off by the plane. When using metal planes, it's important that the surface of the sole or base of the plane be uniformly even and smooth. A plane with a washed out or uneven surface is next to useless. All adjusting mechanisms on the plane must be free from binding. If these adjustments aren't made correctly, the plane will gouge or score the wood and leave an even worse surface than was there before the planing.

The metal plane isn't popular only because you can adjust one easily. Some designs accept a wide variety of different shape and size irons. This means that some planes, especially multiplanes, can replace a whole variety of specialized individual planes, each of which produces a separate, differently-shaped cut. Although the multiplane has largely been replaced by the stationary shaper, many fine craftsmen still choose to work with this tool.

Because of the hand plane's long tradition and the fact that each kind does a different task, a long list of names has evolved to describe the various types. Sizes and names have become relatively standardized in metal planes, but for wood-bodied planes the names can be somewhat arbitrary. The following is a discussion of some different types and sizes of planes, and some of the products that go into each category. In each heading you'll find a discussion of that plane's particular workscope. By comparing the workscope to your own needs, you can determine which planes you require.

The Scrub Or Roughing Plane

This type of plane is used for the initial, rough shaping of wood. It removes a lot of wood. A roughing plane's iron is ground slightly convex to take deep and heavy "hogging" cuts. Commercially-made scrub planes are usually wood-bodied, and have a 10x2-inch sole dimension. This kind of plane also usually beds an iron about 1¼ inches wide. Many craftsmen simply convert an old jack plane or smooth plane for this type of work by grinding the iron to a convex shape. If you have a used plane available, this is a good, money-saving idea.

The Ulmia is a good-quality scrub plane, available from most mail order tool houses. It exhibits good workmanship and top-notch materials. The wedge, or wooden insert, that holds the iron in place is retained by a metal crosspiece—a feature not found on all wooden planes. The sole measures 9 inches long and it beds a plane iron 1⅚ inches wide. This is only one of Ulmia's fine, hammer-adjustable planes. It's available from Woodcraft Supply under the stock number 16C04-0. Approx. Price: $19.50

The E.C.E. scrub plane is produced in Germany. This fine-quality tool exhibits very good workmanship and E.C.E.'s unique form of castellated joinery between the red beech body and white beech sole. Length is 9½ inches, and the iron is 1¼

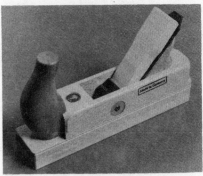

Ulmia Scrub Plane

E.C.E. Scrub Plane

inches wide. It's available from both Garrett Wade (#24P07.01) and Woodworker's Supply (#507-006). Approx. Price: (24PO7.01) $26.00

Fine wooden planes have one special point—each maker has a unique joinery system by which the sole is joined to the body of the plane. This complicated joinery is done automatically and is a tribute to man's ingenuity. The E.C.E. Primus Company, for example, uses a form of "castellated joinery." An edge view resembles the top of a medieval castle or a series of square-topped interlocking indentations. Ulmia uses a system they call "corrugated joinery." This gives a side appearance of a rolling ripple to the mating surface. Denmark's A.B.C. Company uses a combination of "sawtooth and corrugated joinery." Whatever the system in use the purpose is the same: cause an interlocking face and increase the glue area. It is possible, if you know wooden planes well, to recognize the manufacturer even if all the identification is removed, solely by the method of joinery employed.

Bench Planes

"Bench plane" is a catchall term that encompasses a whole series of planes. As the name implies, the purpose of these kinds and sizes of planes is to smooth and prepare wood at the bench. They're not confined to this use, however, and are often

Type		Length, Inches	Iron Width, Inches
03	Smooth	9	1¾
04	Smooth	9¾	2
04½	Smooth	10¼	2⅜
05	Jack	14	2
05½	Jack	14¾	2⅜
06	Fore	18	2⅜
07	Jointer	22	2⅜
08	Jointer	24	2⅝

nuts make the mechanism work smoothly, and with less wear over the long run. Steel is less costly, but is not the best material for this use. The various types of bench planes are generally used in a certain order on a workpiece. Here's how it goes:

Jack planes are used after rough planing with the scrub plane. They are generally 12 to 14 inches long and 2½ to 3 inches wide. You use a jack plane to bring the piece of wood to an initial smoothness and trueness. Many

used on large workpieces and in the field.

Metal bench planes have a standardized numbering system. A number 05 jack plane, for example, would be virtually the same size and shape if it were purchased from Stanley of America, Record-Ridgeway, Great Neck, or Stanley of the UK. What does vary is quality. There are many metal planes sold that exhibit intolerable quality and shoddy workmanship. On metal bench planes of cheaper manufacture, the soles are finished with an abrasive belt rather than by surface grinding. The result is that the "mouth," or slot where the iron projects, is washed out and rounded. The mouth area just ahead of the iron must maintain good contact with the work being planed. If the area is washed out, try to close down the mouth by adjusting the frog forward.

You can't obtain high-class work with a plane having this defect, unless the sole is made perfectly flat. The cost of doing this is prohibitive, so it's much better to buy a quality plane to begin with. Cheaper planes also have adjusting nuts made of steel. Brass is the traditional material for the nuts, and is also a natural bearing surface. Brass adjustment

The "bedding angle" or pitch at which the iron is set into the body of the plane is very important. The lower the angle the easier the cut; but the more likely the chance of tear out ahead of the iron. The higher the bedding angle the greater force necessary to move the plane; but the less chance of tear out ahead of the iron. Most common bench planes today have a bedding angle of 45 degrees, called "common pitch." This is about perfect for softwoods and preliminary planing, but it is not the optimum angle for hardwood. In the latter case, an angle of 50 degrees or "York pitch" is best. There are still some wood planes available that are bedded at this pitch. A very low bedding angle of 20 degrees or less is required in the block, mitre, and shoulder planes. These planes are mostly used for endgrain work and this pitch is better for this kind of cutting.

Block planes always have a problem with tear out. The hole where the iron protrudes through the sole is called the mouth, and by keeping this area as small as possible tear out can be minimized. A good block plane will have a sliding plate in the toe section which is for adjusting the mouth size. In the case of metal bench planes, the mouth opening is adjusted by moving the frog. A small captive screw moves the frog backward or forward in the plane body and by changing the point at which the iron is bedded in the body adjusts the opening of the mouth. Adjusting the mouth opening in a wooden plane has traditionally been a problem. One fairly recent innovation has been the addition of a sliding plate set into the sole ahead of the iron. This allows the mouth to be adjusted in the same way as block planes. Wood bench planes incorporating this particular innovation are known as "reform planes."

craftsmen keep two irons for this plane. One, used first, is ground slightly convex to let you take heavy cuts without leaving unsightly lines on the board (as would be left by sharp corners). The second iron is ground more or less square, but has the corners removed. This is used to bring the surface to further smoothness.

Jointer planes are used after the jack plane to true up critical edges for gluing or a perfect fit. A jointer plane used for this is often called a "trying" plane, but the term jointer can apply to any bench plane over 20 inches long. The long sole of these planes allows the user to true up local imperfections in the board, and get a perfectly true edge along the entire length of the piece. The extra length lets the sole span depressions, rather than follow them as shorter planes do.

Smooth planes are the most useful. Any bench plane from 6 to 9 inches long and 2 to 3½ inches wide is called a smooth plane. This kind of plane is easy to use and feels good in the hand. It's used for smoothing out slight imperfections and bringing the surface to a final finish. The typically small size of this plane makes it good for cleaning up in confined areas and ridding the wood of minor imperfections.

All three types of planes could be used to join two boards together. After scrub planing, you would use a jack plane to true and smooth the surfaces. Next, the edges to

be glued together would be "tried" with a jointer plane. When the edges were square and smooth, they would be butt jointed with glue. After the glue has dried, the joint would be lightly planed with the jack plane. The smooth plane would then be employed to bring the surface to a final finish.

———————————

Stanley Tools now manufactures a fine line of bench planes. Until quite recently, the firm of Record-Ridgeway of the United Kingdom was the only manufacturer of quality metal bench planes. Stanley Tools, like many other domestic manufacturers, was drawn in the direction of mass merchandising and lower prices. The result was metal planes that were cheap, but didn't work well. If you wanted a good plane, you had

to order a Record-Ridgeway tool from a catalog house. Happily, Stanley has improved its line of planes. The high quality and availability of these Stanley tools has caused them to become the best example of metal bench planes.

These new planes have a number of features. The body castings are of a higher grade iron, cast in much finer sand. This results in much smoother unmachined cavities on the top surface. The handles are hardwood, rather than plastic, and the front handle is much higher than before, in the traditional design. The adjusting nut is now brass instead of iron. This, combined with an improved adjusting mechanism, allows much smoother control. Most important, the soles of these planes are ground to absolute flatness. The entire redesign results in planes that anyone can be proud of.

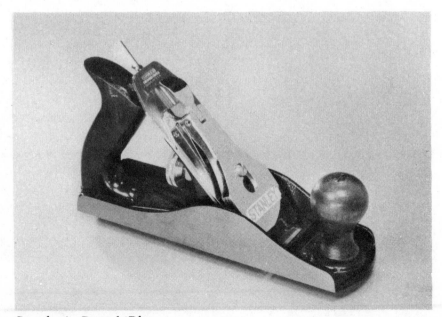

Stanley's Bench Plane

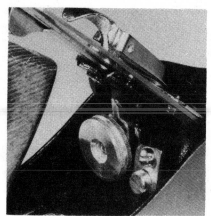

Close-up of Stanley bench plane's brass adjusting nut.

Stanley bench planes are made in sizes ranging from an 03 smooth, measuring 9 inches long, to a huge, 24-inch, 07 jointer. Regardless of size, all the planes look and work the same. Blade height is adjusted by way of a large brass nut, just under the blade and ahead of the rear handle. While planing, you can adjust this by turning it with your forefinger. Lateral adjustment of the iron is done with a regulator level that projects from beneath the iron and over the handle. It's easily moved with your thumb while planing.

The iron itself is of quality, chrome-vanadium steel, with excellent edge-holding ability. Throat adjustment is made by moving the die-cast aluminum frog, and on the 06 and 07 planes there is a captive head screw to make this adjustment easier.

Stanley's 04, 05, and 06 planes are also available with a corrugated sole, instead of the normal, smooth type. The value of a corrugated sole is debatable. The claim is that it cuts down the surface area in contact with the work and makes the plane glide easier due to less friction.

It's a common practice to wax or lubricate the sole to make it move smoothly, and the corrugated sole is supposedly better able to retain the wax. Also, when planing resinous wood, a vacuum sometimes forms between the plane's sole and the wood as it comes to smoothness. A corrugated sole is supposed to break this vacuum. Frankly, the value of the corrugated sole is questionable, as is the fact that you should pay extra for it.

Stanley planes are available at just about any hardware store, and if an exotic model is out of stock, the store will order it for you. But, be sure you're getting a plane of recent manufacture that incorporates the above features. One quick way to check this is to see if the adjustment nut is brass or steel. If it's steel, pass up the plane because it is an inferior tool. Approx. Price: (05) $33.00

Wooden Bench Planes

The E.C.E. Primus bench plane represents the best in wood-bodied planes. This plane has the best adjusting mechanism, which features zero backlash. What this means can be seen when a normal plane is adjusted. If the mechanism is reversed from one direction to the other, there is a small amount of backlash that has to be taken up with the adjusting screw before the iron starts to move. Primus planes have a spring-loaded mechanism that holds this backlash in one direction and allows the iron to be raised or lowered by minute increments. It's so sensitive that you can make shaving thickness adjustments to thousandths of an inch.

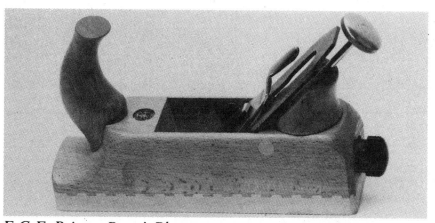

E.C.E. Primus Bench Plane

One disappointment is the lateral regulating mechanism for bringing the iron square with the sole of the plane. It's easier to hammer-adjust this iron for lateral movement, than to use the mechanism. Bulky, cumbersome, and hard to move, the mechanism is hard to adjust because it's held in place by a screw and star washer.

The body is of varnished European beech, and the sole is made of hornbeam. As with all E.C.E. planes, the sole is joined to the body by a unique form of castellated joinery, which increases the glue area and forms an interlocking joint. This plane's sole is 9 inches long, and it beds an iron 1⅞ inches wide. Woodcraft Supply (#17H20-CH), Garrett Wade (#24P02.01), and Woodworker's Supply (#07-001) all carry this fine plane. Approx. Price: (24P02.01) $64.00

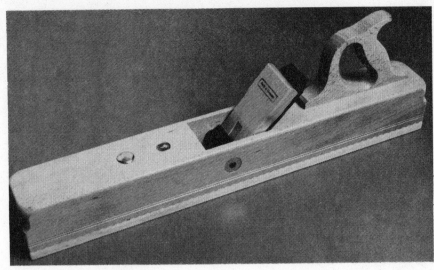

Ulmia Jointer Plane

and the hornbeam sole is laminated with a wavy form of joinery that increases the glue area, while it forms a locking bond. The striking button, used for iron adjustment, is located on the upper body just ahead of the blade. Woodcraft Supply carries this plane as stock #17A01-0. Approx. Price: $45.50

E.C.E.'s Improved Primus plane is another fine product of this company. Adjusting and regulating mechanisms are the same as on other Primus planes, and the criticisms are the same. Technically, this plane is called a "reform plane," incorporating a sliding plate that's let into the sole, just ahead of the mouth. You can

The Ulmia jointer plane is a fine representative sample of the company's entire line of hammer-adjustable planes. Although it takes practice to adjust a plane with a hammer, this type of plane is considerably less expensive than those incorporating the Primus-type adjusting mechanism. In the case of planes like this jointer, which aren't used often, it makes sense to opt for the less expensive models. This plane has a 24-inch sole and beds an iron that's 2⅜ inches wide. The body is of beech,

E.C.E. Improved Primus Plane

adjust the mouth opening by sliding this plate to the rear. However, this plane is so well made that the mouth is rather small as it comes from the factory and works well. If the sole wears down, the mouth opening becomes larger, and you must move the plate to adjust for this wear.

The Improved Primus is made of excellent materials. It has a body of fruitwood and a sole of lignum vitae. The latter is a dense, hard, oily wood that tends to be self-lubricating as it glides over the work. The body of the plane is 8⅞ inches long and it beds a 1⅞-inch-wide iron.

A unique feature of this plane is that the iron is bedded at a York, rather than Common, pitch. Pitch is the angle at which the iron is mounted in the plane. In this case it is 50 degrees instead of the common 45 degrees. This leaves a superior finish when planing hardwoods. It's the only plane that's effective on burl woods, too.

However, it does have one disturbing defect. In spite of the high price, the finish on the wood of this tool leaves something to be desired. It's rough, with disc sanding marks and a bad final finish. Although it doesn't affect the quality of the work, it is esthetically displeasing. Woodcraft Supply (#17J20-CH), Garrett Wade (#24P04.01) and Woodworker's Supply (#507-002) all carry this tool. Approx. Price: (17J20-CH) $62.50

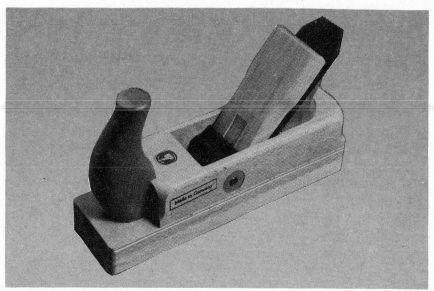
Ulmia Smoothing Plane

Ulmia's general smoothing plane is a good alternative to the Primus, and has a price that doesn't make you shudder. It has typically fine quality and workmanship, and a hammer-adjustable iron. The body is of European beech, with a hornbeam sole attached with corrugated joinery. The body is 9½ inches long and beds an iron 1⅞ inches wide. Woodcraft Supply carries this tool under their catalog #16D03-0. Approx. Price: $24.50

Rabbet/ Fillister Planes

After the jointer or bench plane, the next candidate for a project is the rabbet/fillister plane. You use this type of plane to cut a ledge, or step, along the edge of the wood.

The woodworking terms "rabbet" and "fillister" can be slightly confusing. If the ledge is cut into the face of the work, it's called a rabbet; if it's cut away from the face of the work, it's a fillister. So, the cutout in a picture frame that holds the piece of glass is a fillister, while a similar ledge cut on the outside of the frame would be a rabbet. A common example of a fillister is the glazing bead in a traditional, double-hung window. Much of the wood shapes that are technically rabbets are now cut by machines like the power jointer. But it is sometimes easier to cut them in the traditional manner with a hand plane.

Rabbet planes are offered in a whole spectrum of designs. They range from very simple, square-bodied planes to cut along the grain, to ornate, complicated

Before the advent of the shaper or router, all decorative moldings were done with hand planes. It was not uncommon for a cabinet-making shop to have an inventory of 60 to 70 different molding planes, each cutting one specific molding. Plane making was a large industry in Colonial times; and in 1855 there were about 180 such establishments in England.

Colonial architecture created a demand for heavy, ornate moldings for cornices. Large molding planes were needed to make these moldings. They were referred to as "cornice planes." This kind of plane had a sole whose width varied anywhere from 2 to 6½ inches wide. These large planes often had a handle built into the top to make carrying them easier. A bar or hole was usually provided in the front of the plane. In use, a rope was attached so that an apprentice could pull the plane while the master pushed and guided it. The creation of large moldings was a laborious task and considerable power was required to move these planes into the wood. Even today, picking up one of these planes will give the holder renewed respect for the strength and ingenuity of these artisans.

shearing, cut. In theory, this makes the plane easier to push and creates a better final finish. It also makes the plane much more complicated and expensive, and its benefits are doubtful. In practice, the fence forces the plane to work in absolutely parallel, back-and-forth strokes. Since this stroke is longitudinal, the plane is still taking a shearing cut. It is questionable that the skewed iron is of any value other than to draw the plane into the rabbet and make it slightly easier to guide. You shouldn't pay extra for this refinement.

models with adjustable fences and skewed irons. To use the simplest form of a rabbet plane, you scribe a line for the depth of the rabbet. Then you clamp a fence to the work to guide the plane and set the width. Lastly, you plane away until the gauge line is reached. The simple rabbet plane is only useful for planing with the grain of the wood.

A more complicated version of this plane incorporates an adjustable fence that guides the plane and sets the width of the rabbet. There may also be a depth stop that eliminates the need to mark a gauge line first. Also, the plane may have a spur cutter. This lets you plane crossgrain, because the spur is lowered and it incises the wood ahead of the main iron.

Some better-quality rabbet planes have "skewed" the cutting irons. This means that the iron is set at a slight angle, so that it's no longer square with the sole of the plane. Supposedly, this skewed effect lets the iron take a paring, rather than a

The Record-Ridgeway 778 rabbet/fillister plane's iron can be bedded in either of two spots. For normal planing, the iron is bedded in the rear slot and is fully adjustable with a captive nut. The iron can also be positioned in the front bed, close to the front of the plane.

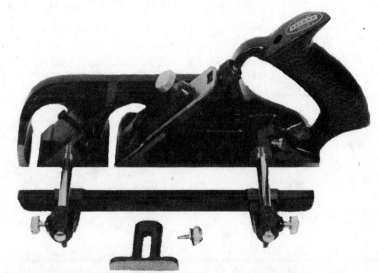

Record-Ridgeway's 778 Rabbet/Fillister Plane

This is done for bullnose work close to obstructions, such as when planing the inside of a drawer. When bedded in the front slot, the iron must be hammer-adjusted.

Overall length of the plane is 8½ inches, and it beds an iron 1½ inches wide. The adjustable fence allows it to make rabbets up to the full width of the iron, and a depth stop permits it to cut rabbets up to $\frac{1}{16}$-inch deep. A spur is also included for crossgrain work. This metal plane is an excellent choice for rabbet and fillister work, because it has all the features to help you produce top-quality work. Woodcraft Supply carries the plane as stock #02D10-R. Approx. Price: $23.00

Although a plane may work satisfactorily as supplied by the factory, it will work even better after the user fine tunes it. First and most important is honing the iron to a razor edge, and in the case of a jack plane you may want to break the corners so it will not gouge. All burrs should be carefully removed from all parts of the iron with a small file.

The cap iron comes next. The leading edge of the iron at the point where it contacts the blade should be honed so that it mates perfectly with the blade. This prevents a wood chip from sliding beneath it and will insure efficient chip breaking during use.

All rough edges and burrs should be removed from the regulating and adjusting mechanisms. These should work smoothly, without any catches. With metal planes the frog should be unscrewed and removed, then deburred. It should seat squarely with the body and adjust easily via the captive head screw. The casting should also be cleaned up. If the sole is not perfectly flat (test with a try-square), it should be either surface ground or lapped to make it so.

In the case of wooden planes, you may want to clean up the throat area and break any sharp edges. It is not unknown for some craftsmen to even refinish wooden planes, simply to beautify them.

All this may seem like a lot of bother, but the results can be spectacular.

The E.C.E. Primus is a simple, rabbeting plane, designed for working with the grain. It lacks fences and stops, so you can't control width or depth-of-cut with the plane. You must provide your own fence by clamping a piece of wood at the appropriate spot. Depth-of-cut is controlled by planing to a gauge line. There is also a zero-backlash adjustment system. The body is made of European beech, with a sole of lignum vitae attached by the castellated joinery unique to this firm.

This model is 11 inches long and beds an iron 1⅛ inches wide. The mouth is also adjustable. Woodcraft Supply, (#18K11-CH),

Garrett Wade (#24P05.01), and Woodworker's Supply (#507-004) all carry this basic rabbeting plane. Approx. Price: (18K11-CH) $53.50

Ulmia's deluxe rabbet plane

gives you everything you want in a wood-body plane. You can use it for planing with or across the grain, and its adjustable fence lets you cut any rabbet up to the maximum width of the iron (1¼ inches). A depth stop allows you to cut any depth up to ⅞ inch, and an adjustable spur severs the

E.C.E. Primus Rabbet Plane

Ulmia's Deluxe Rabbet Plane

wood ahead of the iron for cross-grain work. Corrugated joinery attaches the hornbeam sole to the beech body. It's really a nice plane for cutting a specialized edge. Look for it in the Woodcraft Supply catalog, under the stock #16D01-0. Approx. Price: $47.50

Since its inception in the 1800s, the metal plane has received widespread acceptance by craftsmen because of its ease of adjustment. The Stanley-Bailey type adjusting system allows for precise adjustments with little or no skill required on the part of the user. Wooden planes, as a consequence, do not find ready acceptance.

Yet, many modern craftsmen have turned to the wooden plane again, for either traditional or functional reasons. Unfortunately this love of the traditional often turns to frustration because the user cannot adjust the plane iron properly. The iron in a wooden plane can be adjusted precisely, but a small knack has to be acquired. A light hammer (a 6- or 8-ounce Warrington pattern is good), a little patience, and a good amount of practice will soon develop the skill.

After honing the iron, secure the cap iron in place, leaving a 1/16-inch gap to the cutting edge. Insert the assembled iron in the plane so the edge does not protrude below the sole. Insert the wood wedge and lock it into place with a light hammer blow. Gently tap the back of the iron until it protrudes below the sole in the amount desired. Any lateral correction that is required can be made by a tap on the appropriate side of the iron.

If you should have too much of the iron out and want to withdraw it slightly, simply strike the heel of the plane. This will cause the blade to withdraw and the wedge to loosen. After it has been withdrawn the necessary amount, strike the wedge to retighten it and proceed again. This is also the way to take out the wedge when the iron is to be removed for sharpening.

The idea of striking the wooden plane will usually give most novices pause. Most good wooden planes, however, have a small convex disc called a "striking button" set into the body at some point. This is the optimum hammer adjusting point for that particular plane. Smooth or jack planes usually have the button located at the heel, while on jointer planes it is usually located in the top of the plane just ahead of the iron. If the plane you have does not have a striking button, one can easily be installed. By cutting off the head of a carriage bolt you get a ready-made button. This is inserted into a small hole in the plane, drilled at the appropriate point and secured with epoxy glue. This will do the job as well as a factory installed one and simplify adjustments.

Plough Planes

Plough planes cut grooves. Unless you plan cabinet work that's nothing more than a rude plank construction, you need a plough plane in your toolbox. Years ago, cabinet makers discontinued solid-plank construction for panel construction. This happened because as wood swells or shrinks, solid construction almost always checks or breaks in one place or another. Panel construction allows for this expansion and prevents distortion. It requires a lot of grooving, and this is where the plough plane comes into use.

Most plough planes come with a variety of cutters that allow cutting grooves 1/8-inch wide and wider. An adjustable fence helps guide the plane and place the groove at any spot parallel to an edge. Better-quality plough planes have an adjustable stop to control depth—a feature that's appreciated when a number of identical grooves are made. This kind of plane comes in a variety of prices and models.

Record-Ridgeway's 044C metal plough plane has

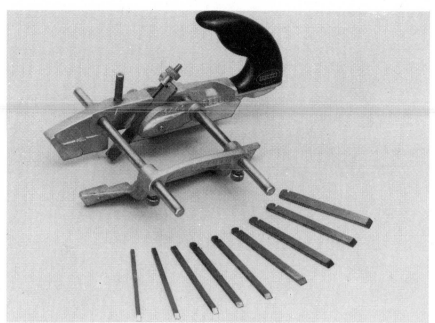

Record-Ridgeway's 044C Plough Plane

wood nuts turning on pear wood screw rods. The six irons that come with this plane range from ⁵⁄₃₂-to ⁹⁄₁₆-inch in width. Woodcraft Supply (#17I20-CH) and Garrett Wade (#24P19.01) both carry this plane. Approx. Price: (17I20-CH) $80.00

Block Planes

interchangeable cutters to cut grooves between ⅛- and ½-inch wide. All cutters, except the ⅛- and ³⁄₃₂-inch are fully adjustable with a captive head nut. The other two must be adjusted by eye. A fence lets you make cuts up to 5 inches from an edge. This fence is also predrilled with two holes. You can easily face the fence with wood to prevent possible stock damage. The body is plated gray iron. You can find this plane at both Woodcraft Supply (#02A20-R) and Garrett Wade (#10P19.01). Approx. Price: (02A20-R) $37.50

The E.C.E. Improved plough plane is a traditional wood-bodied plough plane. If nostalgia is one of the reasons for your interest in woodworking, this plane will send a warm glow through

your heart. It's indistinguishable from a plough plane made in the 1800s.

The adjustable fence permits groove cutting up to 5½ inches from any edge, while depth control is achieved by a depth gauge mortised into the edge of the beechwood body. The fence is held in position by pear

These small planes are designed to cut endgrain. They're called block planes because they were first used by butchers to clean up the face of butcher blocks—which are always endgrained for strength. Blade angle on these planes is usually very low, 20 degrees or less, and the blade is turned upside down so the

E.C.E. Improved Plough Plane

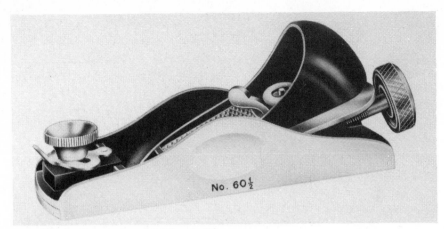

Stanley's Low-Angle Block Plane

bevel is uppermost. Block plane irons don't have a cap iron to turn shavings and are always single. Better planes have an adjustable mouth to prevent "tear out" ahead of the iron. These little planes are very useful and are often chosen for light trim work. They're also one of the few types of planes with a semblance of quality which can still be purchased at a local hardware store.

The Stanley low-angle block plane is made in the United States and beds an iron at an angle of only 12 degrees. It's about 6 inches long and beds an iron 1³⁄₁₆ inches wide. The mouth is adjustable. You can buy this Stanley plane, Model 60½, in most hardware stores. Approx. Price: $16.00

The Record-Ridgeway 09½ block plane has the traditional bedding angle of 20 degrees. This block plane is 6¼ inches long and beds an iron 1⅝ inches wide. The finger and adjusting knobs

are of brass. It's available at good hardware stores or can be purchased from Woodcraft Supply (#02B20-R) Approx. Price: $16.50

Shoulder Rabbet Plane

This version of the common block plane is used mainly for cleaning up the endgrain in the shoulder area of tenon joints. It has a low bedding angle of 20 degrees or less. Even if you're a die-hard machine woodworker, this plane is necessary if you want to have zero-tolerance fits in your tenon joints.

Record-Ridgeway's 311 is called a "Three-in-One" shoulder rabbet plane. Its handy features separate it from the rest of the pack. This plane is furnished with two interchangeable front sections. Mounted with the short front section it becomes a very efficient bullnose plane for working close to obstructions. The longer nose section makes it a shoulder rabbet plane for use on tenon joints. With both front ends removed it is a very handy chisel plane for cleaning up the corners of

Record-Ridgeway's 09½ Block Plane

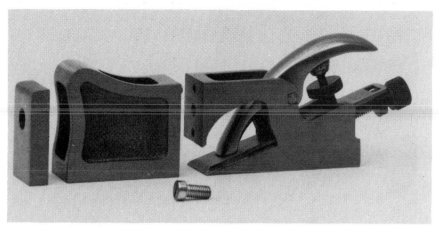

Record-Ridgeway's 311 Three-In-One Plane

work. You adjust the iron of this plane with a captive head screw. Iron angle is set very low for cutting endgrain. Woodcraft Supply (#02D30-R), Garrett Wade (#10P24.01), and Woodworker's Supply (#510-001) all sell this tool. Approx. Price: (02D30-R) $27.00

Spoke Shaves

The spoke shave is a tool that has come down to us from the wheelwright, cooper, and chair maker. It was used in those trades to shape round or long staves. These tools are available in a wide array of shapes and sizes. Like most planes today, you can find models made of metal or wood. But the difference between the two types is more distinctive than with other planes.

Wood spoke shaves are really draw knives placed in a wooden stock. The stock guides the blade and controls the thickness of the cut. On the other hand, a metal spoke shave is just a plane with handles on it, so it can be used as a spoke shave. A wood-bodied spoke shave takes an acute, knife-like cut, while the iron of the metal spoke shave is usually bedded at 45 degrees and takes a planing cut. Both are useful tools, and one of medium size should be in everyone's tool kit. They can often do a job that no other tool can do. Fitting a hammer handle, for example, or cleaning up concave surfaces

are common uses. Best of all, they're inexpensive.

Stanley of the United Kingdom's metal spoke shave is a flat-blade tool with two captive nuts for adjusting the blade vertically and horizontally. The lever cap that retains the iron is a very effective chip breaker. Overall length is 10 inches and the blade is 2⁄16 inches wide. Many good hardware stores carry this tool, or it may be ordered from Woodcraft Supply (#01H10-R) or Brookstone (#E3736). Approx. Price: (01H10-R) $7.50

A chamfer spoke shave is usually not available in most retail outlets, but it does fill a need in the shop—it breaks an edge. This tool is 10½ inches long and mounts a blade 1½ inches wide. Two fences can be set to create chamfers from 0 to 1½ inches wide. By removing these

Stanley of the United Kingdom's Metal Spoke Shave

Woodcraft's Chamfer Spoke Shave

Woodcraft's Combination Spoke Shave

fences, you can use the tool as a normal, round-faced spoke shave. Woodcraft Supply (#01T21-EG) and Brookstone (# E4592) sell it. Approx. Price: (01T21-EG) $8.00

A combination spoke shave is invaluable for fitting hammer and axe handles and for cleaning up difficult and hard-to-reach areas. It's actually two spoke shaves set side-by-side; the left with a concave face and the right with a flat face. The concave blade is 1⅜ inches wide and the flat blade is 1⅝ inches wide. This 10-inch-long, multipurpose tool is available from Woodcraft Supply (#16K20-EG) and Woodworker's Supply (#511-007). Approx. Price: (16K20-EG) $6.00

Scraper Planes

This shaping tool is not really a plane, but is closely related. It's just a stock that holds a simple scraper blade. Traditionally, a scraper, not sandpaper, was used to obtain a final finish on furniture and cabinets. A scraper is nothing but a rectangular piece of tool steel that is pulled over the work surface. Scraper edges are not honed, but burnished — a process which causes a burr to be turned up on the edge of the steel. This burr is the actual cutting edge, and when used properly, produces a superlative finish.

The scraper is often used without the stock, but the scraper plane offers many advantages over hand-holding. Without the stock it's easy to score the work surface by dragging a corner of the blade. The stock holds the blade perfectly square at all times and prevents this. Also, the large handle permits you to apply more force to the work, while eliminating numb fingers.

Scraper planes bed a blade anywhere from completely vertical to 25 degrees forward. Some are available with an optional, serrated blade. This converts the tool to a "toothing plane," used for roughing up a surface before veneer is applied with glue. If you want to produce a superior finish in a traditional manner, using a scraper plane is the way to do it.

An interesting set of two scraper planes is produced by Conover Woodcraft. The larger of the pair is 4 inches long, beds an iron 1³⁄₁₆ inches wide and is intended for

Conover's Small Scraper

Conover's Large Scraper Plane

Woodcraft's Scraping Plane 12

general use. The smaller is 2¼ inches long and beds a small iron ¾ inch wide—perfect for the hard-to-get-at areas and model work. The irons on both planes are held vertically and relieved to an angle of 25 degrees. Each of these planes has heavy brass side plates riveted to a core of solid hardwood. If you appreciate tools the way they were made in our grandfather's time or simply need a good scraping plane,

either of these will be for you. The pair is available under stock #132, or individually. Approx. Price: (the pair) $48.00

Stanley's 80 cabinet scraper is an inexpensive scraping plane that looks a lot like a spoke shave. It's made of cast iron and holds a blade 2¾ inches wide. Optional accessories include both a

fine and a coarse serrated toothing blade for veneer work. Woodcraft Supply carries this tool under stock #16K60-EG, as does Woodworker's Supply (#103-135). Approx. Price: (16K60-EG) $9.00

The scraping plane 12 incorporates all the features required in a fine scraping device. This plane has a large sole area measuring 6¼ inches long by 3⅜ inches wide, and it beds a blade 2¾ inches wide. A knurled adjusting nut lets you change the depth and angle of the blade. This plane is designed to be pushed, rather than pulled. It also does an effective job veneering surfaces with the optional, accessory toothing blade. Woodcraft Supply carries this tool under stock #16044-EG. Approx. Price: $25.00

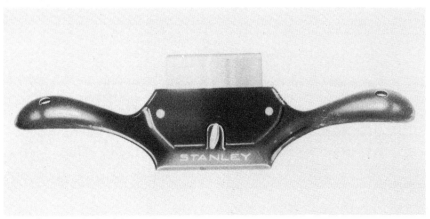

Stanley's 80 Cabinet Scraper

Other And Odd Planes

Here we have the odd and special-purpose planes. They're usually invaluable for one specific task. Because they don't fit in any particular niche that permits a generic description, the actual work that each does will be described in this section. Some of the more exotic ones may fit an odd job you have at hand. But many of these tools are interesting conversation pieces in themselves.

The Record-Ridgeway combination plane is a scaled-down version of the much more expensive multiplane. Even if you're an

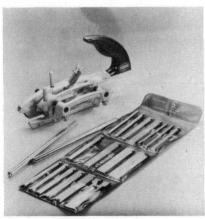

Record-Ridgeway's Combination Plane

Ever since the advent of the metal plane, manufacturers have been trying to develop a plane that will combine the functions of all planes in one. This development reached its high point in the late 1800s with the Stanley Universal Plane No. 55 (and to a certain extent with its predecessor, the No. 45). The number refers to the number of cutters supplied with the plane. The Stanley 55 was an attempt to combine all the planing operations other than those done with a bench plane in one unit. One of the main problems with multi-function tools, however, is that they tend to expand one's workscope, while presenting severe compromises over a tool designed for one specific function. In effect they are a jack of all trades, but the complete master of none.

This is not the case with the Universal Plane. These planes were also manufactured by Record-Ridgeway as their number 405 and by Miller under the name "Combination Plough, Fillister, and Matching Plane." All these companies except Record-Ridgeway have long ceased making universal planes because of limited demand; and now any planes that answer to this designation are referred to as Multiplanes, the Record name.

The Stanley 55 was the most complete plane ever marketed. Listed in the literature as a "molding, match, sash, beading, reeding, fluting, hollow, round, plough, rabbet and fillister, dado, slitting, and chamfer plane," — indeed a "planing mill within itself." This tool was nickel-plated, with solid rosewood fitting. The castings were embellished with scroll and Florentine patterns. This old tool is still sought after by tool collectors and woodworking enthusiasts, and often brings a price far beyond what it sold for originally. It has even fetched prices beyond what a new Record multiplane would bring today. It is difficult to find one with all 55 cutters intact and all the fences to make it complete.

The tradition still lives on, however, in the Record multiplane. This works just as well as the old Stanley 55, though it is not as decorative. To buy one of the multiplanes with all the cutters is quite an investment. The basic plane with 24 cutters sells for $135.00, with several different sets of additional irons adding extra cost. A complete multiplane represents a total investment of about $320.00,

advanced woodworker, this plane can fill your needs. It comes with 18 steel cutters, allowing it to do the work of many special-purpose planes at a much cheaper price than buying many individual tools. A combination plane like this one is the best bet for a single plane purchase, because you get a lot of versatility at a low cost.

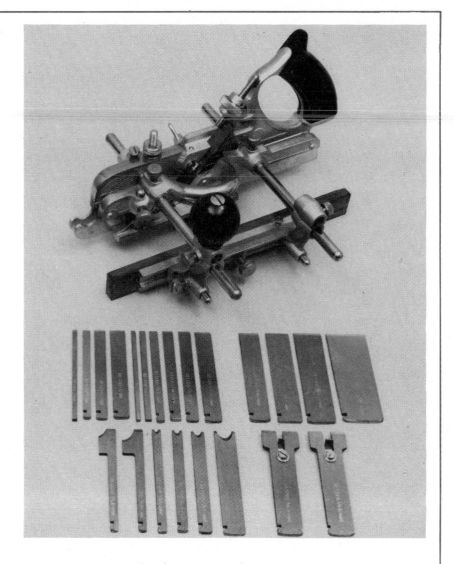

this plane for dadoes, rabbets, and tongue-and-groove work. The body is nickel-plated gray iron, and the handle is of high-impact plastic. A comprehensive instruction book is included with each plane. This combination plane is offered by Woodcraft Supply (#02A10-R), Garrett Wade (#10P20.01) and Woodworker's Supply (#510-033). Approx. Price: (10P20.01) $73.50

The Record-Ridgeway 20 compass plane is a specialized tool, developed for the coach-building industry in the 19th Century. It was used to make the gracefully curving lines that are the hallmark of fine coach building. Compass planes can clean up curved surfaces better than any other hand or power tool.

A compass plane is a bench plane with a thin, flexible steel sole. A screw adjusting mechanism flexes the sole through a pivot point at the heel and toe of the plane. So, you can flex the sole end-to-end to conform to any convex or concave shape. Because of this, you can shave down a radius better than any other tool. The Record 20 incorporates the best features of compass plane evolution at a reasonable price. This plane is 10 inches long and beds an iron 1¾ inches wide. The iron, cap iron, regulating and adjusting mechanism of the plane are identical to other

about the price of a decent-sized power tool.

It should be remembered that this plane does replace a lot of specialized planes, especially individual molding planes. The multiplane comes packed in a wood case, and with a detailed instruction book (practically a necessity). This plane is a limited production, limited availability item produced in one department and hand finished. Demand exceeds supply and only two companies in North America can guarantee reasonable delivery dates on this plane. They are Woodcraft Supply, under catalog #01M10-R and Garrett Wade, catalog #10P30.01.

This combination plane works as a plough plane, cutting 12 different grooves in widths from ⅛ to ⅞ inch, and to a controlled depth of ⅝ inch. An adjustable fence permits cutting parallel up to 5 inches from any edge. It can cut beads from ⅛ to ½ inch, and another cutter can cut a ¼-inch tongue on the edge of a board. You can use

Record-Ridgeway's 20 Compass Plane

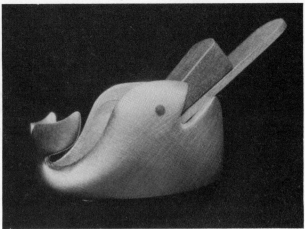

Otner Botner's Finger Plane

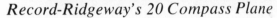

Record-Ridgeway bench planes—excellent. Sole flexibility is adjusted by a screw on top of the plane, and the setting is held by a locking nut. You can buy this tool from Woodcraft Supply (#02B10-R) and Garrett Wade (#10P34.01). Approx. Price: (10P34.01) $51.00

Working up the sounding boards of musical instruments calls for the Otner Botner instrument maker's finger plane. Its design shows both clever engineering and an artistic touch. It's unique, interesting, functional, and simply beautiful. The small, brass body is cast into the shape of a whale. The whale's mouth is the throat of the plane, and the upturned tail is a forefinger rest. An instrument maker requires a plane which is "round both ways." That is, it must be convex in both cross and longitudinal sections, giving it a shape like a ship's

bottom. This makes it easy to carve out the graceful dish-shaped depression encountered in instrument work.

Three sizes are available. The smallest is 1⅜ inches long and beds a ⅜-inch iron. Medium size is 1¾ inches long and beds a ½-inch iron, while the largest measures 2⅛ inches overall and has a ⅝-inch iron. You can purchase them from Otner-Botner, the manufacturer, by mail. Approx. Price: $25.00 each or $70.00 per set of three.

Conover palm planes are another set of miniature planes, but they're more suitable for general cabinet making. They're called palm planes because they have a short, threaded extension rod protruding from the back of the plane, which ends in a wooden knob that fits the palm of the hand. Your forefinger rests in a tiny depression in the front of the

plane, while the thumb and middle fingers rest in flutes on the sides. This provides a very secure grip, much greater leverage, and better control than most other miniature finger planes.

The planes are available in three styles, with scrub, smooth, and beading soles. A number of accessory blades are also available, including a special rabbeting shape with extended wings for forming rabbets and other specialized moldings. Conover's stock numbers for these planes are

Conover's Palm Plane Blades

Conover's Palm Plane

Ulmia Toothing Plane

125, 126 and 127. Those with rabbeting blades have an "R" after the stock number. Approx. Price: $23.00 each or $80.00 per set with blades

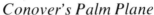

Toothing planes are very specialized tools used for roughing up a surface prior to applying veneer. The iron has a serrated edge, and is held either vertical or close to it. By roughing up the surface with this tool, you increase the glue-holding area and insure a good bond for the veneer. Most woodworkers who do veneer inlaying or surface work simply buy an optional toothing blade for a scraping plane to do this task.

The Ulmia toothing plane is the tool to buy if you don't own a scraping plane. It has a serrated iron that's 1⅞ inches wide, and has an overall length of 9½ inches. The iron is held nearly vertical in the beech body, and the

hornbeam sole is laminated by the intricate, corrugated joinery characteristic of this firm. Woodcraft Supply carries this plane as stock #16D02-0. Approx. Price: $23.00

Bullnose planes are made to solve the problem of cleaning up work close to an obstruction. They have their iron bedded very close to the toe, usually with ⅟₃₂-of an inch gap between the iron

and the front edge of the plane. As with most metal planes, they have a standardized numbering system.

Stanley of the United Kingdom's 75 bullnose plane is a fine tool. Local hardware stores may carry it, but if you can't find it locally, try Garrett Wade (#23P08.01) or Woodworker's Supply (#103-020). Approx. Price: (23P08.01) $9.50

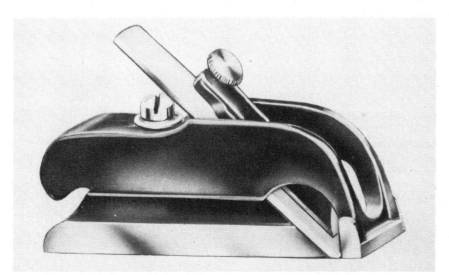
Stanley of the United Kingdom's 75 Bullnose Plane

Although their use is somewhat limited in the full-function woodshop, for the tradesman or those in construction work power planes are almost a necessity. If you need to remove a smidgen of wood or plane down the edge of a door, these tools do the job fast; and they can be adapted to a certain amount of rough surface planing. Relatively inexpensive, they may be well worth your investigation.

Portable Power Planes

Any job that can be done with a hand plane, plus specialized tasks like rabbet planing, can be done faster and easier with a portable power plane. A hand plane in competent hands does give a better surface, but the electric tool is faster and takes less skill to use well. Electric power planes can also accomplish jobs that are normally done on a jointer.

Even people who own these specialized machines add a portable power plane to their tool kit because it can be used anywhere electricity is available — in or out of the shop. You can use it to plane workpieces that are too unwieldy to handle safely and easily on a stationary tool. For example, it's handy for planing a smidgen of material from a door to make it open and close properly. Any piece of lumber that needs an edge smoothed,

needs to be slightly reduced in width, or is too long to cut on a jointer or table saw without table extensions, is a candidate for the portable power plane.

You can also use a power plane to dress stock — smooth rough boards — but if the board is wider than the tool, you'll have to do some fancy tool handling. Smoothing a 12-inch board is a simple task involving one pass on a thickness planer, but a 2-inch power plane has to do the job in a great many passes. The cuts will also overlap, resulting in ridges and even gouges in the work. So, the portable power plane is not designed to replace a jointer or surface planer. And using it as a substitute for these tools should be only a last resort. However, it's great for squaring up an edge, removing a small amount of stock quickly, rabbeting, and

some other planing tasks.

Portable power planes look a lot like standard planes, but they work like an inverted jointer. Handles and the motor are on top, while the cutterhead and its knives turn between a gap spaced between a front and rear "shoe." The shoes form the base that rests on the work. They're comparable to the infeed and outfeed tables of the jointer. The rear shoe, which forms the bulk of the base, is fixed in position. The shorter, front shoe is adjustable for controlling the depth-of-cut. This depth-of-cut adjustment varies from tool to tool — from as little as $\frac{1}{64}$-inch to as much as $\frac{1}{8}$-inch.

You should note that a light tool with a minimum depth-of-cut can remove just as much material as a larger-capacity power plane — it just takes more passes and more time. Also, a ⅛-inch-deep cut is a heavy cut, and even if your machine has the capacity to do this in one pass, you'll get better results if the planing is done in gradual stages. The power plane is most useful for removing small amounts of material, and this is its basic reason for existing.

Power planes can do more than just smooth edges and surfaces. All of them can be used with an adjustable fence that helps produce a planed edge that's square with an adjacent surface. Locked at an angle, the fence serves as a guide for making chamfers and bevels, and most units can make rabbeting cuts. Fences either come with the tool or are available as optional accessories.

These portable electric planes produce the smoothest cut when their cutting blades are super sharp. There are two kinds of cutter mounts. A conventional cutterhead grips straight knives in the same way as a stationary jointer. You can hone these by standard sharpening methods. Some power planes have a spiral-type cutter that's maintained best with a special, accessory grinding attachment. Both types of cutterheads work well, but only if sharp.

Power planes are designed to have a minimum opening around the cutterhead, but the blades are *always* exposed. For this reason, you should always keep your hands on top of the tool and allow it to stop completely before you put it down. It's also important to make sure the tool is operating at full speed before it makes contact with the wood — otherwise it can bounce and chatter. You should be careful when using this tool. A power plane can remove skin as easily as it shaves wood!

These planes should never be forced into a cut, and this shouldn't be necessary if the cutters are sharp. You can tell how well the tool is cutting by listening to its motor noise. When all is going well, the motor noise is not drastically different from when the plane is running without a load. Excessive slowdown or stalling indicate that the cut is too deep and may be going too fast. Feed speed is affected by the density of the wood — you can plane softwoods faster than hardwoods. However, a feed speed that's too slow won't accomplish much, and can dull the cutters faster because they'll be doing more scraping than cutting. The right feed speed and a reasonable depth-of-cut keep the tool cutting consistently without undue strain on the motor.

Planes do an excellent job of smoothing edges on plywood and particle board, both of which are notoriously difficult to smooth well. Minimum cuts of under 1/32 inch produce the best results. The same goes for planing crossgrain on board ends. Some feathering or splintering will occur, but you can reduce this by slowing down the feed speed when the plane approaches the end of the cut. This problem can be eliminated by clamping a piece of waste stock to the end of the work. Then the splintering will occur on the scrap.

Power planes are really limited-use tools, but they can be very handy for some kinds of surfacing tasks prior to final finishing. In a small shop they can take the place of a stationary jointer because, used with care, they can cut a uniform rabbet in very long stock.

Some power planes provide an adjustable fence that rides along the edge of the stock and controls the width of the eventual rabbet. Depth-of-cut is regulated by the number of successive passes. It is better to take a number of even, smooth cuts along the length of stock rather than one heavy cut. Doing the latter will often result in uneven cuts and a stalled motor, which neither improves the outcome of the project nor leads to long motor life. It is important when using a power plane for any operation that the stock be firmly held or clamped prior to use of the plane. This will prevent unexpected tilting and possible loss of control of the tool. Power planes will remove flesh as efficiently as wood, but it is much easier to repair a mistake in the latter than in the former.

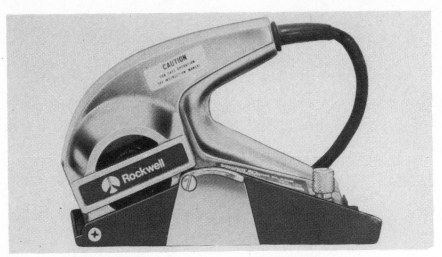

Rockwell's 4690 Portable Electric Block Plane

Rockwell's 4690 is an electrically-powered block plane that you can hold easily in one hand. This little tool can do a host of tasks that you'd otherwise have to do with a file, sandpaper, spoke shave, or scraper. As its ¹⁄₆₄-inch depth-of-cut indicates, it's not for heavy-duty chores. But for removing see-through shavings from a door or drawer, it can't be beat. Width-of-cut is 1¹³⁄₁₆ inches—just enough to smooth the edges of nominal 2-inch material. Although you can use this plane for surfacing work, it's not designed for such work.

The cutterhead turns at a fast 24,000 rpm and this results in *very* smooth cuts. Other assets include small size, light weight, and adequate power. The shape and size of the tool make it usable for shaping and smoothing contours, and a bevel planing fence (#18270) is available as an extra-cost accessory. Approx. Price: (4690) $90.00

Wen's 931 is a heavy-duty, professional model—a no-nonsense machine with a price within reach of the home shop owner. Its two handles are large and easy to grip, and the total shoe length of 16 inches makes it easy to keep this tool flat when planing edges. A ½-hp motor drives the twin-bladed cutterhead at 14,500 rpm. Depth-of-cut is adjustable to a maximum of ¹⁄₁₆ inch, and width-of-cut is a full 2⅛ inches. A bevel planing fence, adjustable to 45 degrees, comes along with the plane. This tool is a good choice for the professional or home shop owner who wants a power plane with good power and capacity, plus excellent performance—all at a reasonable price. Approx. Price: $65.00

Craftsman's 1732, from Sears, Roebuck and Co., has a capacity almost as large as a small jointer. This is 10 pounds of tough tool, with a width-of-cut wide enough to plane the board side of a nominal 2x4 in a single pass. Depth-of-cut is adjustable up to ¹⁄₁₆-inch and it can be used for light and heavy cuts.

This electric plane does its work with a ⅜-hp motor that drives a two-bladed cutterhead at 15,000 rpm. It has a rabbeting capability, a built-in chute that spews shavings away from the operator, is double-insulated, and comes equipped with a fence. One interesting design

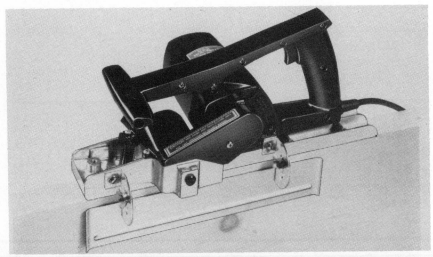

Wen's 931 Heavy-Duty Electric Plane

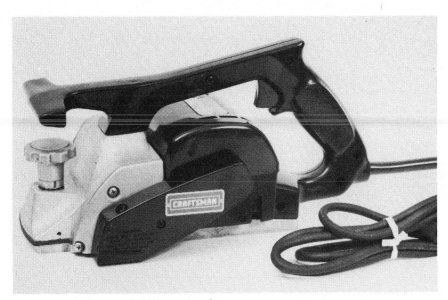

Craftsman's 1732 Electric Plane

tools, but it's enough to allow removal of a lot of material with successive passes. A ⅔-hp motor turns a two-knife cutterhead at 15,000 rpm. The tool is double insulated, and features rabbeting capability, a built-in chip chute, and a guide fence.

It also has a compact design. The main handle is fairly well-centered, which is helpful when you need to bear down on the plane. If you require a powerful machine that will operate without trouble, the Powr-Kraft 85001 is a good investment. Approx. Price: $80.00

touch is a V-groove that runs down the center of the front shoe, which makes it easier to guide the tool when doing a chamfer cut.

It's a large tool, but well balanced, and has a large main and auxiliary handle for good control. The Craftsman 1732 is an excellent tool to select for general, all-purpose planing. Approx. Price: $80.00

The Powr-Kraft 85001, from Montgomery Ward, is an electric plane that's on the borderline between home shop and professional tools. It has a very large width-of-cut capacity at 3⅝ inches — enough to plane the wide side of a 2x4 in a single pass. Depth-of-cut is small, however, at ¾₄-inch. This isn't as much as normally available on professional

Rockwell's 4692 is a giant among power planes, with an overall length of 16 inches. A long plane like this has an advantage when used on long edges and surfaces. This is because it provides more bearing surface on the work. The Rockwell 4692 has a very low profile and an attractive, streamlined design. Weight is so well-distributed that even amateurs find it easy to handle. Although it's made for the tradesman, its ability to smooth long boards often makes it the choice of home shop owners as a substitute for a stationary jointer. It can't perform all the functions of the stationary machine, but it doesn't take up any floor space, either.

Maximum depth-of-cut is ³⁄₃₂ -inch, and a calibrated

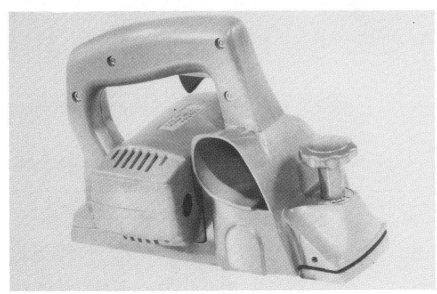

Ward's Powr-Kraft 85001 Electric Plane

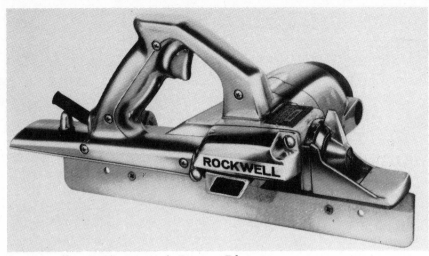

Rockwell's 4692 16-inch Power Plane

scale lets you read settings directly. Width-of-cut is a little better than 2⅜ inches. A powerful, 1½-hp motor drives the cutterhead at a fast 25,000 rpm. Both spiral and straight blades are available, and you can opt for an optional, carbide-tipped cutterhead (#43263). This optional cutterhead is especially good for smoothing particleboard, and it's worth the extra cost, since it stays sharper longer than regular steel blades. The plane has a 60-degree bevel planing range, and a chip chute. Also, a raised post at the rear of the back shoe lets you situate the electric cord on either side of the tool to keep it out of the cutting area. Altogether, this is a fine, well-designed plane that's especially suitable for planing long stock. Approx. Price: $150.00

Skil's 100 is an outstanding example of an electric plane made specifically for

constant, heavy-duty use. It may be too much plane for the average craftsman, unless he does a lot of remodeling work. Maximum depth-of-cut is a full ⅛ inch. This setting is adjustable by means of a lever that clicks to a positive stop for each 1/64-inch change. These small-increment stops let you do precise work that requires a light touch as easily as heavy, hogging cuts.

Maximum width-of-cut is a whopping 3 inches. Although it's generally not advisable to use an electric plane as a

substitute for a stationary jointer, you can do it with this tool. A 1½-hp motor drives a twin-bladed cutterhead at 15,000 rpm. Steel knives are standard, but longer-wearing, carbide-tipped knives are optional (#73279).

Despite its super capacities and impressive power, this isn't an unwieldly tool. Its 18-inch length provides a good bearing surface for the stock. Weight is a bit over 10 pounds, but that's quite acceptable .

Several exclusive features make this plane very convenient to use. You can direct a topside chute to deflect chips to either side of the tool. The edge guide-fence can be attached to either side of the tool, and is adjustable to 45 degrees for bevel cuts. Also, at the rear of the back shoe there's a deflector that moves the cord out of the way. All in all, this is one of the best portable planes available. The only extra you could ask for would be someone to operate it for you! Approx. Price: $275.00

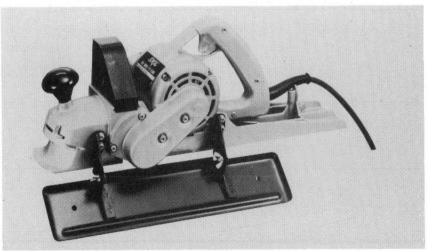

Skil's 100 Heavy-Duty Electric Plane

Jointers are most commonly used to assure an edge square with another flat surface on the workpiece. But they are versatile enough to do other operations: tapers, rabbets, tenons in round stock and within limitations, some surfacing and angle work. They are required tools for joinery or furniture work.

Jointers

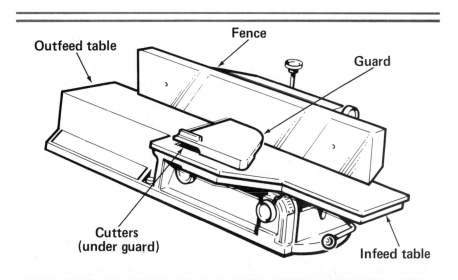

Outfeed table

Fence

Guard

Cutters
(under guard)

Infeed table

The toughest part of any joinery operation is to make the two mating surfaces true and smooth. Traditionally, this was usually done with a hand plane, and still is for much fine cabinet work. Used properly, a hand plane can give you a fine, smooth edge on any wood, but this takes time to learn and time to do. On small jobs, the extra time needed to use a hand plane may not matter. But for large pieces of furniture, the time saved by using a jointer can be substantial. Besides, a jointer can also be used to make some of the special mating joints used in woodworking.

The jointer has always been considered the perfect complement to the table or radial arm saw as the rough edges created by their blades could be smoothed quickly with one pass through the jointer. One typical operation in which the two machines were used in combination was ripping a board to a specific width. One edge would first be passed through the jointer — this would be the edge held against the rip fence while the board was being sawed. The blade-to-rip fence setting, which determines the actual board width, would be deliberately set a little wide. This extra amount was removed by passing the board through the jointer again. The result was a board of the exact width needed, with perfectly smooth edges. This, however, is not any longer a critical operation, due to the modern super-sharp circular saw blades. These blades leave edges smooth enough to be used without further attention.

Today, the jointer's usefulness comes from its ability to do more than just smooth edges. You can use it for a number of other operations and, unlike other tools, it doesn't require extra-cost accessories. Although it's not a substitute for a machine called a "thickness planer," you can

A QUICK LOOK AT JOINTERS AND PLANERS

NAME	REMARKS	TYPICAL USES
Jointer	uses short (10 inch) horizontally-mounted cutters — adjustable infeed and outfeed tables	surface smoothing of edges ("joining") for glue work — used to do rabbets or tapered chair legs
Planer	uses long, horizontally-mounted cutter (up to 4 feet in large models) — power head has automatic feed — cutters always guarded	used to surface-plane large areas of stock — will make 2nd face parallel to flat surface

use it for light surfacing operations on narrow boards. Whether or not the opposite faces of the stock will be parallel depends upon the operator's skill. Some common wood distortions can be removed by making cuts on a jointer, as long as the width of the stock is within the capacity of the tool. A board that's warped across its width can be made flat on that surface by several passes on the jointer, with the concave side of the wood down. The opposite, convex surface can also be flattened, though this takes some care because the stock can rock in the machine. It's better to smooth the concave surface on the jointer, and then resaw the convex side on a band saw.

The jointer can also be used to make some of the most common joints used in woodworking. All of the following can be cut with a jointer in the correct setting:

Rabbets are L-shaped cuts used to mate two pieces or join them at right angles. This joint is often used in corners in place of a butt or miter joint.

Tongues are one of the mating shapes used in a tongue-and-groove joint. Make a rabbet cut on the top and bottom of the same edge of a board and a tongue results.

Chamfers are angle cuts that only remove the edge of the corner. This is usually done for decorative purposes.

Bevels are angle cuts across the entire edge of a board. Although this can be done for decorative purposes, it is usually part of a joint. Two pieces cut at a 45 degree bevel form a 90 degree corner when they are mated together.

Tapers are made by successive passes through the machine. How many passes are required depends upon the degree of taper that's needed. A tapered chair or table leg is produced by making taper cuts on all four sides of a square piece of stock. Often a taper is only required on two adjacent sides.

Tenons are the projecting parts of a mortise-tenon joint, the mortise is often cut on a drill press with a mortising attachment. A wide rabbet cut is made on each surface of the same edge of a board; the result is a "stud" tenon. A "true" tenon results when all four edges are treated similarly, leaving a projecting piece of wood that fits into the mortise and is glued.

The jointer is a squat machine. A cutterhead, holding two or more knives, rotates in a gap between an infeed table and an outfeed table. The cutterhead rotates clockwise. Work is placed on the infeed table and moved forward manually against the direction of the cutterhead's rotation. The outfeed table provides support as the work comes out and over the cutters. Most jointers have an outfeed table that's fixed and nonadjustable, with its surface tangent to the cutting circle of the knives in the cutterhead. The infeed table, on the other hand, can be raised and lowered by means of a knob or handwheel. This sets the depth-of-cut — the amount of wood that will be removed in one pass through the machine. The front infeed table will always be set lower than the back outfeed table by the amount of depth the cut takes.

Jointers also have a fence that you can move across the entire face of the tables. The fence also tilts to create either an open or closed angle in relation to the horizontal plane of the tables. Usually, the fence is used to provide an edge against which the work rides for stability. For regular operations, it's locked at 90 degrees in relation to the jointer tables. A tilted fence is used to put a chamfer or bevel on a piece of wood.

A jointer fence is also equipped with adjustable stops, to let you set most common angles quickly. You should expect at least three on any quality machine: 45 degrees forward (closed angle), 90 degrees (at a right angle to the tables), and 45 degrees back (open angle, actually 135 degrees to the tables).

Jointer fences are mounted either at the front end of the infeed table or at the center of the machine's length. End-mounted fences can have a degree of flex which can cause inaccuracies in jobs like rabbeting, especially in large machines with longer tables. And long fences can pivot around their mounting point much more easily than short ones. Center-mounted fences don't have this potential problem because they're supported at one or more points directly behind the cutterhead. This gives the work support where it's needed most, so the center-mounted fence is the best.

Many jointers also have a "rabbeting ledge." In this case, the cutterhead end of the infeed table broadens and has a narrow projection that extends past the cutting area. This supposedly provides support for the work that is being rabbeted on the jointer. But many manufacturers are dropping this feature because the federal government has ruled that rabbeting ledges are extremely unsafe. If your jointer has this ledge, follow the manufacturer's instructions very carefully to avoid injury.

The size of a jointer is described by the length of the cutterhead's knives. A 6-inch jointer, for instance, can plane down boards that are 6 inches wide. Another important capacity is the amount the infeed table can be adjusted. This can range from ¼ to ½ inch, but it's not an indication of how much wood can be removed in a single pass. It only tells you how deep a rabbet you can

---

Obtaining a uniform taper can be a difficult task with hand tools, but one that is relatively easy with a jointer. Tapers on one or all sides of a length of stock are often used as a design element in furniture, or to produce a graceful line in chair or table legs.

To get a taper on a piece of stock that is shorter than the infeed table, first set the depth-of-cut to the amount that you wish the final depth to be. The stock is then placed so that the starting point of the taper rests on the forward edge of the outfeed table. For a 10¼-inch taper, for example, mark the stock 10 inches from the end and set the infeed table for a ¼-inch cut. Rest the stock at the 10-inch point on the outfeed table and pull it across the cutters. This will result in the required taper.

Tapers in excess of the jointer's maximum depth can be achieved by repeat passes. When the requirement is for a taper on stock longer than the infeed table, say 20¼-inch, it must be done differently. The stock is marked in two 10-inch divisions and the infeed table set to ⅛-inch. The initial pass is made from the first 10-inch mark, and the second from the other 10-inch mark. This will produce a uniform taper for the whole length.

If it is a four-sided taper on the same stock or identical pieces are required, stop blocks clamped to the jointer fence will give positive stopping and starting points. Such stop blocks will also make midpoint tapers possible. Be sure when making any taper to keep the work firmly on the table, or it will not result in a uniform cut along the length of the stock.

With or without an integral rabbeting ledge, it is easy to cut a rabbet on a jointer. It is, however, dangerous. This is because the cutter is completely exposed for the width of the cut. When doing rabbeting on a jointer it is necessary to be extremely careful — or else you may lose skin or a finger.

Width of the rabbet to be cut is set by locking the fence at the correct distance. If there is a guard, it must be removed first. This exposes the cutter knives. The distance between the fence and the end of the cutterhead is the width of the resulting rabbet.

Depth of the rabbet is controlled by the setting of the infeed table. The maximum depth that the rabbet can thus be cut is the amount that the infeed table can be lowered. On most home machines this is at least ½-inch, ample for most rabbeting requirements. If the rabbet is to be more than ¼-inch in depth, it is wise to make successive passes in order to reach the correct depth. This will prevent excessive strain on the motor and result in a smoother cut.

Mark the end depth and width of the rabbet on the stock with a pencil. Put the workpiece on the infeed table, snug against the fence, and bring it over the knives. If successive passes are required, adjust the infeed table accordingly. When the pencil marks have been reached, the result is a rabbet of the correct depth and width.

You can also create a tongue in the wood by flipping it end for end and running it through the cutters. When working with endgrain, it may be necessary to make more shallow cuts and feed the work into the machine at a slower rate. This will help to reduce the feathering and splintering that can occur in endgrain and make the cut smoother.

cut. The maximum depth-of-cut possible on any jointer depends upon motor horsepower, cutter sharpness and wood density. In most surfacing operations, minimum cuts are best. They are easier to do, don't tax the machine or the operator, and result in the smoothest cuts. When a lot of wood must be removed, or an especially deep rabbet must be formed, several successive cuts will do a better job than one on this machine.

Overall length of jointer tables varies among machines. Longer tables give better support for the work. Even a small jointer can be used to plane stock of any length, but work support is the operator's job. This is true on even the largest machines. They have longer tables, but not long enough to relieve you from the duty of supporting longer work with your hands. In most furniture construction, it's unlikely that any piece will be longer than 6 feet. This length work isn't difficult to handle on any jointer. In shops that deal with repeated numbers of longer boards, workers extend the basic length of the machine's tables by setting up special support sawhorses or tables.

Jointers are narrow machines, and even 6-inch versions aren't longer than 4 feet. They don't occupy much floor space, but work space needed depends upon the length of wood which will pass through the machine. Normally, 6 feet on either side of the machine is sufficient. Jointers are not so large or heavy that they can't be moved into an open area when you need more work space for longer work. The machine is often placed on the left side of a table saw, where it's handy to use after you cut the wood.

For safety, jointers have a guard that's mounted on the fence or tables. This guard is spring-loaded and moves in a horizontal plane to keep the cutters covered. It slides aside as work is fed past the cutterhead and returns automatically to the covering position. On some of the better machines, the spring is adjustable. This spring action should be very positive, and the guard should return immediately to cover the cutterhead as soon as the work has passed the cutters. If this is not the case, you should remedy the matter with an immediate adjustment. This is especially important when the fence is set so that only a small part of the cutterhead is used, as it's not advisable to have any part of the spinning blades exposed when the machine is running.

When planing wide boards, you may be tempted to remove the guard—don't do it. For some types of work, like rabbeting, the guard must be removed, which is why OSHA regulations have banned the use of jointers for making this particular cut. If you do remove the guard for a rabbet, make sure you know where your hands are in relation to the cutters at all times. The use of a wooden device called a "pusher-hold down" is a must. This safety item resembles a wooden trowel, and should be used for all surface-planing tasks, rabbeting, and any operation where the cutterhead is exposed. Many manufacturers include a set of these hold downs with the jointer.

In some types of planing, the fence is so far forward that a portion of the cutterhead is exposed behind the fence. Center-mounted fences often have an auxiliary guard to cover this portion of the cutterhead. On other models, the normal guard can be mounted to cover this portion of the cutterhead. They should be used at all times.

In any case, possible safety hazards with a jointer increase as the size of the work decreases, simply because your hands are brought closer to the work. Also, all jointers have a lower limit on the length of a piece of stock that can be run through the machine. If the wood doesn't rest securely on the tables as it passes through the cutterhead area, it can tip or grab, throwing it up or back toward you. Reading the jointer's owner's manual will give you helpful hints for safe use, and you should study the instructions carefully. Jointers are very dangerous tools.

If you're thinking of buying a jointer, you must consider that they are limited-use tools, despite their potential for doing a variety of jobs. Unless you do a lot of woodworking or are involved in fine furniture work, it's hard to justify the cost of a jointer. You should learn to use a hand plane in any case, because some jobs are faster to do with this hand tool, even if you own a jointer.

Rockwell's 37-130 is a 4-inch jointer designed for the layman, but it has some features found on larger, professional machines. Also, some commercial shops with limited space choose this machine because of its small size.

Unlike most jointers, the infeed and outfeed tables are both adjustable. Its adjustable outfeed table lets you perform operations not possible on some other

Warped or cupped boards can often be straightened out by using a jointer. It is tempting to use a planer to do this, but because pressure is applied during the feeding process the board is actually flattened before it reaches the cutter. The board simply springs back to its original shape after it passes through the planer.

One easy way to remove the dished or cupped surface is to run the concave side across the cutter in the jointer. The high points provide a good bearing surface for the initial passes until it is flat.

Removing the convex side is more difficult. The most accurate way to achieve this is to plane down the concave side first with the jointer, then use that side as a bearing surface against the rip fence on a table saw. This "resawing" will result in two flat sides that are of equal thickness along the length of the board. Resawing can also be done on a band saw if it is equipped with a rip fence on the table, and it is usually the most practical solution if the stock is wider than 3 inches.

The convex side of a warped board can also be removed on a jointer. It is difficult, though, and you have to be careful to keep the surfaced side parallel to the table or the board will not have parallel sides when you have finished. Better results can be achieved by resawing, and you will not lose as much stock in the process.

Rockwell's 37-130 4-inch Jointer

The Sprunger J450 is a small jointer produced by people who have an established reputation for building great machinery. Its capacity is a little larger than most jointers of this size — it permits planing on boards up to 4½ inches wide, while the maximum depth for rabbeting is ⁵⁄₁₆-inch. The tables are both 31 inches long, approaching the lengths found on some of the larger, 6-inch machines. Like most Sprunger tools, the emphasis in this machine is on rugged functionalism, not fancy knobs or chrome covers. This is simply a jointer.

The fence on this model is front-mounted and has a dual-purpose locking handle. Adjustable automatic stops are provided for the two 45-degree positions and the basic 90-degree setting. A three-knife cutterhead rotates at 4300 rpm and can be powered with either a ⅓- or ½-hp motor. The larger motor should be used if you want to have a full-capacity machine or are planning heavy-duty operations.

Any small shop owner who wants the most in function but does not have the room

machines. One such operation is called "recessing." This is a planing cut that's often found at the bottom of table legs — a slot or groove confined within the ends of a workpiece.

The maximum depth-of-cut is only ¼ inch, which is smaller than that of most 4-inch machines. The fence of this Rockwell machine is front-mounted and a single control handle locks the fence in for positioning or angular settings. Adjustable stops are provided for 45- and 90-degree settings.

Tables on this jointer are 27¼ inches long, and the three-knife cutterhead turns at 4200 rpm. This particular model includes stand, built-in dust chute, and a set of pusher-hold downs, but no motor. At least a ½-hp unit is recommended. The Rockwell 37-130 is capable of all the heavy-duty work of the average shop, but it's not a production machine. Approx. Price: $260.00

Sprunger's J450 Jointer

Toolkraft's 4671 Jointer

Toolkraft's 4691 6-inch Jointer

or the money for a larger unit can be very happy with this machine. It will do the job, and what more could be asked of any machine? Approx. Price: $250.00

Toolkraft's 4671 is about as compact as a 4-inch jointer can get. This is one of those motorized tools, which means that the motor is an integral part of the machine. It is fully enclosed in the base and there are no pulleys or belts to worry about. Because it requires little space, Toolkraft's 4671 is a good choice for anyone with a small shop.

Basic necessities of a good jointer are not ignored on this machine. Depth-of-cut is ⅜ inch, the end-mounted fence tilts, and the ⅞-hp motor turns the three-knife cutterhead at 4800 rpm. This higher speed is because of a direct-drive motor. Table length is a bit small at 22¾ inches, but extra wide. Although the tool's basic capacity is only 4 inches, the tables are 6½ inches wide. As a part of the jointer package you get an adjustable table stand and a set of pusher-hold downs. Approx. Price: $260.00

Tooklraft's 4691 is simply a larger, 6-inch version of the company's model 4671. Here, the tables are almost 3 feet long and are a bit more than 7 inches wide. Maximum depth-of-cut is a full ½ inch, and the enclosed motor develops 1⅛-hp. It's extremely compact for a machine with such good capacity. If you require a jointer that can do a maximum number of planing tasks yet take up little space, then this is a good one to select. Approx. Price: $350.00

The Powermatic 50 is an industrial-type 6-inch jointer—the kind most often found in commercial shops. Yet it's not an unreasonable purchase for the woodworker who demands the most from his machines, or for the person who is assembling a

Powermatic's 50 6-inch Jointer

"dream shop."

This rugged, heavy machine is built to take abuse and lots of use. It has an extra-long, center-mounted fence with one rather

interesting feature. In addition to being tiltable and movable across the table, you can also swivel it so that any work can cross the blades at an angle, instead of feeding directly into the cutters. Advertisements claim that it improves the cut on exotic woods like cherry and curly maple, and this may be possible. But it does help to keep the work tight against the fence, and this in itself is a useful feature.

Both infeed and outfeed tables are adjustable to allow some offbeat planing cuts on the machine. The adjustable outfeed table also makes it easier to set the cutterhead knives to cut exactly on plane. Automatic stops set the 90-degree position and the front and back 45-degree settings. The knives are always covered, regardless of fence position, because a secondary guard is attached to the fence.

The machine's tables are over 4 feet long and 7 inches wide. Also, the infeed table broadens out to form a rabbeting lip, though this design feature has been discredited because of its inherent danger. Depth-of-cut is ½ inch, the three-knife cutterhead turns at 5000 rpm, and it's powered by either a ½- or ¾-hp motor. The smaller motor should be sufficient for anything but the most heavy-duty commercial applications or continuous use. This is quite a tool, but its purchase can only be justified if you plan to use it extensively. Approx. Price: $650.00

A tenon on round stock can be very difficult to achieve, especially if several pieces are required and the fit is critical. One way to make tenons is to use a jointer to cut them. The result will be a uniform, completely centered tenon of the required diameter.

This effect is achieved by rotating the stock against the direction of rotation of the jointer's cutterhead. The fence can be used as a stop to control the length of the tenon, or a guide jig can be clamped to the table. If the jointer you are using has a rabbeting ledge, the stock can be rested directly on the ledge and fed into the cutterhead. If it does not, the piece must be braced against the guide and brought slowly into the cutters. To form the tenon the work is slowly rotated until the desired depth is obtained. Tenon diameter is controlled by the position of the guide and the depth of the infeed table. It is wise to practice this cut several times on scrap pieces first, since the position of the guide is very important. You must also be careful not to feed the stock too fast, or it may jam in the cutterhead or make a ragged, uneven cut.

The planer's one function is the surface planing of rough lumber; but it does this woodworking task better than any other power machine.

Thickness Planers

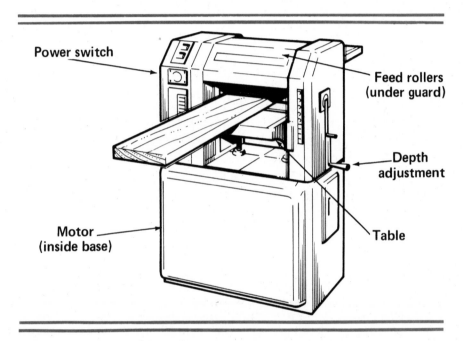

Power switch

Feed rollers (under guard)

Depth adjustment

Motor (inside base)

Table

Normally, stock purchased from a lumberyard is of somewhat dubious thickness and the surface may be smooth or have a grain like an old washboard. The tolerances allowed commercial lumber producers may also mean that two separate pieces of stock can vary as much as ¹⁄₁₆-inch or more in thickness. While this doesn't matter much with 2x4s used for house framing, putting together a table top is another

story. Here, an uneven surface looks terrible and is a sign of bad craftsmanship. Aside from laborious work with a hand plane, the only other way to an even and smooth surface is to use a thickness planer. Planers can give you stock that's sized and smoothed to your specifications, and they can also save you money. You can purchase lower-cost, rough lumber in quantity at a 20% to 50% savings and surface it yourself. And if

you plan to make fine cabinets or furniture, a thickness planer will simplify the job and give you a finer end product.

Thickness planers will not correct board distortions like warp—a concavity across the board—or wind, which is a twist in the board. The infeed rollers on planers are powered, and they will temporarily flatten the board as they move it into the cutterhead. The outfeed roller will also keep the board flat temporarily. When the planing is finished, the board will undoubtedly be thinner, but unfortunately, it will still have the original shape and distortion.

To eliminate such distortion, the board must first be flattened on one side to at least some approximation of a true surface. This can be done on a jointer-planer, with a hand plane, or by resawing on a band saw. The piece is then moved into the thickness planer with this flat surface down to achieve the desired result—a flat board.

Thickness planers are

simple machines, with three major components. A "bed" supports the work, and this is where the wood rests as it is being planed. A "cutterhead," situated below the bed and adjustable for height, turns two or more knives which do the actual planing. A set of "feed rollers" keeps the work flat on the bed and moves it past the cutterhead. Rollers are parallel to the cutterhead, with an infeed roller on one side and an outfeed roller on the other. Both rollers and the cutterhead rotate under power, but at different speeds and in opposite directions. The cutterhead rotates counterclockwise at high speed, while the rollers rotate slowly clockwise. This is done so the wood is fed *against* the direction of rotation of the cutterhead. The speed of the rollers determines how fast the wood moves past the cutterhead, and is expressed as feet-per-minute, or FPM. Common feed speeds range anywhere from 12 to 25 FPM.

When using a planer, very little effort is required on your part. You just place a rough-surfaced board on the entry bed and move it forward into the infeed roller. The machine does the rest. The stock is moved by the cutterhead, woodchips spew out like cornflakes, and the smooth-surfaced board appears on the outfeed table. This machine is a simple, hands-off pleasure to use.

Just about the only control found on this machine is a handle or wheel that adjusts the distance between the bed and the cutterhead. This is a simple adjustment to accommodate different stock thicknesses.

All thickness planers produce the smoothest surface when you feed the work into the machine so that the cutterheads cut *with* the grain of the wood. Usually, it's easy to determine grain direction, since grain patterns often have a "V" shape. The point of the V should point

Aside from simple surfacing, a planer does not find much use around the shop. Yet even with these limitations it is possible to create some unusual crafted pieces. Butcher block tables have become popular and functional kitchen and decorating items whose beauty is matched only by their expense. The possession of a planer enables the craftsman to turn out those tables by the dozen, limited only by the amount of scrap hardwood available and the bed width of the planer.

The high cost of even minimal thicknesses of butcher block is directly related to the difficulty in surfacing it. Hand planing with a block plane can take forever, and there is the likelihood of splitting and tear out. Using a planer to get a smooth and uniform surface is much simpler, leaving a minimal amount of finish sanding to finish off the piece.

To make a butcher block table, use a jointer or hand plane to smooth the sides of long 2-inch-square stock. Maple is the traditional material, but any hardwood can be used. After side planing, the stock is cut into equal lengths of 2 or more inches. These blocks are glued side-to-side using a bar clamp, with the endgrains facing up and down. The resulting long strips are glued together side-by-side, until a square area is obtained the length and width of the finished table. Allow some extra stock to permit surface finishing on the edges.

When the table blank has dried thoroughly, hand plane off any excess glue lines (to prevent any damage to the planer cutters). Pass the blank through the planer on both sides, taking minimal cuts to assure smoothness. Do not make so many passes that the resulting thickness of the butcher block table will be less than 1½ inches, otherwise the table will lack rigidity and may split. The sides of the blank are cut with a table saw and finished off with a sanding block, as is the surface.

If the butcher block blank is to be used in the kitchen as a work surface or countertop insert, the top and edges must be sealed carefully. Otherwise, water or oil will soak into the block and result in warping or splitting of the individual pieces.

down toward the cutterhead. If you feed the wood into the machine incorrectly, the machine will emit a staccato sound instead of a smooth purr. The waste will also contain splinters of large chips, and the planed surface will look like a washboard.

The size of a thickness planer is determined by the length of the cutterhead's knives. This tells how wide a piece of wood the machine can handle. Sometimes the maximum thickness of stock that can be planed is included in the description. A 12x4-inch machine, for example, can handle stock that is up to 12 inches wide and 4 inches thick. Commercial machines can handle wood as large as 4 to 5 feet wide, but these are obviously not candidates for the home shop.

There is no limit on the length of stock that can be fed into a thickness planer. The only restriction is width. So little space is needed on either side of the machine, but lots of room is needed on the infeed and outfeed sides. If you plan to feed 10-foot-long boards into the machine, then you need 10 feet of space on both the infeed and outfeed sides of the machine. This can create a problem in a small shop. But you can handle this problem by placing the infeed end close to a door. This way you can open the door and feed work into the machine from outside the shop, reducing the space required inside by 50%.

Even the smallest thickness planers are hefty, dangerous machines that should be treated with respect. They can remove 1/8-inch or more from the surface of a board as easily as a sharp knife can slice cheese for a sandwich. You should never place your hands even close to the cutterhead when the power is on. All planers come equipped with protective covers that include a chip deflector. Its purpose is to insure that the waste which is produced by the cutterhead is lifted away from the stock and directed away from the cutting area. The waste is thrown toward the outfeed end. Usually, these are small shavings that can do little harm, but once in a while a splinter or piece of knot is ejected. A good practice is to stand at the side of the machine when it's in operation, and help support the work as it emerges from the outfeed roller.

Some curious people can't resist the temptation to lift the guards to view the action—this is a stupid move. The best way to see how a planer works is to pull the plug and look at it then. This is also the only way you should change the knives on a cutterhead. Pull the plug and take great care when working around the knives. Even a dull knife on a cutterhead is sharp enough to cut fingers severely, and use of gloves is recommended.

Read the machine's instructions carefully to find out the maximum recommended depth-of-cut, too. If you go too deep on one pass, the machine will jam or chatter. In addition, a piece of wood shorter than the distance between the two rollers will result in poor cuts, a jammed machine, or the machine will spit the wood out in dangerous little pieces. For safe, efficient operation, follow the directions carefully and use your head.

The Inca 510 is a Swiss-made, combination large-capacity jointer and automatic-feed thickness planer. It's a compact tool that requires less than half the floor space of two separate machines and accomplishes the same functions.

As a thickness planer, this machine has a capacity of 10x6 5/16 inches, giving a width-of-cut that's smaller than most machines, but adequate for furniture making. Width-of-cut capacity when set up as a jointer is also 10 inches, which is wider by some 4 to 6 inches than typical home-version jointers. Unfortunately, the infeed and outfeed tables are on the short side, so longer boards require roller stands for jointer operations. The changeover from jointer to planer capabilities takes less than a minute.

The two-knife cutterhead turns at 6000 rpm, which gives you 12,000 cuts-per-minute. You can set the automatic feed at either

Garrett Wade's Inca 510 Jointer/Thickness Planer

many small shop owners reduce costs, and prompted others into retirement or moonlighting—making extra cash from sales of moldings and other standard pieces.

A 1-hp motor can drive this machine, but it's designed for motors up to 5-hp. A 2- or 3-hp powerplant is a happy medium for the small shop owner. Planer capacity is 6x12¼ inches, and the cutterhead turns 4100 rpm with recommended pulleys and motor. Automatic feed speed can be either 12 or 22 feet-per-minute. But the higher speed only makes sense with a motor over 1-hp when mass production is the goal. Approx. Price: $640.00

11½ or 16½ feet-per-minute by simply changing a belt. The automatic feed speed determines how many cuts are made on a given piece of wood. Slower speeds give you more cuts than higher speeds. Softwood requires a fast feed, while hardwoods are planed best at slower speeds.

This machine has a good guard system, and a chromium-plated planer table minimizes friction. You control depth-of-cut with a handwheel, and read the settings on a built-in scale. The scale has measurements in English feet on one side, and a metric scale on the other. To switch them requires removing only two screws and flipping the unit over. A drawing for a special wood stand is included, but a

motor is not. At least a ½-hp motor is recommended to get the fullest use of this machine. Approx. Price: $1089.00

The Belsaw 910
Planer-Molder-Saw is basically a thickness planer, but it lets you mount shaper knives in place of blank planing knives and add a circular saw blade for ripping. This lets you plane, mold and cut a board to width, all in one operation, or you can use the features independently. Perhaps the average amateur doesn't need a multi-purpose tool with such a wide workscope, but this machine's capabilities have helped

The W-7S molder-planer from Williams & Hussey Machine Corporation, weighs only 80 pounds and uses only a 1-hp motor. But it's no sissy, since it can plane off ¼-inch of stock in a single pass. This machine has an open-end design which has been attempted unsuccessfully by a few other manufacturers, but which works in this machine. It works because the machine is made of gutsy steel and cast iron, assembled to prevent possible deflection of the topside cutterhead unit. The cutterhead is designed to use shaping knives as well as blank planing knives for good versatility. Cutterhead rotation is a good 7000 rpm; output capacity, with power feed, is a respectable 15

Williams & Hussey W-7S Molder-Planer

Close-up of W-7S

feet-per-minute. The machine allows you to work with stock as thick as 8¼ inches, but the standard width capacity is only 7⅛ inches. This small width capacity is not really a drawback because of the open-end design. You can make one pass with the stock, flip it around, and make a second pass to double the width capacity. Also, you can save quite a bit of money if you're willing to settle for a non-power feed version. Approx. Price: $445.00

Rockwell's Uniplane is a unique, giant of a machine with the delicate touch of a surgeon. It's a highly sophisticated rotary planer that at first glance doesn't look like a jointer-planer. But a closer look reveals a

dynamically balanced cutterhead, mounted on a vertical plane and resembling a thick, 8-inch diameter pancake. The cutterhead secures and turns eight high speed steel cutters, which resemble machine shop tool bits. Four of the cutters are set to score, and four do a

Rockwell's Uniplane

shearing cut. Overall, this produces exceptionally fine finishes. Although this machine, operated with a ¾-hp motor, can easily handle a ⅛-inch cut on hardwood, its fascination lies in how *little* material it can shave away. Depth-of-cut is adjusted with a "Micro-Set" knob, having a collar calibrated in 64th-inch gradations. This capacity lets you do everything from getting a respectable finish on the end grain of a 6x6-inch timber to forming a flat on a matchstick. Other functions include jointing, planing, beveling, chamfering, tapering and doing a ready-to-assemble finish on simple or compound miters. Cutterhead speed is 4000 rpm, which gives a total for the eight bits of 32,000 cuts-per-minute. Approx. Price: $615.00

Every project requires some shaping, even the most simple. This may be light filing or chiseling, or many lathe-turned parts with decorative, shaped fluting. Here's where you'll find the right tool to do it correctly — every time.

Shaping Tools

Files/Rasps

Today the file is often overlooked by the craftsman. This is mainly because few people have any way to learn the art of hand filing. Many eagerly sought-after antiques are a tribute to this art. The Pennsylvania rifle, for example, is a case in point. Most weapons and machines made prior to 1750 had metal parts and screws that were all made by hand filing. Even when working with wood, the file is a handy item to have around. It can clean up small areas very quickly, and is especially useful for removing that last 1/64-inch for a close-tolerance fit.

Originally, all files were handmade, and often entire families specialized in their manufacture. Many of these file-making concerns were located in the Alps region of France and Switzerland.

Even today, the finest files are still made in these regions, and the term "Swiss" has become synonymous with quality files. Nicholson, which makes the majority of files in

North America, markets "Swiss Pattern Files." These are actually made by the Grobet firm in Switzerland.

There are two basic types of files — chisel-tooth and rasp. Chisel-tooth files are for both wood and metal working, while rasps are solely for working with wood. The surface of a chisel-tooth file can be described as a line of minute, continuous wood chisels arranged in a pattern. When you push the file over the

The technique of learning to use a file may seem very cumbersome and it does take some time to get the knack. One of the first problems anyone has in using one is to "hold a flat." Usually what happens is that a user intends the surface to be flat, but the final result is rounded. It is easier to "hold a flat" if you do not move the file both ways along the surface. Instead, cut only on the forward stroke and lift the file from the work on the return. This technique should be used during all metal filing because it results in a better surface and makes the file last much longer. Another trick which helps to hold a flat surface is to place the thumb of the leading hand on top of the file's tip and the first and second fingers under it. This hold is much like what you would practice if you were going to bend the file. When combined with lifting the file during the return stroke, this hold helps to promote a true flat surface in the material.

work, the chisel teeth actually cut away as they pass over it. A rasp, on the other hand, is like a small board with nails sticking out of it. When a rasp is pushed over a piece of wood, the nail-like projections abrade the material, rather than cutting it away.

In the days when files were handmade, the worker first used a cold chisel and hammer to make a series of cuts in a steel blank. This raised a series of teeth. After the cutting process, the tool was heat-treated. To make a rasp, a series of projections were raised on the blank before heat-treating. Today, of course, all files are made by machine.

Machine-made chisel files come in two varieties: "single-cut" and "double-cut." Single-cut files have only one row of teeth cut diagonally across the file. Double-cut files have two rows of cuts made diagonally across the file, at about a 30-degree angle to one another. Each type has advantages and disadvantages.

A single-cut file generally yields a smoother surface than a double-cut of the same grade. Double-cut files, however, have the advantage that the second cut acts as an effective chip-breaker. The file doesn't "load up" or clog with material as readily. Only single-cut models can be used for a technique called draw-filing, which is used on long pieces that must have a cylindrical or curved surface. In this procedure, you turn

Length

This is measured exclusive of tang from point to heel. Desired stroke length, type of material, and its size will determine length required.

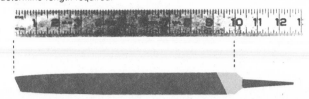

Coarseness

Work to be accomplished, roughing or finishing, will determine type of teeth and coarseness for each application.

Comparative Coarseness 10" Mill

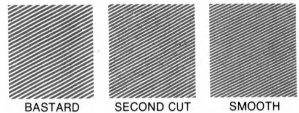

BASTARD   SECOND CUT   SMOOTH

The degree of coarseness is greater in longer files, but differences between bastard, second cut, and smooth are proportionate.

Area to be filed will determine specific cross section: round, square, knife, flat, etc., to be used.

Kinds of Teeth

Single cut and double cut are the two choices of chisel cut teeth.

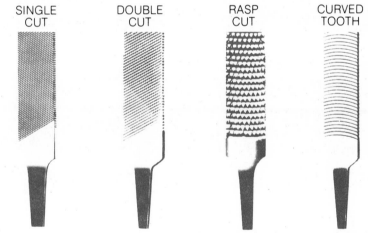

SINGLE CUT   DOUBLE CUT   RASP CUT   CURVED TOOTH

single cut, one series of parallel teeth double cut, two series of teeth, over cut and up cut

Shape

Area to be filed will determine specific cross section; round, square, knife, flat, etc., to be used.

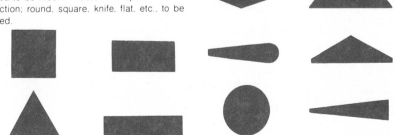

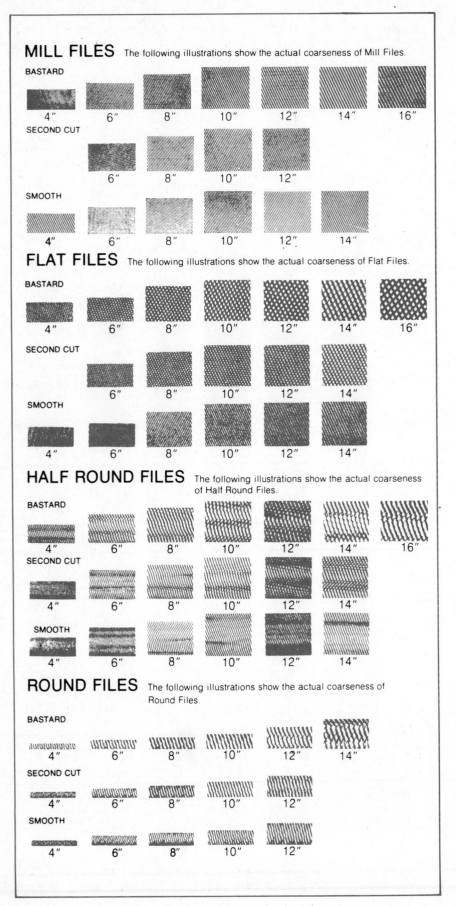

MILL FILES
The following illustrations show the actual coarseness of Mill Files.

BASTARD
4" 6" 8" 10" 12" 14" 16"

SECOND CUT
6" 8" 10" 12"

SMOOTH
4" 6" 8" 10" 12" 14"

FLAT FILES
The following illustrations show the actual coarseness of Flat Files.

BASTARD
4" 6" 8" 10" 12" 14" 16"

SECOND CUT
6" 8" 10" 12" 14"

SMOOTH
4" 6" 8" 10" 12" 14"

HALF ROUND FILES
The following illustrations show the actual coarseness of Half Round Files.

BASTARD
4" 6" 8" 10" 12" 14" 16"

SECOND CUT
4" 6" 8" 10" 12" 14"

SMOOTH
4" 6" 8" 10" 12" 14"

ROUND FILES
The following illustrations show the actual coarseness of Round Files.

BASTARD
4" 6" 8" 10" 12" 14"

SECOND CUT
4" 6" 8" 10" 12"

SMOOTH
4" 6" 8" 10" 12"

the file sideways, about 90 degrees to the work surface, and draw it along the work. The file has a tendency to move sideways, but if you're careful and apply moderate pressure, the work progresses fast. The material is literally planed away as long, thin shavings peel away from the back of the file.

In any type of filing, there's always the problem of having the file clog with waste during the cut. When material builds up between the teeth, cutting virtually stops. At this point, the loaded-up file is said to be "pinned." This is more of a problem when filing metal than wood. One way to partially prevent this is to chalk the file with an ordinary piece of blackboard chalk before using. Once a file does become pinned, it must be cleaned. You do this with a "file card" — a brush with very short, steel bristles inclined slightly in one direction. As this file card is pulled parallel to the teeth, it removes the waste and cleans the file.

Figuring out what file to buy isn't easy because they come in so many sizes, shapes and cuts. The common file shapes are: flat, pillar, square, taper (sometimes called three-square), half-round, and round. These names refer to the file's cross-sectional area. A file may be tapered for its entire length, or may maintain the same thickness throughout. Files may also have teeth on all sides, or one or more sides may be "safe."

A safe side has no teeth, permitting work in corners or areas where you only wish to cut one surface.

Files are also sold in various "cuts," a term that refers to the relative coarseness of the teeth. Cuts run from bastard (coarsest), to second-cut (medium), and smooth (finest). A shop should be equipped with at least a flat, round, half-round, and three-square file. For general use, a coarse bastard cut is recommended, plus a selection of rasps. If you do metal work, some of the finer bastard cuts as well as second-cut and smooth can probably be put to good use.

If you do a lot of filing, a file handle is a useful accessory. This is just a simple wood or plastic handle that fits over the tang of the file. You only require one, because you can switch it from file to file. A handle promotes a higher quality of work in that it assures you of a good grip. Consider a file handle necessary if you intend to do any draw filing or dressing any sharp edges.

Most of the files found in retail outlets and offered by catalog houses look and cost virtually the same regardless of brand name. This is because the majority of files made for the North American market are manufactured by Nicholson File, a part of The Cooper Group. This company's dominance in the consumer and trade fields is tremendous. Even if a particular file carries a brand name that is not Nicholson, it is probably made by that company and sold under a different label. There is only one way to make a good-quality file. Because of this we favor the Nicholson files, either under their own name or their Black Diamond brand.

Some typical file shapes and their uses are:

Pillar files: These files have a thicker, more rectangular cross-section than flat files. They are used mostly by machinists for cutting slots and keyways in metal work. Approx. Price: (10 inch, bastard) $4.00

Flat files: The standard, all-purpose file used for

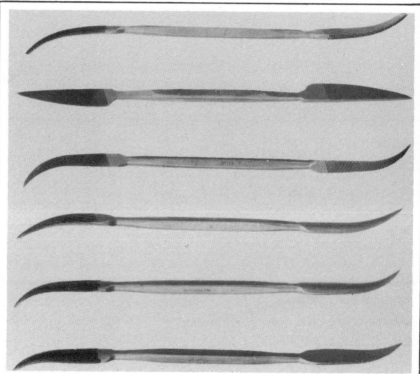

Like any tool, files come in a wide variety of shapes and sizes. What is important, perhaps, is the kind of work which the file is intended to do. "Riffler" files are a special pattern that is very handy for getting into small, narrow spaces. These files are cut onto the ends of round shafts, then bent at an angle to that shaft. These facilitate the filing of difficult shapes in hard to approach areas. They find most of their application in jewelry and fine detail work, but can also be used in other kinds of shaping. Rifflers are expensive, and not worth the purchase unless you do this kind of small, precise shaping. But, once you have taken the plunge and invested in a set, you'll wonder how you got along without them.

Nicholson's Flat File

Nicholson's Taper File

Nicholson's Round File

machinist's work, shaping metals, draw filing, and metal finishing. Available in lengths of 4 to 16 inches, and degrees of coarseness of bastard, second-cut, and smooth. Flat files are usually made single cut on both flat edges. Approx. Price: (10 inch, bastard) $3.50

Square files: Large sizes in these files are often preferred over corresponding flat files because they have four filing surfaces and a thicker cross-section. These files are used for general surface filing, keyways, and slots. Approx. Price: (10 inch, bastard) $4.00

Taper files: Also called triangular files because of their three-sided cross-section. Most often used for filing handsaws and

for narrow cuts close to an obstruction, they are available in regular taper down to double extra slim. Only one kind of cut is available. Approx. Price: (10 inch, slim) $3.00

Half-round files: These files have one flat surface, with the other semi-circular in shape. Half-round files are used for filing contours and other shapes in metals. They are available in bastard, second cut, and smooth. Approx. Price: (10 inch, bastard) $5.00

Round files: These files taper slightly to a point with a completely round cross-section. Normally used to file circular openings or concave surfaces, they are often called "rat-tail" files because of their shape.

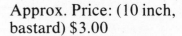

Approx. Price: (10 inch, bastard) $3.00

Cabinet rasps: These are very similar in shape to the half-round file, only the radius of the curved edge is much greater. Available in a coarseness of regular (actually a second-cut) and smooth, these are used for coarse cutting of wood by cabinet/furniture makers and woodworkers. Approx. Price: (10 inch, smooth) $10.00

Surforms/ Abraders

In spite of their efficiency, files and rasps are unpopular because they have two unavoidable problems. One of these is "pinning" or clogging. Both tools will quickly pick up material from the work, which lodges in the crevices between the cutting edges. Even chalking the file or rasp will not prevent this. Periodically you have to stop and clean off the tool. The other problem is learning how to hold the tools so as to assure the desired shape in the work. They should always be used with a handle and the correct grip on the free end. When held this way, they will do an excellent shaping job. It does require some practice and a slight knack. Many users do not take the time to practice and, after a bad initial experience, throw the file or rasp in a box and forget it.

There are products on the market, however, which are a clever union of the traditional file or rasp and modern technology. In form these tools are nothing but an abrading surface with a permanently attached handle, and they are used in much the same manner as a standard file or rasp. Pinning is prevented in these tools because the cutting surface is open, allowing shavings and particles to pass through and be shaken off the tool. The problem of holding the tool correctly is also partially solved because of the design. A wide variety of shapes is available that can conform to even the most awkward shaping space—be it round, square, hole, or corner.

Because they can be adapted to so many odd uses on a wide variety of materials, this type of shaping tool can be useful around any shop. Wood, tile, plastics, and metals up to the hardness of mild steel can be shaped or trimmed with these tools. Their body shape can be as varied as the different spaces where they are used. A plane shape with attached handle is probably the most generally useful. They are also available as shavers, traditional round or flat file types, and even round drums

for use with power equipment.

While they do not completely replace the traditional file or rasp (they cannot be used to "draw file," for example), they are a useful adjunct in the shop where shaping and forming materials can often be a problem. Power tools are useful, but they cannot do shaping operations where they can't fit. Surform tools or abraders are different, for with these you can choose the tool to fit the work at hand. One of them is always the right shape, no matter what task they are required to do.

Stanley's Surform tools are perhaps the best known hybrid union of a rasp and a permanent handle. The blades or cutting surfaces of these tools are semi-circles

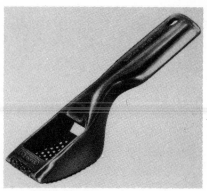
Stanley's Surform Shaver

punched through a metal plate, with a raised, razor-sharp metal lip. The metal lips do the actual cutting, while the material that is shredded or sliced away passes through the holes and prevents clogging.

Blades on the Surform tools are replaceable, and can be purchased with either a regular or fine cut, and with either a flat or half-round surface. Body shapes include flat and round files with attached handles; a variety of plane shapes; shavers, and

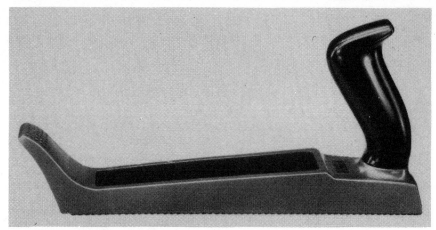
Stanley's Surform Plane

Stanley's Surform File

No matter what the cutting tool, it will only cut as well as the sharpened edge. Chisels, gouges, planes, irons — any edged tool in fact — have to be sharpened properly. Although most small shops will have a bench grinder to true up a ragged edge, that final keenness can only be obtained by using a whetstone. If you wish to get the most use out of your tools, a whetstone is a necessity. There is no finer variety than natural Arkansas stones.

Arkansas stones are manufactured from an almost pure natural silica rock called Novaculite that occurs around the city of Hot Springs. There are four basic grades of this whetstone: Washita, Soft, Hard, and Black Hard Arkansas. Washita is the fastest cutting, with the others producing a progressively finer edge due to increased hardness. Black Hard Arkansas is often called "surgical" Arkansas because it is used to sharpen medical instruments, and will produce a razor-sharp edge. Soft Arkansas is probably the most general grade, and will produce a fine edge in a minimum of time.

Arkansas stones are always used with honing oil, and should always be cleaned after use with a little kerosene. They are also expensive, but with reasonable care will last a lifetime. If you require the finest of cutting edges on your tools, purchase of an Arkansas stone is more than a necessity, it is indispensable.

etched into a stainless-steel sheet. These pillars are all of uniform cutting height and non-directional, which allows the Abrader to be used in any direction without gouging.

The cutting surface or sheet is permanently bonded to a plastic handle which can be square, full round, or several other odd shapes. The flat-faced models can be bought in either a coarse or fine grade, while the round and half-round are sold only in a coarse grade. Although they are not made for cutting metals, they are ideal for shaping/sanding tasks in wood or plastics, removing paint, and other smoothing jobs. They are a welcome addition to the shop and once you've bought one, you'll wonder how you did without it. Approx. Price: (square) $7.00

drum styles. The latter is for use with a portable electric drill or a drill press. All of the Surform tools will produce straight, contour, or odd-shaped cuts in soft materials. These tools are widely available in most hardware outlets. Approx. Price: (plane type) $8.00

Disston's Abraders are made for use on wood and soft materials. Abraders will sand wood more rapidly than sandpaper, while leaving a finish that is smoother. The cutting edge of these tools consists of hundreds of chrome-plated teeth or pillars

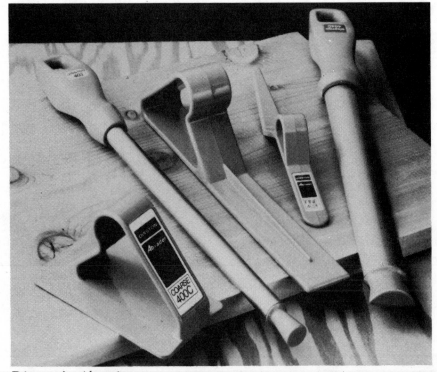

Disston's Abraders

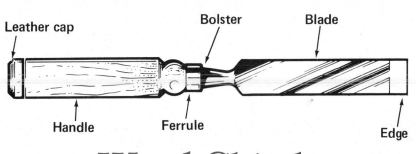

Leather cap — Bolster — Blade

Handle — Ferrule — Edge

Wood Chisels

Every woodworker, from cabinetmaker to rough-house framer, needs at least a couple of wood chisels. A wood chisel is a simple tool—just a blade attached to a sturdy handle—but when one is needed, nothing else can take its place.

Chisels have their own jargon, resulting from tradition and long use. This vocabulary can seem strange at times. The chisel most people think of as a "carpenter's chisel" is technically called a "firmer" chisel. Firmer chisels are designed to be struck with a hammer on the end opposite the cutting edge. These chisels are flat with parallel sides, and are intended for general use. The sides of a firmer chisel can take one of two forms. One is a bevel edge, in which the sides of the chisel are ground at an angle to the cross-section of the body. These sides fit better in tight spaces, and are used for work on the dainty side. Square-ground sides give the chisel body a boxy cross-section. Chisels with square-ground sides are used for tough cutting, like mortise holes and deeper slots in wood. This is because square-ground sides give greater strength to the corner of the chisel.

Handles are attached to firmer chisels in several ways. Most commonly, a "tang," which is a sharp projection from the chisel blade, is driven into a hole in the handle. Usually there's a metal bolster at the beginning of the tang to prevent the handle from going all the way down the chisel and splitting it. Traditionally chisel handles were made of wood, but these eventually split after repeated blows. Now they're also made of plastic, which is virtually indestructible.

Tang design has been improved by the insertion of a leather washer between the bolster and the handle. The leather takes some of the shock out of repeated pounding, and greatly extends handle life. Washers are usually added in combination with a brass hoop or ferrule around the end of the handle. This also tends to retard splitting. Both of these design improvements are found in most quality chisels, and are a sign of careful manufacturing.

A firmer chisel may also have a "socket handle"-type handle attachment. The chisel blade itself ends in a conical or round mortise hole. The handle is made with a tapered tenon that fits into this socket, and it's usually capped with a leather washer to prevent breakage. Socket chisel handles have several advantages, the best of which is that they can be used interchangeably among chisels. They're also better for rugged work, because more force can be transmitted to the blade without breakage.

Regardless of type of handle attachment, firmer chisels can be purchased individually or in prepackaged sets of from three to five chisels. For the average shop, a four-piece set is best. It should include chisels with blades ranging from ¼- to 1-inch wide. Unless you intend to do a lot of cutting by hand, rather than with a hammer, stick with plastic handles. They last longer and require less care than wooden handles.

When buying a chisel, the most important consideration is the quality of the blade's steel. Usually, the more expensive the chisel, the better the quality of the steel

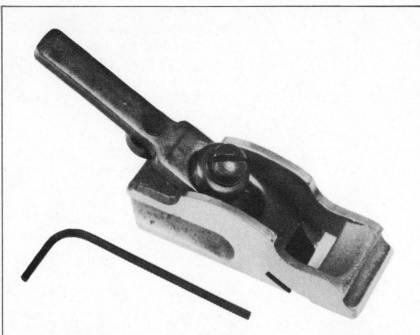

In cabinet and finish carpentry the most common fastener used is the finish nail. This does not have a head like a common nail; instead, there is a slight swelling with a dished depression on the top. A punch called a "nail set" is used to sink the nail below the surface, with the hole being filled afterwards to conceal it. These holes are never completely hidden, however, and if a clear finish is used they tend to be very noticeable.

A trick to get around this problem is called "blind nailing." To do this a craftsman will use a narrow wood chisel to raise up a curl of wood at the point where a nail is to be driven. The finish nail is driven into the trough under the curl. Afterwards the chip is glued down. Once dry and then sanded, the nail is completely hidden.

The trick in doing this, aside from a little practice, is to first dampen the area where the chip is to be raised. This will allow the chip to be raised without breaking. A good, sharp, narrow chisel about ⅛- or ¼-inch wide is best. Using light hammer blows to move the chisel will result in the best curl, but it is wise to practice this procedure on scrap first. Blind nailing, when done incorrectly, can produce mistakes that are difficult to cover up afterwards without a lot of extra work.

An alternative to the normal blind nailing technique is to use a tool designed for this task. Conover Woodcraft manufactures what they call a "blind-nailer" — a small brass body with an adjustable iron. To use it the wood is dampened first, the blind-nailer set into place, and tapped lightly with a hammer. This produces the required curl of wood with a minimum of fuss. At $21.00, it may be just the tool you need for delicate cabinet work.

used in its manufacture. So this is a good way to judge quality in chisels of the same size. This price-quality relationship holds true for chisels more than it does for any other tool.

The Stanley 64 firmer chisel set is one of the company's top-of-the-line sets, containing four chisels in ¼-, ½-, ¾- and 1-inch sizes. Each tool has a 3-inch-long blade and a two-tone plastic handle with a black bolster and cap and an amber center section. This is a fine starter set for the craftsman, and includes a convenient plastic case. Other chisels in Stanley's "best" line are available in sizes up to 2 inches wide. Approx. Price: $26.00

The Stanley H1252R chisel set is part of the company's "handyman" line. It includes ¼-, ½-, ¾- and 1-inch size firmer chisels of adequate quality for most casual chisel work. This "handyman" line of chisels, however, does not offer as wide a range of sizes as Stanley's "best" line. Approx. Price: $15.50

Greenlee sells a professional set of firmer chisels which is made by Marples of England. These chisels have a traditional design, with beechwood handles bound with a hoop. They also have a leather washer in front

Greenlee's Marples Mortise Chisel

of the bolster. The sides of these chisels are not beveled, so they are correctly called "mortise chisels." Blades are of high-quality, high-carbon Sheffield steel, with excellent edge-holding ability. They are available in ¼-, ⅜-, ½-, ⅝-, ¾-, and 1-inch sizes. Approx. Price:(½-inch) $8.00

or mail order house also sells paring chisels individually. This way, you can replace chisels, or add to your set more economically. Also, ask if the handles are replaceable. Paring chisels with replaceable handles can save you money in the long run. Some companies make paring chisels without handles, too. This is because many woodcarvers make their own handles to save money and assure a good, comfortable grip.

Paring Chisels

Paring chisels are used for woodcarving. They're designed to be pushed by hand, rather than hit by a hammer. So, their handles are not as sturdy as those of firmer chisels, and are smaller to fit comfortably in the hand.

A wide variety of sizes and shapes is available. One visit to a woodcarver's shop will quickly give you an appreciation of the investment a carver must make in paring chisels.

Although designed for hand use, all woodcarvers strike them occasionally with a wooden mallet that looks much like a rolling pin. Striking is not necessary unless the wood is extremely dense and tough, or if a heavy cut is needed.

Paring chisel sets range from small sets of three to five, to comprehensive sets of 15 to 20 tools. It's probably best to choose a set of five to 10 chisels to begin with. When you buy the set, be sure to find out if the store

Woodcraft Supply's "Swiss Carving Tools" are probably the best available. All of the paring chisels in this extensive line are recommended as high-quality tools. Woodcraft Supply sells these chisels individually and in large (#13D16-D) and small (#13D17-D) sets which include a book on woodcarving, an Arkansas slipstone, and a Belgian honing stone. Approx. Price: (13D17-D) $49.50

Carving Parquet (1760s)

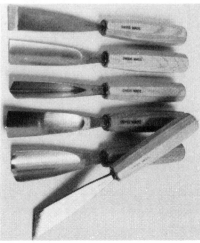

Woodcraft's Carving Tools

Greenlee's Marples Paring Chisel

Greenlee's extensive line of paring chisels is made by Marples of England. You can buy these chisels, catalog #3030, in sets or individually from mail-order houses and some craft shops. These chisels come in ¼-, ½-, ¾-, 1-, 1¼-, and 1½-inch sizes. Quality is good, although the tools are not the best. Approx. Price: (1-inch) $11.00

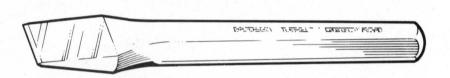

Cold Chisels

Cold chisels are designed to cut metal—not wood. A quality model is made of a tough, forged-steel blank that's heat-treated to withstand the repeated shocks of metal cutting. Although a cold chisel looks much like a wood firmer chisel, it doesn't have a wooden handle. The shank is usually octagonal in shape, and ends in a simple, slightly spherical, head. To prevent the edge from breaking during the high stresses of metal cutting, it's not as thin as that of a wood chisel.

A cold chisel is commonly used for cutting off bolts and cutting light sheet metal, like that on the top of an oil drum. The most useful type of cold chisel is the flat, standard-blade type, ½-inch or more wide. Some cold chisel sets give you a diamond-point, round-nose, and cape chisel in addition to the standard type. These other chisels have special applications. The cape chisel, for example, is used to correct a drill hole where the drill has wandered off center. If the set you buy has these special-purpose chisels, you are probably wasting your precious money. They can always be bought individually whenever you have a need for them—if ever.

A "drift" and a "punch" are much the same. They're used for "drifting," or punching-out pins and rusted bolts during machine setup. A punch is tapered throughout its length and ends in a flat point; a drift is one diameter overall. Punches can withstand greater striking forces because the tapered body tends to strengthen the point. But a drift can follow a pin down into a hole and gain access where a punch can't. Usually, a punch is used to start the pin or bolt, and the drift is used to push it through. The drift gets its name from this technique, which is called "drifting the pin."

Center punches are used for marking and layout work, and are usually employed for marking points for holes to be drilled. Hitting a center punch with a hammer leaves a slight indentation or hole that's easily picked up by the drill point. You should always use a center punch for marking a drilling location in wood or metal, because it almost eliminates the drill's annoying tendency to drift when started on a smooth surface. Center punches are available individually, and are also often part of a cold chisel and punch set. This type of set is an economical way to obtain the cold chisels and punches commonly needed. It usually contains a center punch, in addition to several standard cold chisels and a drift or punch.

The Stanley Tools 18-905 five-piece punch and cold chisel set is just right for everyday shop use. This set includes a center punch, two cold chisels, a punch and a drift. All of these tools are made of fine-quality steel, with the added convenience of a vinyl coating on the shank of the tool. This coating has a practical, shock-absorbing effect when you hold and use the tools. The set is available in most hardware stores. Approx. Price: $13.00

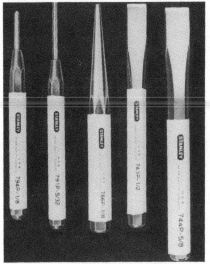

Stanley's 18-905 Five-Piece Punch and Cold Chisel Set

projection that fits into a hole in the wood handle. The socket-type handle fits into a circular mortise in the chisel body. Both do the job, but the harder-to-find socket variety is more useful, because handles are interchangeable between several gouges. Although gouges are less in demand than other types of chisels, you can find them in better hardware stores and most catalog houses dealing in woodworking tools.

Gouges

Gouges are wood chisels that have their blades bent into a specific radius. This curvature can vary greatly, depending upon the tool's design and intended work. For this reason, there's a wider selection of gouges than other chisels.

"In-cannel" and "out-cannel" varieties are available. This terminology refers to the direction in which the bevel at the end of the blade is ground. An in-cannel gouge has a bevel ground on the inside of the curved blade and is used for removing material from a concave surface, such as the inside of a bowl. An out-cannel gouge has the bevel ground on the outside of the curved blade for removing material from convex shapes like the outside of a bowl.

Gouges are available with either "tang"- or "socket"-type handles. With tang-type handles the blade has a

Greenlee's socket-handle, out-cannel gouges are fine tools that exhibit quality workmanship. Greenlee is also one of the last large firms to make this type of gouge. These gouges have handles of selected hickory, fitted with a leather tip for longer service life. They have a medium sweep (curved) blade of tempered alloy steel, with excellent edge-holding capability. The Greenlee socket-type firmer gouges are available in ¼-, ⅜-, ½-, ¾-, 1-, and 1½-inch sizes. Approx. Price: (½-inch) $14.50

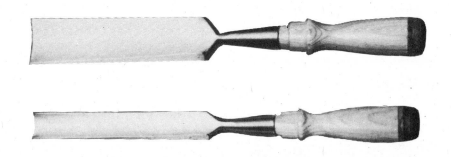

Greenlee's Socket-Handle Out-Cannel Gouges

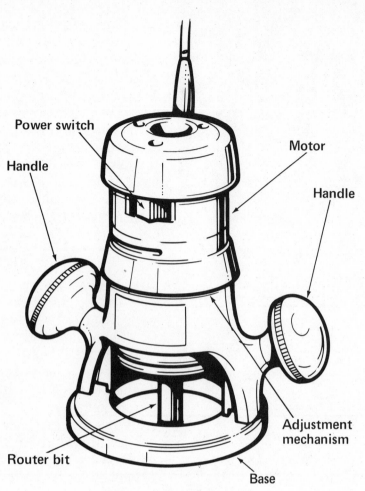

Power switch

Handle

Motor

Handle

Adjustment
mechanism

Router bit

Base

Portable Routers

If an experienced shop owner had to make a choice between a router and a shaper, the router would win hands down. You can use this small, portable tool to form any decorative edge, as well as practical ones like those required for a drop-leaf table joint. Dadoes, grooves, rabbets, and the more-complicated joint forms like the mortise-tenon can all be made with this tool. With the proper template, you can even make a dovetail joint. Routers incise and carve, cut circles, pierce, trim out plastic laminates and form cutouts for electrical outlets in wallboard or paneling. You're only limited by the number of accessories you have for this easy-to-use tool.

This is a lot to say about a power tool you can carry around in one hand, but it's true.

For all its versatility, the router is a simple machine. It's no more than a vertically mounted motor whose rotating shaft ends in a chuck that grips a variety of cutting tools. The motor sits on a base that keeps it in a vertical position, and this base can be adjusted up and down to control the amount the cutter protrudes. This motor turns at high speeds approaching 30,000 rpm, which accounts for the router's exceptionally smooth cuts across the grain of wood.

The method used to control the motor's vertical adjustment can vary between tools. One common system incorporates a helical action that works like a screw thread. The motor threads into the base. Turning the motor clockwise lowers it and the attached chuck and cutter. Turning the motor in the opposite direction raises the cutter and motor.

Another system has a rack-and-pinion arrangement. The motor has a rack that is affixed to the base. An external knob turns the gear and racks the motor up and down. In many cases, the housing that encases this mechanism has a built-in scale that gives you a direct read-out of depth-of-cut adjustments. Regardless of the vertical adjustment system, there's always a lock or handle that secures the motor's position. The precision and positive locking of this vertical adjustment mechanism is critical to the function of the router. It must operate positively, smoothly, and lock in place once it's in the correct position. Any looseness here is a reason to pass up the machine.

The chuck fixed to the end of the shaft is of the collet type. Turning a threaded collar with a wrench causes the collet to grip the shaft of the inserted cutting tool. Some tools require two wrenches—one to turn the collar, and another to prevent the shaft from turning. There are some routers on the market that have a built-in device to lock the shaft. This makes adjustments easier and reduces profanity in the shop. The ability of the collet to grip the cutter is of critical importance. It should grip firmly, without slipping.

Two handles are always attached to the base of the tool. These range from simple knobs to fancy pistol grips, but they should offer you a secure grip for moving the tool around. Some pistol-grip types have a built-in on-off switch with a lock. This lets you lock the switch in the "on" position, yet turn the machine off quickly by pressing the trigger again. The arrangement is an advantage, since you can shut off the machine without releasing one of the handles.

All router bases accept an "edge guide." This is an adjustable fence that guides the router when making parallel cuts along an edge.

Routers are very handy for making a wide variety of decorative cuts. One of the easiest to do with a router is "tapered flutes," where the depth-of-cut varies along the length of the flute. Often this is done around a circle to create a rosette pattern. This is difficult to do in any other way and makes a distinctive decorative effect.

The way to do this is to make a template. If a slot is cut in a board that is already shaped like a ramp it can be used as a template to form tapered cuts in another board. A template "guide" (available from most router manufacturers) is attached to the base of the router. The slot in the ramp-shaped board is cut to this width so that the router can follow it smoothly.

The technique is simple: Make a straight cut that is guided by the ramp-shaped slot. As you go down the ramp the cutter will make a progressively deeper cut into the bottom board. The degree of the final taper is determined by the amount of slope in the ramp; the length can be as long as the slotted ramp template. The result will be a tapered flute almost impossible to duplicate in any other way.

You can also use this guide for other purposes, among which is cutting perfect circles by pivoting the machine on the guide. These guides are either standard equipment or are available as extra-cost accessories. If you do a lot of routing, they are indispensable.

The size of a router is usually described by the horsepower of its motor. There's little difference in physical size between a light- and heavy-duty tool, but there is a difference in weight. A ½-hp router, for example, may weigh in at 5 or 6 pounds, while a 1-hp machine can be 3 to 4 pounds heavier.

A ½-hp or lighter motor usually puts a router in the light-duty category, while machines with motors of ¾-hp or better are heavy-duty models. If you use a router only occasionally, a light-duty machine is sufficient. It can do almost any job the heavier machines can, but it takes more time to make the cuts. A heavy-duty router can often form a good-sized dado in a single pass, while the lighter tools usually require two or three progressively deeper cuts.

Heavy-duty routers can stand up to consistent, full-function use which would overtax a lighter machine. Routers have their own way of indicating abuse. If the cutter slows up excessively, stalls, overheats, or if it takes a lot of pressure to keep it cutting, the machine is trying to tell you something. The construction of a router has a lot to do with its efficiency and durability.

Total ball-bearing construction, for instance, usually indicates a good quality tool, as does solid heft and feel. If the machine is designed and made well, it'll take a lot of punishment without complaining.

Most routers have a standard collet capacity. All routers grip cutters with ¼-inch shaft diameters, the normal size for router bits, although some industrial models accept ⅜- or ½-inch collets on their motor shaft. All the tools and cutters used with a router are available with ¼-inch diameter shanks, so the ¼-inch collet capacity of standard routers does not limit your workscope.

Routers are fairly safe to operate because most of the work done places the housing between you and the cutters. This is only true, however, if you keep your hands on the handles, and not below the base. Often, people leave the machine running while moving from one section of a project to another. This practice is only as safe as you are alert. Router bits cut flesh easier than they cut wood. They can also snag clothing. So, it's a good idea to shut the machine off whenever it's not cutting.

A router's chuck should grip the bits securely. If they slip they won't cut well and can loosen enough to be thrown by the force of the motor. The shaft of the cutting tool should penetrate the chuck far enough to assure a tight hold — ¼ inch is minimum and ¾ inch is better. Never minimize this insertion depth to get a greater depth-of-cut. That adjustment should be controlled by the position of the motor in the base.

Always use two hands to grip the machine firmly and guide it. For proper operation of this tool, it's important that the motor be at full speed before making contact with the work. Otherwise, the motor may be damaged. If you want a router to give you good service, you have to use it properly.

When viewed from the top, the cutters rotate clockwise. Since a router works best when the cutter tends to push against the material, routine passes should be made from left to right. If a pass is made in the opposite direction, the cutter will tend to travel along by its own action. When this happens, you have to exert force to make good contact and prevent the tool from being drawn into the work. The router will walk along the cut ("climb mill") and more force will be necessary to maintain control.

Smoothest cuts are made in the direction of the grain of the wood, rather than against or across it. If you do have to cut across or against the grain, feed the machine into the work much more slowly. The router should also be kept on a level plane, since tilting it may cause the cutter to gouge the work.

Never force a router. Something is definitely wrong if you have to use muscle to keep the tool moving. The cut may be too deep or the pass is being made too fast. Let the tool do the work. If you need to use a

---

Hanging a door is one of those household tasks that you may be called upon to do at one time or another. Owning a router can make this considerably easier. Hinge slots on the jamb and the door itself must be mortised or inset into the wood the same depth as their thickness, otherwise they will not fold flat. The old-fashioned, hand-method of doing this is to use a firmer chisel after marking out the dimensions of the hinge on the door and jamb. An easier way is to use a router to make the correct depth-of-cut.

Depth-of-cut in this operation is important, since the hinge surface must be flush and not below the surface or it may pull. To assure the correct depth, use the hinge itself as a depth gauge. Set the bottom of the cutter so that its end is flush with the bottom of the router's baseplate. Unfold the hinge, and using it as a depth gauge, lower the motor until it is at the correct depth. This will give precise control.

Many hinges now sold have square corners. With these you will still have to do some chisel work after cutting the hinge recess with the router. You can also purchase hinges with rounded corners which simplifies the process considerably.

lot of force, you might as well have the satisfaction of using a hand plane, where force is sometimes necessary. A fairly consistent motor noise, a feed that doesn't require a lot of pressure, and smooth results indicate proper use of the router. After some practice, you can use these factors to judge the correctness of your technique.

A router is fun to work with and its uses are limited only by your imagination. A good quality machine will give you years of service and pleasure. Even if you know little about tools, a router can quickly broaden your woodworking horizons.

just simple knobs, and power is turned on by way of a slide-action switch on the motor housing. Precise depth-of-cut adjustments are made by a ring that turns on the motor housing and sits on the top edge of the router's base. Turning the ring moves the motor up and down. It's not very tiring to use this machine, since it weighs only 5 pounds. Construction is all ball bearing. As long as you don't abuse this machine, the Craftsman 1735 can satisfy for a long time. Approx. Price: $30.00

Light-Duty Routers

The term "light-duty" only refers to motor horsepower and doesn't mean that the tool is limited in function. A ½-hp router has ample power for most routing work, as long as it's not expected to perform on a production line. If you need a router for occasional use, a light-duty model is a good, cost-conscious choice. Even if you later find that you need a more powerful model, you can still use the light-duty model for small tasks. Professionals in shop work often have a small router as a second machine. They use it especially for touch-up work, where a heavy machine would be unwieldy. A light-duty machine may take more time to set up, and the cut may take longer than with a heavy-duty model, but the quality of the work will be just as good.

The Craftsman 1735, from Sears, Roebuck and Co., is a light router with a ½-hp motor and a no-load shaft speed of 25,000 rpm. This is a double-insulated tool with a helical-type motor adjustment to set the depth-of-cut. The handles are

Rockwell's 4619 is a ½-hp router with a shaft speed of 28,000 rpm. This is a light, basic router that's quite popular with craftsmen. It has a helical-type motor adjustment, and precise settings are accomplished by a ring gauge. You guide this

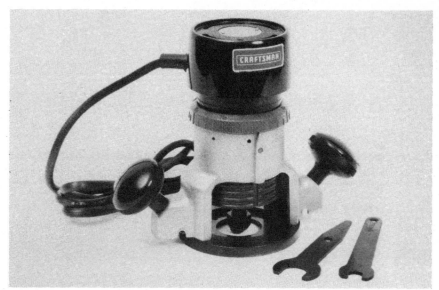

Craftsman's 1735 Light-Duty Router

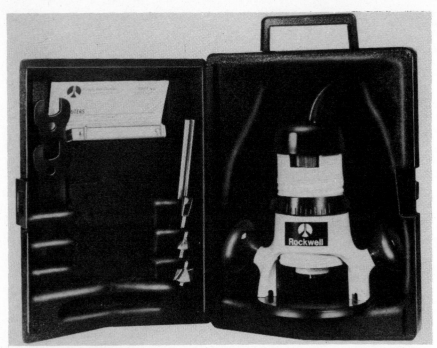

Rockwell's 4619 Router

with sleeve bearings, which are not as long-lasting as ball bearings, but the tool should give you lots of trouble-free service if you don't work it too hard. Approx. Price: $37.00

Heavy-Duty Routers

Routers in this classification are for serious woodworkers who expect the tool to perform in a professional fashion. These tools are often chosen for commercial purposes. Use techniques and work quality don't differ from that of light-duty machines, but these routers can stand up to continuous use and reduce work time. Most of the tools in this category also have special features that make them more convenient to use and reduce set-up time. They are heavier and larger because of the increased size of the motor, but the average craftsman can handle any of them. As usual, price generally increases with power.

Stanley's 91-267 is one of the routers that has earned this company the reputation it has for producing quality

tool with two good-sized handles and turn it on and off with a slide switch on the motor housing. It's double-insulated and features complete ball-bearing construction. Included with the router are three commonly used router bits, an edge guide and a plastic case for the router and accessories. The Rockwell 4619 gives you extra value for the money, since the bits

Ward's 8911 Router

and edge guide are usually not supplied with a router. Approx. Price: $60.00

Montgomery Ward's 8911 is an economy router, but it offers some features usually found on more expensive tools. Its ½-hp motor provides a shaft speed of 25,000 rpm. An unusual feature of this model is its two pistol-grip handles, with one containing the power switch. This is a definite convenience, since you can stop or start the motor while gripping the tool firmly. Adjusting the motor height for depth-of-cut is done by rack-and-pinion gearing, with an exterior knob to move the motor up and down. A scale is provided for direct readings of height adjustment. It is constructed

machines. Most of their units are used in the building and furniture trades, and this particular machine may only be available in a tool supply house. A 1½-hp motor drives the shaft at a speed of 27,000 rpm. This tool weighs in at 9 pounds and has all ball-bearing construction. It comes with ¼- and ⅜-inch collets so that you can mount heavier tools when the work calls for it. Handles are wing types, not quite pistol grips, but quite comfortable to hold. They have a sufficient span to give the operator good control. Motor adjustment is of the helical variety, but it is very precise. A good size lever secures the setting. This is a professional tool at a very expensive price—worth it, however, if you plan some heavy routing work. Approx. Price: $111.00

Rockwell's 4684 Heavy-Duty Router

Stanley's 91-267 Router

Black & Decker's 7625 router is designed for the building trade, but its price is not out of reach of the serious amateur. It weighs slightly more than 6 pounds, and its 1¼-hp motor provides a shaft speed of 23,000 rpm. The dual handles are sculptured to fit the user's hands. These handles and the tool's good balance make this an easy router to control. The toggle power switch on the housing has a small ledge to prevent accidental starts. You control motor height on this machine with a rack-and-pinion system calibrated in ¹⁄₆₄-inch increments. This Black & Decker router is constructed with all ball bearings to withstand the heavy use its designed for. Approx. Price: $70.00

Rockwell's 4684 is a professional machine with a specially designed base that gives you some options in tool handling. In addition to the convential knob-type handles, the base has an integral D-shaped handle (like that on handsaws) with a built-in, lockable trigger switch. This lets you guide and operate the tool with one hand. It also has a shielded toggle switch on the motor housing. Other features include a 1½-hp motor, 22,000 rpm shaft speed, precise helical motor and depth-of-cut adjustment, and all ball-bearing construction. The Rockwell 4684 weighs 10 pounds and is solid and compact. It also has power for the most demanding work. Approx. Price: $110.00

Millers Falls' 7900 Router

Skil's 297 Router

Millers Falls' 7900 is a professional router that takes the most demanding jobs in stride. Its 1¼-hp motor provides a 24,000 rpm cutting speed, and the tool has a lot of good features for its weight — about 8½ pounds. The machine has two different kinds of handles. One is T-shaped; on the opposite side of the base is a pistol-grip with a built-in, lockable trigger switch. An interesting feature of the pistol-grip is that it can be rotated to adjust your work position for better control. Another convenience is a push-button spindle-shaft lock that makes it easier to secure bits in the chuck. This router also takes ⅜- and ½-inch collets, in addition to the standard ¼-inch variety. The Millers Falls 7900 has a helical-type motor adjustment and is an interesting tool with lots of staying power. Approx. Price: $130.00

Skil's 297 router is light in weight, but heavy in performance. This 6½-pound tool's 1-hp motor drives the shaft at 22,500 rpm. The wing-type handles are contoured for a comfortable grip, and one of them has a lockable trigger switch. A unique feature on the router is a built-in light that illuminates the cutting area when you press the trigger. Other features include a shaft lock for easy bit changing, and a plastic shield around the open end of the base. This shield prevents chips from flying around and permits close visual inspection of the work. Motor height adjustment is helical, and a depth scale gives quick adjustment readouts. This Skil router, with all ball-bearing construction, is a professional tool. Approx. Price: $90.00

Router Accessories

variety of different-shaped cutters. The only limitation is that they can only be used for edging operations, and not for internal cutting.

Router bits, like the three-lip cutters used with stationary shapers, come in many shapes and sizes. Straight bits form dadoes, grooves, and rabbets; profile cutters are for making attractive, decorative edging on furniture; fan-shaped bits are used with a template/jig to do the classic dovetail joint; and specialty bits are designed for specific purposes like trimming plastic laminates.

The common router bits used for edge forming have an integral shaft and pilot. The shaft is gripped in the router's chuck, while the pilot follows the edge of the stock to control the width of the cut. Depth-of-cut is controlled by the height of the tool's motor relative to the base. Because the pilot turns at the router's normal speed, it can create enough friction to burn or gouge the wood if you exert too much pressure. Good tool handling minimizes this possibility. Simply move fast enough and with only as much pressure as needed to keep the cutter working.

Bits with ball-bearing pilots are also made for edging work. They eliminate burning and gouging because the pilot rides against the work and doesn't turn at the high rpm of the motor. This type of edging bit is more expensive, but it does a better job by minimizing friction and riding along the work more easily.

Another type of cutter is actually an assembly. It consists of a shaft, a variety of interchangeable cutters, and either a solid or ball-bearing pilot. This design works as well as the solid, one-piece cutters. You can also save some money by selecting them because the single shaft can be mounted with a

Edge guides are used to guide the router along a predetermined line parallel with the edge of the wood. Most designs consist of twin rods that lock into the router base and support a small guide fence that you adjust in relation to the position of the cutter. They're mostly used for cuts parallel to the edge of the wood, but you can also use them as a pivot point to make circular cuts. Edge guides are not interchangeable between brands of routers, so you must purchase them from the manufacturer of the machine.

One of the most intricate joints used in quality furniture work is the dovetail. This sign of craftsmanship is difficult and tedious to cut with hand tools, but a router makes it (almost) a snap. All you require is a jig and template and the required dovetail bit. The rest is practice. With some scrap wood and patience you will soon reach the point where it will take only a minute or two to produce each corner in an average size drawer.

The template's function is to hold the two sides or pieces of wood in a fixed position. The shapes for the dovetail are cut at the same time, thus assuring a perfect fit. The jig fits on the router's base and permits correct spacing and action as it rides on the template. Dovetail templates are common items sold by most tool manufacturers. You should make sure that the one you purchase will fit your router; other than that it is simply a matter of following the directions to the letter. With a little practice the result will be a perfect dovetail—every time you do it.

Dovetail templates look like complicated assemblies, but they're easy to use once you get the hang of it. These templates enable anyone to form the classic dovetail joint in a professional manner, though not the true full-blind dovetail. These fixtures hold the wood and a finger template, which is a guide for the router. All you need to do is guide the router along the template. In one operation, dovetail sockets are formed in one piece, while dovetail tails are cut into the mating piece. The result is a very precise, neat mesh of the individual pieces. Detailed instructions are usually provided with the fixture. These templates have taken much of the drudgery out of the process of creating this joint, and are an excellent accessory for anyone who wants to produce quality furniture.

Typical dovetail fixtures:
Sears' 2571 for wood up to
  12 inches wide and from
$\frac{5}{16}$ to 1½ inches thick.
  Approx. Price: $32.00
Wards' 8559 for wood up to
  12 inches wide and from $\frac{7}{16}$
  to 1½ inches thick.
  Approx. Price: $50.00
Rockwell's 5008 for wood
  up to 12 inches wide and
  from $\frac{5}{16}$ to 1 inch thick.
  Approx. Price: $43.00

Router Tables are small, table-sized jigs that let you mount the router beneath in an inverted position. This way you can use the router much like a stationary shaper. A router table is a practical alternative to a stationary shaper at a much lower cost in money and floor space. These tables are simple, but provide most of the necessary shaper components—a work support surface mounted on short, steel legs, a means of attaching the router, adjustable fences, and a miter gauge groove. You should note that they are not a complete substitute for the full-sized shaper, but for small pieces and occasional use they're fairly functional.

Sears' 25444 is a sophisticated router table—handsome, sturdy, and provided with a hinged guard that covers the cutting bits when they're not in use. A miter gauge is part of the package, and the table can also be used to hold portable saber saws. Approx. Price: $40.00

Ward's 8913 is an economy router table, but it does include a miter gauge. The fences are very small, but the support surfaces can be extended by adding wood facings. This is a usable table with one good feature—it has a low price. Approx. Price: $17.00

Laminate trimmer kits are useful accessories for projects like kitchen counters and cabinets, which involve plastic laminates. The usual procedure is to cut the piece of laminate ¼-inch oversize and then glue it down to the base surface. The excess is trimmed off by running the

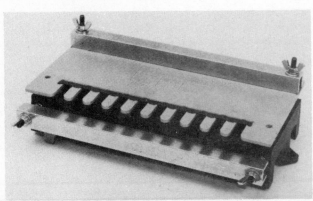

Sears' 2571 Dovetail Template

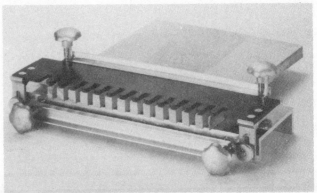

Ward's 8559 Dovetail Template

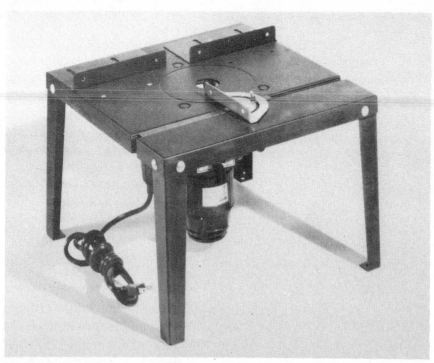

Ward's 8913 Router Table

any machine, but you must equip the router with a special accessory, called a "guide bushing." This bushing locks onto the base of the router and has a projecting flange that rides against the templates while guiding the router for the cut. Guide bushings are not interchangeable, so you must buy them from the manufacturer of your machine. Also, you must make sure that the bushing you purchase fits within the template you use.

Router bit sharpening kits usually consist of two separate parts — a grinding stone with a shaft that chucks into the router like a regular bit, and a special router base with an adjustable clamping device. This clamp secures the router bit to be sharpened, and lets you move the bit across the revolving grinding stone to sharpen the cutting edges. This is the easiest and most convenient way to keep router bits sharp. Sharp cutting bits produce the best quality cuts and contribute to safety, since not as much force is needed to get the job done.

Sharpening kits are often made specifically for a particular brand of router. Check carefully before buying.

Typical brands include:

Sears' 6650 — Approx. Price: $25.00
Rockwell's 5011 — Approx. Price: $35.00

router along the edges of the project. Usually, the kits contain cutters with carbide-tipped blades, and fit any router. The guides, however, are not usually interchangeable. So, it's smart to purchase the entire package from the manufacturer of your router.

These kits are normally used for trimming outside edges. For internal cutouts, like a sink hole in a counter, another special bit is required. One common kind is a straight-shank type whose cutting end has a drill-type point, a smooth area to serve as a pilot bearing, and the actual cutting surface. The names for these bits vary, but two common ones are "flush-cut trimmer" and "hole and flush-cut trimmer." Typically, they are used by first cutting the sink cutout in

the base, and then applying the laminate. The special bit in the point of the cutter creates its own starting hole, while the pilot follows the edge of the cutout as the cutters trim away the laminate. Another popular method for doing this operation doesn't require a special router bit. In fact, it doesn't even require a router. You just make the entire cutout, including the mounted laminate, in one operation with a carbide-tipped saber saw blade. This is much simpler, but it depends upon which tool you have.

Letter and number guides are templates used with a router to carve nameplates, house numbers and signs. These templates can be used with

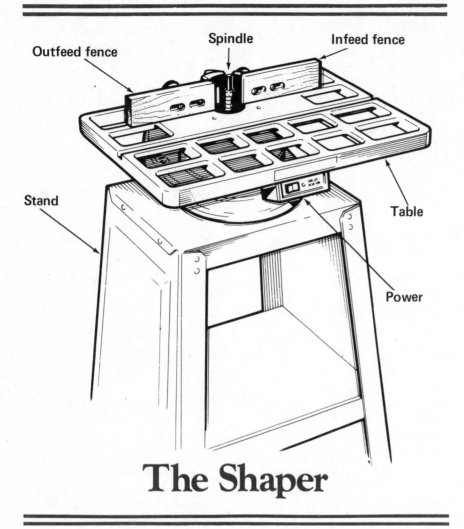

Outfeed fence Spindle Infeed fence

Stand

Table

Power

The Shaper

To the dedicated woodworker, the shaper is an indispensable machine. Yet to others, even those familiar with woodworking, this tool is somewhat redundant. They can't understand why they should spend cash for a separate machine, when accessories on a power saw or drill press can accomplish the same tasks. The point they miss is that such adaptations are almost always a compromise. The setup may work, and may let you increase your workscope at a minimum cost, but they are seldom full-function substitutes for the tool engineered to do the particular job.

This applies especially to the shaper. The machine runs at a higher speed than most drill presses, and gives better, smoother cuts. It's also designed to withstand the heavy stresses created when work is forced against the cutters. The spindle is under the table, so you don't have to contend with topside obstructions as you do when using a table saw or drill press. Lastly, a well-designed shaper has attachments and mechanisms that provide easier and more convenient working. This is true even when dealing with curved edges, which are difficult cuts to make on substitute machines.

Many shapers also let you change the direction of rotation of the spindle and cutters — useful for some kinds of work. Often, the machine also permits working with the cutters above as well as below the work. This can dramatically increase the number of shapes a single cutter can produce, and provides a measure of safety in that when the cutter is below the work, the wood acts as a guard.

Too often the shaper is viewed primarily as a tool that merely does decorations. It has many practical applications like performing shape cuts for tongue-and-groove joints, forming parts for a window sash and frame, and making lips on cabinet doors.

The shaper is a simple machine. It consists of a flat table, below which is a motorized spindle that's adjustable vertically and protrudes through a hole in the table. This spindle is threaded so that cutter blades can be secured with a nut. The vertical adjustment is necessary to position the cutter assembly in relation to the wood. After you make the adjustment, you lock the assembly in place.

A shaper has individually-adjusted infeed and outfeed fences that provide guidance for straight cuts. The two fences are set in a straight line when you want to cut only a part of the stock's edge. You place them out of line, with the outfeed fence set forward of the infeed fence when you need to remove the entire edge of a piece of wood. In this way, the wood is supported throughout the cut. The infeed fence supports the part of the wood not yet reduced in width by the cut, and the outfeed fence supports the narrow width cut portion of the wood.

A workpiece that's oval, circular, curved or which has irregular edges, cannot be shaped by using the fences. In this case, the fences are removed, and special "collars" are mounted on the spindle along with the cutters. These collars resemble very heavy steel washers, and are available in various thicknesses and diameters. They provide support for the work when it's pressed into the cutter, and they control the amount of material the cutters remove (depth-of-cut). You can use the collars under or over the cutter, and even between two cutters to provide special shapes. Since these cutter/collar combinations rotate together, they create friction. It's essential that you keep them clean and smooth when not in use.

Working against collar/cutter arrangements is called freehand shaping. Since the fences are removed, many machines are equipped with "fulcrum

Shapers are essentially uncomplicated tools that do one task well—but only if used properly. It is important to work with sharp cutters, a reasonable rate of feed, and depth-of-cut settings that are not excessive. If the wood is hard and the cut too deep during the initial pass you will notice obvious burn marks. These can be hard to get rid of, especially if the shaping cut you are making is for a close tolerance fit. Excessive slowing down of the motor during use is a sign that you are moving too fast. It will do you no good to use the machine if the final result is unsightly or cutting it destroys the motor.

When cutting crossgrain work on a shaper you have to do it slowly, otherwise there will be chatter and some chipping out of the work. On pieces where more than one edge is to be done, do passes on the crossgrain edges first. There is a possibility that chips will be taken out when you reach the end of a pass. Subsequent passes along the grain will remove these blemishes.

pins" to provide support for the work. These are short, steel pins about ⅜ inch in diameter, which are set in threaded holes in the shaper's table. Two are present, one at each side of the table. The correct way to use them is to brace the work against the first pin, and then slowly move it into the cutters until it is frrmly supported by the collar. The second pin is used to support the work as the pass goes through and to the end of the cut. Although these fulcrum pins are sometimes considered a nuisance and removed, they do provide an element of safety when using the machine freehand.

Most shaper tables also have a groove in the top surface that accepts an optional miter gauge. The miter gauge is used much the

same as that on a table saw. You use it to support and guide the work.

The way a shaper is used, especially in freehand work, makes it very difficult to provide the machine with adequate guards. Often, safety assemblies consist of a ring or cone that is attached to the end of an arm. This arm rides above the table by means of a post, and is adjustable so the guard can be positioned over the spindle and close to the work. You should use this guard system whenever possible, but always remember that it cannot keep you completely safe.

Never attempt to shape pieces that are so small that they might be torn from your grasp. Small pieces also bring the hands dangerously close to the cutters, which rotate *extremely* fast. You can lose a finger before you realize it's gone! The best way to shape a slim molding, for example, is to use the shaper to cut the edge of a wide board, and then cut off the molding strip on a table saw. Whenever possible, position the work so the cutter is under the wood. All passes through this machine should be made only fast enough to keep the tool working. Forcing cuts produces unsatisfactory results and increases the possibility that your hands may slip. When work is placed against collars for freehand shaping, it is essential that they provide adequate support surface for the wood moved against them. Smooth, clean collars reduce friction so the work passes through easily and lessen the chance that the collars will mar the work surface. The shaper is a useful tool. But beware—this machine often bites the hand that feeds it wood.

Shapers, even industrial models, are not large machines and demand little floor space. A couple of square feet of floor space for the machine will do, but the operator should have free access to all sides of the tool. And, if you're making long molding, it's necessary to situate the machine in an open area. If, for instance, you wish to shape a 6-foot-long board, you need 6 feet of room on both the infeed and outfeed sides of the machine.

If you were to compile a list of necessary tools, it's doubtful that the shaper would be near the top of the list. On the other hand, a full-function wood shop wouldn't be without one. Other power tools (or hand tools like specialized planes) can duplicate the results obtained with this machine. But none of them can do the job as easily as the shaper. If you have the shop space and the money, a shaper can make your shop life easier and your finished projects finer.

Rockwell's 43-115 is listed as a light-duty shaper, but the description is only relative to an industrial model that's three times heavier. For the small commercial shop or home shop, it can be considered a full-function machine, suitable for the advanced woodworker. And it doesn't lack the features of the larger machines, either.

This shaper has interchangeable spindles, not often found on smaller machines. This increases your workscope, because a "stub spindle" can be used with special cutters to form intricate joint shapes used to assemble window frames and doors with inset panels.

Rockwell's shaper uses either a ½- or 1-hp motor to drive the ½-inch diameter spindle at 9000 rpm. The ½-hp motor has a special drum switch that permits it to reverse; the 1-hp motor has

Although a shaper is basically an edge forming machine, you can perform a lot of different tasks within these limitations. The fence, of course, permits straight line shaping, while the fulcrum pins allow freehand cutting on irregular-shaped workpieces. You can also use the machine to shape the outside edge of a circle. This is called pivot work.

To organize the machine for pivot work you must first cut a hardwood bar to fit into the miter gauge slot on the shaper's table. A nail is driven into the end of the bar to serve as a pivot point for the circular work. To use this setup, the work is placed over the pin and the hardwood bar kept loose as you hand-feed the workpiece into the cutters. When you obtain the depth-of-cut required, the machine is turned off and the bar clamped to the table to give a secure pivot point. Holding the workpiece firmly, the machine is then turned on and the stock turned against the direction of rotation of the cutter blades.

You must be careful when doing pivot work, because if you do not use a firm grip the cutter can take over and spin the work out of control. The feed should be slow and the depth-of-cut kept light. This operation on a shaper should not be tried unless all your attention is completely on the work at hand!

an integral reversing switch. Choose the larger motor if you want to use the machine extensively and to its fullest potential. Table size is 15½x18 inches, and a slot for an optional miter gauge and holes for the fulcrum pins are provided. The shaper comes with a stand and 1-hp motor. Its miter gauge and ring guard are extra-cost accessories. Approx. Price: $380.00

Craftsman's 23928N3, from Sears, Roebuck and Co., is a tool designed specifically for the small shop market. As such it lacks a few of the features found on industrial machines, but none essential for quality furniture construction. It doesn't have interchangeable spindles, but does take special cutters necessary to shape the joints used in window and panel door construction. The table is good sized — 19x27 inches — larger than most machines for the small shop. It is grooved for a miter gauge and has threaded holes for fulcrum pins. This machine has a ½-hp motor that drives a ½-inch spindle at 9000 rpm — quite adequate for smooth, accurate cuts.

The machine comes with motor, stand, belt guard and a cone-type guard for use in freehand shaping. The on-off switch includes a locking device, which is quite handy for keeping inquisitive fingers out of the machine. This is a fairly complete tool in one package and useful for anyone who wants to do shaping work. Approx. Price: $266.00

Toolkraft's 4256 is like many of the tools in the company's line — it's "motorized," having a built-in, totally enclosed drive system. This results in a very clean, compact design, with no belts, pulleys, or motor outside the tool's base. The motor drives the spindle directly, and this eliminates power loss from belt slippage. Its power and speed are exceptional for a tool in its class. A 1-hp motor spins the ½-inch spindle at 18,000 rpm. This high speed is especially good for producing

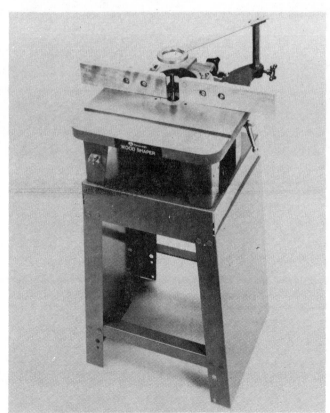

Rockwell's 43-115 Shaper

Craftsman's 23928N3 Shaper

Toolkraft's 4256 Shaper

Cutter Assemblies

smooth cuts across the grain of wood and when working with materials like plywood and particle board.

The table measures 15¼x18 inches, and it has a miter gauge slot and provisions for mounting fulcrum pins. When you buy this tool it's ready to plug in and use, and includes a cup-type guard for freehand shaping and a stand. This machine is a very good, basic shaper that both expert and beginner can use with a minimum of fuss. Approx. Price: $250.00

Gilliam Manufacturing's 441-K is a shaper that comes as a build-it-yourself kit. If you need a shaper, but don't want to foot the bill for a commercial unit, this is a good avenue to explore. All the necessary metal components are supplied and ready to install. The only really hard part of building the machine lies in constructing the wooden cabinet and table. The kit includes detailed plans and patterns for the wood parts required, and the only tools you really need are a saw and portable drill. However, the plans take for granted that you already have a basic knowledge of woodworking. Unless you're already highly skilled in cabinet construction, the result will not be a great machine.

Many builders of such kits have made the machine more attractive by using higher-quality wood than the plywood called for in the plans. This way you end up with a functional as well as good-looking piece of equipment. The kit doesn't include the motor, pulley, or drive belts, but the company sells these separately. Approx. Price: $45.00

The most common cutting tool used with a shaper is called a "three-lip shaper cutter." This is a one-piece assembly with three integral cutting edges and a centered hole for mounting on the shaper's spindle. It comes in standard profiles and all units fit all shapers as long as the spindle hole is the correct diameter. Some of these cutters are designed for a particular function.

Others are combination cutters, like the cove-quarter round, which can be used to round off an edge (quarter round) or form a concave shape (cove). Quite an assortment is available and a full set is expensive. The best way to accumulate a set is to buy a few at the beginning and then add cutters.

For the beginner, a good starting set includes a combination bead-quarter round, a cove and bead molding cutter, door lip cutter, and perhaps a glue joint cutter.

You should note that all cutters are really combination tools. The resulting cut with any cutter depends upon how far the spindle protrudes above the table and how the fences are set. You merely use as much of the cutter's profile as you need for your project.

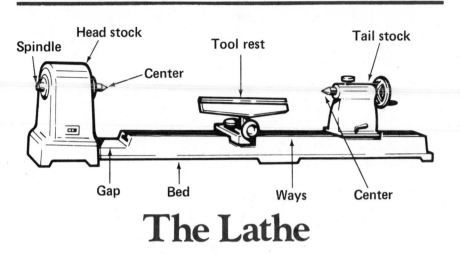

Spindle
Head stock
Center
Tool rest
Tail stock
Gap
Bed
Ways
Center

The Lathe

Lathes are probably the most intriguing of all woodworking tools. Based on a concept as old as working with wood itself, all these machines really do is hold a blank of wood and spin it. Using "turning tools," you can shape the blank into decorative and functional items.

In lathe work, the artisan has complete control over the shapes that are formed, and there is ample room for creativity. Many enthusiasts justifiably consider lathe work to be an art form. The lathe is their only power tool. If other equipment is present, it's usually used only to size blanks for eventual turning on the lathe. These turners indulge in lathe work for the satisfaction of creating beautiful wood objects, and the result is often a real work of art.

Cabinetmakers and those who design fine furniture also appreciate the lathe for its ability to expand their creativity. If you're interested in advanced furniture making, you should definitely investigate the possibilities a lathe opens to you.

The lathe is one of the few tools on which a project can be done from start to finish. Making a large bowl is an example. A suitable wood block or blank is mounted on a "faceplate," which is a device to fix the work to the machine and keep it turning. Then the blank is formed to the desired shape by using a variety of turning tools and techniques.

After this process, you can sand the piece as it revolves at high speed on the lathe—the amount of sanding necessary depends on the amount of skill you apply during the forming process. Advanced techniques allow a much finer finish to be achieved with the turning tools themselves. Even the final finish can be applied to the work without removing it from the lathe.

One popular final finish is called "French Polishing," which is simply an application of linseed oil and orange shellac while the work is turning on the lathe. This provides a very quick and beautiful finish once the technique is mastered. All that remains after final finishing is to remove the faceplate.

It's fascinating to watch a blank of wood transformed into graceful shapes and curves by applying cutting tools to the spinning stock. The final shape can be planned in advance and checked with a cardboard template as you work, or you can visualize and execute the design as you go. A template is a necessity when turning a replacement for a broken part, such as a chair rung or table leg. Working without specific plans is more creative, and can be likened to shaping clay on a potter's wheel—although wood is a much less forgiving medium than clay. With clay the process can be reversed if too much material is removed. This is not so with wood.

The lathe is a fun machine to work with, but too often it's viewed only as a hobby or craft tool. Up until World War II, turning was a vast cottage industry practiced in England. Many turners there made their living shaping utilitarian items for everyday use, a situation that can be duplicated today by the home shop owner. Due to the emphasis on straight geometric design in modern furniture, the lathe was ignored as a power tool for

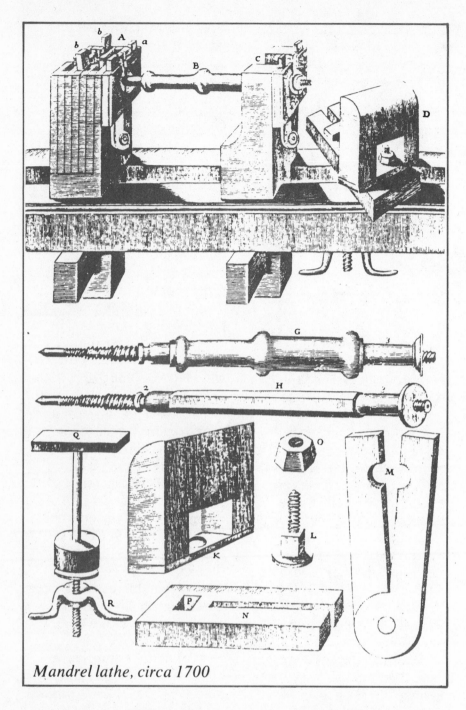

Mandrel lathe, circa 1700

these members or "ways," are attached upright stands called "stocks." At the left is a fixed stock, called a head stock, which contains the spindle that's driven by a motor. At the right is a movable tail stock. Unpowered, this can be slid along the fixed ways and provides adjustment for different sizes of blanks put between the stocks. The tail stock also has a spindle, which can be extended or withdrawn via a handwheel. Both head and tail stock spindles share a common axis, which is parallel to the bed.

Spindles are designed to seat a variety of appliances to hold the work. The most common is to hold a blank between centers or short shafts which have been ground to a 60 degree point at one end. The center in the head stock is called the live center because it's powered and driven by the spindle. The center in the tail stock remains immobile and is called the dead center. Because of its immobility, a considerable amount of friction is created between the wood blank and the center. So, it's customary to use a small amount of lubricant to eliminate excessive heat buildup. A nice luxury is a tail stock center-mounted on ball-bearings. This creates, in effect, a second live center and the work turns more freely and with less friction. Live centers also have a variety of forms, the most common being a spur center.

many years. A current trend of nostalgia and the interest in antiques has resulted in craftsmen rediscovering the lathe in recent years. Anything, even straight geometric lines, can be downright boring when done to excess. The lathe is one way to remedy this.

In concept, all lathes are the same, but they do differ in size, weight, capacity, and features. The lathe is a horizontal machine. The basic supporting structure is called a "bed," which can be mounted on a stand or work bench. The bed usually is formed of two horizontal members fixed in a parallel plane. At the end of each of

This is a point surrounded by a series of radial knife edges which are driven into the wood in order to hold it. Another type is the screw center — merely a wood screw mounted on a small platform at the end of the shaft. This is screwed into the work to hold it firmly, and can be useful for holding small workpieces.

When work is held between centers, the process is called spindle turning. Turning components like chair rungs or table legs is best accomplished by spindle turning. Bowls and hollowed out pieces cannot be held between centers and the tool used to fasten them into the lathe is called a faceplate. It's a flat metal disc, available in several sizes, and screws are used to mount the work to it. The faceplate is threaded in the center so it can be screwed onto the spindle in the head stock and turned by it. Most lathes come equipped only with a live spur center for the head stock and a cup-shaped dead center for the tail stock. Such features as screw centers, faceplates and ball bearing centers are usually optional, extra-cost accessories.

Mounted on the bed of the lathe between the head and the tail stock there is a "tool carriage," or tool rest. You can slide this along the bed and lock it at any point. The tool rest support carries a T-shaped bar, which is adjustable vertically and can be pivoted about the central mounting point. This tool rest supplies support for the turning tools when they are in use. You can adjust the rest to best support the turning tools and position them in relation to the work that is being done.

The basic size of a lathe is called its "swing." This is twice the height of the center over the bed. The measurement expresses the maximum diameter of a piece that can be turned between the two spindles. Some lathes also have a "gap bed." In this case, the bed has a U-shaped depression directly in front of the head stock. The gap bed increases the maximum diameter of the work which can be mounted on the faceplate. For this reason, the swing of such a lathe is expressed as two numbers. For example, 11/14 means that the basic swing of the lathe over the length of bed is 11 inches, but faceplate work of up to 14 inches can be done in the gap.

Another lathe capacity is the maximum length of work which can be mounted between centers. Most lathes can handle spindle work 30 inches or better between centers. This may seem to limit the length of work you can do on a lathe, but it really doesn't. You can make projects as long as you want, simply by turning separate pieces and joining them. If you examine most long turnings, you can see where these joints have been made.

Lathe speeds can be changed in two ways — through the use of step pulleys or a variable-speed mechanism.

The latter method is best because it lets you change speeds more easily, and you can select an exact speed for a particular job. Although matching the speed to the work must be learned from practice and experience, there are some general rules.

Usually, lower speeds of 750 to 850 rpm are used for roughing out work or for large diameter faceplate turning. Intermediate speeds around 1100 rpm are normal for average spindle turning. Finishing and sanding is done at the higher speeds of 2500 to 3600 rpm. If you have a doubt about which speed to use, select the slower one. Step-pulley lathes normally offer these three-speed ranges; variable-speed machines, of course, have infinite speed adjustments within a given range. A lathe owner's manual gives you some useful suggestions and details which speeds are best to use.

There's a certain amount of danger involved in lathe work because the work spins and the tools are fed into the wood. It's extremely important that you fix the work firmly between the centers or on the faceplate. Loosely-mounted work can fly off the machine with results best left to the imagination. Also, you must be careful about speed selection when dealing with large diameter pieces and during initial roughing stages.

You must also have a firm grip on the turning tool at all times. A light cut is always better than a deep one, because there's less chance for the tool to snag in the wood and be torn from your hands. The position of the tool rest can be crucial in preventing this. Read your owner's manual carefully before ever using the lathe, and try to find an experienced turner to explain to you exactly what to expect. The design of the lathe makes it impossible to install protective guards, so it's up to you to protect yourself.

Since the size of the workpiece is limited by the size of the machine itself, the lathe requires only floor space for itself and the operator. Even large, heavy-duty models need an area no larger than 3x6 feet. Also, you only need operating space in front of the lathe, unless the machine is designed for "outboard turning." This design lets you mount a faceplate on the left side of the head stock, and is used for turning work that's too large in diameter to be turned over the bed.

Theoretically, this increases the faceplate work diameter to twice the distance from the spindle to the floor. But average lathes don't have the power or structural strength to turn such a large piece without shaking themselves apart. Outboard turning, however, does increase capacity for projects like trays and bowls. But the extent of this capacity depends upon the size of the lathe, motor power, and how the stand is mounted on the

Woodcraft's Collet Chuck

Probably the hottest new item in lathe work is the "chuck." Chucks are fixtures that are screwed or fastened into the headstock spindle in place of a faceplate. Most varieties are adaptations of metal turning chucks, standard equipment on all metal turning lathes. The purpose of these chucks is to center, grip, and hold work that is placed within their jaws.

The universal, three-jaw chuck is probably the most common. This has three jaws that close simultaneously as a key is turned, and are often called scroll chucks because of the internal spiral scroll that activates the three jaws. Occasionally a used chuck can be found—too inaccurate for metal turning but adequate for woodworking. The backs

floor. If outboard turning is possible on your machine, you need work space to the left of the machine as well as in front of it.

Many neophyte woodworkers shy away from the lathe because it seems to be an expert's machine, with the results directly related to the operator's skill. To a large extent, this is true. But gaining the skill is more a question of practice than inborn talent. Advanced turning techniques are just a matter of time and practice. Elementary techniques like scraping are simple and effective, and any beginner

can be immediately productive.

With a workscope that can range from postage-size goblets to porch columns, the lathe offers much to beginner and expert alike. Plastic and even soft metals can be turned if you use carbide-tipped or tool steel turning chisels. On heavy machines you can even do some metal spinning to make items like pewter plates or a set of serving dishes.

The lathe is a functional and useful machine that offers much to anyone who uses it. Adding one to your equipment can bring some

Woodcraft's Coil-Grip Chuck

may have to be machined to fit into the head stock of the wood lathe, but they are a good value if they can be found.

Woodcraft Supply carries two varieties of chucks for use in the wood lathe. The collet chuck is reasonably priced and comes with three collets of ½, ¾, and 1 inch. A tendon is turned in the work to one of these three diameters and then inserted into the chuck. They also sell a chuck, an import from Great Britain, that is a new development. This "coil-grip" chuck holds a workpiece by four different methods, and was developed by Peter Child, a well known authority on lathe work. Any chuck will increase the turner's workscope and is worth the investment if you do much lathe work.

old-time craftsmanship back to your shop, as it has done for many other woodworkers.

Sprunger's L1036 is a 10-inch, gap bed lathe that's built for performance rather than inherent beauty. Lacking chrome plating and fancy plastic handles, it's simply a rugged, cast-iron tool designed to be used and used and used. Suitable for the amateur, this is a machine to learn on and to use forever afterwards.

Capacities and features are more than adequate for any job you're likely to run into in the average shop. Both head and tail stocks are oversize and rest on an extra-wide bed—two features that lower vibration and contribute to precision turning. It has a 10-inch capacity over the bed and 13 inches over the gap in front of the head stock. Center distance between the spindles is 38½ inches. Both ⅓- and ½-hp motors are recommended, with the larger one best for full-function use. Step pulleys provide four specific speeds—875, 1150, 2250, and 3500 rpm. These are very good for usual turning tasks. You can also perform outboard turning on this machine, and it comes with the usual complement of tool rests and spur centers. In all, the Sprunger L1036 is a functional machine that can do justice to any turning task. Approx. Price: $300.00

The Rockwell 46-451 can do any lathe task, including light metal turning and spinning, with the correct accessories. This machine is designed for the professional. It's a heavy-duty, industrial-grade machine that can fill the dreams of any lathe enthusiast. For occasional turning, the amateur should look elsewhere.

Capacities are 12 inches over the bed and 16½ inches over the gap, with 38 inches between centers. Outboard turning is possible. Features of this machine include a

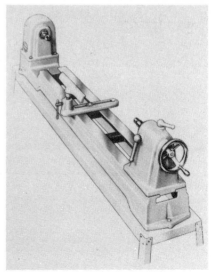

Sprunger's L1036 Lathe

Montgomery Ward's 1916 catalog advertised lathes and scrolls saws.

built-in, mechanical drive device that provides a range of variable speeds. Depending upon the rpm of the motor used, this range can be either 340 to 3200 or 250 to 2135 rpm. The low-speed range is valuable for metal turning and spinning.

This Rockwell lathe has what is called an "indexing head." It allows you to perform operations like cutting reeds or flutes along the length of a column. In this type of operation, the work does not spin. The lathe becomes merely a holding device for the work, as you use special accessories to do the cutting. The indexing head provides automatically spaced stops, so that the decorative cuts can be spaced equally around the work's circumference. In this particular case, there are 48 stops, or one for every 7½ degrees. Dividing by any even number permits accurate spacing that can meet the needs of most situations.

A motor isn't included with the lathe, but it does come with a heavy steel cabinet base that houses the variable-speed drive. You can count on this Rockwell machine to do just about any turning task you can dream up. Approx. Price: $1235.00

Rockwell's 46-150 is a basic lathe with a cast-iron bed,

Rockwell's 46-451 Lathe

Rockwell's 46-150 Lathe

head and tail stocks. This gives you all the rigidity needed for work likely to be done in the average shop. The lathe's capacity is 11 inches over the bed and 14 inches over the gap. Spindle turning up to 36 inches can be done between the centers. Step pulleys give you four specific speeds of 990, 1475, 2220, and 3250 rpm.

This model includes an open steel stand and a few extra accessories for the basic price. A 3-inch faceplate, two sizes of tool rest, and an offset tool rest are included. The offset tool rest has a right-angle turn, and is especially useful for inside turning—like when doing the inside of a deep bowl. A motor isn't included, but either a ⅓- or ½-hp power plant can be used. If you intend to perform mostly faceplate operations, the larger motor is best. Approx. Price: $340.00

The only problem the editors had in considering the Shopsmith Mark V was deciding which chapter to put it in. The Shopsmith is not really any single tool at all, but rather an ingenious device that is virtually a whole workshop combined in one machine. We have put it in the lathe section because the basis of this machine is a lathe. Using the lathe bed as a mounting base and the head stock as a power source, an array of accessories can be fitted to the machine, turning it into such things as a table

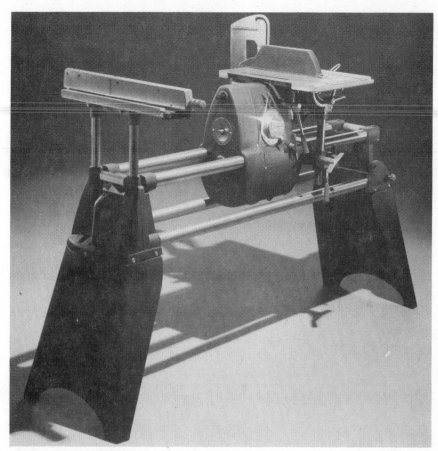

Shopsmith's Mark V Multipurpose Tool

saw, a disc sander, a drill press, a band saw, a jointer, a belt sander, or a jigsaw.

The purchase price of this machine includes enough accessories to start you off with a basic wood shop. By purchasing a Shopsmith you instantly have a lathe with a 16½-inch swing and 34 inches between centers, a 10-inch table saw, a horizontal boring machine, a 12-inch disc sander, and a drill press with a 16½-inch capacity. Additional accessories can be purchased which turn the machine into an 11-inch band saw, a 4-inch jointer, a 6-inch belt sander, or an 18-inch jigsaw.

You do pay a compromise for all this versatility. A

considerable amount of setup time is often needed to convert the Mark V from one machine to another. Since many advanced woodworking projects call for a sequence of many operations, the constant necessity of rearranging the machine can get a bit nerve-racking.

On the other hand you get a lot of tools at a reasonable price. A further economy lies in the fact that only the one motor in the head stock is needed to drive all of the machinery. The band saw, jointer, belt sander, and jigsaw can also be mounted on their own stand and motorized separately, which may be a good idea when the budget

allows. Although some of the accessories represent a compromise over a machine designed specifically for the purpose, they still do a very adequate job.
Approx. Price: $925.00

Toolkraft's 4712 is a motorized lathe. This means that it has a built-in motor, and is ready to use as soon as you uncrate it. In the trade this is called a "turn key" installation. The drive unit is also built-in. It's an electronically-controlled, solid-state device that gives you infinitely variable speeds from 800 to 2800 rpm — attainable by dial as easily as tuning in a radio. The Toolkraft 4712 is a lathe designed for good-sized projects. It has a 14-inch swing over the bed; 36½-inch swing between centers; ⅝-hp ball-bearing motor plus positive gear drive; a 12-inch tool rest and one-piece steel bed. It's good looking, too, with no exposed belts or pulleys for the operator to get caught up in. Approx. Price: $265.00

Turning Tools

Adequate turning tools are available from lathe manufacturers, mail order catalogs, and general retail outlets. They may be purchased individually or in sets, and many types of points and sizes are commonly offered. A beginning set should include the following: roundnose, gouge, spear point, and skew. Carbide-tipped turning tools are also available for use on plastics, soft metal, and, of course, wood.

Lathe turning tools come in two categories — "standard strength" and "long-and-strong." These names don't indicate quality, but rather tell you what the tool was designed for. Standard strength tools are for spindle turning and long-and-strong tools are for faceplate turning. If you do mostly spindle turning, except for an occasional bowl or two, standard strength tools are the best bet. If large bowls, platters and lamp bases are your bag, then the long-and-strong variety are a must. If you do a variety of turning, you may need both kinds. You can use standard strength tools for faceplate turning and vice-versa.

Tool descriptions also include the terms "hand" and "unhand," which simply tells you whether or not the tool has a handle. Going the unhand way saves you about $3.00 per tool. But that's not really the point. Tools are offered without handles because lathe enthusiasts often like to add handles that are custom made to fit their hands.

Robert Sorby & Sons turning tools are highly recommended. These superb tools are made in Sheffield, England. They are forged with exacting care and hardened and tempered to perfection. The high-quality carbon steel provides a long edge life, yet maintains a degree of flexibility to withstand sudden shocks that could bend other tools. Handles are of substantial length and diameter, and have strong and well-set ferrules. Sorby lathe tools are listed in the Garret Wade and Woodcraft catalogs. Approx. Price: (8 Standard) $54.00; (8 Long & Strong) $71.00

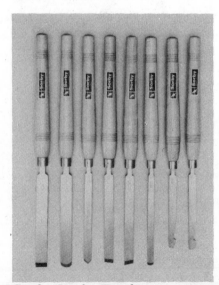

Sorby Lathe Tools

"Smooth as silk" is a common phrase;
but how many projects really have that
kind of loving finish? Our selection of
sanding equipment lets you get
maximum results with minimum effort.

Smoothing Tools

Sandpaper

There is no secret to cutting, shaping, and final fastening of materials together. It requires nothing more than careful attention to detail in the original shaping and assembly. However, once the piece is put together there always remains one final operation. It must be smoothed and a final surface finish applied. The final finish is put on to protect and beautify the work, but it will only be as good as the preparation and smoothing that goes before it. There is no better sign of craftsmanship than a final finish that is smooth and free from surface blemishes. Twenty hours can be spent on constructing a piece, only to be wasted and the piece ruined in one hour of inadequate final finishing. Careful attention to this step will result in something any craftsman would be proud of, even if it is only a simple shelf.

No matter what the method used to form a workpiece, it is a sure bet that final smoothing will be done by using sandpaper. A sheet of sandpaper appears deceptively simple, but there is a wide variety of types available. It pays to know the differences because some types are only suitable for certain kinds of smoothing work. This depends upon the characteristics of the sandpaper itself.

All sandpaper is constructed of three parts. Glued to a paper or cloth backing (which may be waterproof) will be grains of natural or man-made abrasive. "Open-coat" or "closed-coat" designations will tell you how much of the backing paper is covered with the abrasive grit. All-over coverage means closed-coat, while open-coat varies between 50 to 70 percent coverage. A closed-coat sandpaper will produce the smoothest finishes, but it has a tendency to clog more easily. An open-coat sandpaper does not clog quickly, but cuts slowly. In use, closed-coat sandpaper is best for obtaining the final smoothness; open-coat paper is better for rough sanding or removing old paint or finishing materials.

Because of the abrasive particles glued onto it, sandpaper is actually a cutting tool. It will remove particles of material from a surface in varying degrees, depending upon the coarseness of the abrasive grit. The coarser the abrasive grit on the paper, the more easily you will be able to feel the ridges left in the surface. The general procedure that is followed when using sandpaper is to start with the

A QUICK LOOK AT SANDPAPER ABRASIVES

NAME	REMARKS	TYPICAL USES
Flint	natural hard form of quartz — clogs quickly in use — softest of common abrasives — low cost	removing old paint and finishes — rough sanding on uneven or washboarded surfaces
Garnet	natural mineral with typically red color — harder and sharper than flint — wears longer	sanding hard or soft woods — any soft material like horn or plastic
Aluminum Oxide	manmade with a bauxite base — brown — cheaper to use than garnet because it lasts longer — costs more per sheet	hardwood and soft metals — will abrade mild steel — ivory and plastic
Silicon Carbide	manmade — harder and more brittle than aluminum oxide — cuts very fast — most costly of papers	will cut all materials including glass and cast iron — wet sanding — final finish work

A QUICK LOOK AT ABRASIVE GRITS

NAME	GRIT NUMBER	GRADE NUMBER	TYPICAL USES
Very Coarse	16 20 24 30	4 3½ 3 2½	extremely rough work — often used on unplaned or unsurfaced work — use in place of a rasp or file to round edges
Coarse	36 40 50	2 1½ 1	for initial sanding on most woods — prepares the wood for later medium/fine work
Medium	60 80 100	½ 1/0 2/0	remove roughness — intermediate sanding prior to fine work
Fine	120 150 180	3/0 4/0 5/0	final surface work before application of sealers or stains
Very Fine	220 240 280 320 360 400	6/0 7/0 8/0 9/0 10/0	polish and smooth between finishing coats — smooth after final coat — super fine finish on raw wood — use after shellac for final smooth, silky feel

coarsest grades and progressively work into the finer grits. Often the coarser grades of paper can be left out altogether, since much of the wood used today has already been surfaced to some degree before purchase or during construction.

There are three basic types of grit abrasive used in sandpaper. Natural flint particles are the least expensive, but they cut slowly and dull rapidly. Garnet is another natural abrasive, but it costs more. With similar size grit and on a similar sanding job garnet will last up to five times longer than flint paper. Aluminum oxide or silicon carbide grit cut as well if not better than garnet paper, but last even longer. Both are more expensive but worth the extra cost if you have a large amount of sanding to do. The backing on either of the latter types of grit can be paper or cloth, and they are the first choice for power-sanding equipment. They cut faster and last longer than the natural abrasive grits and will take the punishment which would cause the other two to disintegrate.

The back of any sandpaper sheet will be marked with various designations depending upon the manufacturer. It will usually list the type of backing, the kind of abrasive grit that is used, and the size or grit/grade number of the abrasive. It is important that you select the correct grade or grit size for the particular sanding task at hand. Coarse sandpaper should be used for any rough cutting, with fine or very fine paper used for finish work.

Using sandpaper is fairly easy and does not require any long training period. Although cutting it to size and using one's hand as a backing is almost traditional, better results can be gotten by making a sanding block. This will provide a firm backing for the sandpaper and prevent it from tearing when you bear down. Sandpaper should always be used *with* the grain of the wood during final finishing, otherwise ridges will be left that are difficult to remove. If it is absolutely necessary to smooth the piece across the grain during final sanding, it is better to use a piece of steel wool. This does not cut as well as sandpaper, especially in the finer grades. Used with patience, however, it will produce a smooth surface without the danger of sandpaper scratches left by normal crossgrain sanding.

Almost all of the portable sanding tools use sheet sandpaper as a cutting tool. This will be either a third or quarter of a normal size sheet, and sometimes even a half-sheet. Selection of a proper grit size is no different in using a power sander. You start with the coarsest grit necessary and work through progressively finer grit until the desired smoothness is obtained. Disc/belt sanders move their abrasive surfaces at faster speeds than a finish sander and because of this should be mounted with a better grade of paper with a heavier backing. This will help to prevent them from tearing as readily. You will obtain a superior surface by using a quality sandpaper to begin with.

Perhaps the commonest use for the belt sander is removing old finishes, especially paint or layers of varnish. If you do this, however, you will often discover that even an open-coat abrasive belt will clog quickly. This is because the old finish, paint especially, will soften under the heat and friction of the belt's passage.

There is a method that can be used to partially prevent this problem. Instead of the conventional method of pushing the sander forward and letting it move under its own speed, with this technique you pull the sander towards you. All sanding should start from the end of the workpiece that is furthest from you. You will, in effect, be moving the sander from those areas already abraded back onto the finished ones. This means that you will be sanding with the rear of the machine, instead of the toe.

This will help to prevent belt clogging, but the belt should always be examined at regular intervals. Using a stiff brush frequently will help to keep it clean as you work.

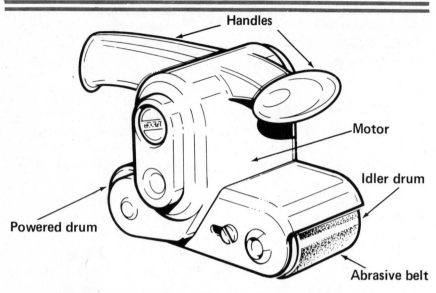

Handles

Motor

Idler drum

Powered drum

Abrasive belt

Portable Belt Sanders

Portable belt sanders are much like the larger, stationary ones in concept—they incorporate a moving abrasive belt powered by a motor. Reasonably light and small, they're easy to hold and apply to the work. A portable belt sander can be a workhorse in a small shop, accomplishing tasks usually done by large stationary machines in extensively equipped shops. Fast, flexible workers, portable belt sanders can be used to smooth rough, unplaned lumber, resurface kitchen cutting boards, and sand lumber and panels of any length and width. In a complete shop, such jobs would be delegated to the surface planer or jointer, and in many cases, to the hand plane. But portable belt sanders are versatile—and

with the right kind of abrasive belt, they let you sand metals, slate and even concrete.

Portable belt sanders are usually used prior to final sanding with a pad or finishing sander. A portable belt sander can deliver a finishable surface, since it can be used with very fine abrasives. But the pad sander was designed, and is still largely used, to add the final touch. It's easy to handle on smaller surfaces and has a stroke action that's intended to produce the smoothest, finest finish possible.

The portable belt sander uses an endless loop coated with an abrasive. This belt is mounted on and travels over two drums mounted beneath the machine. There is a platen between the rollers. The rear drum is turned by a shaft powered by the

tool's motor. The front idler drum is adjustable so you can mount new belts, keep the belt taut, and correct tracking. The spring-loaded front drum makes belt tensioning automatic. Tracking adjustments are made by turning an external knob to tilt the front drum one way or the other, depending upon the action and bias of the belt.

You can mount belts with relative ease because the front drum moves back to shorten the distance between the two drums. After you center the abrasive belt over the two drums, a lever moves the front drum into a working position by a spring.

The opening between the two drums at the bottom of the tool is spanned by a platen, or backup plate, for the abrasive. The surface area of this platen determines how much abrasive area contacts the work. If a tool has a larger platen area it will sand a project faster. As a tool increases in power and size, so should its platen area.

Some belt sanders are designed to work with a dust collector that's either standard or offered as an option. Sanders can envelop you in dust in a jiffy. A dust collector is good health insurance and makes housekeeping a lot easier.

Flush sanding is possible with some models. They let you sand things like the perimeters around a floor, the shelf area of a cabinet, and adjacent components in a construction. Most models are open on one side to allow this kind of sanding. And it's a point to check if much of this type of work is planned.

Belt sanders are rated by horsepower and belt size. Weight of the tool generally increases with the belt size and horsepower, but production increases in proportion to the amount of abrasive surface that contacts the work. Common belt widths are 3 to 4 inches; lengths can vary from 18 to 24 inches. Belt length doesn't indicate the overall length of the tool. This is a measurement of the length of the belt if it were cut and measured laterally. Longer lengths and wider widths usually go together.

Speed of a belt sander is listed in surface-feet-per-minute, or SFPM. This tells you how many feet of belt travel over the platen in a minute. Higher speeds permit faster sanding, but not necessarily better sanding. You can compensate for a slower tool SFPM by moving the sander more slowly over the work (using a slower feed speed).

For the best results, you have to handle a portable belt sander correctly. The platen must always be held parallel to the work surface. Smoothest results are obtained when the sander is stroked or moved parallel to the grain of the wood and when the strokes overlap 25 to 50 percent of the time. Strokes made across the grain or at an angle remove the largest amount of material in the shortest time. This is only advisable when

the material is very rough or the thickness must be reduced significantly. Cross-grain sanding produces scratches that you have to sand with the grain to remove anyway. Lateral or cross-grain sanding with any power sander leaves scratches that cannot be hidden by any finish.

Weight of these portable belt sanders is normally sufficient for good contact between the tool and the work. Forcing, in an attempt to make the sander work faster, is not a good practice. You only succeed in clogging the belt, straining the tool and pooping yourself out. Quality sanding is only obtained when you let the tool do the job at its own pace.

One of the belt sander's peculiarities is that the abrasive belt can move off the drums if you don't adjust them correctly. Read your owner's manual carefully before using the machine to find out how to perform this adjustment. Even a correctly tracked belt can wander off the drums if used in a side or lateral movement. Be aware of this and allow the sander to run free of the work for a moment to see if the belt returns to a correct alignment. If it doesn't, a small twist of the tracking knob can solve the problem.

In certain respects, portable belt sanders are like self-propelled toys. Set them down with the power on and they'll walk away from you if you don't hang on firmly. Make sure the machine is started and at full speed

before contacting the work, and make the initial contact with the full surface area of the platen. Once on the work, keep the tool in motion and set firmly. Allowing a belt sander to stay in one spot or permitting it to tilt always damages the surface it sits on — resulting in a very smooth, deep spot or dents and gouges.

Belt sanders are handy, but not indispensable. Speed is their main advantage over other sanding methods. But for a low price they give you convenience and save you some work. For these reasons, you might want to consider one for your shop.

Black & Decker's 7451 portable belt sander is a neat and compact machine. A very low profile puts the bulk of the tool's weight as close to the work surface as possible. This helps to keep the tool stable and minimizes the possibility of tilting and gouging. The B&D 7451 is designed for home use by one of the best of the power tool manufacturers, but its quality approaches that of professional equipment.

This sander uses a ¾-hp motor to run a 3x24-inch belt at 1200 SFPM — that's a belt travel of ¼-mile each minute. Platen area is about 14 square inches, which is small when compared to tools with a 4-inch belt, but adequate. Control handles are good sized. The main D-shaped one at the rear has a built-in

Black & Decker's 7451 Belt Sander

Craftsman's 1178C Belt Sander

trigger switch; an auxiliary handle is topside and over the platen, so extra pressure can be applied if necessary. Dust-collection equipment is standard, as is double insulation. And the whole outfit weighs less than 9 pounds. This is undoubtedly one of the best sanders designed for the small, noncommercial shop. Approx. Price: $80.00

Craftsman's 1178C, from Sears, Roebuck and Co., is a heavy-duty portable belt

sander that can make short work of any sanding job. A 1½-hp motor drives a 4x24-inch belt at 1300 surface-feet-per-minute, and the tool has a platen area of a full 24 square inches. The motor is located directly above the platen area, and its weight aids in maintaining firm contact with the work. Double insulation and dust-collection equipment are standard. This hefty, 13-pound tool is only for the serious woodworker who wants to remove a lot of material quickly. Approx. Price: $100.00

Wen's 919 is a small but gutsy portable belt sander that's suited for sanding chores around the small shop. This light, 7-pound tool works with a ⅔-hp motor to drive a 3x18-inch belt at 1000 SFPM. It's double-insulated, and the integral handles follow a straight line parallel to the platen. The trigger switch, located beneath the handle, can be locked so you can keep the tool running if your hand is too far back on the machine. Although the belt size is small, this tool is adequate for most small shop work. Approx. Price: $60.00

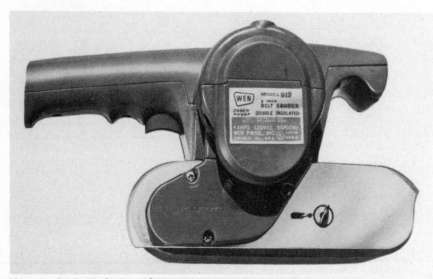

Wen's 919 Belt Sander

Rockwell's 4460 is a popular tool because it's compact enough for small projects, yet is capable of heavy-duty work. This sander has a ¾-hp motor, which drives a 3x21-inch belt at 900 SFPM. The main D-shaped handle, the auxiliary handle in the front, and the motor are close together — making one compact package over the platen area. This concentrates the tool's weight and makes work contact easy to maintain. Other features include automatic belt tensioning, easy tracking adjustments, an open side for flush sanding, double insulation and a lockable trigger switch. It's a full-function sander with all the desired features. Approx. Price: $90.00

Skil's 448 is a professional's tool built to industrial specifications to stand up to consistent, heavy-duty work without burnout or failure. This is definitely too much tool for the casual, amateur woodworker unless the workscope includes much rough lumber smoothing, remodeling, or outdoor deck work.

The tool uses a 1½-hp plus motor to turn a 3x24-inch

> *Belt sanders find most of their application on wood, but they can also be used on metals with the correct abrasive. You can obtain a satin finish or a polish on metal simply by using a fine grit paper (3/0 or 4/0 grit, aluminum oxide or silicon carbide abrasive). This provides enough abrasive action to remove surface blemishes and smooth out the finish.*
>
> *Another technique is to make a polishing lubricant by mixing kerosene and heavy oil in a 3 to 1 ratio. This mixture is applied to the metal surface. A fine belt is mounted on the sander (make sure it has a waterproof backing) and you go over it as if sanding wood. You should be careful with this mixture, since it is very flammable, but it will give a superior polish to most metal surfaces.*

belt at 1500 SFPM. Its main D-shaped handle at the rear of the tool has a lockable trigger switch, while the motor is on top, over the platen. This puts the bulk of the tool's weight where it should be—over the working area of the belt. A knob-shaped auxiliary handle can be mounted in one of two positions. Total weight is 14½ pounds—a necessary evil that should be expected from a pro machine. This portable belt sander upholds its manufacturer's reputation for building quality, professional power tools. Approx. Price: $290.00

Rockwell's 4460 Belt Sander

Skil's 448 Belt Sander

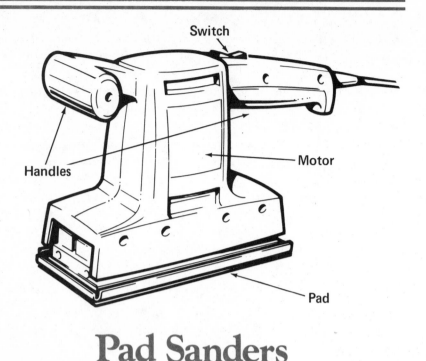

Switch

Handles

Motor

Pad

Pad Sanders

The pad sander is often called a "finishing" sander because it's the only type of powered smoothing tool that can produce a glass-like, satiny surface on wood. It's designed to move sandpaper that is stretched taut over a flat, resilient pad of material, usually rubber or felt.

Too often a sander is judged solely on the speed with which it can remove material. Even a pad sander, if fitted with a coarse abrasive, can exhibit good sanding speed. The more important criteria for a pad sander is the quality and smoothness of the finished surface. This sander is the one to use to make the final touchup before the application of finish material like stain or varnish.

There are several varieties of pad sanders. "Orbital" sanders move the pad in tiny circles. "Straight-line" sanders move the pad in a back-and-forth movement. Some units are designed so that they can work either way, depending upon which mode you think will best accomplish the work. Since sanding with the grain produces the best results, the straight-line action is usually recommended for the finest finishes. The orbital action results in faster wood removal. Swirl marks—circular scratches left by an orbital action—are obvious when a coarse abrasive is fitted on the pad and the tool is moved very slowly. Any good sander can give you a smooth finish, but sanding with the grain is necessary for top-grade work.

A QUICK LOOK AT PORTABLE SANDING TOOLS

NAME	REMARKS	TYPICAL USES
Belt Sander	uses small, endless belt that rotates on two drums—belts available in wide variety of grit sizes—relatively heavy tool	rough surface finishing—some heavy cutting of stock with coarser grit abrasive—removal of paint or old finishes
Pad/Finish Sander	mounts square cut from single sheet of standard sandpaper—orbital or straight line action—pads replaceable according to hardness desired in job	final surface finish prior to application of stain/varnish—sanding between surface coats—satin brush finish on metals

A multiple-action sander does offer some options. Coarse abrasives with an orbital motion result in fast stock removal. Straight-line action and fine abrasives will result in a fine surface. You pay extra for a multi-action sander, but it's worth the cost.

All pad sanders come equipped with a soft pad mounted on the bottom of the tool. This is usually either a third or quarter of the size of a standard 9x12-inch sheet of abrasive. The pad has just the right degree of flexibility for average work but because different wood species have different characteristics, it may not be the best backing for the abrasive. A grain pattern, for example, that has hard and soft areas will have more wood removed from the soft areas if a soft pad is used. The soft pad conforms to the softer areas and produces a wavy surface that you can actually feel. In this kind of situation, it's better to switch to a harder pad or slip a piece of thin hardboard between the pad and the abrasive. This enables the pad to span the gap across the grain and take hard and soft parts of the wood down together.

On the other hand, you sometimes need a pad that's even softer than the one that comes with the machine. Softer pads are useful for sanding contours, columns, and dowels. One successful improvisation is to use a piece of rug or foam rubber as a backing material in the pad. Or you can purchase a softer pad.

Pad/finish sanders usually come equipped with a bottom pad of felt. This has a certain amount of flexibility that is about right for average work. Often a hard rubber pad is also available — either as an extra-cost accessory or standard item supplied with the machine. If however, you are using the sander as a honing tool, or sanding woods with a prominent hard-and-soft grain pattern (like fir), you may find an even harder pad useful. Unless one is commercially available with your machine, you will have to make one yourself.

With most machines, the original pad is secured to a baseplate by screws. If you wish to make a hard pad, remove the original one and use it as a pattern. The new pad can be attached in the normal fashion. A different way to do this is to drive some small nails or brads through the new wooden pad and then into the pad that is already on the sander. This does not fasten it so securely that it cannot be removed easily, but is sufficient to enable the harder pad to function well. You may also find it necessary to cut sanding sheets a little longer or wider than normal to compensate for the increased pad thickness.

All pad sanders have a means of fastening the sandpaper over the pad and holding it taut. A loose abrasive reduces sanding efficiency, and if really loose, the pad will just rub the paper a little and accomplish nothing. Methods for mounting the paper vary with the manufacturer. One method uses pressure rollers on either side of the pad. The paper is placed under one roller, stretched taut against the pad, and the opposite end placed under the second roller. Then you use a screwdriver to turn the roller to make sure the paper is held firmly. Another common method incorporates spring-powered clips, somewhat like those found on clipboards to hold paper. You just place one end of the sandpaper under one clip, pull the paper taut, and place it under the second clip. Both methods of paper attachment work, but the roller type is more convenient and allows for a certain degree of adjustment after the paper is in place. What matters most is that the paper is held taut — otherwise you'll accomplish little.

Except for skinning a finger, you can't really hurt yourself with a pad sander. The dust created by the sander can be a health hazard, however. Some of the more costly units come with dust-collection equipment, otherwise it is optional. This type of attachment makes sense if you do a lot of sanding. However, it must be removed when it interferes with a work procedure. So it's sometimes better, and less expensive, to use a respirator instead.

If you put a pad sander on a flat piece of work and flick the switch, it'll move off on its own. It won't run away from you like a belt sander, but it will do a sort of disco dance and finally tumble over. You need to keep a firm grip on this tool at all times.

A pad sander is easy to use. This tool has to be kept moving, slowly but consistently. Grip the tool firmly to control it, but don't apply pressure. The tool's weight is usually sufficient for good contact between the abrasive and the work. If extra pressure is required, never apply so much that the motor sound changes. A sound change indicates that the motor is being strained, and it can be damaged.

Whenever possible, stroke the tool so sanding is done parallel to the grain. This goes for straight-line as well as orbital sanders. Less pressure is required when edges are being sanded because the softer pad curls up over the edges and rounds them. Use a hard pad if you want to maintain a square edge.

General sanding rules call for using progressively finer grits of sandpaper until the necessary finish is obtained. But much depends upon the original condition of the wood. Lumber purchased through commercial outlets is usually planed down and has a respectable finish. Often simple sanding with fine

Rockwell's 4480 Pad Sander

sandpaper can produce a finish ready to stain or clear coat.

Rockwell's 4480 pad sander is a compact tool that's easy to grip with one hand. It doesn't have the largest of pads, at only 4⅛x4½ inches, but this is in accord with its design. The purpose of this sander is to produce the smoothest finishes, and it does this very well. Its construction provides good balance and minimum vibration.

This tool works with one of the smallest orbits in the business — ¾₄ - inch. Orbits-per-minute (OPM) is 12,000. With such a speed, swirl marks are not a problem. This speed and small orbit make this sander a finesse tool, though it has the guts to do heavy work with

coarse sandpaper. It weighs in at 3½ pounds, holds abrasive with spring clamps, and has a removable pad. A replacement pad is made of thick, sponge rubber to produce good results when used for fine sanding on curved or round surfaces. A standard 9x11-inch sheet of sandpaper can be cut to provide four sander-size pieces for use on this tool. The Rockwell 4480 is a useful tool and well worth the price. Approx. Price:$65.00

The Black & Decker 7404 has a price so low that it almost makes this orbital sander disposable. This sander has the conventional pad sander shape — with a rectangular pad and dual handles on top for a firm grip. The main handle has a built-in slide switch positioned naturally under the operator's thumb. Although it only weighs 3 pounds, it works smoothly enough to require only a one-handed grip for most work.

The pad takes a paper size of 3⅝x9 inches, which is a third of the standard size sheet of abrasive. It produces 10,000, ³⁄₁₆-inch orbits-per-minute. It's also double-insulated and comes with a 10-inch cord. The short cord makes the tool easy to store, but it also means that an extension cord is required for all work. One interesting item that's available as an extra-cost accessory is a dust-collection attachment (#74-001),

Black & Decker's 7404 Orbital Sander

Millers Falls' SP6080 Pad Sander

designed to work with most tank-type vacuums. This attachment works, but the trailing hose can be a nuisance during many sanding tasks. Approx. Price: (7404) $19.00; (74-001) $10.00

Miller's Falls' SP6080 is a professional tool for heavy as well as light work. This sander only weighs 3½ pounds and is constructed for smooth orbital action with minimum vibration. An adjustable, T-shaped handle provides an auxiliary grip that you can position to suit yourself. This contributes to good control and uniform abrasive-work pressures, regardless of the task. Paper size is 3⅝x9 inches — a third of a standard sheet of sandpaper. It gives you 10,000 orbits-per-minute for a good amount of sanding action. The sander is double-insulated and comes with a 10-foot cord. The long cord is a nice feature because

you can do a lot of work without an extension. Approx. Price: $60.00

Skil's 459 orbital sander can give you the smoothest finish possible with a power tool. This is a sander for the dedicated woodworker who spends as much time preparing wood for a final finish as he does shaping and assembling the pieces of a project. The sander gives you 10,000 ¹⁄₁₆-inch

orbits-per-minute. Pad area is large, requiring a 3⅝x9-inch sheet of sandpaper to cover it. This tool has an integral, dual-grip handle — both ends of which are sculptured to fit fingers and palms. It's double-insulated and the power switch is conveniently located on top of the main handle. The tool grips abrasive paper by means of spring clips, but the clips have an extension that protrudes toward the top, so they're easy to use. Approx. Price: $35.00

Skil's 459 Orbital Sander

Wen's 300 (PR 30) is a multi-action sander that's as attractive in appearance as it is in performance. The tool is compact, light, and has a shape that's easy to handle by anyone. Both the auxiliary and main handles are well-designed for good control, and permit one-hand or two-hand operation.

A lever lets you switch easily from orbital to straight-line operation. It gives you 4000 orbits-per-minute or 4000 strokes-per-minute. Lever-type clamps hold the paper—not the easiest or most efficient method, but adequate if the directions are followed. The motor is ½-hp, but since the tool weighs only 3 pounds, you can use it for long periods of time without tiring. This is one of the better models among multi-action sanders. Approx. Price: $40.00

Craftsman's 1168

Pad sanders are usually used to create a final smooth surface on wood before the application of a finish. You can also use them to sand between finish coats. Using lacquer, shellac, or varnish usually means a number of layers in the finish, with light sanding between each. This final sanding is also given to the top coat to add a final gloss.

The usual technique is to use a commercial rubbing compound that can be bought at most hardware outlets. This is applied on the surface of the workpiece. A piece of carpet or burlap is mounted on the sander in place of the regular pad and paper, and then the sander is used on the work. This will produce a superfine finish with a high gloss—one of the distinctive marks of quality craftsmanship.

multi-action sander, from Sears, Roebuck and Co., has its own dust-collection equipment. A shroud completely encloses the sanding pad and the dust is sucked up a tube and deposited in an attached bag. This is a heavy-duty tool with a hefty, 9-pound weight to match. The ½-hp motor drives the extra-large, 4½x9-inch sanding pad at either 4000 orbits- or strokes-per-minute. This can help you sand broad areas rather quickly. Main and auxiliary handles are good-sized, which is necessary with a tool this big. It holds paper by means of a lever that's easy to use, and the machine has a lockable trigger switch and double-insulation. Approx. Price: $80.00

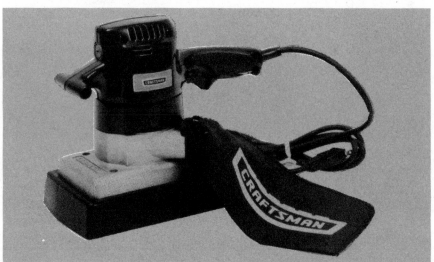

Wen's 300 (PR 30)   *Craftsman's 1168 Multi-Action Sander*

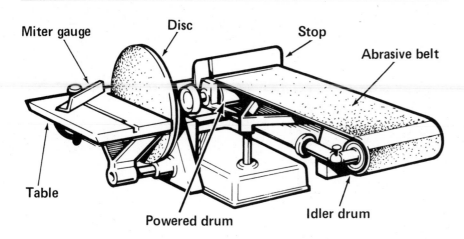

Miter gauge · Disc · Stop · Abrasive belt · Table · Powered drum · Idler drum

Stationary Disc/ Belt Sanders

Both the disc and belt sander are available as separate tools, but this is a case where it makes sense to have two tools on one stand. Usually combination tools are a compromise, but this is not the case with the disc/belt sander. By mounting the two sanders on one stand you need only one motor to drive both tools, and you save floor space. Also, having them so close together is handy, because you can easily switch the work from one machine to the other as necessary.

Why have one of each? Quite simply, because each does a particular job better than the other. Here's how they work.

The belt sander moves abrasives with the grain of the wood — an action that produces the smoothest surface. This sander is not designed to smooth large surfaces, but it's unbeatable for finishing project components before final assembly. The smoother each part is before final assembly, the less work you have to do before the finish is applied. Also some projects, like box drawers and picture frames, can be sanded on the belt sander even after final assembly. The belt sander is also excellent for smoothing endgrain, and most can handle up to a 4x4-inch piece of wood without problems. It's this straight-line capability that makes the belt sander so valuable in the shop.

The disc sander, on the other hand, is basically a flat, metal circular plate on which abrasives are mounted. This disc revolves in a circular motion, which means that regardless of how the work is applied, the sanding action is always crossgrain. This particular limitation makes the disc sander a poor choice for finish sanding. But it's superior for "truing up" a surface. Because a table is mounted at right angles to the centerline of a very flat plate covered with abrasive, anything brought up against the disc is sanded at right angles. Disc sanders give you a much higher degree of accuracy than belt sanders because the belted abrasive has a certain amount of float — the belt flexes slightly as it travels over the wood. The disc sander's rigidity makes it the perfect choice for sanding endgrains, finishing miter cuts, and smoothing outside curves. There is, however, one hitch to using a disc sander. You must remember that the abrasive on the perimeter of the disc moves faster than the abrasive on the center of the disc. So, when you hold a piece of wood against the disc, the part that's against the perimeter of the disc is sanded faster than the part held against the center. For this reason, you must apply more pressure toward the center of the disc surface to sand the wood evenly and to prevent the outside from being sanded faster than the inside. A miter gauge placed in the slot on the table helps correct this tendency, because it helps insure that the piece is held at the desired angle to the disc surface.

As you can see, it's very beneficial to combine these

237

> On almost all disc/belt sanders, the belt sander portion of the machine is constructed so that there is a backup plate only at the front. This design allows you to use the back portion of the belt for such tasks as sanding knobs, ball shapes, and rounding off pieces to break an edge. You will find it easier to do these jobs if the belt tension is slackened a little first, allowing the belt to conform to the contours of the workpiece.
>
> Commercial users of disc/belt sanders often mount "slashed" belts for these kinds of tasks. They simplify rounding-off because the belt can conform to an odd shape more easily. This kind of belt is not found in most hardware outlets. A way around this problem is to slash cut a belt yourself. Select a belt with a fine-grit abrasive. With a sharp knife cut slits on the back (paper) side of the belt. These should be 4 to 6 inches long and about ¼ inch apart. Do this across the entire width of the belt, leaving about ½ inch of solid belt on either side. The entire length of the belt should be slit, though an inch or so should be left between groups of slits.
>
> The result will be a belt that will conform to odd shapes and make rounding-off operations much easier. Do not put too much pressure on the belt once it is mounted on the machine. Slashing does weaken the belt and it may part under too much strain.

two tools into one machine—the disc/belt sander. Now that you know the individual functions of the tools, let's delve into the nitty-gritty of how they operate.

The belt sander portion of the machine works with an endless, abrasive-coated belt that travels over two metal cylinders called "drums." The drum closest to the disc sander is rotated by a motor-driven shaft, and causes the belt mounted on the surface of the drum to rotate. The second drum is an "idler," and only rotates because the belt moves over it. This entire section of the belt sander is mounted on a mechanism that lets you vary the distance between the drums, and tilt them. You need to adjust the distance between the drums to maintain proper belt tension to keep the belt tight on the drums. The tilt controls assure that the belt tracks properly and does not veer off to one side.

Mounted between these two drums is a backup plate called a "platen." Both drums are slightly crowned in the center to make the belt track correctly. Properly adjusted, the platen should be about $\frac{1}{64}$-inch above the height of the drums' crowns. The platen provides support for the belt when work is pressed against it. The back area of the belt (or the lower area, when the sander is in the horizontal position) is not supported, which leaves it slightly flexible at this point. This back area is often used to smooth compound curves or knobs. Many industrial machines are totally enclosed, except for the area directly in front of the platen—a design that promotes safety and facilitates dust collection. Ducting leads to an attached shop vacuum to suck away virtually all sawdust. This design does, however, prevent you from using the slack, back belt area.

Most machines have a removable guard mounted on top. It's easily removed so you can use the curved surface of the belt for sanding inside curves. This is a handy feature on the belt sander. All belt sanders have a "stop," a metal ledge that you can rest the work against to prevent the belt travel from ripping the workpiece from your hands. A belt sander may also include a full-function, tilting table with a slot recessed in the top for a miter gauge. The table is a great asset, but it's not often found on home shop tools.

Most belt sanders swing 45 degrees so they can be used in a vertical, as well as horizontal, position. You can also lock the sander in any intermediate position. These adjustments let you position the tool for convenient use, depending upon the task at hand.

The disc sander portion of the machine shares a

common motor shaft with the belt sander. It has no adjustments and is only a flat, circular plate that turns counterclockwise and is covered with an abrasive paper. All disc sanders have a table mounted in front of them. This table usually tilts through 45 degrees, is slotted for a miter gauge, and is fixed either at or slightly above the center-line of the disc. This means that the work is applied against the upper half of the rotating disc. For normal operation, you set the table at 90 degrees to the surface of the disc, but you can tilt it for sanding chamfers and bevels. This adjustment allows for supported sanding of compound angles.

Work is usually done on the lefthand side of the table because the counterclockwise rotation of the disc forces the workpiece down toward the table. You can use the other side of the table, but you risk having the work lifted by the motion of the disc and torn from your hands. At best, this leads to inaccurate work. At worst, it could be dangerous. Sometimes a project may call for removing the table and using the entire surface of the disc. In such situations, you should grip the work firmly and press it very lightly against the abrasive.

Abrasive papers are usually attached to the disc with some kind of adhesive. The traditional way to do this was to apply a type of stick shellac to the turning disc until it was coated evenly.

Then the paper was stuck on. This method still works well, but modern glues make the job easier. There are a number of brushable and sprayable adhesives that are quite superior. Also, you can buy abrasive discs that have a pressure-sensitive backing. You just peel away a protective paper backing and apply the sheet of abrasive to the metal disc. All disc adhesives are nonhardening, allowing you to remove a worn sheet quickly. When you change abrasives, always check the metal disc for large particles of dirt clinging to it. The dirt can cause bumps or unevenness under the new disc and may lead to tearing or scoring on the wood being sanded.

Size of a disc sander is determined by the diameter of the disc, with 9 inches being common for home shop tools. The size of a belt sander is expressed in terms of the width and length of the belt. A common size is 6x48 inches, meaning the belt is 6 inches wide and would form a strip 48 inches long if cut and measured linearly.

A disc/belt sander doesn't take up much floor space—just a few square feet. And you need standing room at the disc and belt side of the machine. If you normally use the belt in the horizontal position for sanding long boards, extra space is required in the belt's line of travel. Actually, you have a lot of options when positioning the disc/belt sander in the shop, because it's light enough to move

easily from one location to another.

Even though sanders have no blades, you can still get hurt when using one. With equal impartiality, the abrasive particles can remove softwood, hardwood, metal and flesh—the last with quite a bit of pain on your part. Be sure to hold workpieces, especially small ones, so that your hands stay clear of the abrasive surface. Position tables and stops so there is a minimum gap between them and the abrasive surface—just enough to provide clearance. This is to prevent small or thin pieces of material from being pulled between the abrasive and the table edge—a definite possibility if the gap is too wide.

When working with long pieces of wood on the belt sander it's impossible to use a stop to brace the work. On these occasions, remember that the belt travels much like a treadmill, and anything you touch lightly against it can be torn from your hands if you don't grip the piece firmly. And you might find yourself dodging a flying piece of wood.

Also, you must mount new belts carefully. The belt should be taut, but not so stiff that the motor strains to turn it. After some use, a new belt may need additional tensioning, and maybe a small tracking adjustment. Read your owner's manual to find out how to do this correctly.

All belts for a belt sander have an arrow on the back

that tells you which direction the belt should revolve. This arrow should point in the direction of the drive drum's rotation. The correct belt rotation is necessary because of the lap joint that ties the belt into a loop. When the belt is turning as it should, the workpiece slides smoothly over the joint; incorrect mounting causes the work to snag at the joint and tear the belt.

With both belt and disc sanders, it's often tempting to rest the corner of an object on a table or stop and tilt it against the abrasive to "break a corner" or round an edge. Avoid this practice, because it's easy for the workpiece to become wedged and dig into the belt or disc. At the least, it'll rip the abrasive surface and may ruin the piece. And there's always a possibility of injury to yourself. The correct method is to do it freehand, and touch the abrasive without resting it on anything. When using a belt sander, you should remember that the top of the workpiece tends to be pulled slightly deeper into the belt than the bottom. To correct for this, you should put a little more pressure on the bottom of the piece to insure an even job.

After mounting a new disc on a disc sander, it's a good idea to stand back and let the machine run awhile before doing any work. This way, you make sure the abrasive is mounted correctly and that the bond is strong enough to keep the abrasive disc from flying off.

Use of a dust mask is an excellent precaution when using fine abrasive, since you may find yourself in a substantial cloud of dust. It's a must when sanding any metal. Copper is toxic — a fact to remember when sanding this metal, bronze or brass. You can connect a vacuum or blower system to most machines. A vacuum attached to the sander reduces airborne dust and particles, and greatly improves your working conditions. Also, there won't be a fine layer of dust from one end of the shop to the other.

As a finishing tool, the belt/disc sander is an excellent investment. It provides working ease, convenience and speed. You still need to touch up the workpiece before applying a final finish, but the task is considerably easier if this machine is used first. It's a "must have" machine for any full-function shop.

Craftsman's 22584L3, from Sears, Roebuck and Co., is a sturdy, full-function disc/belt sander designed for the home shop. It's about as big as such a machine comes, with a 9-inch disc and 6x48-inch belt. This Craftsman machine gives you plenty of sanding area against which the work can be applied, because it has a 17½-inch backup plate. The belt section of the sander has a removable work stop. And the 6¼x12-inch table can be used with both the disc and belt portions of the machine. This versatile table also tilts 45 degrees and has a slot for an optional miter gauge. The dual function table is a sign of a full-function machine, and is necessary for precise work.

Like most tools designed for the small shop, the belt isn't completely shielded, and the top area is always exposed. The back area of the tool is only exposed when the sander is used in the vertical position. This doesn't affect procedure when using the belt section of the machine, but it does mean you have to be careful. The disc is guarded by a cover plate in the back, so the only exposed area is where the abrasive is mounted.

Craftsman's 22584L3 Disc/Belt Sander

Both belt and disc sections have dust traps that take a 2½-inch diameter hose. So you can easily attach a shop-vac to suck away most of the sanding dust. When you buy this sander you get a complete outfit—belt/disc sander, stand, ¾-hp motor, pulleys and drive belt with guards. You can operate this machine with a ¾-hp motor, which is a good idea for heavy-duty work and sanding large surface areas frequently. You have a nice machine here, with just about all the necessary goodies in one package. Approx. Price: $250.00

Toolkraft's 4337 disc/belt sander is an excellent candidate for the home shop. It has all the convenience features craftsmen look for, and a standard 9-inch disc and 6x48-inch belt. The belt stop is removable and the 6¼x12-inch table can be

Toolkraft's 4337 Sander

It is possible with the disc portion of a disc/belt sander to sand perfect circles or arcs. The best way to do this is to make a jig setup. The simplest is a piece of plywood through which a nail is driven for use as a pivot. The plywood is clamped to the table in front of the disc sander, with the nail approximately centered in the downward rotating portion of the disc. Distance from the abrasive sheet and the nail should equal the radius of the circle to be sanded. To use this jig is easy. The center of the circle to be sanded is first marked, and the pivot inserted in a hole drilled at that point. It doesn't matter which way you turn the circle against the disc, but best results are obtained if it is rotated very slowly.

positioned for disc or belt use. This table is also slotted for a supplied miter gauge and tilts 45 degrees. A 16½-inch platen supports the work area of the belt—ample for most home shop work.

Construction is very good. The tool's rugged cast iron can stand up to considerable use and abuse. Belt and disc shielding is minimal—a standard practice in home shop machines. Cost of the sander includes all the necessities: sander and stand, ½-hp motor, drive belt and guard, pulleys, and the miter gauge. It's ready to go right from the crate. Approx. Price: $290.00

AM&T's 271-A388 disc/belt sander is definitely a low-end tool—an economy machine from a company whose basic business is producing no-frills, functional tools at flea market prices. It's a good choice for the craftsman who wants the basics at a rock-bottom price. This machine is small when compared to most disc/belt sanders—disc size is 6 inches in diameter and the belt measures 4x36 inches. You have enough surface area here for most tasks. All necessary features are present: belt tensioning and tracking mechanisms, belt

AM&T's 271-A388 Disc/Belt Sander

mechanism adjustment for horizontal and vertical use, 4x12-inch, tiltable disc sander table that's slotted for a miter gauge, and a work stop for the belt. You have to supply your own motor, however, but that should be expected in such a low-cost model.

A bonus feature on this machine is its removable disc. You can remove the disc from the drive shaft and put other tools in its place: a small drum sander, buffing wheel, grinding wheel or wire brushes. This is a light tool with a shipping weight of only 17 pounds. It can't do everything, but it's a lot better than not having a disc/belt sander at all. Approx. Price: $52.00

of the disc and belt. Side, top, and back guards shield the belt, though all of them can be easily removed for special applications. The disc sander is shielded by a cover in the back and a flange that covers most of the rotating edge. Belt size is the standard 6x48 inches, while the disc has an extra-large 12-inch diameter. Two separate, tiltable tables are provided. A 7⅜x14¾-inch unit is made for the belt area, and a 9¾x16¼-inch table serves the disc. Each is slotted to receive a miter gauge.

Physically, this tool is not larger than most of its type, but there is a difference in weight. At 158 pounds, this tool is more than twice the weight of most tools in this

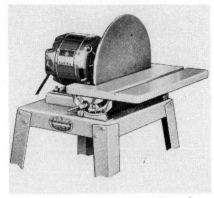

Sprunger's DS-1200 Sander

category. The cost of this disc/belt sander only includes the basic machine. Stand, motor and miter gauge are all extra-cost items. Although the average worker may find this machine a bit expensive, its superlative performance will pay off in the long run. Approx. Price: $553.00

Rockwell's 31-710 is a fantastic machine and a prime example of a disc/belt sander built to satisfy industrial needs. It's a rugged, powerful machine suited for school shops, commercial woodworkers and the advanced home shop owner who demands tools that match his skills. The fact that it is made to operate with a 1½-hp motor (hopefully on a 220-240 volt circuit) says much about its design. It can handle everything from light touchups to continuous heavy-duty jobs.

Because this machine is partially designed for commercial applications, it's as shielded as possible. The only exposed abrasive areas are the actual working areas

Rockwell's 31-710 Sander

Sprunger's DS-1200 is a single-purpose disc sander for the person who wants a separate belt sander or thinks he can get by with a portable belt sander, although metal surfacing is best done on a stationary belt sander. This tool is extremely simple—disc, table, and motor all sitting neatly on one stand. To cut costs, the 12-inch disc is mounted directly on the motor shaft. The table is a good-sized 9x16 inches and tilts through a 50-degree range. It's also slotted for a miter gauge, which is optional. It's not a great machine, but it can do the job. Approx. Price: $85.00

Because screwdrivers, wrenches and hammers are used every day, they are taken for granted. In actuality, the marketplace offers a dazzling array of types at a variety of prices.

Tightening And Fastening Tools

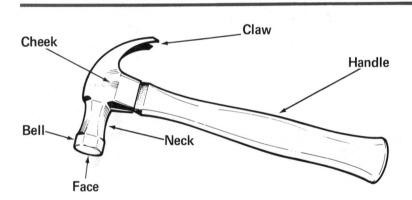

Cheek

Claw

Handle

Bell

Neck

Face

Hammers

The hammer is one of the oldest tools known to man. However, its evolutionary process has been rather gradual and innovations are still being made in striking instruments. For a good part of the last century, a hammer was a locally produced item, beat out on the anvil by the local blacksmith. These hammers weren't very durable, and their faces quickly mushroomed from use. This was because they were made out of iron. As technology progressed, the smith was able to achieve a longer wearing hammer by case hardening it. Mild steel, which a blacksmith used to fashion an item, lacks the necessary ingredient — carbon — for hardening. Case hardening is a process by which carbon is induced into the pores of the steel, so that it will surface harden. A blacksmith does this by a process known as "pack carborizing." In this process, the hammer head is "packed" in charcoal inside an airtight metal box. This is then put in the forge and brought to a high temperature for a long period of time. The longer the piece is "soaked," the deeper the carbon is induced into the surface of the metal. This in turn determines how deep the surface hardening extends into the hammer head. After soaking, the piece is heated to a bright cherry red and quenched in water or oil.

243

This results in a hard, durable surface extending 10- to 15-thousandths of an inch deep, and a shock-absorbing, mild-steel core. Toward the turn of the century, less time consuming liquid carborizing processes were developed for mass production. Liquid carborizing also gave a greater depth of hardness.

Near the end of the 19th Century, processes were developed which could produce steel with an established carbon content. This meant that steel could then be "through hardened" to a very exact hardness. By controlling the carbon content and adding other material to "alloy" the steel, steels of great "toughness" could be made. Toughness is the metallurgist's measure of a steel's ability to withstand shock. Hardness and toughness are equally important in the making of a high-grade hammer head.

Today hammer manufacturers use steel that's made by a computerized, monitored process to carefully control carbon content and alloying materials. A manufacturer of a high-grade hammer takes a blank of this steel and hot forges it into the hammer's basic shape. Hot forging is a process in which a blank of molten steel is put into a die and a powerful mechanical press hammers, or "forges," the metal into the die cavity to form a hammer head. This hot forging process, sometimes called "drop forging," compacts and aligns the grain molecules of the steel to produce a tough, high-grade end product. As a part of the process the eye of the hammer, which is the hole into which the handle is fitted, is also pierced.

Cheaper hammers are made of cast steel. Never buy this type of hammer, because it lacks the durability of a forged tool. A cast hammer's head is usually entirely painted, and it has a rough texture from the sand used in the casting process. The head also has a ridge running through the middle, another result of the casting process.

After forging, the hammer is heat treated and then finished. For the most part, hammer-head polishing is still done by hand. Higher-grade hammers have a face carefully ground to shape and the entire head is brought to a high polish. Economy hammers only have the areas around the face, cheeks, and claw

COMMON AND BOX NAIL SIZES																	
Size-Penny (d)	2	3	4	5	6	7	8	9	10	12	16	20	30	40	50	60	
Length In Inches	1	1¼	1½	1¾	2	2¼	2½	2¾	3	3¼	3½	4	4½	5	5½	6	
Common Nails Gauge	15	14	12½	12½	11½	11½	10¼	10¼	9	9	8	6	5	4	3	2	
Approximate # Per Pound	845	540	290	250	165	150	100	90	65	60	45	30	20	17	13	10	
Box Nails Gauge	15½	14½	14	14	12½	12½	11½	11½	10½	10½	10	9	9	8	–	–	
Approximate # Per Pound	1010	635	473	406	236	210	145	132	94	88	71	52	46	35	–	–	

The traditional grading system used for nail sizes was by weight—a system still in use. It takes about 1010 2d (penny) nails to make one pound by weight of that size nail.

highlighted with an abrasive belt.

Originally, all hammer handles were made of wood. But now there are also handles made of steel and fiberglass. Wood is still used extensively today, and many craftsmen prefer it. Wood has great resilience to absorb shock, and it's a strong, lightweight material that gives a hammer good balance. It also provides a good grip. Although it's durable, it can't take abuse that other materials can. A 10- to 12-ounce wooden-handled hammer used by one person in a cabinet making shop could last a lifetime. But a 20- to 22-ounce framing hammer used by a rough carpentry crew often has a short service life. Pulling nails with this type of hammer puts a high strain on the handle, and the handle usually breaks just back of the head.

A wooden handle is attached to the head by inserting it into the eye of the hammer and driving wedges. Most hammers made today have an adze eye, which was developed here in the U.S. by a blacksmith named David Maydole in 1840. The adze eye has been improved by making a projection at the base of the hammer, so the eye can be longer and taper gradually. The longer eye gives a greater bearing surface to withstand the forces of prying better. And, since the eye is tapered, the head is much less likely to come off after the wedges are put in place.

Often it is not recognized how much environment and technology mesh to produce the everyday things in our lives. An example of this is "balloon framing." This technique is the forerunner of the present stud and plate construction now used almost universally in house construction.

Early construction in the North American colonies closely followed the patterns of the home countries. Tradesmen had no difficulty in reproducing the classical, medieval or Queen Anne lines of the old country's buildings, but wood replaced stone. This was because of the lack of qualified stonemasons to construct buildings of cut stones, and the ready availability of wood in a world where wood was free.

This practice of following old patterns in construction continued until the 1830s, when two technological developments brought new construction techniques. The introduction of mechanical sawmills created large quantities of planks and boards, while manufacturing techniques improved to the point where the mass-production of nails was possible. Together they permitted a building technique in which one man could erect an entire building using only hammer and saw.

This frame construction consists of closely positioned studs (vertical members) connected by joists (horizontal members). A ground or floor plate anchors the bottom, while a head plate supports the roof rafters. The entire structure is further strengthened by diagonal boarding across the outside. The result is a building that uses a minimum of material, offers increased structural rigidity, and can be constructed by one or two men moving relatively small pieces of wood.

Balloon framing was usually used with studs two stories high, while another technique used single-story studs, with each successive story added to the one below. Both used the frame technique of studs and joists. There are few wooden buildings constructed today which do not use the same technique—testimony to the mesh between the tradesman and technology.

The forged steel handle is the strongest made. It's another U.S. innovation, patented by Ernest Estwing in 1926. The handle is either made separately from the head and then joined permanently, or the head and handle are forged in one piece. The problem with steel handles is that they transmit, and even magnify, shock rather than dampening it. For this reason, they have either a leather wrapping or, more commonly, a heavy rubber cover. Steel hammers are very popular with construction workers, cement contractors and the like.

Fiberglass handles are the most recent on the tool scene. This material has the resilience of wood, but is much more rugged. The latest development has been the introduction of hollow-core fiberglass handles, which are very effective at dampening shock. While fiberglass handles strike a happy medium between the shock-dampening qualities of wood and the strength of steel, the steel handle is still the strongest.

There are many hammer manufacturers, and each manufacturer makes several different grades of hammers. For this reason, it's difficult to make hard and fast brand recommendations. It wouldn't be fair to compare one maker's low-line products with another's high-priced line. So, in this chapter you are presented with the different types of hammers, and given highlights of one or two representative brands. You can use this information to make comparisons.

Standard Claw Hammers

When the average person hears the word "hammer," he

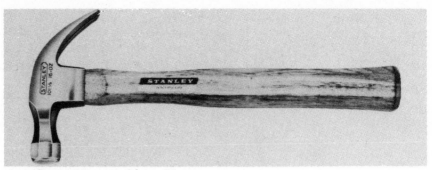

Stanley's "Best" Claw Hammer

thinks of a standard claw hammer. This type of hammer has been around since Roman times and is still the most popular. Designs vary, but most have an octagonal neck and a round or octagonal bell. The face may be either flat or slightly convex. The convex face is preferred for a couple of reasons. First, the convex face corrects for striking the nail at a slight angle. Second, a nail can be driven down to a surface more easily without producing a hammer bruise on the wood—a sign of poor craftsmanship.

Traditionally, the claw was well-curved, and many hammers are made this way today. But modern, large ripping hammers have a claw that's almost straight. The curved claw gives you a higher mechanical advantage for nail pulling, but to pull long nails, you must put a block of wood under the hammer to get enough height.

Standard claw hammers are available in weights ranging from 6 to 24 ounces, with all sorts of handle configurations. For general household use, a bell-faced, 16-ounce curved claw model with a wood or fiberglass

handle is a good choice. Although it's hard to make specific recommendations without knowing a person's workscope. House building and rough framing usually call for a 20- or 22-ounce straight-claw framing hammer. You may want to choose a framing hammer with a waffle face. This kind of hammer has a flat face with a checkered pattern machined into it. It's strictly for rough framing, and offers great advantages when large spikes are set with heavy blows. Glancing is much reduced.

If your work is of a more precise nature, you might want a much lighter hammer than those just described. For work such as model building and cabinet making, a 6- to 10-ounce model with a wood handle and curved claw offers more precision than heavier hammers.

The Stanley Tool Company makes a fine line of claw hammers sold in most hardware stores. These hammers are also marked "good," "better," and "best," to let you know which grade you are buying. Common weights from 7 to 22 ounces are offered with wood, fiberglass or steel handles. Approx. Price: (22 oz.) $16.00

The Vaughan Company makes a particularly fine line of hammers. Their finish is superlative, making them a pride to own. The best grade is the Professional series, available in all weights and options. Their medium-grade 999 series is probably equal to other companies' top grade. Although this series has long been popular with professional people, Vaughan is now aiming it toward the do-it-yourself market. Vaughan's economy, or "good" grade is what they call their "super steel" hammers. In the company's

sales literature, Vaughan claims these hammers are for the handyman and differ from their more expensive models only in finish and polish. Approx. Price: (10 oz. "Little Pro") $9.00; (20 oz. "999") $15.00; (16 oz. "super steel") $11.00

Millers Falls also markets a line of hammers. Although the company has no grading system, you can consider Millers Falls hammers to fit into two grades — "better" and "best." The company's "better" wood-handled hammers have epoxy bonding, while the "best" grade incorporates double steel wedging. This, incidentally, is a good way to evaluate other brands of hammers which don't have a grading system. True Temper is also a maker of good

hammers, and this company makes many of Millers Falls' models. Approx. Price: (20 oz. "better") $12.00; (16 oz. "best") $12.50

Ball-Peen Hammers

The ball-peen hammer is the stock in trade of the tool and die maker, machinist, tinsmith and other metal workers. Its neck is shorter than that of a claw hammer, and it has a bell-shaped ball called a peen, instead of a claw. The peen is used mostly when metal must be "moved," such as when riveting. A rivet is inserted through a hole in the work and placed on an anvil. Striking the rivet's peripheral area with the peen causes the rivet metal to move outwards. Then the other face of the hammer is used to finish the job. Ball-peen hammers are also useful for removing small dents from sheet metal, although there's an extensive line of special auto body hammers for this purpose.

The ball-peen hammer is useful to have around, and should be a part of any good craftsman's tool chest. Such

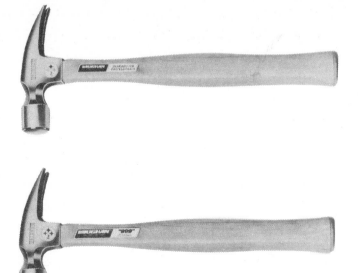

Vaughan's Little Pro Hammer (top) and 999 Hammer (bottom)

things as center punches, cold chisels, and drifts are properly struck with a ball-peen hammer and not a claw hammer.

It's much easier to select a ball-peen hammer because they're usually available in only one grade, and almost all come only with a wood handle. A wood handle on this type of hammer can withstand heavy pounding, and it's not subjected to the nail pulling stress encountered with claw hammers. A few fiberglass-handled models are available, however, which you might want to consider.

Most manufacturers of claw hammers also make ball peen hammers. Purchasing a ball-peen model is simply a matter of picking one that looks and feels good to you. But don't expect the same quality of finish as found on claw hammers because a ball peen hammer is more of an industrial item. A good weight for general use is 16 ounces. Ball-peen hammers weighing 16 ounces and less are available for jewelry making, and they range upwards in weight to as heavy as you can swing.

The Compo-Cast Company of Indianapolis, Indiana makes a very unique model. It's a dead-blow type ball-peen hammer that works like the company's dead-blow soft-faced mallet. For a description of this dead-blow principle, see the soft-faced hammer section under Compo-Cast Dead Blow Hammer.

Soft-Faced Hammers

Whether you're an amateur or professional, sooner or later you'll need a soft-faced hammer. A common type, available in most hardware stores, has a metal head and wood handle. One end of the head is usually covered with a rather hard, composition plastic material. The other end of the head has a hard rubber covering. You use the rubber side when the work surface is very susceptible to damage, and the hard plastic side is used when more *oomph* is needed.

Another type is the rubber mallet. This is usually just a rubber, mallet-style head with a wooden handle. You can use it for everything from driving tent pegs to assembling furniture during gluing. Before rubber mallets were in existence, the traditional rawhide mallet did the job. This is a piece of rawhide leather, rolled into a cylindrical shape to form a hammer head. Although they've been largely replaced by rubber mallets, rawhide models are still available and work very well.

Wood is another material often used for soft-faced hammers. Wood hammers are made in many forms and are often homemade. They're used extensively by wood carvers, because they're easy

on chisel handles and are very controllable. Cylindrical models, shaped like a rolling pin, are especially liked by woodcarvers. The handle and head are turned in one piece. These hammers are made from maple, oak, and sometimes lignum vitae.

Other types of soft-faced hammers common in industry are those made of lead, Babbitt, brass and bronze. These are all mallet-style hammers, and generally, but not always, have wood handles. Babbitt and bronze hammers often have metal handles. These types of hammers are used anywhere a drive fit in metal is necessary, and the work must not be harmed.

Of all the soft-faced hammers on the market, the Compo-Cast Dead Blow Hammer is highly recommended. This unique, patented hammer is made from polyurethane. Compo-Cast's polyurethane is a souped-up formula they call Compoethylene. Handle and head are molded in one piece. However, inside the head there is a metal canister and inside the handle is a steel core. The canister is filled with chilled magnum shot. This gives the hammer what is known as a "dead-blow" effect.

One of the biggest problems with using a soft-faced hammer is that the hammer tends to bounce back with the same force with which it was struck.

This means that if you hit something hard enough, its possible for the hammer to bounce back and hit you in the forehead! With the Compo-Cast hammer there is no rebound, because the chilled shot rebounds inside the hammer and absorbs the recoil. Also, the plastic material of the hammer is almost indestructible, and you can strike sharp objects with little or no effect on the plastic.

It's an excellent product that virtually replaces all other types of soft-faced hammers. You can use it for everything from assembling furniture to tasks that would otherwise require a hammer with a head made from Babbitt. The hammer comes in sizes from 14 ounces to 4 pounds, although the No. 1 model, weighing 1½ pounds, is good for general use. Approx. Price: $12.00

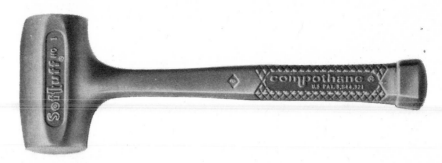

Compo-Cast's Dead Blow Hammer No. 1

Warrington Hammers

For those deeply interested in cabinet making and other fine woodworking, the Warrington hammer is a happy alternative to the claw hammer. The cabinet maker doesn't need the claw because he wouldn't use it to pull a nail anyway — it would mar the work surface. And the claw also gets in the way when working in confined areas.

Warrington hammers generally have a convex face and an extended bell and neck. In place of the claw there's a flat bill called a "cross peen." This cross peen is great for starting small nails and brads because it can slip between your fingers. Warrington hammers aren't found in general hardware stores, but some mail order tool houses carry them. Weights range from about 6 to 14 ounces. The best for most cabinet work is probably 10 ounces, but don't be afraid to go a couple of ounces in either direction when choosing one. They're available from Woodcraft Supply, Garrett Wade, Woodworker's Supply, and Conover Woodcraft. Approx. Price: (8 oz.) $5.00

Framing Hammers

Here's a tool for picture framing, not house framing. This clever hammer solves the problem of driving small brads or glazing points. The square-shaped head makes it easy to work against the glass, as does the hammer's handle. The head is ½-inch square and 3 inches long, and it has a steel shaft ending in a hardwood handle. Length overall is about 12 inches, and weight is 8 ounces. The hammer is available from Brookstone, stock number 4583. Approx. Price: $8.50

Brookstone's Framing Hammer 4583

Axes And Hatchets

Although the pioneer used an axe for felling trees and cutting firewood, today the chain saw has taken over this function. Modern needs for an axe run more toward brushing out an area so a chain saw can be used, notching a tree for felling, and splitting logs.

Axes come in a variety of traditional patterns, such as Dayton, Michigan and Hudson Bay. Also available are a variety of weights, handle lengths and both single- and double-bit heads. A single-bit axe has a single cutting edge with a square face at the back for light pounding. Double-bit axes have a cutting edge on both sides of the blade. This type of axe is popular with lumbermen, because one edge can be ground to a very thin, sharp edge for fine work, while the other edge can be kept thicker for hogging cuts. While these double-bit axes are handy, they're also dangerous. Axe weights commonly vary from 1½ pounds for a camp axe with a 14-inch handle to 3½ pounds for a Michigan double-bit axe with a 36-inch handle. If you're interested, even heavier models are available.

For average use, a Dayton or Michigan single-bit axe with a 3½-pound head is a good choice. Stay away from the short-handled camp axe. This type of axe brings the blade too close to the body, making it easy to hit your legs if you're not careful. Also, you can do much more work with a long-handled model.

A hatchet is a short-handled axe designed for various trades. Most hatchet heads are different from camp-axe heads in that they have a long, straight edge instead of a curved one. Also, there's usually a notch in the lower edge of the head for pulling nails. One of the best examples of a special purpose hatchet is one designed for roofers. This is often called a "shingle hatchet," and is designed for getting under shingles and removing them for repair.

Splitting Wedges

Using a splitting wedge is the easiest way to split any sizeable piece of firewood. It's nothing more than a large, forged steel wedge that you drive into the wood. Sizes vary from about 8 to 10 inches long and from 1½ to about 2 inches wide. A single wedge is useless, so you have to buy a pair. It's not unusual to drive a single wedge into the wood as far as it will go, without splitting the wood. When this happens, you use a second wedge to both rescue the first and split the wood.

A wedge gets hard use, and the top edge tends to mushroom badly. If the mushrooming is allowed to progress, the tool becomes unsafe. So, you should dress the wedge by filing or grinding away the mushroomed metal after each splitting session. Of course, safety goggles should be worn during any type of wood splitting.

The Chopper I improved splitting axe offers a radically new design in handheld splitting equipment, and is very worthy of consideration for gathering firewood. The key feature that makes this axe so effective is a combination of spring-loaded levers in the axe head. These levers extend through slots in the axe head and rotate on individual shafts. Since the levers are fixed on opposite sides of the blade, they are forced to rotate as the blade enters the log. As they rotate, they transform the downward force of the axe head into a more efficient, outward splitting force. This axe is technically three to four times more effective than any other handheld splitting tool. The friction normally associated with wedges,

The Chopper I Improved Splitting Axe

Vaughan's Mini Bar

mawls and axe blades is eliminated by the splitting force in the outward direction. The maker claims that Chopper I can split most varieties of wood with a single stroke. And it makes hard-to-split woods, like elm and sycamore, easier to deal with, too. This is because the levers prevent the axe from becoming wedged in the work. If a piece doesn't split on the first swing, it's easy to withdraw the axe head and try again. This is a very clever tool and a tribute to American ingenuity. It's available at many local hardware stores. Approx. Price: $33.00

made the original one, which they call the Super Bar. A pry bar has a large hook or claw on one end for pulling large spikes, and a less-curved claw on the other for ripping open packing crates and such. Stanley Tool makes the Wonder Bar, which is identical to Vaughan's Super Bar. Vaughan also makes a miniature Super Bar, called the Mini Bar. It's only 5½ inches long and is great for pulling upholstery tacks and small nails. Approx. Price: (Super Bar) $6.50; (Wonder Bar) $6.00; (Mini Bar) $1.50

Ripping Bars

If you plan any demolition work, like knocking out a wall in your house or pulling down the back shed, you need a ripping bar. This tool is often called a crowbar. It's usually made from ⅜-to ¹¹⁄₁₆-inch forged hex stock and can be from 12 to 36 inches long. One end is usually bent into a claw, while the other end has a slightly offset chisel for prying.

Pry Bars

A small pry bar about 15 inches long and made from flat steel stock is a useful tool for the average homeowner. Vaughan claims to have

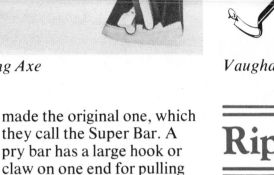

Vaughan's Super Bar

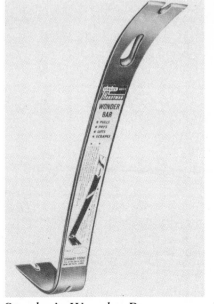

Stanley's Wonder Bar

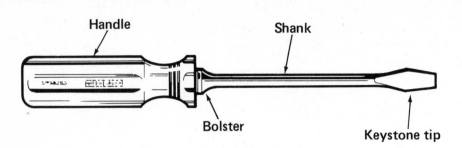

Handle   Shank

Bolster

Keystone tip

Screwdrivers

Screwdrivers come in a wide variety of types and sizes and can be purchased at very low prices. But it's better to stay away from the bargain counter when buying these tools. A little extra money spent on a quality screwdriver will be returned in longer service life and less butchered screw heads. Good quality tool steel and sturdy handles are indications of a quality screwdriver. There are also other aspects to look for, which are discussed in the following information pertaining to specific types of screwdrivers.

Conventional Screwdrivers

The regular, flat-tipped tool everyone has seen is a conventional screwdriver. In this type there is probably more variation in price and quality than any other. One of the easiest ways to spot a quality conventional screw driver is to look at the tip. The tip of a quality tool is cross-ground, rather than ground longitudinally. This helps to prevent the tip from slipping out of a screw slot during use. Low quality screwdrivers are not ground at all, and the corners of the tip are rounded instead of square. High-class tools also have a heavy bolster area just ahead of the handle. And they often feature a flat square or hex built into the bolster so you can apply a wrench for extra torque.

A screwdriver may have a wood or plastic handle. Wood, of course, is the traditional material, and is still used extensively. Many prefer wood for its good looks and nonslip grip. Many fine screwdrivers are made with plastic handles, too. So, the type of handle material doesn't indicate good or bad quality. Plastic is light and durable, and can even withstand light pounding. It's also a good insulator, so you should use a plastic-handled model for any type of electrical work. You should note, though, that the dielectric strength of plastic handles varies greatly. If you work with high voltages, make sure that the tool is designed for high voltage use.

Although plastic-handled screwdrivers can take a beating, you should still resist the temptation to use them for pounding and prying. Use cold chisels and pry bars for these purposes, and save the driver for screw turning. Once the handle is broken, the tool is useless, unless you have a replaceable handle model like that made by Snap-On.

Phillips-Head Screwdrivers

The Phillips-head screw is popular today because it lends itself well to mass

Screw Diameter Inches	18	16	14	12	10	9	8	7	6	5	4	3	2
STANDARD WOOD SCREWS													
Screw Diameter Inches	.294	.268	.242	.216	.190	.177	.164	.151	.138	.125	.112	.099	.086
Pilot Hole Twist Drill Dia. In Inches	5/32	9/64	1/8	7/64	7/64	3/32	3/32	5/64	5/64	5/64	5/64	1/16	3/64
Auger Bit Number	4	3	3										
Body Hole Twist Drill Dia. In Inches	19/64	17/64	1/4	7/32	3/16	3/16	11/64	5/32	9/64	1/8	7/64	7/64	3/32
Auger Bit Number	5	5	4	4	3	3	3	3					
Countersink Auger Bit Number	10	9	8	7	6	6	6	5	5	4	4	4	3

production. This screw has two slots that cross one another, and they take the form of a small, conical cross in the screw head. The corresponding screwdriver for these fasteners has a four-point, 30-degree, cone-shaped tip. Manufacturers like the Phillips-head screw because this cone shape makes the screws self centering, and easy to use with power driven screwdriver bits. If you use a spiral-ratchet screwdriver or an electric drill for installing screws, you can use Phillips screws to advantage, too. Not only is the self-centering feature useful when using these tools, but the screw's design reduces the risk of having the driver tip slip off the screw and mar the wood.

Because of the unique shape of the Phillips-head screw, drivers for these fasteners must be of high quality. Make sure the tip is ground to close tolerances, and that high-quality, heat-treated steel is used in the tool. Low-quality Phillips-head screwdrivers don't fit the screws properly and soon ruin the screw heads.

Other Screwdrivers

Cabinet pattern screwdrivers are one of the hottest-selling items among tool purveyors today, but four or five years ago they were an endangered species, almost forgotten by tool distributors. The woodworking renaissance created a new demand for these tools, whose design dates back to about 1880. Now they are made by three major English companies—Clay, Footprint, and Marples. The American company Greenlee markets the Marple-made tools under its own label.

No matter which company manufactures them, they all look alike, and a standard set contains 3-, 4-, 5-, 6-, and 8-inch screwdrivers. This length refers only to the amount of blade sticking out of the handle, and not the overall length. They all have large, comfortable handles

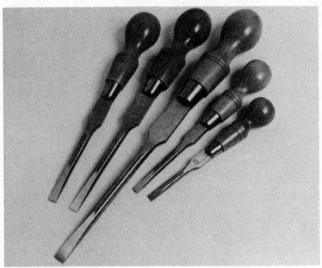

Cabinet Pattern Screwdrivers

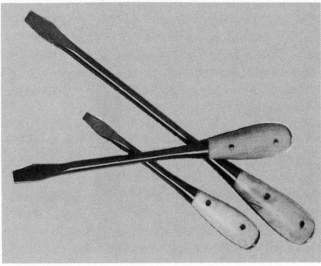

Irwin's Slab Handle Auger Screwdrivers

turned of European beech. And they also have a convenient flat just ahead of the handle that lets you use a wrench to turn stubborn screws. Cabinet pattern screwdrivers also differ from conventional models in that they have a "cabinet," rather than a common "keystone", tip. The cabinet tip is flush from the tip of the screwdriver back, which allows you to turn screws in recessed holes.

These are quality screwdrivers which, of course, are cross-ground. They're generally available from all the major tool houses, such as Woodcraft Supply, Garrett Wade, Woodworker's Supply, Frog, Brookstone, Princeton and Conover. Approx. Price: (5) $18.00

Irwin auger screwdrivers have been around since the late 1800s, and now are very popular items at tool supply houses. They were originally designed for tradesmen and others who put screwdrivers to very hard use. This is why the tool houses market them under names like "Century," "100 Year," and "Lifetime."

They differ from other screwdrivers in that the handle, shaft, and blade are forged in one piece. Two small slabs of wood are riveted into a pocket that is milled out on either side of the metal handle. A large metal striking area is left at the top of the handle. This striking area, plus the one-piece metal construction, allow you to pound the screwdriver without damage. And the wood handle sections give a firm grip, too. The cross-ground tip is of the keystone type, which gives extra strength to the business end of the tool, but doesn't allow you to set a screw in a recessed area.

Although they are available in a wide range of sizes, most major tool houses sell these tools in sets of three, in 5-, 7-, and 10-inch sizes. The measurement indicates only the length of the shaft and blade ahead of the handle. Some better hardware stores and industrial supply houses also carry these tools, but they usually only sell them individually, rather than in sets. Some tool houses that offer these screwdrivers are Woodcraft Supply, Brookstone, Garrett Wade, Frog, Woodworker's Supply, Princeton, and Conover. Approx. Price: (3) $12.00

Stanley's 100 Plus line contains high-quality screwdrivers that are available at local hardware stores. The tough, plastic handles are an amber color, and have deep, black flutes for a good grasp. Blade and tip are made of good-quality steel that has been well heat-treated. The shanks end in an increased bolster area, which

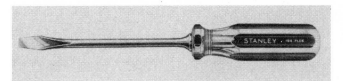
Stanley's 100 Plus Screwdriver

Stanley's Jobmaster Screwdriver

gives the blade extra strength for pounding and prying. And the tips are carefully cross-ground.

The Stanley 100 Plus line gives you a complete selection of standard screwdrivers with keystone tips, as well as a selection of cabinet tips and two varieties of stubby screwdrivers. A stubby is a very short screwdriver, seldom more than 3¾ inches long. It's handy for tight places. The line also includes pocket, instrument, and spark-detecting screwdrivers, in addition to Phillips-head, Pozidriv, clutch head, and Robertson styles.

The company also has a line of cheaper screwdrivers called "Jobmaster." These are a good choice if you don't need, or can't afford, the higher-quality tools. Approx. Price: (100 Plus Standard 6-inch) $4.00

The Snap-On round-shank series screwdrivers, which have stock numbers SSD-1 through 12A are the ultimate in rugged screwdrivers. And if the blade or handle should break, either can be replaced. This does, however, take a Herculean effort and a vise to make the handle and blade separate. The bolster is built up and made in the form of a hex, so a box wrench can be used to help turn stubborn screws. The tip is cross ground, and the entire shaft is chrome plated. This tip is also vapor blasted, which is a chemical etching process that prevents the chrome from peeling from around the tip—a quality touch. As with all Snap-On tools, these

Shop for threading worms and screws. (Detail from 1700s print)

screwdrivers are not available in retail outlets. Approx. Price: (SSD-1) $3.50

The standard ratchet type screwdriver is the predecessor to the spiral ratchet screwdriver. It looks like a standard screwdriver, but has a ratcheting mechanism in the handle. By slipping a little catch at the base of the handle, the mechanism can be made to ratchet in either direction or lock entirely. When locked, you use this tool like a conventional screwdriver. It's handy for working in tight places and can be used with one hand because you never have to release your grip on the handle. Although you can still find this type of screwdriver in hardware stores, it's becoming scarce. Its scarcity is due to the popularity of variable-speed drills, electric screw guns and spiral ratchets.

The Brookstone Company still markets a line of quality ratcheting screwdrivers. The blades and shaft are of high-carbon steel, heat-treated to exacting industrial standards. They're available in pairs of two sizes. The larger pair has a standard screwdriver for screw sizes 5 through 9, while the second driver is for No. 2 Phillips. This pair is available under stock number 5253. The smaller pair has one standard driver for screw sizes 2 through 4, and another driver for No. 1 Phillips. This pair is sold under Brookstone's stock number 5224. Approx. Price: (5253) $12.00; (5224) $6.00

A spiral ratchet screwdriver has a plunger with a spiral cut into it. By pushing downward on the handle of the tool the blade turns clockwise or counter clockwise, depending upon how the ratchet is set. Most ratcheting mechanisms are

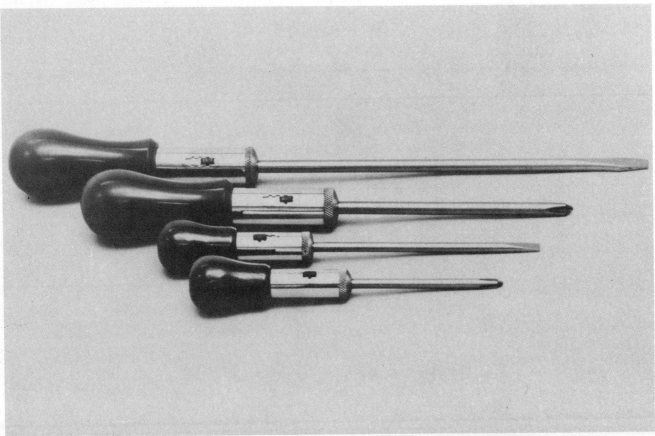

Brookstone's 5253 (top pair) and 5224 (bottom pair) Ratcheting Screwdrivers

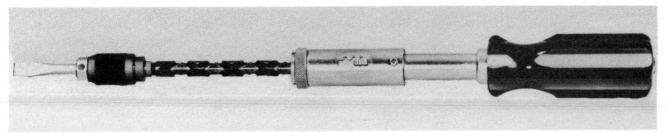

Brookstone's 4686 Spiral Ratchet Screwdriver

set via a small sliding button. There are two general types of ratchet screwdrivers—quick return and manual return. The plunger of quick-return models returns to the normal position when pressure is released from the handle. It takes two hands to run the manual return types because you have to pull the shaft from the handle manually. The quick-return type is better for home use, while manual-return models are popular on assembly lines. You can use one ratchet screwdriver for a wide variety of screw types, because an assortment of interchangeable tips is available for each tool.

Stanley Tools makes an extensive line of spiral ratchet screwdrivers under the old Yankee trade name. For general use, the 130A all-purpose quick return

screwdriver is recommended—although you should look at the entire line to see if there's another model more suited to your needs. This particular model has an overall length, with the plunger extended, of 20¼ inches. It comes with two screwdriver bits—a ⁷/₃₂ -inch-wide standard tip and a No. 2 Phillips bit. Stanley put a great deal of research into this tool's handle, and it has paid off with a very comfortable grip. Approx. Price: $23.00

The Brookstone 4686 spiral ratchet screwdriver is manufactured in Great Britain. It has a very compact, chrome-plated steel body, and is only 11¾ inches long with the plunger extended. And its high-impact plastic handle is fluted for a good grip. This tool comes with a good

selection of bits. You get two sizes of slotted screw bits and two Phillips-head bits as well as a ⅛-inch diameter fluted drill for drilling small pilot holes. Approx. Price: $12.00

When access to a screw is too limited even for a stubby screwdriver, the offset screwdriver is called upon. Available in both standard tip and Phillips, an offset screwdriver has a blade on both ends. These ends are offset 90 degrees to the shank. Also, the blades are set at 90 degrees to one another. This allows a screw to be turned in quarter-turn increments by using the two ends of the driver alternately. Used this way, the going is slow, but it's often the only way to get a job done. Stanley makes a line of offset screwdrivers, which are available in hardware stores. Approx. Price: (669) $2.50

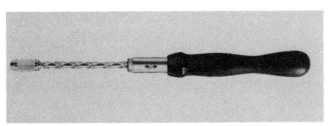

Stanley's 130A Spiral Ratchet Screwdriver

Stanley's 669 Offset Screwdriver

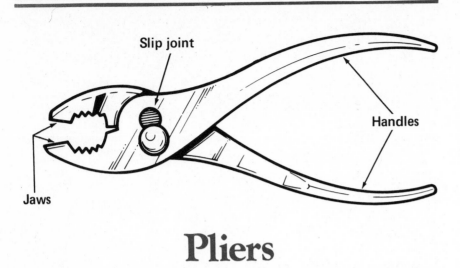

Slip joint

Handles

Jaws

Pliers

Almost every trade has developed one or more specialized types of pliers. For example, there are lineman's or electrician's pliers, fence pliers for installing wire fences, water pump pliers, gas pipe pliers and a multitude of jeweler's pliers. Since the function of pliers is fairly self-explanatory, this section will concentrate on a few specialized types and on what makes a quality plier.

Pliers are called upon to perform a host of really tough tasks like wire and nail cutting, bending, crimping, nail pulling, and light nut and bolt turning. Because of this, it pays to choose a quality tool. The rugged work causes poor materials and shoddy workmanship to show up quickly. There are a lot of foreign-made pliers on the market whose quality ranges from excellent to deplorable. Quality pliers have strong joints. The best have boxed joints — one arm of the plier fits through a slot cut in the other arm and is pinned in place. Also, look for high-grade steel and careful heat treating. Most cutting-type pliers today have an induction-hardened edge. Induction hardening entails heating the metal by electronic means. It's a highly-controlled process that ensures very uniform treating.

Cutting Pliers

Cutting pliers range from miniature tools for cutting jewelry wire to gigantic bolt cutters for cutting reinforcing bars used in road construction. You should always be careful not to "overwork" cutting pliers. They're designed for cutting copper and brass wire and mild steels, such as found in nails. Never use them to cut piano wire. For cutting piano wire and other hardened materials, you need special, expensive music wire pliers. Cutting piano wire with normal pliers results in a half-moon shaped nick in the jaws. Also, cutting oversize work and putting high stress on the pliers will spring the joints. The pliers will be ruined because the jaws will never again mate perfectly.

Diagonal cutting pliers, sometimes called side cutters, are the most common type of cutting pliers. They're useful for all sorts of cutting tasks, such as trimming electrical wire to length and shortening small nails. You can also use them for pulling nails. This is done with the help of a small block of wood next to the nail. You grasp the nail with the pliers, and rest the tool on the block of wood, which acts as a fulcrum.

Multipurpose pliers often have a U-shaped notch on each jaw in the joint area. This forms two "gates," which are used for cutting wire, nails, and small, mild-steel rods. The object to be cut is placed between the gates. Squeezing the plier's handles causes the gates to move toward one another and shear the object in two.

Another type of cutting plier is the bolt cutter, which is designed for cutting mild-steel bolts and large-diameter, mild-steel rods. They're used extensively by cement contractors for cutting cement reinforcing bars, and are a favorite tool of thieves and burglars.

Vise Grips

Vise Grips are patented tools that have a cam-type lock built into the handle. You adjust Vise Grips to the desired size, and then lock them with a squeeze of the handle. Squeezing another small lever inside the handle releases them. They're excellent for light nut and bolt twisting, but they do tend to mar the fastener badly. Another use is to hold two objects together during soldering or welding. In fact, there's a whole series of special Vise Grip clamps for this purpose. These are a spin off of Vise Grip pliers, and have clamp-type jaws. Peterson Mfg. has recently come out with a new pair of pliers, Model 10WR, which is automatically adjustable. This tool does not tend to work nearly as well as the original Vise Grips. Turning the knurled screw is worth the extra effort. Approx. Price: $6.00

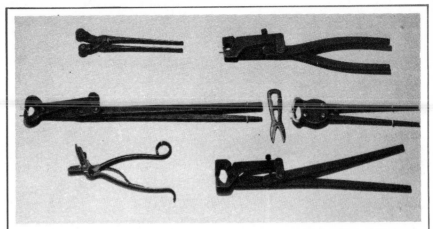

Tool manufacturers and users are traditionalists, as the picture here indicates. All of these tools are handmade, date from the late 1800s, and with the exception of the Bicycle Wrench in the center, are still manufactured and sold as either farrier's (horseshoer's) tools or for the normal hardware trade. Starting from the upper left hand corner and moving clockwise there is a Clinch Tong (to bend over nails after they are driven into a horse's hooves), Compound Nipper (for cutting off nails and wire), another Clinch Tong, a Compound Hoof Shear (used to trim hooves), a Compound Hoof Parer, and another Hoof Shear. Any of these patterns can still be found on the market as active items.

Other Pliers

The tongue-and-groove plier is often called a "channel lock" because Channellock was the first company to manufacture it. This tool has parallel jaws and a high mechanical advantage. The joint slides and locks at various points by a series of tongues and grooves. Channellock pliers are excellent for all sorts of holding and light nut and bolt work. Plumbers also find them useful for turning drain nuts and the like. Approx. Price: $5.00-$11.00

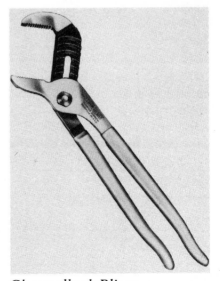

Channellock Pliers

Water pump pliers are very similar to channel locks, and derive their name from the early automotive era. Early autos had water pumps that needed to be packed regularly with water pump grease. This grease acted as a sealant. Modern rubber "O" rings and high-quality rubber gaskets make this unnecessary. Water pumps are usually located on the front of an engine, just behind the fan. Because of this location, removing one is a ticklish task. Water pump pliers answer the need. They consist of a parallel set of jaws with a high mechanical advantage and a slip joint. The joint locks via a series of holes and a stem, which has two flat spots in it. By aligning the two flat spots with the elongated joint, one arm of the pliers can be adjusted to any desired hole.

jaws. The jaws can be used for all kinds of crimping and twisting tasks. They are very good for pulling nails. Many electrician's pliers also have a set of gates in the joint for cutting heavier material.

Although they're not really pliers, a pair of surgeon's hemostats are an excellent shop item. Their original purpose is to seal blood vessels and arteries during surgery. The serrations on their thin jaws interlock, and a series of catches on their handles cause the jaws to clamp shut. During surgery, they're simply clamped over a blood vessel and the catches hold them in place. Despite their rather gory background, they have great usefulness. They can be bought in many shapes and sizes and with jaws offset.

Another plier-type item that can find a niche in the

shop are watchmaker's tweezers. The very best are made by A. Dumont & Sons, in Switzerland. The metal alloy this company uses and the heat-treating process is a family secret. Watchmakers swear by them and buy little else. The Brookstone Company sells a fine line of watchmaker's tweezers which are made in Switzerland, but not by Dumont. You can choose from a wide variety of models made of either spring steel or anti-magnetic stainless steel. The latter are useful in certain kinds of electrical work, but they do not hold up as well as spring steel. Anti-magnetic tweezers are also more expensive, and are probably not worth the extra money unless the work you are doing demands their use. Approx. Price: (Brookstone) $9.50-$12.00

There are many other types of pliers, among which is the needle-nose type. This kind is necessary for electronic and jewelry work. They're also handy for automotive work, and can be used to hold a nut while it's started in a hard-to-reach spot. Needle-nose pliers come in a variety of lengths, and sometimes have jaws bent at a 45- or 90-degree angle for working in limited-access areas.

Electrician's pliers are a valuable household tool. They consist of a large, heavy pair of side cutters, in combination with broad, flat

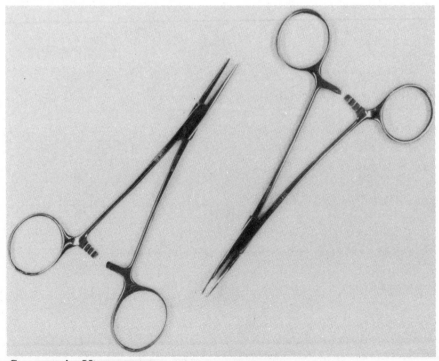

Surgeon's Hemostats

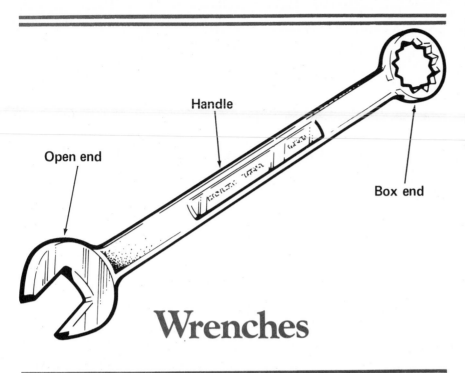

Handle

Open end

Box end

Wrenches

If you're even slightly do-it-yourself oriented, you'll need a wrench at some time. Your needs may range from a simple, adjustable wrench to a comprehensive inventory of box, socket and special-purpose wrenches. An extensive collection of wrenches is only needed by persons who get involved in a lot of automotive work, however. Since this book is for the woodworker, this section covers only the basics of nut-turning tools. This will give you the basic knowledge you need for tackling household and appliance repairs and light automotive work like changing spark plugs and eliminating rattles.

Nut and bolt work has its own specialized vocabulary. The screwing of a bolt into a threaded hole or a nut onto a bolt or stud is divided into three distinct phases— starting, running, and setting or torquing. The removal of a fastener has two phases—breaking and running. Starting is nothing more than finger twisting the fastener down a couple of threads. Then you run the fastener farther down the threads until it contacts the surface of the work. If the hardware is new and clean, this can be done with your fingers. When dirt or corrosion is present, a wrench is needed for this second phase. Setting is always done with a wrench. In this last phase, you put enough torque on the fastener to ensure that it will stay in place. If the torque pressure is critical, such as when tightening engine head bolts or preloading bearings, a torque wrench is used. A torque wrench gives you a direct reading in either inch-pounds or foot-pounds. When using a torque wrench, you have to make sure that the fastener actually turns. If it doesn't, a torque value higher than that desired has already been set up on the fastener. As you gain experience in nut and bolt twisting, you'll acquire a knack for applying the right amount of torque without a torque wrench. Many old-time mechanics laugh at the idea of using a torque wrench for anything but critical operations like bearing and engine-head work.

When removing a fastener, the running stage is the same as just described. And, of course, the breaking stage requires a wrench. You should always make sure there's a clear path for your hands when breaking a fastener, because you could get hurt if the wrench slips or the fastener starts to turn suddenly.

Removing a fastener that has been in place for a long time, or which is badly corroded, often presents a problem. If the fastener doesn't break loose with a reasonable amount of torque applied, it can crack or be damaged by further twisting. You're not faced with much of a problem if you're working with a simple nut and bolt combination. You just replace the fastener. If the fastener is a bolt in a blind, tapped hole, the situation gets a bit more sticky. You are faced with having to remove the broken bolt end from the hole. A device called a "screw extractor" can sometimes do the job, but often the hole must be drilled out and retapped. The trick is to get a feeling for what a bolt's terminal torque is. This knack of knowing just how much you can twist a bolt before it cracks is something only learned through experience and some cracked fasteners.

There are some aids to help you remove frozen fasteners. The most popular is penetrating oil—a special preparation available in hardware and automotive stores. As the name implies, it penetrates into the threads of a fastener and loosens rust and corrosion. The longer the soaking time, the better your chances of removing the fastener easily. Soaking times vary considerably with the situation. A frozen nut may require only 10 minutes soaking time, while a bolt in a deep hole may need more than a day. If penetrating oil doesn't do the trick, you can try applying heat with a propane torch, or preferably a map gas torch. When loosening a fastener this way, it's better to heat one side of the nut, rather than the entire

nut. The heating causes the nut to expand and contract quickly, breaking the corrosive bond. Simply apply heat to one flat of the nut, and get it as hot as you can. If the fastener is very badly rusted, look for a friend who owns a welding torch and knows how to use it safely. Have him heat the fastener to a cherry red color. This often works when a map gas or propane torch doesn't.

Adjustable Wrenches

An adjustable wrench is probably the first wrench you should own. If you use a wrench very seldom, it could get you through a lifetime. Adjustable wrenches have one jaw, which can be moved by turning a knurled worm gear. This type of wrench is often called a "crescent" wrench, because the Crescent Tool Company was one of its first developers. It's handy for light repair work and adjusting

machinery. The tool's main disadvantages are that it can't apply high torque without damaging the fastener slightly, and it can't get into tight places. An adjustable wrench only grips the fastener on two opposing flats, and its adjustable nature prevents the precise fit of a fixed wrench. When you apply force to a fastener, the adjustable wrench tends to round the corners. And in extreme cases, it may slip right off the fastener—ruining the fastener's head.

Adjustable wrenches are all look-alikes, regardless of brand. Common sizes are 4, 6, 8, 10, and 12 inches overall. The baby 4-inch size can handle fasteners up to ½ inch, while the whopping 12-inch one can handle fasteners up to 1⁵⁄₁₆ inches. A joy to behold, the 4-incher is great for a bicycle repair kit and dandy for keeping on your keychain. The 10- and 12-inch sizes qualify as weapons. Most manufacturers offer adjustable wrenches in either black or chrome finish. The black finish is less expensive and popular with industrial

Sears' 44603 Adjustable Wrench

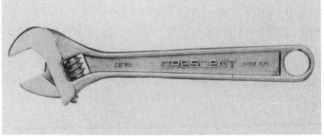

Crescent's 4-inch Adjustable Wrench

users. Tradespeople and homeowners generally choose the more corrosion-resistant chrome finish. All local hardware and automotive stores carry adjustable wrenches. The original Crescent, as well as Proto and S-K, are all good brands of adjustable wrenches. They are also sold extensively under private label by all the major merchandising chains, such as Sears, Montgomery Ward, and J.C. Penney. Approx. Price: (Crescent 8-inch) $5.00

Socket Wrenches

Socket wrenches have a more universal application than any other type of fixed wrench. Compared to other types of fixed wrenches, they are relatively economical. And, especially in the six-point variety, they do the least damage to the fastener. These are all good reasons for ownership.

A socket wrench merely consists of a cylindrical piece of steel with a socket forged into one end to accept a certain sized fastener. The other end has a ¼-, ⅜-, or ½-inch square forged into it. Both 6- and 12-point sockets are commonly available. The "points" are the protrusions that line the inside of the

Snap-On Tool Company caters to the professional mechanic; they manufacture wrenches, socket sets, and other tools that have earned a reputation for high quality. Unfortunately their marketing system does not use normal distribution channels. Instead, their tools are marketed through independent peddlers who purchase a van and fit out the inside with a display of Snap-On tools. Then, like old fashioned milkmen, they call on automotive shops and gas stations in their territory on a regular basis. This allows the mechanic to buy right on the job and, since Snap-On dealers offer financing, it is convenient for both the seller and the purchaser.

If you are not a professional mechanic, however, it may be somewhat difficult to find a Snap-On dealer. The easiest way is to go to a gas station and ask a mechanic who the local dealer is and give him a call. Another method is to use the phone book and find out where the distribution point for your area is; they will be able to tell you who the local dealer is. Once you have discovered who the wagon peddler is, it is only a matter of contacting him and discovering where the two of you can meet. Sometimes it is possible for you to go to his home. Do not be surprised if he will not come to yours; since he works on a volume basis, he will lose money if he only sells you a socket set or extension. His bread and butter is the professional mechanic who spends upwards of $1000 on tools. Servicing a small account would be done only for your good will—but Snap-On does make one of the best lines of tools in America.

socket and grip the fastener. These two common types of sockets are designed for hex fasteners, but special 8-point sockets are marketed for use with square nuts and bolts—particularly useful for farm machinery and tightening carriage bolts. For hex nuts and bolts, most professional mechanics prefer 6-point sockets because they let you apply higher torque and damage the fastener less. Inexplicably, 12-point sockets are now very popular and 6-point types are hard to find. The popularity of 12-point sockets has brought down

their price, because they are now produced in high volume. For household use, 12-point sockets are fine. If you plan a lot of nut twisting, especially at high torque, opt for the 6-point type.

Sockets are commonly available in ¼-, ⅜-, and ½-inch "drive." This refers to the size of the square that's forged into the back of the socket, and which lets you mount the socket on various types of driving implements. A ratchet handle is the most common driving implement. It allows you to apply torque in one direction and ratchet in the opposite direction. The ratchet mechanism is, of course, reversible. A ratchet handle's main advantage is that you needn't remove the socket from the nut to make successive, partial strokes. This speeds up work considerably when clearance for the opposite, swinging end of the wrench is limited.

For very high torque situations, such as the breaking of a frozen nut, a "breaker bar" is valuable. This is nothing more than a sturdy, forged handle with a square pinned in the end. The square can usually be pivoted through 180 degrees. When a great many nuts must be run and mild torque applied, a "speeder" comes in handy. A speeder looks much like a bit brace, but has a square on the end instead of a chuck.

The problem of turning a nut in a recessed area is solved by extensions. An extension is merely a round bar, fitted between the socket and driver. Although they're available from 2 to 36 inches, a 3- and 6-inch model can take care of average tasks for most people. The "universal joint" solves another problem—that of turning a nut that's around a corner. U-joints let you bend the direction of force by up to 45 degrees. They are inserted between the socket and driver or extension.

Of the three drive sizes, ⅜-inch is the most popular and most usable. And, it's probably the best choice for the average homeowner. If you plan a lot of work on washers, dryers, and other appliances, a ¼-inch set is

very handy. For trucks, farm machinery and other robust work, the ½-inch drive is a necessity. Professional mechanics usually have all three sizes.

Sockets with ¼-inch drive are readily available from ³⁄₁₆- to ½-inch sizes in ¹⁄₃₂-inch gradations. Those with ⅜-inch drive range from ¼ to 1 inch, in ¹⁄₃₂-inch increments. The ½-inch drive sockets range from ⅜- to 1½-inches. The smaller ½-inch drive sizes come in gradations of ¹⁄₃₂-inch, while larger sizes are only available in ¹⁄₁₆-inch gradations.

Socket Sets

Many socket sets are available, and they can save you a considerable sum over buying each item *á la carte*. The sets vary widely in size as well as price. Simple sets give you a half dozen sockets, a ratchet, and an extension or two. More comprehensive sets add more sockets, a breaker bar, a universal joint, and more extensions. Plus, they often contain a speeder, deep-wall sockets and a spark plug socket. Deep wall sockets are used when normal sockets can't reach a nut because of a long stud. In the extensive selecton of socket sets, there's sure to be

one to fit your needs and your budget.

The Craftsman 21-piece set standard size (33227), from Sears, Roebuck and Co., is a ⅜-inch drive socket set that is adequate for most people's needs. The set includes seven 6-point deep sockets, seven 12-point regular sockets, a spark plug socket, reversible ratchet, universal joint, and three extension bars. All are contained in a Permanex plastic case, and the set is available in both English and metric sizes. Craftsman wrenches are an attractive buy, because if any part of the set should ever break, it will be replaced by Sears with no questions asked. Also, if you wish to add sockets to the set, they can be purchased from Sears. Approx. Price: $35.00

The Snap-On 222-FSP set is ⅜-inch drive and includes 22 pieces. You get a nut speeder standard handle ratchet, 11 6-point standard sockets, a universal joint, and a 1½-inch extension bar. If your work is of a professional nature, or if you just want to own the finest tools available, this is a set to consider. Snap-On Tools takes great care in the manufacture and heat-treating of its sockets, which results in a socket with a thinner wall that fits in tighter places. The sockets also have a patented flank drive, which is less damaging

A "wobble-drive" extension is a handy little tool that is not usually available because it is only sold by the Snap-On tool company through their distribution network. Like many great tool ideas the principle of these extensions is amazingly simple. The squared end of the extension is ground to a diamond shape. This allows the extension to "wobble" about 15 degrees in any direction. This play greatly eases running or setting nuts in many situations, especially where access is somewhat limited. This wobble extension often eliminates the need for a universal joint. Many professional mechanics put a 3-inch wobble extension on the ratchet and leave it there. It is inexpensive and once you have one you'll wonder how you got along without it.

to the fastener. This set is available in English and metric, and the metric sockets have a black ring around them for easy identification. Since Snap-On tools aren't available through normal distribution channels, consult page 263 to find out how you can buy them. Approx. Price: $107.50

Other Wrenches

When you can only gain access to a fastener from the side, an open-end wrench, with its C-shaped opening, is what you need. This opening grips the opposing flats of a hex or square nut. A box wrench is called a "ring wrench" in German, and this is a fitting name. It's a handle with a ring forged on the end. The ring has 12 serrations, or points, which grip the corners of a hex nut. Open-end and box wrenches usually have a different size wrench head on either side of the handle. This way, a set of six wrenches can cover a comprehensive range of sizes. A combination wrench has an open-end wrench on one end and a box wrench of the same size on the other. The combination wrench is handier, but it takes a set of 12 wrenches to cover the same range of sizes that a six-piece box or open-end set covers. That professionals prefer the combination wrench is reflected by the fact that Snap-On Tools, which caters to the professional market,

S-K's 4520 ⅜-inch drive socket set is available at local hardware stores. It gives you 20 pieces which includes four 6-point standard sockets, five 12-point standard sockets, eight 6-point deep sockets, 1½-inch extension, 3-inch extension, and ratchet. The entire outfit comes packaged in a metal box. This is a quality set, and sockets and accessories are available individually when you wish to add to it. Approx. Price: $39.00

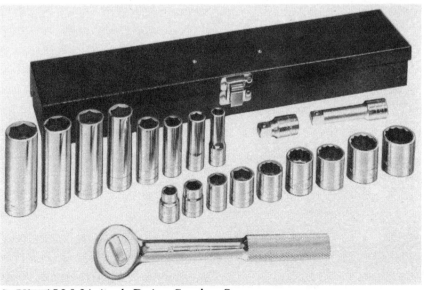

S-K's 4520 ⅜-inch Drive Socket Set

does not offer either box or open-end wrenches. The company only sells combination wrenches. For the average user, however, it's best to buy a set of both open-end and box wrenches, and shun the combination wrench. The single-design wrenches are offered by Sears, Montgomery Ward, and other merchandising chains at reasonable prices. You can often purchase a set of both box and open-end tools for less than an equivalent range of sizes in combination wrenches. Besides, this gives you two wrenches of the same size, which comes in handy when a nut and bolt must be held from both sides.

The Craftsman 6-piece box wrench set (4461), from Sears, is an excellent starter package. It includes all the common sizes, from ⅜ to 1 inch, that the homeowner or amateur mechanic is likely to need. You should note that although you get 12 wrench

heads, you get only 11 sizes. This is because the ⁹⁄₁₆-inch wrench head appears on two wrenches. As with all Sears tools, you get an iron-clad guaranty. Each wrench has a bead-blasted finish, polished highlights, and chrome plating. Metric sizes are available. Approx. Price: $18.50

S-K's 360 long pattern 12-point box wrench set offers 11 sizes from ⅜ to 1 inch, with the ⁹⁄₁₆-inch size opening repeated on two separate wrenches. S-K may not be as competitive as Sears, but then you can find a complete range of S-K wrenches at nearby hardware and automotive stores, which may be more convenient for you. Approx. Price: $27.00

Craftsman's 6-piece open-end wrench set (4451), sold by Sears, Roebuck and Co., covers the sizes from ⅜ to 1 inch. The ¾-inch opening is found on two separate wrenches, giving you 11 sizes. These quality wrenches have a chrome-plated, bead-blasted finish with polished highlights. Metric sizes are also available. Approx. Price: $16.50

The S-K 550 5-piece open-end wrench set is sold at local hardware and

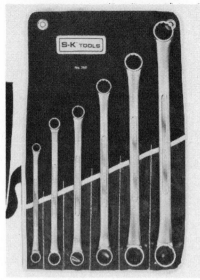
S-K's 360

automotive stores all over the country. It offers opening sizes from ¼ to ¾ inch, with the ⁹⁄₁₆-inch opening repeated on separate wrenches. As all S-K hand tools, these are nicely finished and offer a high degree of durability. Approx. Price: $16.00

The Craftsman 10-piece combination wrench set (4496), from Sears, Roebuck and Co., is one of the better values in combination wrench sets. This fine-quality

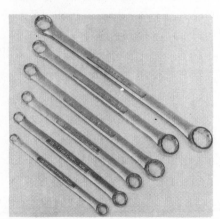
Craftsman's 4461

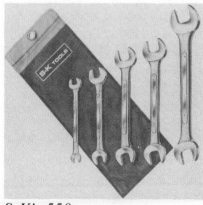
S-K's 550

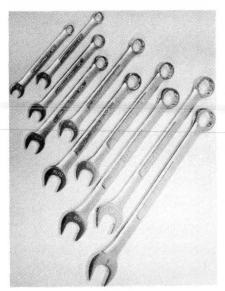

Craftsman's 4496

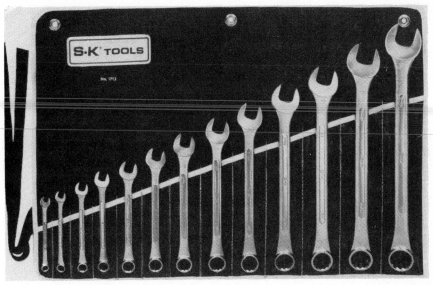

S-K's 1713 Combination Wrench Set

set includes open-end and box openings in sizes from ⅜ to 1 inch. As all combination wrench sets, this one offers you a lot of convenience. For instance, you can lay the wrenches out in the toolbox in the order of their sizes—making it quicker to pick out a particular size. But you should be aware that for four dollars more than the cost of this set, you can buy two individual 6-piece open-end and box wrench sets from Sears. This combination wrench set exhibits Craftsman's usual fine tool quality and is available in metric. The wrenches have a chrome-plated finish with polished highlights. Approx. Price: $31.00

S-K Tools' 1713 13-piece combination wrench set is quite a comprehensive tool set. It includes sizes from ¼ to 1 inch, and can take care of

most people's box and open-end wrench needs. You will, however, need additional wrenches or an adjustable wrench if you encounter a nut and bolt combination that needs to be held at both ends. Approx. Price: $53.00

The Snap-On 15-piece combination wrench set OEXS-715-K is for the person looking for top quality. It offers a wide range of opening sizes from ¼ to 1 inch. If you work in limited access areas, these Snap-On wrenches offer some advantage over Sears and hardware store wrenches. The web areas around both the box and open end of the wrench are much thinner than garden variety wrenches. Because of this thinner web area, you can turn bolts in areas where other, less expensive, wrenches can't fit. Snap-On

wrenches are also brightly polished and chrome-plated over their entire surface. Lower-cost wrenches have only polished highlights. The set is available in metric sizes, as well as many style and size options. This set is the short standard length, but the same wrenches are also available in the long handle style. If your work is very demanding, this is the set to consider. Refer to page 263 for details on buying. Approx. Price: $117.50

Ratcheting box wrenches are somewhat of a cross between a regular box wrench and a socket-and-ratchet combination. They consist of a handle made up of two flat, stamped pieces of steel with a 6- or 12-point wrench head at either end. These wrench openings are built in the shape of a wheel. The wheel and a ratcheting mechanism

267

are held between the two metal stampings. As with all double-ended box wrenches, each wrench covers two sizes. The ratcheting mechanism of this type of wrench doesn't reverse. Instead, you merely turn the wrench over to twist nuts in the opposite direction. Most designs have one side marked "on" and the other side marked "off" so you can easily tell which way force can be applied.

Principally, this wrench is used where a ratchet-socket combination won't fit, but where you want more speed than is offered by a simple box wrench. The only disadvantage is that the web area around the wrench is fairly substantial, so it can't fit in some areas where a regular box wrench can.

Good-quality ratcheting box wrenches are expensive. There are some very inexpensive models on the market, but these usually have leaf-spring ratcheting mechanisms which give way with a little use. Make sure the one you buy has a pawl-type ratchet.

The Craftsman 5-piece ratcheting box wrench set (4368), from Sears, Roebuck and Co., gives you good quality at a reasonable price. The wrenches range in size from ¼ to ⅞ inch and they are made of chrome-plated steel with a plastic shroud to seal the ratcheting mechanism, which is very positive, from dirt. They also come in metric sizes. Approx. Price: $18.50

The Snap-On RB-606S-K 6-piece ratcheting box wrench set offers very high quality and sizes from ¼ to $^{15}\!/_{16}$ inch. All wrenches are 6 point except the ⅞- and $^{15}\!/_{16}$-inch sizes, which are 12 point. Snap-On offers ratcheting box wrenches in metric sizes. Approx. Price: $75.00

Nut runners are used extensively in certain service fields, such as appliance repair. Appliances, such as washing machines and dryers, are put together with many self-tapping sheet metal screws. Because these screws require a higher setting torque, they're often made with a hex-head like a bolt, rather than being slotted like a normal screw. There are also a number of special screw heads, such as clutch and pozidrive, being used in the appliance field today. These are improvements on the Phillips head design, made for high-speed, automatic screw setting equipment used in industry.

With nut runners, you can quickly run, set, and break these small, hex-head screws. They are also very useful for other small nuts and bolts often encountered in service-type work. A nut runner is nothing more than a socket wrench with a shaft and screwdriver-type handle. They usually come in sets of five to 10. Their effectiveness stops at screws over ½ inch in head diameter, because you can't apply enough torque with the screwdriver-like handle.

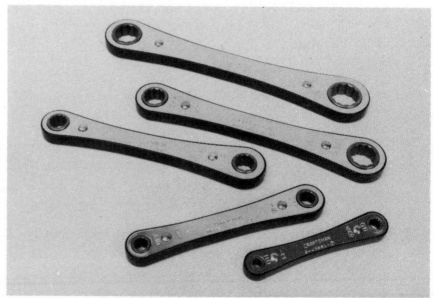

Craftsman's 4368 Ratcheting Box Wrench Set

If you're economy minded, you might prefer to choose one of the good ¼-inch socket sets over a set of nut runners. Many of these sets have a screwdriver-type handle, which can be fitted to any of the sockets in the set. If this handle isn't included with the set, you can buy it as an option. This makes an effective nut runner set, and when extra torque is required, you can use the set's ratchet. The only inconvenience encountered with the socket set is that you must change sockets every time a different size fastener is encountered. In nut runner sets each tool has its own attached handle.

The Craftsman 7-piece nut driver set (4196), from Sears, Roebuck and Co., covers the sizes commonly encountered in household appliance repairs. The tools have

hardened sockets and plastic handles, and metric sizes are available. This is a set of good quality, and the price is reasonable. Approx. Price: $16.50

Snap-On's ND-1070-K set includes seven nut drivers ranging from ¼ to ½ inch. All have 6-point openings. This set is of the highest quality and carries a correspondingly high price tag. Both English and metric sizes are available. If you work with both systems, you will appreciate the fact that metric models have amber handles and English models have black handles. This makes for quick identification at the bench. Approx. Price: $34.50

The Stanley Tools 66-525C Hex-A-Matic nut driver has

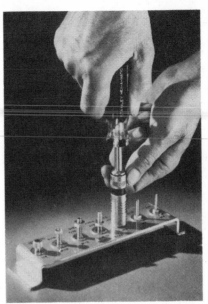
Stanley's 66-525C Nut Driver

a chuck design that fits all hex nuts between ¼ and ⁷⁄₁₆ inch. It also fits all hex-head bolts from No. 6 to ¼ inch. To use this tool, you just place it over the nut head and push down. Pushing down causes the chuck to close around the hex head and lock onto it. Then you just keep a slight pressure on the tool while turning it. The one disadvantage of this tool is that its design sometimes makes access to tight places difficult. This same tool is offered by Sears under the stock number 41991. Approx. Price: (41991) $6.00

Although the average shop owner or homeowner has little use for torque wrenches, you should know something about them. Basically, a torque wrench lets you tighten a fastener to a specific torque. Models are available which read in inch

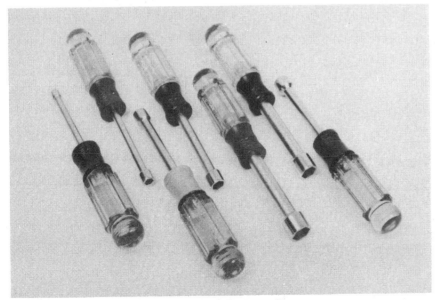
Craftsman's 4196 7-Piece Nut Driver Set

pounds, foot pounds, and meter kilograms. Homeowners and backyard mechanics who wish to purchase a torque wrench will find models that read from 0 to 150 foot pounds most useful. Inch pound wrenches are for torquing small fasteners and are used in industry and aircraft work. Meter kilogram models have doubtful value, since most foreign car service manuals give torque values in both English and metric systems. Besides, there are always conversion charts available to help you through occasional metric situations.

There are several types of torque wrenches, but the most inexpensive is the beam type. This type of torque wrench costs between $15.00 and $20.00, and is accurate enough for most automotive work. The beam-type torque wrench has a relatively thin metal shaft, ending in a handle. When torque is applied to a nut or bolt, the shaft bends a specific amount, depending upon how much pressure you apply. A pointer sticks back from the head of the instrument to a scale attached to the handle. This scale gives a direct reading of the torque applied.

For professions such as aircraft work, however, the beam-type torque wrench is not accurate enough. So, a dial-type or the newer, snap-type torque wrench is used. This is one tool that has come down greatly in price in the past five years. Even Sears is selling wrenches of this type today at fairly

reasonable prices. These wrenches can be made to torque within 3 to 6 percent accuracy, which is necessary for very specialized work. Even so, in work like that involving aircraft, a torque wrench's accuracy must be checked by a certified calibration service at specific intervals. In some trades, this interval can be as short as 90 days.

Staplers

Once the stapler was strictly a professional tool, but it's now becoming as commonplace as the hammer in households. Manual staple guns get their staple-driving power from a large spring that's cocked and released by squeezing a handle. An alternate pattern is the hammer stapler, in which the action of a hammer-type blow provides force for driving the staple. Air powered, automatic staplers are not suitable for home use because they require attachment to an air compressor. They are used almost exclusively in industrial applications. But automatic, electric-powered models are fine for home use. They use the action of an electro-magnet to drive the staple, and are activated by a switch.

Staple guns are used because of their speed and because of the good holding power staples provide. Staples are now commonly used for fastening fragile materials like upholstery and insulation, and have largely replaced the tack for these purposes. Tacks are slow to set, and even though they have enlarged heads, they often pull through the material.

The Bostitch Model T-11 Tackler is much smaller than most tools of this type and drives a smaller staple. It has a lighter tension spring to let you use it longer without tiring, and is adequate for upholstering and craft work. This is a good-looking tool, and it comes with a supply of 600 staples. Approx. Price: $9.50

The Duo-Fast Model CT859A Staple Gun can tackle jobs such as carpet laying, because it can drive a $\frac{9}{16}$-inch-long staple. For average use, however, this tool uses a $\frac{5}{16}$-inch-long staple, and comes with a supply of them. Power is variable on this gun, which is a useful feature. You vary the power by turning a knob located at the top of the gun. This allows you to attach fragile materials without crushing them. Look for this high-quality tool at hardware and discount stores. Approx. Price: $20.00

Bostitch Model T-11 Tackler

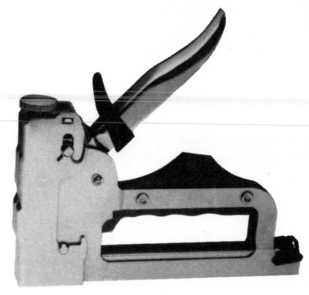

Duo-Fast Model CT859A Staple Gun

The Bostitch Model H2B Hammer Stapler is less tiring to use than a hand-operated staple gun, especially if you intend to install a great deal of insulation. The only drawback to this tool is that it's rather specialized, and can't be used for a variety of purposes. Approx. Price: $31.00

The Duo-Fast HE5018

Electric Staple Gun drives staples from ¼- to ⁵⁄₁₆-inch-long at the touch of a switch. This is a fairly expensive tool, but could pay for itself quickly in some applications. For the professional or semi-professional upholsterer, this tool would be invaluable. It runs on standard 115-volt, 60-cycle AC house current and has a positive safety lock to guard against accidental triggering of the gun. The main body of the tool is green, high-impact plastic, and all metal parts are nickel-chromed steel.

The same tool is also made in a nailer version, and Duo-Fast supplies nails in four different colors to go with the gun. This gun is intended for installing house paneling, but can be used for picture frames and molding installation. It has a limited workscope, and a price tag equal to that of the stapler version. Approx. Price: $70.00

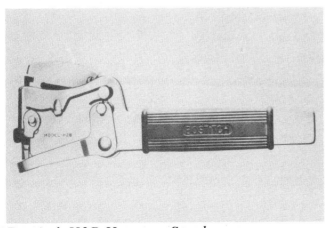

Bostitch H2B Hammer Stapler

Duo-Fast HE5018 Staple Gun

Although more are always needed, we're limited to two hands. Workbenches, vises, and clamps provide those extra hands when you need them.

Gripping Tools

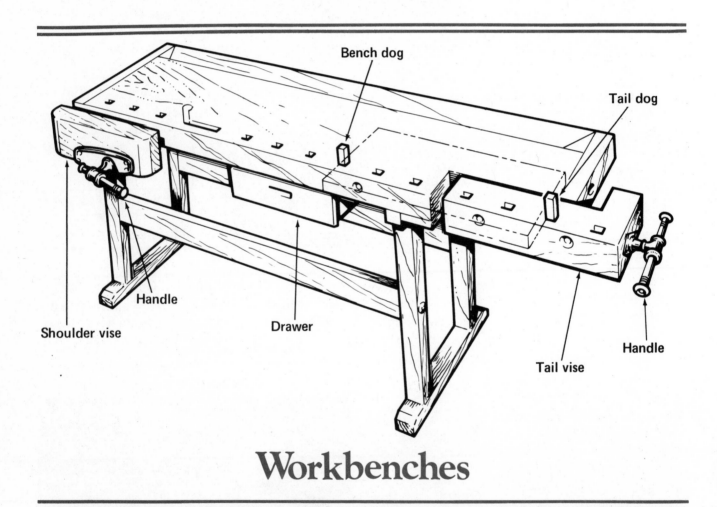

Bench dog

Tail dog

Handle

Shoulder vise

Drawer

Tail vise

Handle

Workbenches

A workbench is an indispensable item in the shop. It provides a sturdy, stable platform, and allows you to work at a convenient height. Most have one or more vises, and storage cupboards or drawers below for tools. To most Americans born in this century, a workbench is a homecrafted item with a top usually fashioned from 2x10s and legs made from 2x4s or 4x4s. And sometimes the top is covered with Masonite. With the increasing cost of lumber, many people are now using prefabricated steel legs for their workbenches.

To a European, or an American working before 1925, a workbench is a different animal. To such a craftsman, a workbench isn't built into a corner of the shop. Rather, the bench is the focal point of the workshop and the shop is built around it. For the purpose of this discussion, this type of bench can be called a "European-style workbench," although benches of this style have been known all over this country, in England and on the Continent since about 1600.

Although most European-style workbenches are made in Europe, at least one reasonably good example, the Garden Way Research bench, is made in this country. The most common construction material for this type of bench is European beech, because the wood is commonly available in Europe. It's the only decent hardwood the Europeans have left. Beech is a good, tough hardwood that makes an excellent choice for workbenches. An American manufacturer would probably use rock hard maple, which is what Garden Way Research uses.

In looking through major mail order company catalogs, you'll find advertising phrases such as "Swiss Cabinetmakers Bench," "Danish Carpenter's Bench," and "Scandinavian Mastercraftsman's Bench." The truth is that whether the bench is made in Sweden, Denmark, Germany, Holland or Switzerland, the style and function are virtually the same. As all benches are based on a basic pattern, which has not changed since the 1600s, the only variables in these benches are size, weight and quality.

A European-style workbench has a fairly narrow working surface, which ranges from about 10 inches on smaller benches to about 12 inches on larger ones. These benches also vary from 55 to 80 inches in overall working length. Most have a tool tray conveniently located somewhere at the rear, or sometimes to one side. The most endearing feature of a European-style bench is its clever system of vises and holds, which allows it to grip virtually any piece of wood. Its standard layout includes one horizontal vise. This vise is the conventional type familiar to American craftsmen, and it takes care of most of the routine woodworking jobs like sawing, planing, and mortise chiseling. When the work needs vertical, rather than horizontal holding, a second vise, called a "shoulder," or "tail" vise is used. Because it's for vertical, rather than horizontal holding, this vise is unencumbered by spindles through the jaw area. The shoulder vise is ideal for sawing tenons, shaping ends, and working with round stock. In conjunction with the shoulder vise, there's a system of dogs, which allows large, bulky items to be held. The front top edge of the bench is pierced by a series of holes. Into these holes, a steel, or sometimes wood or plastic, dog can be inserted. There are also three or four holes in the shoulder vise which accept dogs. A large, flat piece can be gripped between two dogs by placing one in an appropriate hole in the bench and another in the shoulder vise. This type of clamping system is particularly valuable during hand planing.

A quality European-style workbench is indispensable for craftsmen who work exclusively with hand tools, but it's optional for the person who prefers power tools. Although you can place this type of bench against a wall, it's better to place it in an open spot in the middle of the shop. This placement allows large pieces to hang over the bench and greatly aids working. Another point in favor of the European-style workbench is that the dog system can be used as a bar clamp.

European-style workbenches are available in a wide range of sizes, shapes and prices. You can buy one for as little as $250, although current high prices run close to $750 when the freight is added in. These prices are steadily rising, too, because of the dollar's unstable nature.

The professional model benches are the most expensive, and of the highest quality. Of these, the benches built by Lachapelle in Lucerne, Switzerland are probably the best. They are handled by Garrett Wade and run from $625.00 to $795.00, depending upon size and options. Another bench of extremely good quality is the Ulmia, which is manufactured in Germany. This extremely rugged, very heavy industrial-style workbench ranges in price from $380.00 to $550.00. It's sold by Woodcraft Supply and Garrett Wade. Ulmia also makes a bench with a double row of dogs, specially for the Garrett Wade Company. A bench that's about equal to the Ulmia is the Steiner, sold by

Garrett Wade. You can choose from two sizes, which are priced at about $550.00 and $600.00.

Aside from these heavy, industrial benches, which are designed for professional shops and vocational training schools, there are many less expensive models made for the home shop. Here are some of them.

The Garden Way home workbench is manufactured in Vermont, and is sold by Garden Way directly as well as by Sears, Roebuck and Co. It's a good looking bench crafted from hard maple. The vise and dog system, however, is very poorly

done, virtually eliminating this bench from consideration as a craftsman's tool. Approx. Price: $300.00

The Sjöbergs is a very good looking bench, and works flawlessly. Some corners have been cut, however, to save cost. It has plastic, rather than steel, dogs. But they seem to work well. The center of the bench has a plywood section instead of solid beech as in most benches. Also, the undercarriage is made of Swedish pine, and is slightly on the rickety side. Sjöbergs sells their benches with or without storage cupboards. Storage cupboards make sense for some situations, but

Interior view of woodworker's shop showing European-style workbenches. (circa 1760)

Sjöbergs Work Bench With Drawers   *Sjöbergs Work Bench*

their small dimensions limit the number and size of tools that can be stored. You can obtain this bench from the Brookstone Company (#3162). Approx. Price: $295.00

Hobitek's benches are well constructed and reasonably priced. They're not quite as cosmetically appealing as the Sjöbergs, but they do have a no-nonsense approach to quality where it counts. The top of this bench is of solid construction, and the undercarriage is of European beech rather than pine. It has steel dogs and large, smoothly-operating vises. Three models are available, one of which has storage cupboards very similar to those on the Sjöbergs. Hobitek benches are sold by the Princeton Company and Conover Woodcraft. Approx. Prices: $250.00 to $360.00

Vises

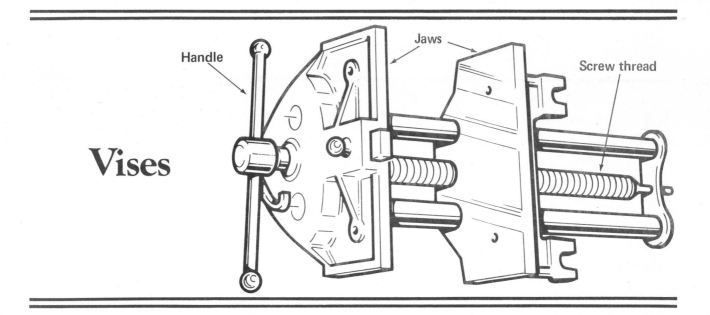

The vise is among the first tools you need to buy when assembling a shop. It's a basic tool for any kind of crafting, and because of this, the marketplace is flooded with them. Vises run the gamut from excellent quality to absolute rubbish. Since a vise is basically nothing more than two iron castings, it's easy to manufacture. For this reason, developing countries like India, Korea and Taiwan have taken up vise making and export a great many to the U.S. Some of these tools are well-made and competitively priced. However, since it would be impossible to cover the entire, vast number of vise brands, this chapter will stick to discussing a few established brands for which spare parts are readily available.

There are woodworking vises, metalworking vises and tools that can be used for both types of work, due to interchangeable jaws. But all vises are essentially two parallel jaws, which close by the action of a screw thread. To get extra leverage on the screw thread, there's usually a long handle located on the front of the tool. Turning the handle actuates the screw thread and closes and opens the jaws.

Metalworking vises have serrated, iron jaws that are usually pinned in place and held fast by a flat-head screw. For finish metalwork, the jaws are often faced with brass. Since these jaws take a beating, replaceable jaws are a good feature on a metalworking vise.

Woodworking vises have large, broad, flat jaws, and there's usually a provision for facing the jaws with wood to protect the work. Two nice features usually found on higher-quality vises are "dogs" and "quick actuation." A dog is a sliding steel pin, at the top of the vise, which can be raised. It has two purposes. You can use it as a stop in operations like hand planing. In this

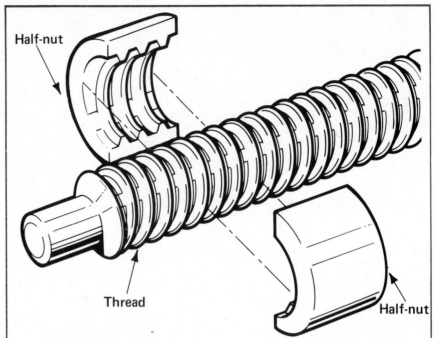

Detailed view of the split nuts used in woodworking and other vises. When a lever is thrown in the front of the vise, the two "half-nuts" move apart. This permits the spindle to slide freely in the vise's body.

case, you place a board against it to keep the work from moving. Also, if the vise is mounted on the end of a bench, the dog can be used in conjunction with a line of holes and another dog to hold long work.

Quick actuation means that you can open and close the jaws quickly without turning the spindle a lot. This is usually done with a "split nut," which is often called a "half-nut." When you throw a lever located at the front of the vise, a nut moves away from the spindle in two halves. With the nut open, you can slide the jaws open or shut without turning the spindle. Interrupted screw threads is another method of quick actuation. These threads are the same as those used in the breech of military

howitzers. They let you open and shut the vise jaws quickly and then tighten them in the usual fashion.

Good vise spindles have special types of threads. The most common thread used in this country today is the American Standard thread, which has flanked angles of 60 degrees. This thread lends itself well to mass production and is commonly used for fasteners. It is not the best for continuous operation, however. Other threads—the Acme, Square Cut, and Buttress—have been developed to give longer service life. The oldest of these threads is the Square Cut, which is very strong and long-wearing. The Acme thread has a profile much like the Square Cut, but is better suited to mass production manufacturing. Acme threads have a flanked angle of 29 degrees. Finally, a Buttress thread is for very high stress in one direction. It's used for some very large, sturdy woodworking vises.

The Ulmia Universal Patternmaker's Vise is excellent for craftsmen and artisans who do precise work on intricate pieces of wood. It's well-made and you can mount it on any bench top. Mounting is done by inserting a threaded spindle on the bottom of the vise through a hole drilled in the bench top. The vise is then locked in place by a large, cast-iron wing nut. The vise can swivel 360 degrees and the wood-faced jaws pivot to hold oddly shaped objects. These jaws open up to 6¼ inches and are faced with red beech. This is an excellent vise for cabinetmakers, woodcarvers, musical

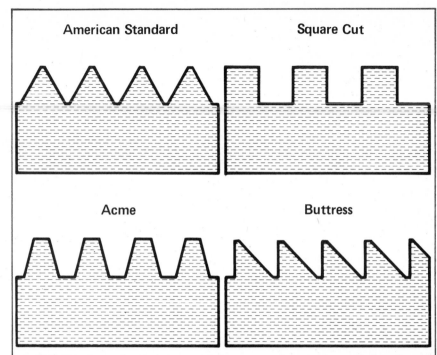

While thread cutting would seem to be a minor point for consideration when buying a vise, it has much to do with the wearing qualities of the tool. In this drawing are the four most common thread styles used in vises.

instrument makers, and, of course, patternmakers. It's available from Garrett Wade Company (#90G02.01) or Woodcraft Supply (#18A01-0). Approx. Price: $174.00

Record-Ridgeway vises are high-quality tools, and the line of these British-made vises includes a size and shape to fit everyone's needs at an affordable price. All have the same design features, regardless of size. Record's vises are quick acting, through split-nut construction. The rugged and long-wearing spindles have Buttress threads. A nice feature is that the jaws have a slight toe-in, to give them a firmer grip at the top of the vise for holding small objects. Some models have bench dogs, and some don't. The choice is yours. There are provisions to face the jaws with wood, which all careful craftsmen want to do. Record vises are available from Woodcraft Supply, Garrett

Ulmia Universal Patternmaker's Vise

Record-Ridgeway's Steel Bench Vises

particular working position with a large, T-handle located at the rear.

Also, the jaws are interchangeable. It comes with two sets of jaws — one smooth set for woodworking, and one hardened, serrated set for working with metal. Further versatility is added by a built-in set of pipe jaws, which are located below the main jaws. These hold round stock from ⅜ to 1⅜ inches in diameter. The price is reasonable, too. Approx. Price: $25.00

Wade and Woodworkers Supply. Approx. Price: (medium vise) $66.00

The Wilton Flip-Grip II vise is a versatile tool that's valuable for the homeowner and do-it-yourselfer. And it incorporates just about all the features you could want. It has a "flipping" feature, from which the vise gets its name. You can swing it down, completely out of the way, or it can be adjusted to hold the work at any desired angle. You lock the vise in a

Clamps

If there were any sure-fire way to tell how long a person has been a woodworker, it would be by how many clamps he owns. The walls of many old-time woodworking shops are literally lined with clamps of all shapes, sizes, and descriptions. Fast-drying, modern glues have reduced the number of clamps necessary in a woodworking shop, but clamps are still very much a part of the business.

Clamps hold two mated parts together while glue dries. You can also use them to secure something temporarily, such as a fixture on a table saw or a wood fence to a board when using a rabbet plane.

Wilton Flip-Grip II Vise

NAME	REMARKS	TYPICAL USES
C-Clamp	cast-iron, "C" shaped body — threaded rod applies tension — sliding rod on spindle allows precise tension	most common of clamps — used for holding small pieces together — temporary fixing of guides to tables
Screw Clamp	two parallel wood jaws — tension applied by two wood spindles with file handles — jack-screw action	basic woodworking clamp — majority of force is in jaw tips — useful for small, odd-shaped pieces
Bar Clamp	long metal rod or pipe on which paddles slide — tension applied by threaded spindle once clamp is fitted on work	used for gluing up boards for table or furniture — long lengths (3-8 feet) allow use on wide surfaces
Web Clamp	simple band or web of nylon with sliding tensioning clamp — will not mar work	useful for four-way tensioning on odd-shaped or four-corner pieces

C~Clamps

The C-clamp is the most common type of clamp. It's a cast-iron "C," one end of which ends in a pad-like anvil. The other end of the C has a threaded spindle running through it. The end of the spindle inside the C has a round pad, which is free to float on a ball and socket joint. You adjust the spindle by either a large, wing-nut style handle or a rod fitted in a hole cross-drilled in the end of the spindle. This latter method of adjustment is better, because you can slide the rod completely to one side to clear an obstruction. Cheaper C-clamps have a spindle with V-threads, while better ones have Acme or Square Cut threads.

Hardware stores carry C-clamps that range in size from tiny to huge. These clamps are extremely handy for holding small pieces together during gluing as well as securing jigs and fixtures to machine tables. When clamping wood for gluing, it's best to protect the wood piece by putting scraps of wood between the jaws of the clamp and the workpiece. This way, you won't mar the finish of the piece you're working on.

Screw Clamps

Screw clamps are probably the most basic woodworking clamp. They consist of two parallel wooden jaws, which are adjusted by two threaded spindles. Most modern screw clamps have metal spindles. But this type of clamp was traditionally a homemade item with threaded, wooden spindles. The spindles are turned by two file-like handles, one on each side of the clamp. These spindles are arranged so you can grasp one in each hand and turn the entire clamp in a cranking motion to open or close it quickly. When it's adjusted to the desired opening, you place the clamp over the work and turn the two spindles simultaneously until the clamp is snug. Then you turn only the rear spindle to put pressure on the work. This way, the rear spindle acts as a jack screw, while the front spindle acts as a fulcrum. The jaws act as two levers, and the majority of the force is concentrated at the jaw tips. An important

Jorgensen Screw Clamps

feature of modern steel spindle clamps is that the nuts are full-floating, and by turning the spindles a different amount, you can make the jaws nonparallel. This greatly helps to hold odd-shaped pieces.

You can often find old-style wooden spindle clamps at antique shops and flea markets. If priced reasonably, they're a good value. Although wooden spindle screw clamps can't be adjusted in a nonparallel fashion to the degree steel spindle models with floating nuts can, they're still very useful. Actually a considerable degree of adjustment is possible with 10- and 12-inch wood-spindle clamps. This is because the wood spindles spring slightly, and the fit of the wood threads is quite sloppy.

The Adjustable Clamp Co. is so well-known for making Jorgensen screw clamps that this type of clamp is often called a Jorgensen.

There are also many other makers of quality screw clamps besides this company, however. This clamp comes in a variety of sizes and is classed by jaw length. For general woodworking, 10- and 12-inch screw clamps are the most useful. Small 3- and 4-inchers are used for small work, while monstrous clamps measuring 16 inches and larger are used for barn building and the like.
Approx. Price: (12-inch) $14.50

Bar Clamps

Bar clamps are used for tensioning larger furniture sections during gluing and for "gluing up stock." This latter procedure is the term for gluing several boards together to make a wider piece of wood, like a tabletop. The boards may be simply planed square and butted together with glue, or tongue-and-groove or spline joints may be incorporated for extra strength. Bar clamps are used to hold the boards together while the glue dries. They consist of an I-beam, which has a threaded spindle attached to one end. This threaded spindle is much like one end of a C-clamp. On the other end of the bar, there's a sliding, paddle-like device, which you can lock at any point on the bar. Bar clamps are available in sizes from 3 to 8 feet, and any well-equipped shop should have at least two. A clamp pad, which is a rubber cushion that fits over the jaws to protect the work, is a useful accessory.

A set of bar clamps can present a considerable investment. An inexpensive solution to the problem is supplied by a very ingenious clamp, which converts any ¾-inch standard black or galvanized water pipe into a bar clamp. The clamp is part of a kit that includes a head and sliding paddle. You fit the parts on a length of pipe to form a bar clamp. Most major mail order tool houses and many hardware stores sell these kits for about $9.50

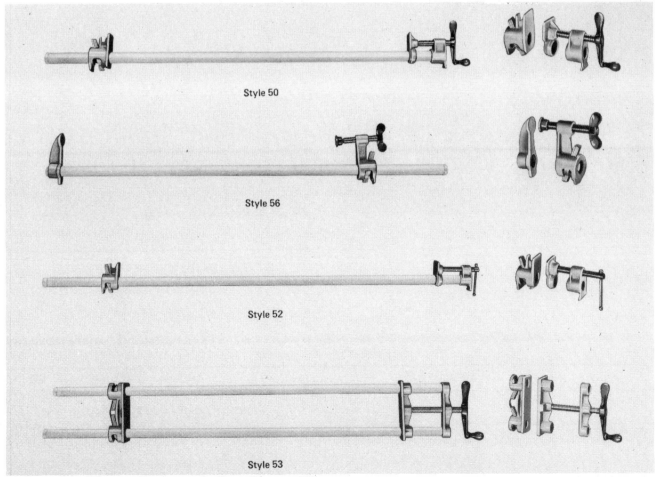

Adjustable Clamp Company's Bar Clamp Kits

Instead of buying a clamp for that once in a lifetime job, it may be better to improvise one. An inexpensive variety of web clamp can be constructed out of a piece of old garden hose and a length of bailing wire. This makes a dandy clamp for fixing that old rickety chair that has finally fallen to pieces. The length of hose is cut to fit around the chair legs and the bailing wire threaded through it. After glue is applied to the rungs and legs of the chair, a stick is used as a toggle to tighten up the wire. If this is a once in a lifetime repair, you'll save yourself some money by not having to buy a web clamp to do the job.

Another very handy, inexpensive clamp can be made from an old inner tube. This is really a very large rubber band (which also makes an excellent improved clamp for modeling and other small work). Smaller bands can be made by cutting through a cross-section of the tube, while very large bands can be made by cutting out a section along the circumference. The strength of this clamp can be adjusted to a certain degree by the width of the strip of rubber. This type of clamp makes a nice fit for round or off-shaped work where a conventional clamp would be difficult to fit on the workpiece.

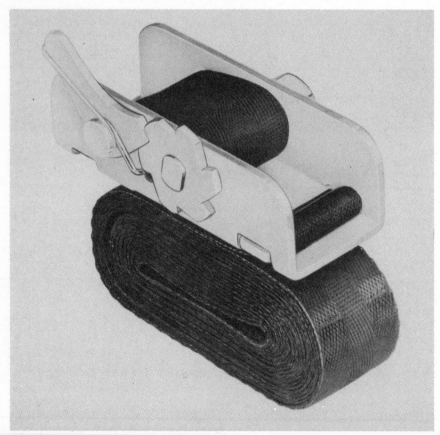

Stanley's 41-159 Web Clamp

each. So, you can have a set of bar clamps for about $25.00 if you buy the pipe, and for about $20.00 if you scrounge the pipe. The clamps can be ordered from Garrett Wade (#13F04.01), Woodcraft Supply (#15101-AR), and the Adjustable Clamp Co. (#50, 56, 52 & 53). (#13F04.01) $9.50

Web Clamps

A web, or band, clamp consists of a length of nylon strapping with a tensioning device. It's handy for gluing such things as chair bottoms, where four-way tensioning is necessary. You can find a lot of uses for them around the home and shop. Plus, they're inexpensive and can't mar the work.

The Stanley 41-159 web clamp has a very strong, 12-foot nylon webbing strap. This clamp is easily tightened with a wrench or screwdriver, and a ratchet mechanism keeps the webbing tight when you achieve proper tension. It's a clamp for all but the most gargantuan projects. Approx. Price: $6.50

Directory Of Manufacturers And Suppliers

A

Adjustable Clamp Co.
417 N. Ashland
Chicago, IL 60622

American Machine & Tool Co., Inc.
4th Avenue & Spring St.
P. O. Box 70
Royersford, PA 19468

Anglo-American Distribution Ltd.
P. O. Box 24
403 Kennedy Blvd.
Somerdale, NJ 08083

Arco Products Corporation
110 W. Sheffield Ave.
Englewood, NJ 07631

Arrow Fastener Co., Inc.
271 Mayhill St.
Saddle Brook, NJ 07662

B

Belsaw Machinery Co.
3574 Field Bldg.
Kansas City, MO 64111

Black & Decker Mfg. Co.
701 E. Joppa Rd.
Towson, MD 21204

Bostitch
Division of Textron Inc.
420 South Kitley Ave.
Indianapolis, IN 46219

Brett-Hauer Co., Inc.
Dept. WN
Putnam Valley, NY 10579

Brookstone Company
475 Vose Farm Rd.
Peterborough, NH 03458

C

Channellock, Inc.
Meadville, PA 16335

Chopper Industries
P.O. Box 87
Easton, PA 18042

Compo-Cast
2222 N. Olney St.
Indianapolis, IN 46218

Conover Woodcraft Specialties, Inc.
18123 Madison Rd.
Parkman, OH 44080

Consumers Bargain Corp.
109 Wheeler Ave.
Pleasantville, NY 10570

The Cooper Group
P.O. Box 728
Apex, NC 27502

Craftsman Wood Service Co.
2727 S. Mary St.
Chicago, IL 60608

Crescent
(*See* The Cooper Group)

D

DeWalt
Division of Black & Decker Mfg. Co.
P.O. Box 540
Lancaster, PA 17604

Disston Inc.
1030 W. Market St.
Greensboro, NC 27401

Dremel Mfg.
Division of Emerson Electric Co.
4915 21st St.
Racine, WI 53406

Duo-Fast Corporation
3702 River Rd.
Franklin Park, IL 60131

E

Emco-Lux Co., Inc.
2050 Fairwood Ave.
Columbus, OH 43207

Exact Level & Tool Mfg. Co., Inc.
High Bridge, NJ 08829

F

Frog Tool Co. Ltd.
541 N. Franklin St.
Chicago, IL 60610

G

Garden Way Research
Dept. 80731
Charlotte, VT 05445

Garrett Wade Company
302 Fifth Ave.
New York, NY 10001

Gilliom Manufacturing Inc.
1109 N. 2nd st.
St. Charles, MO 63301

Greenlee Tool Co.
2136 Twelfth St.
Rockford, IL 61101

H

Haddon Tools
4719 W. Route 120
McHenry, IL 60050

Homelite
Division of Textron, Inc.
P. O. Box 7047
14401 Carowinds Blvd.
Charlotte, NC 28217

Husqvarna, Inc.
224 Thorndale Ave.
Bensenville, IL 60106

I

Irwin Hand Tools
The Irwin Auger Bit Co.
Wilmington, OH 45177

L

Lee Valley Tools Ltd.
P.O. Box 6295
Ottawa, Ontario
Canada K2A 1T4

Leichtung, Inc.
701 Beta Dr. #17
Cleveland, OH 44143

Lufkin
(*See* The Cooper Group)

M

Makita U. S. A., Inc.
390 Crossen Ave.
Elk Grove, IL 60007

Mayes Brothers Tool Mfg. Co.
P. O. Box 1018
Johnson City, TN 37601

McCulloch Corporation
P. O. Box 92180
Los Angeles, CA 90009

McGraw-Edison Co. (Shopmate)
1801 N. Stadium Blvd.
Columbia, MO 65201

Millers Falls
Division of Ingersoll-Rand
Greenfield, MA 01301

Milwaukee Electric Tool Corporation
13135 Lisbon Rd.
Brookfield, WI 53005

Minnesota Versatil Inc.
5100 Edina Industrial Blvd.
Edina, MN 55435

Montgomery Ward (Powr-Kraft)
Montgomery Ward Plaza
Chicago, IL 60671

N

Nicholson
(*See* The Cooper Group)

O

Otner Botner
P.O. Box 6023
Providence, RI 02940

P

Parker Manufacturing Co.
Trojan Tools
149 Washington St.
P. O. Box 644
Worcester, MA 01613

Peterson Manufacturing Co., Inc.
(Vise-Grips)
DeWitt, NB 68341

Pootatuck Corporation
R. R. 2, Box 18
Windsor, VT. 05089

Portalign Tool Corporation
P.O. Box A-80547
San Diego, CA 92138

Powermatic Houdaille Inc.
Morrison Rd.
McMinnville, TN 37110

The Princeton Company
P. O. Box 276
Princeton, MA 01541

R

R.A.K. Products, Inc.
5605 W. Hemlock St.,
P.O. Box 23426
Milwaukee, WI 53223

Remington Arms Co., Inc.
939 Barnum Ave.
Bridgeport, CT 06602

Rockwell International
Power Tool Division
Suite 600, Poplar Tower
Memphis, TN 38138

Ross Tool Co.
257 Queens St. West
Toronto, Ontario
Canada M5V 1Z4

S

Sands Level & Tool
Division of Harmon, Inc.
225 W. Lewis
P. O. Box 147
Wichita, KS 67202

Sandvik Inc.
1702 Nevins Rd.
Fair Lawn, NJ 07410

Saw-Mate Corporation
P. O. Box 49383
Los Angeles, CA 90049

Sears, Roebuck and Co. (Craftsman)
Sears Tower
Chicago, IL 60684

Shopmaster
1212 Chestnut Ave.
Minneapolis, MN 55403

Shopsmith, Inc.
750 Center Dr.
Vandalia, OH 45377

S-K Tools
Dresser Industries, Inc.
3201 N. Wolf Rd.
Franklin Park, IL 60131

Skil Corporation
4801 W. Peterson Ave.
Chicago, IL 60646

Sperber Tool Works, Inc.
Box 1224
West Caldwell, NJ 07006

Sprunger Corporation
P.O. Box 1621
Elkhart, IN 46514

The Stanley Works
Stanley Tools
195 Lake St.-Box 1800
New Britain, CT 06050

Stihl Inc.
536 Viking Drive
Virginia Beach, VA 23452

T

Toolkraft Corporation
250 South Rd.
Enfield, CT 06082

V

Vaughan & Bushnell Mfg. Co.
11414 Maple Ave.
Hebron, IL 60034

W

Wen Products, Inc.
5810 Northwest Hwy.
Chicago, IL 60631

Williams & Hussey Machine
Corporation
Milford, NH 03055

Wilton Corp.
2400 E. Devon Ave.
Des Plaines, IL 60018

Woodcraft Supply Corporation
313 Montvale Ave.
Woburn, MA 01801

Woodworker's Supply, Inc.
11200 Menaul, N.E.
P.O. Box 14117
Albuquerque, NM 87112

X

X-Acto
45-35 Van Dam St.
Long Island City, NY 11101

Index